CRUISERS' AA
(Accumulated Acumen)

JACKIE & NOEL PARRY

Warning

Every effort has been made to maintain accuracy of information. However, we (the authors/publishers) disclaim responsibility for any errors and/or omissions in the work. The medical advice and procedures outlined in this book should not be taken without first consulting a doctor or trained paramedic.

We take no responsibility and bear no responsibility for accidents or near misses. It is up to you, the reader, to research and seek professional advice on safety, medical issues, navigation, boat handling and all aspects covered within this book and on our website.

That said, we hope you enjoy our book.

ISBN: 978-0-9875515-0-4

ACKNOWLEDGEMENTS

We are indebted to friends for sharing their vast knowledge in cruising and editing! And supporting us through the insanity of editing this book. Our deepest gratitude goes to:

Colin Parry, Val Franks, Brenda Parry, Andrea Stafford, Peter Taylor, Julia Smallbone, Rachel Amphlett, Ruthie Sandven, Chris & Gilli Dicker, Trevor Impett, Helen Wheeler & Matt Delaney, Angus & Rolande Ramsey, Lesley Grimminck, Dianne McLeod, Trevor Elias, and Jonathan Tickle for designing our marvellous webpage and front cover: http://www.webdiversiondesigns.co.

Additional thanks to marketing consultant and editor extraordinaire: Julia Smallbone www.littlebone.co.uk. And Rhiannon Templeton for professional and fast editing rhiannon@wideband.net.au

Also, to Rachel Amphlett, author extraordinaire (www.rachelamphlett.com) for handling my incessant writing and self-publishing questions. She handled these as well as she handles her own stories, with patience and finesse. (Rachel's thrillers: White Gold and Under Fire).

And special thanks to both our families. Our adventures and love of life is all thanks to you; without your support it would simply not be possible.

Particular love and thanks to Val & Roy Franks (Jackie's mum and dad), Brenda Parry, Alma Parry, Margaret Hendrie & Colin Parry. This book is dedicated to you.

READER'S NOTES

Mariah and Pyewacket are officially Mariah II and Pyewacket II. For ease of reading I have omitted the II most of the time. I have also used the pronoun 'I' a lot throughout the book, this 'I' is Jackie talking as I typed up the text and do most of the talking!

Throughout the book you may spot alternative spellings, e.g. meter (American) and metre (UK). Please just deal with it.

We refer to cruising people as 'cruisers' or 'boaties' or 'yachties'.

Radio 'Scheds' and radio 'Nets' are 'Schedules' and 'Networks'. This just means that they are a planned meeting of people on the radio at a set time and frequency.

SV means Sailing Vessel.

During the Navigation section we have capitalised True, Variation, Magnetic, Deviation, Compass, North, South, East and West. We have done this to highlight the importance of these terms.

Most tips and ideas are in alphabetical order with a few exceptions for ease of reading.

Internet website and book recommendations are noted throughout the book, in appropriate sections. They are also listed at the end of the book.

Useful resources for the reader are noted as 'Resources'. Acknowledgements are noted as 'Resource'.

Any recommendations of food, drink or medication are just ideas of what we, or our friends, have used or ingested. Please seek medical advice before trying anything new.

CONTENTS

& drift, sextant, speed/distance/time calculations, speed, speed vs. wind, waypoints, weather at sea, wind apparent & true, resources

Cruisers' AA

INTRODUCTION
How we did it

Searching for our first boat, I had no idea this cruising world existed and I felt like I had been dumped onto another planet. The beings on that other planet spoke another language. Back when I was living in England I was in total control of my corporate life until I lost someone very dear to me. My counsellor advised me to stay and face my emotions. Of course, I completely disregarded this advice and ran away. All of a sudden I was thrust into a new culture (Australia), I fell in love and married a man I had only known for six months and faced a whole new maritime language - it was a daunting time.

On the back of Noel's motorbike, cruising up and down the east coast of Australia viewing boats I asked him, 'So, what's it going to cost, running a boat?'
He replied, 'Everything we've got.'
A little perplexed, but not yet deterred, I then asked, 'What's so great about sailing anyway?'
Noel, with his brutal honesty and years of experience with boats replied, 'Getting into port.'
Good grief, I thought. After about two hours of silence while I digested these little gems, I said, 'Why do it then?'
Without hesitation Noel responded, 'It's the closest thing to freedom I know.'
It was right then that I was sold on the idea. Fifteen years later I still see the wisdom in his answers.

On board there was just Noel and I with our combined skills and resourcefulness carrying us to where we wanted to go. At times the good stuff in life is in balance with the not-so-good stuff, terror and delight are usually at the cost of one another. The freedom is balanced by the knowledge that you are responsible for your partner's life and surviving the fear makes moments of enjoyment that much sweeter. Every day is different. Every day is alive. These are some of the reasons why Noel and I go cruising.

We are fascinated with how others live on board and many cruisers have shared some great ideas with us. Some of those ideas we have not employed, simply because time, effort and reward seem to be off balance - for us. We have a wealth of information, but we do not know everything. For most of the sections in this book an entire book could be written on each. At times I feel like a lazy sailor as there are so many more things we could do to save money. Yet then I would be working harder at it, leaving less time for enjoyment, and if it is not about enjoying life then I am not sure what the point is.

The idea is to go cruising now, create happiness on board and in your life. As you read through our book, you will figure out what does and does not work for you in order to step closer to a contented life. Most importantly, remember that you will not have the time to take on everyone else's opinions or ideas - do what is right for you. It is all about your adventure and the self-discovery your journey will bring. Do write, we would be interested to know what *you* discover. www.jackieparry.com

WHAT'S THIS BOOK ABOUT?

If you are an aspiring cruiser, already on passage towards the great life or, if you just enjoy dreaming, this book provides a peek through a port hole to the cruising life and how cruisers live.

If you are already a cruiser, this book will help you make cruising life much more enjoyable and stretch your budget to allow more years of living freely.

If you are a firm landlubber, are interested in knowing what happens 'out there' and want some great tips that could help you improve your life too, take a look - you might be surprised at what you find.

Living on board

It could cost millions or next-to-nothing to live this lifestyle - we have met both extremes. We are somewhere in the middle and definitely budget conscious.

There are thousands of great cruising books available. The problem is if we followed *all* the advice on what to have and how to do it, we would still be firmly anchored and working on land to create funding for the trip. **The point is to do the best with what you have and get going**. We hope this book helps you change tack to that direction.

Who are we?

My name is Jackie Parry. Together with my husband Noel we've spent four years compiling this book. For more about us, please see our website: www.jackieparry.com

Our qualifications for writing this book?

We have sailed around the planet (including The Great Loop in the USA plus Canada's Great Lakes and the French Canals), in addition we have:

- Traversed the Pacific Ocean twice: the first time on the 'milk-run', the second time exploring further south to Easter Island, Pitcairn and the Gambier Islands (aka Mangareva Islands).
- Skippered commercial vessels internationally.
- Taught commercial maritime and skippered Marine Rescue boats.
- Written several hundred magazine articles worldwide and co-written a pilot book (in America).

In addition to all of these recent and full-time experiences, Noel has a lifetime of boating adventures. We are not rich but simply found a level of freedom that worked for us. At times we have worked very hard to continue this life - but it was for us and us only - that's the difference.

What's included

This is a reference book with really useful information to plan for and go cruising; or to improve life on board if you are already on your way. It also includes short stories, published articles and unpublished articles. We hope this blending of information shows you better, different and clever ways to live on board.

Get going!

When you get going, remember that you simply cannot escape everything. You still have to live with yourself. If you see the world through troubled eyes, it will be the same when you cruise - it all starts with you and don't forget *This Is It* (see 'This Is It' article in Fun, Games & Pleasure section).

MARIAH II

Mariah II was a tough but pretty boat and she felt very homely within her timber cabin. She looked after us in bad weather and taught us a lot.

Double diagonal Kauri, cutter rigged sloop with a canoe stern:

Owned us from 1998 - 2006
Length Overall: 12 metres
Deck length: 10 metres
Beam: 3.4 metres
Draft: 1.5 metres

Specifications:
- Designer: Baum
- Year of manufacture: 1985
- Similar to Colin Archer design
- Builder: Henderson
- Built in New Zealand
- Deck material: ply-epoxy
- Kauri cold moulded
- Kauri & Rimu interior
- Flush deck
- Hard dodger
- Full keel, cut away fore-foot
- Displacement: 9.5 tonnes
- S/Steel/lead keel

Engine:
- Yanmar 40hp (fitted new 2000)
- Model: 3JH3E
- Diesel
- Cylinders: 3
- Flexi drive shaft coupling
- 85W alternator on engine
- Dual filter fuel system
- Fresh water cooling
- Max speed: 7 knots
- Cruise speed 5.5 knots

Tanks:
- Aluminium diesel tank (225 litres) with inspection hatch
- 260 litre water tanks (three tanks: 2 fibreglass, 1 bladder)

Equipment:
- 80W solar panel
- Electric auto-helm
- Aries wind vane

PYEWACKET II

Pyewacket II was our home for almost two and a half years. We bought her in San Francisco and sailed her back to Australia, allowing us to experience other parts of the Pacific Ocean.

Cutter rigged sloop, an Aleutian 51. She was built to incredibly high standards with no money saving tricks. We felt very safe on board. She sailed beautifully and went to wind better than we did! We achieved several 200+ mile days.

Owned us from 2009 - 2011
Length Overall: 15.5 metres
Water line: 13 metres
Beam: 4.2 metres
Draft: 2 metres

Specifications
- Designer: S. Huntingford
- Aleutian 51
- Builder: John Nissen
- Built in Canada
- Deck/hull material: Fibreglass, Balsa cored above the waterline
- Year of manufacture: 1980
- Interior: Timber
- Hard dodger, canvas enclosure
- Three-quarter keel
- Displacement: 15 tonnes
- Encapsulated lead keel

Engine:
- Chrysler Nissan
- Model: M6336
- Diesel
- Cylinders: 6
- 55 amp & 65 amp alternators
- Duel filter fuel system
- Fresh water cooling
- Max speed: 9 knots
- Cruise speed: 7 knots

Tanks:
- 2 x fibreglass diesel tanks fore & aft (750 litres total)
- 864 litres water (two separate, baffled tanks)
- 60 litres holding tank

Equipment:
- 2 x 120 Watt solar panels with Charge Controller for maximum amp output
- 2 x Airex, 30 amp max, wind generators
- Teleflex wheel, hydraulic steering
- Wagner autopilot, Raymarine autopilot and Aries wind vane.

BOAT EQUIPMENT
(See BOAT HANDLING for more equipment)

The amount of equipment available to purchase is practically unlimited. You have to choose what is essential and what you can do without. Over time our opinions on this have changed. We did not have radar on Mariah and what we didn't have we didn't miss. On Pyewacket there was full colour radar and now we wouldn't go to sea without one!

Air Conditioning
The best air conditioning units are canvas shade, good ventilation and fans.

The canvas cover on Pyewacket (in Panama) looks small but is actually very large and heavy. However, it did a tremendous job keeping the boat cool.

The cover was designed to be easily furled if big winds developed. We folded up the sides so it lay along the boom, minimising windage.

Power consumption: Regular air conditioning units use considerable power, keep you permanently at the marina and take valuable stowage space. Powering the unit underway is achieved by running a generator, thus creating noise and heat.

Fans: Search auto shops for the twelve-volt type fans; you will need several to keep the air circulating in warmer climes. Computer fans can be good, test them first if you can, some are noisier than others.

Fan location: Mount a fan near your companionway. If it is raining when underway, all your hatches are closed and you are running your engine, a fan near the companionway will help suck in and circulate fresh air.

Alarms
Watch alarms: Use a portable oven alarm to enable you to take short naps when on watch. If we become tired on watch we set the alarm to go off every eight minutes. *(See 'Standing Watches' in the Voyage Preparation section.)*

An approaching ship with a speed of 26 knots coupled with your speed of 6 knots is a combined speed of 32 knots. Over a distance of five nautical miles (approximate horizon view to ship, dependent on height of eye), it would only take a little under ten minutes before collision.
(See 'Speed, Distance, Time Calculations' in the Navigation section.)

Anchor alarm: We use our GPS anchor alarm at most anchorages. It wakes us up if we have moved more than our pre-set range. *(See 'Anchoring' in the Boat Handling section.)*

Binoculars
Configuration: Binoculars are described by two numbers. The first number refers to magnification: the higher the number, the more powerful the magnification. The second number refers to the diameter of the outer lens: the larger the number, the more light transmitted to the user's eye which is very useful at dusk.

The greater the magnification the harder it is to hold the binoculars steady. This is especially true with over seven times magnification.

Recommended: We like the Steiner binoculars 7x50, made in Germany. They are sturdy, waterproof, have a rubber encasing and a compass that can be lit, which is very useful for taking bearings. *(See 'Bearings' in the Navigation section.)*

Blocks & Tackle
A heavy weight can be lifted with a fraction of the force when using an arrangement of pulleys and ropes. Tackles are systems of blocks and lines that increase pulling power and are named according to the number of sheaves in the blocks that are used.

Mechanical advantage (MA) is the power of the tackle.

Disadvantage: If the 'fall' (end of the line) finishes at the fixed block and you are pulling in the opposite direction to the movement of the weight, then the tackle is roved to disadvantage. Disadvantage = number of sheaves (MA).

Advantage: If the 'fall' finishes at the moving block and you are pulling in the same direction as the weight is moving then the tackle is roved to advantage. Advantage = number of sheaves plus 1 (MA+1). Main sheets are usually 4:1.

1 to 1 ratio:	Called Single Whip. A single fixed block and fall. There is no increase in power unless rigged to advantage, i.e. the block is on the weight to be moved. The gain is height of lift or change of direction (e.g. used on a jib reefing line to avoid it catching on other equipment).
2 or 3 to 1 ratio	Called Gun Tackle. Two single blocks. If the line is roved to advantage the power - Mechanical Advantage is 3:1, if roved to disadvantage the MA is 2:1.
3 or 4 to 1 ratio	Called Luff Tackle. One double block and one single block. If roved to advantage the MA is 4:1, roved to disadvantage 3:1.
4 or 5 to 1 ratio	Called Two-Fold or Double Tackle. Two double blocks. If roved to advantage the MA is 5:1, if roved to disadvantage the MA is 4:1.

Technically the mechanical advantage is a little less than stated due to friction.

Bosun's Chair
Integrity: These can be as simple as a rope and a plank of wood. Always double check the knots and integrity of the chair. Testing the chair with four or five times the weight that will be using it is a

good idea (if possible). If I am the one being lifted, i.e. sitting in the chair, it is my responsibility to check the integrity of the knots, chair and lines, even if someone else has checked them first.

Comfort: Specially designed chairs do make you feel more secure. If you are uncomfortable with heights buy a purpose made chair. *(See 'Mast Climbing' in the Maintenance & Repairs section.)*

Dive Hookah
A dive hookah is a good alternative to dive tanks for fun and to assist you in cleaning the bottom of your boat at anchor. Generally the air compressors are petrol or electric engines; there are pros and cons for both. We had a petrol hooker and it worked very well. *(See the Personal Equipment section for more uses.)*

Electric: The electric type is quieter but drains the batteries quickly.

Petrol: The petrol type is noisier, but it is cheaper (in power terms) to run and can be used away from the mother ship.

Safety: Ensure you understand all the safety issues before using dive equipment. As well as cleaning the boat, we use ours to check our anchor is set in deeper water or free a fouled propeller if necessary.

Etiquette: Try to avoid running the engine too late or early in the day and not more than one hour at a time to avoid upsetting neighbouring boats. At particularly pristine and quiet anchorages where other boats are enjoying the tranquillity, we avoid using the hookah unless absolutely necessary.

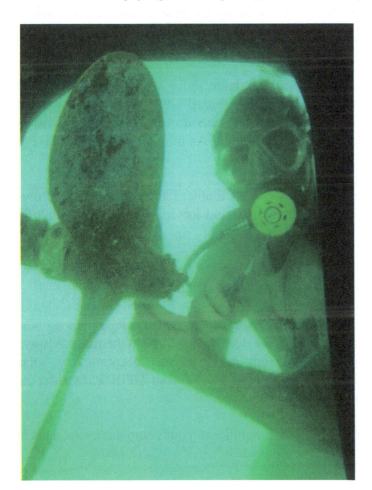

Our Dive Hookah on Pyewacket was brilliant. This equipment was unnecessary on Mariah's five foot draft but invaluable on Pyewacket's seven foot draft.

Noel scraping Pyewacket's prop.

Diving & Snorkelling

Convenience & care: We use our stern platform for our gear if we want a 'free' swim after using fins and snorkel/dive gear. Putting a net or a box (that is tied on) on this platform for our gear means we don't have to worry about it slipping into the water. Thereafter the box is easy to lift into the cockpit for a fresh water wash down. Ensure all your equipment is washed in fresh water and thoroughly dried before stowing, to avoid corrosion and rotting.

Additional uses: Snorkel gear is not just for snorkelling. Keep your mask handy in a storm, whether in port or at sea. Sometimes the wind and driving rain is so fierce you will need to wear your mask in order to be able to see on deck, or in an open cockpit. *(See 'Storm Preparation' in the Boat Handling section.)*

Emergency Tiller

An emergency tiller is an important back up to have on board. Stow the tiller in an easy-to-grab spot while at sea. Ensure everyone on board knows where it is and how it fits together and operates. A sea trial in a calm, relaxed situation is the time to test the emergency tiller. If the opportunity arises, try it out in heavier weather, it may prompt a redesign. *(See 'Emergency steering' in the Maintenance & Repairs section.)*

EPIRBs & GPIRBs (Emergency Position Indicating Radio Beacon & GPS Position Indicating Radio Beacon)

How it works: The position of a 406 MHz EPIRB is determined by calculations using the Doppler shift in the beacon's distress signal, which occurs as satellites approach and recede in overhead orbits. The number of signal bursts received by the satellites determines the accuracy of the calculation. Accuracy is enhanced when a satellite passes directly overhead, because the satellite receives the greatest number of signal bursts. The only real problem with the system is that it takes time for an accurate fix to be acquired.

GPIRB: The GPIRB (GPS and EPIRB) takes an active role in determining its own position. When activated, its internal GPS finds its own position, just like an onboard GPS. When it has located itself, it broadcasts its identity and position on 406 MHz. It then shuts down for twenty minutes to preserve power and after twenty minutes it starts the process again. As long as the unit is active it will continue this process in twenty minutes cycles.

The advantage of a GPIRB: An accurate fix is almost instantly available; its frequent update allows rescuers to calculate set and drift accurately, sending the Search and Rescue (SAR) teams directly to you.

Testing: Test your unit every few months, utilising the test button. Keep your unit clean (free of dust and dirt) as they do collect a lot of dust over time, which may affect performance.

Signal: GPS uses the reflective plane qualities of the water surface to enhance its reception signals. Therefore it is better to mount your GPS antenna closer to the deck rather than up the mast. Always ensure that there are minimal overhead projections that may interfere with reception (e.g. solar panels). And if you find yourself in a situation where you have to use your GPIRB, consider its location for the very best chance of being found!

Mounting: Mount the unit in an easily accessible place, for example, in your companionway. This is an ideal spot to enable you to grab the unit as you leave the boat.

Turned on in error: If your EPIRB is inadvertently switched on, switch it off immediately and inform authorities (local marine authority or rescue association). If this is a genuine accident and authorities are notified, there will be no penalties.

Eyelets & Eyelet Punch
Purchase an eyelet punch and eyelets to use on your canvas. Over time you will adapt the shade canvas and probably collect more canvas. This way you can rig it up yourself and maybe even use it to catch water. *(See 'Water' in the Voyage Preparation section.)*

Fiddles
Fiddles are the lip at the edge of your cupboards and around a table to stop items sliding out/off. A small length of timber, screwed and glued in place is ideal. Ensure your table fiddles are not too high, making eating uncomfortable.

Short story On Mariah the fiddles on the saloon table were two inches high which made eating very uncomfortable, so we took them off. On Pyewacket there were no fiddles on the saloon table. We rarely sat there when underway as most of the time we were in the cockpit (it was the same on Mariah, even with an exposed cockpit). If it was really calm, one of us might sit at the table for a change when underway. The table was primarily used in port, so we did not miss the fiddles.

Fire
Theory: There are four elements that must be present for a fire to occur:
- Fuel
- Heat
- An oxidizing agent (usually oxygen)
- A chemical chain reaction

A fire is extinguished by removing one or more of these four elements from the combustion process.

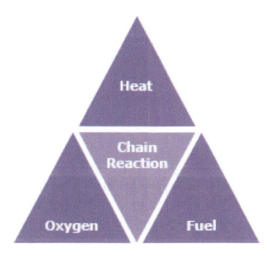

Strategy: Have a planned strategy. Where does everyone muster in the event of a fire?

Know the equipment on board: Know where all of your fire extinguishers are and ensure they have not passed their expiry date. Everyone on board, including guests, should know the location of the extinguishers, their contents, purpose and how to use them.

Maintenance: Regularly check your extinguishers for corrosion. Some manufacturers recommend shaking or turning the dry chemical extinguishers upside down every so often, to avoid the powder 'compacting'. However, some authorities say this could cause further problems (blocking the tubes if there is 'caking'). Talk to your supplier for pertinent recommendations.

Safety: Entry and exit points should be highlighted, some people may think they can get through the hatch but in reality it could be too small and it is too late to find out when there is a fire.

Emergency alternatives: Baking soda from the galley can be used to smother a small fire of most types. Baking soda is the ingredient contained in Dry Chemical extinguishers (denoted by a white stripe on a red cylinder in Australia). However, a fire blanket is much more efficient and far less messy to clean up.

Fire fighting procedures:

- Call for help. Even if it is a small fire, it can grow very quickly. If you manage to extinguish the fire you can always call off the assistance, but if it is out of control it may be too late to call for help.

- Get everyone who is not engaged in fighting the fire out on deck. Tackle the fire if it is not dangerous to do so.

- Cut off the air supply to the fire by closing off ventilation hatches. Close off the fuel delivery if the fire is in the engine room.

- Use extinguishers, blankets and/or water. Ensure water is not used on electrically started fires or oil fires. On oil fires water will cause the oil to spread violently and therefore the flames too. Using water on electrical fires (i.e. a fire started by an electrical fault) could give you an electric shock. *(See 'Safety' further on in this section.)*

- Turn off the gas (LPG).

- Fires can re-ignite easily, especially if you have used a foam extinguisher or a blanket. If you part the foam or lift the blanket, the fire may well blaze back up. Allow everything to cool and have additional means at hand to fight a secondary fire.

- Attending a fire-fighting course is highly recommended.

- Install fire alarms.

Fire Extinguishers

Learn which colour extinguishers fight which types of fire. The extinguishers you purchase for your vessel will have a label which lists all this information and ingredients, but instant identification is important in an emergency situation. Older extinguishers that are still in use may vary in colour.

Identification: Colours may not remain the same internationally. If you crew on a foreign flag boat, make sure you find out their colouring system. International authorities are trying to align the colours; but you may find silver extinguishers with coloured banding (that denotes the type) as opposed to red extinguishers with banding (as in Australia).

Where different types of extinguishers for different fire types are situated together they must be properly labelled to prevent confusion in a panic.

Safety: Using the wrong type of extinguisher on a fire can be very dangerous, (water on an electrically started fire as mentioned above). If you use water on an oil fire, the water will spread the oil and the flames will explode up causing other parts of the vessel to catch fire.

If an extinguisher has been used, always lay it on its side (safely) to indicate it is empty and needs refilling. If an empty extinguisher has been put back in its bracket, it may be forgotten about. (Of course, if you are at sea, laying it down inside a cupboard is a better idea, so it cannot roll around and cause damage.)

Requirements: Check your country's safety requirements, as there are legal requirements for most boats to carry extinguishers. Either way you would be foolhardy to have none. Requirements will vary with the size of vessel.

Re-charging: Re-charging times and survey/safety requirements vary for extinguishers and countries, check the manufacturer's instructions for maintenance. Check with the local marine authority to ensure the safety requirements have been met on your vessel.

Location: Install a fire blanket in the galley. Extinguishers should be situated on escape routes. They should be fixed in a location where the extinguisher can be reached quickly. The best location for a fire extinguisher is near a door leading to a place of safety or near to a specific risk. They should be fixed where they can be easily seen. Do not place extinguishers over cookers or heaters or in places of extreme temperatures.

For special risks (engine room) extinguishers should be near the risk but not too close to prevent use in the event of a fire occurring (i.e. having to reach over the engine to get the extinguisher).

Operation: Where possible the method of operation should be similar for all extinguishers. Everyone on board should be capable of handling all types and sizes of extinguishers recommended for your boat.

Short story On Mariah there was a large timber step, located over part of the engine. One night we had a mosquito coil burning on a plate on one side of this step. I had a wash in the galley and dried my face, hanging the towel to the side of the mosquito coil, a fair distance away. At 2 a.m. I awoke for some water. On the step was a mound of black stuff. Confused (and dopey), I looked up at the sky (through the companionway hatch) to see where it had come from! Then I moved the mound and realised it was warm. I woke Noel up, he moved what we then realised was ash, to see the step smouldering. We poured a cup of water on the ash to put it out. When I had hung up the towel I must have lightly brushed it over the lit mosquito coil. By pure dumb luck there was no wind that night and the towel just smouldered completely away (a full size towel at that!). If there had been any breeze, flames would have developed and the situation would have been very serious. The fire would have prevented us leaving the boat. There was a large hatch over the bed, which we covered with a tarp. This tarp was lowered at night so the hatch could stay open if it rained (air getting in, rain not). After that incident we installed a knife near that hatch in case we needed to escape. I still shudder when I think of that night. (Addendum: instead of a plate for our coil, we now use the enclosed tins with holes in the side and top – they are a lot safer!)

Flares

<u>Which flares & where</u>: Read the instructions on each flare and understand them prior to an emergency: they are not all the same. There are different types of flares to use during the day (smoke) and night (parachute). Know which types you carry on board and where they are located.

<u>Requirements</u>: Never use a flare just for fun, it is illegal. Different countries have different (and changing) requirements for carrying flares.

Short story Once upon a time in Australia we were able to use out-of-date flares for training. Due to short-sighted bureaucrats this is now illegal. Over the years during training, we practiced on old flares and 99% of them worked. Appropriate rescue authorities and police were notified prior to a training night and it was a great opportunity to learn about the safety and operation of a flare. (Addendum: good cruising buddies have recently told us a story of a flare backfiring during a demonstration. The girl that fired it was lucky as it only burnt a hole in her glove and shirt. However, this is a good reminder for us all that flares are pyrotechnics and things can go wrong!)

Flare training with Shoalhaven Marine Rescue in NSW, Australia.

We all said a silent prayer in the hope that we never have to do this in a real emergency.

<u>Storing</u>: Store your flares in a sturdy plastic, sealed container to help prevent the damaging effects of moisture.

Gadgets

The more gadgets you have the less likely you are to leave port! Meaning, the more you have, the more likely something will break or need repair, which will prevent you from leaving.

Grab Bag/Ditch Bag

We had one large grab bag on Mariah, ideally it should have been split in two (1) Absolute necessities and (2) Necessities. Our bag included ideas gleaned from experience, as well as ideas from other cruisers. *(See article 'Ditch Bag' further on.)*

Our bag carried:

Survival suits	Sun hats x 2
Sunglasses	Whistle
Wind-up torch	Barley sugar
Hand held radio (VHF) & spare batteries	Hand held GPS & batteries
Spirulina (nutrient source in powder form)	Leatherman knife (multi-use knife)
Survival sheets (space blankets)	Cereal bars
Hand Watermaker	Puncture repair kit
Toilet roll	Water packets
Water	Spectacles (old, spare)
String	T-Shirts x 2
Fishing line & hooks	Tea towel
Signalling mirror	Wet wipes (baby wipes)
Knife	Sanitary products
Seasick tablets	Flares
First aid kit with extra strong painkillers	Plastic bags
Sea-marker dye	Lighter
Paperwork (passports etc)	Sunscreen

Additional items:(suggestions from others): shampoo, canned food, can opener, cookies. Note: be careful of sharp items in the inflatable raft.

Regular checks: Every six months check your bag for out of date medications, food and sunscreen. Check torch batteries are still working and that nothing has leaked or corroded. Water should be changed and if you worry about leeching (plastic into water) then change the bottles too.

EPIRB: Our EPIRBs (Emergency Position Indicating Radio Beacon) are mounted in the boat and if necessary will be grabbed at the same time the bag is grabbed.

Emergency water: Should the unthinkable happen, as part of the 'grabbing' process (if we have time), we would grab the water jugs and tie them to the life-raft. They will float, provide extra water and a container for catching more water. (Seawater is denser than fresh, so you can leave fresh water jerry cans almost full and they will still float.)

Addendum: Our great friends, Chris and Gilli, on board West Wind make a good point. 'We have always thought that an EPIRB in the life-raft makes a lot of sense. You not only have to grab the EPIRB when leaving the boat, but you also have to keep it with you somehow.'

ARTICLE: Published in Australia by Modern Boating magazine.

Ditch Bag
by Jackie Parry

Your grab bag, ditch kit, flee bag (sounds like my old dog), jump-and-go-bag should include stuff to measure your own priorities and capabilities. What would you need? Who is on board and where you are going? Does everyone on board know where it is?

Align your inclusions with distance. Seasons don't count, anyone on the water knows you can experience all four seasons twice in one day. However, thinking about the sea temperature is important; hypothermia has insatiable hunger. The sea gods also have an unquenchable greed and anything in your boat that you think you need should have a piece of string (lanyard) fitted, to give you a fighting chance of hanging on to it. Common sense, speedy reaction and lack of panic should be mentioned, although I am not sure how to pack those things. The bag obviously needs to be watertight and waterproof, a bright reflective colour is a good idea (boats don't just sink during the day).

Each to their own; some people include their obituaries - how very odd . . .! Other cruising buddies suggest a book and a mattress! All very nice, but I can think of several more important items. I'd rather have an extra bottle of water than reading material.

The Obvious
At the very least have water, flares and attention grabbers, surviving is nice, but being rescued is even better. The ditch kit should contain items for immediate use and possibly some months. Short-term think injuries, hypothermia and signalling devices. Mid to long-term survival, think water and food. Are you going to make water or catch it? Can you catch fish? Provision for prevention of sun exposure is imperative if you don't want to end up like a crisp.

How much?
I have seen lists for short-term (minutes to hours), mid-term (hours to days), medium-term (days to weeks) and long-term (weeks to months). All very useful but how do you know which bag to collect when your boat sinks? Do you take all four? Think necessity not holiday!

Can the bag be snatched quickly? Paperwork is a good one, your passports and boat papers have to be somewhere, why not in the grab bag? Add a few dollars (American dollars are the most widely accepted if you are travelling overseas). Think of all the bureaucratic bits of paper that cause major headaches and gnashing of teeth, if you had to replace them.

As terrifying as it sounds, one day you might need it; now's the time to think carefully about what it should contain. Grab bags provide thought-provoking conversations to all boat people. (Young, 'Include my favourite toy', old, 'Put in the fine Scotch dear'), both would argue that their life depends on it.

Research suggests forgetting everything you have seen in the movies, on TV and in novels. But I tend to disagree, who's to say what happens - survivors of course, but what of those who don't. That monumentally dramatised scene could be precisely what happens. We've met a survivor whose boat took fifteen minutes to sink. He had 'all the time in the world' to grab stuff from cupboards. He now thinks all boats take this long to be swallowed in to the deep. Most of us know a story where a boat vanishes within seconds; those brief moments may give you enough time to grab your survival bag.

Our Bag

We have one big bag on our boat, which ideally should be split in two (1) Absolute necessities and (2) Necessities. However, it's not and at the time of writing we are firmly welded to a mooring (for now). Our bag includes years of ideas gleaned from chatting to other people on boats as to 'what's in yours?'. It has (in no particular order): survival suits, sunglasses, wind up torch, handheld radio (VHF) and spare batteries, Spirulina (nutrient source in powder form), survival sheets (space blankets), hand Watermaker, toilet roll, water, string, fishing hooks/line, signalling mirror, knife, seasick tablets, First Aid with extra strong painkillers, flares, sanitary products, wet/baby wipes, tea towel, plastic bags, sea marker dye, lighter, paperwork (passports/boat papers/money), sunscreen, t-shirts, whistle, barley sugar, handheld GPS and batteries.

Diving into the bag after a year I am surprised to see that the wet wipes are still moist and the Spirulina still edible (mind you, it does look and smell remarkably like mould - even when new). Clearly, batteries should be replaced regularly, as should water in plastic bottles (leeching). Sunscreen and tablets/pills will have use by dates to be aware of too. We have spent over three weeks at sea in one go and been 1,500 miles from the nearest land, hence a fairly comprehensive bag. In compiling our kit, we gave careful thought to all the yummy stuff already included in our life-raft when it was last surveyed. Our EPIRBs are mounted in the boat, perhaps one should have been in the bag. Now, I would also include the Leatherman and some cereal bars. But the bag is heavy already.

Watermaker

Our small Watermaker was purchased in America (US$600). In Puerto Rico we met a guy who spent 66 days in a life-raft, in the Pacific Ocean, with his wife. They were attacked and holed by a pod of whales, 'they were so lovely, riding alongside us and suddenly they turned . . .' (Note to self: do not enjoy company of whales, turn on engine and shoot flares into water if same happens). He claims that they would be dead if they had not had the Watermaker in their grab bag. Before setting sail into the mighty Pacific, we purchased one. The emotions of coughing up the equivalent of almost a thousand Australian dollars were an odd mix; unwillingness to part with a large chunk of our cruising budget, conflicting with the thought that should we find our lives depended on it, it would seem a remarkably small amount of money. The Watermaker is still in its bag, unused and lonely, long may it remain so!

Other suggestions from friends:	*My humble opinion*
Chemical heat packs	*Space blanket is smaller and works well*
Petroleum jelly	*A necessity?*
Book to read	*Really?*
Wool and rubber work gloves	*Maybe one pair*
Enema sack for rehydration	*I'd rather drink the water*
Inflatable splints	*Great idea*
Repair kit	*Already in life-raft*
Swiss Army knife, sharpening stone, tube of oil.	*Make sure knife is sharp to start with*
Sextant	*Way too hard to use in life-raft*

Sponges	In life-raft already
Chemical light sticks	Good idea
Navigation kit	Maybe
Sea anchor	Good idea
Dried fruit and chocolate	I'd never say no to chocolate (ensure fruit is not already in chocolate - this stuff can really go off)
Survival ship's biscuits	Good idea
Multiple vitamins	A necessity?
Small plankton net	Hmmmm
Photocopies of all essential crew documents	Yup (or the originals)
Shore survival items in case you land in an uninhabited island: waterproof matches, flint, wire saw	It's all getting a bit much
Self-inflating foam pad or air mattress	What about a snugly blanket and a cuddly teddy bear too - really . . . !
Spare prescription glasses	Good idea - these are in our life-raft
Pack all gear into separate waterproof bags	Not a bad idea

We hope you found this article useful. It was compiled with ideas from many different cruisers and survivors. They all openly expressed their survival considerations, experience and concerns.

Halyards

Spares: Have your spare halyards sheaved and ready to go before putting to sea. Chafing can occur right at the top of the mast where it is difficult to check regularly.

Care and etiquette: Banging halyards at anchor? Use elastic with hooks at either end (bungee cord/Occy strap). Hook one end on the rigging, the other on the halyard; it keeps them away from the mast. This is far easier than trying to winch the lines tight enough to prevent banging. Check your halyards won't bang all night if leaving your vessel, especially if you have an aluminium mast. Otherwise you may drive your neighbours a bit dotty! *(See 'Lines' below for further information.)*

Jack Lines

Types: These are lines that run along the port and starboard deck to allow you to be harnessed on and roam freely up and down the length of your vessel. You can buy jack lines that lie flat on the deck. We use seatbelt webbing, which is very strong. You could use 16mm halyard rope.

Use: We have a rule on board: the person on watch is always to be clipped on, in all but the most benign conditions (and is always clipped on during any deck work). One of us could fall overboard at any time and the other may be asleep and not find out about it for hours.

MOB: If MOB (Man Overboard) occurs in nasty weather, it is sometimes impossible to turn your boat around to carry out a MOB procedure. In addition, if the waves are steep and the person in the water only has their head above water, they will disappear in the ocean swells immediately and you will be very lucky to spot them again. *(See 'MOB' in the Boat Handling Section.)*

Maintenance: Check your jack lines have UV protection and regularly inspect the lines for wear. Once in port, wash the saltwater off your lines with fresh water to help preserve them. Dry them thoroughly before furling up and stowing out of the sun.

Set up: We have cruising buddies who use two lines from their harnesses to the jack lines. This means they are always clipped on with at least one line at all times. When they traverse equipment on the boat and it is necessary to unclip, they unclip one line at a time and clip that one back on again before unclipping the second line.

Some cruisers prefer their jack lines in the middle of the vessel, with the tether short enough to prevent them going over the side. They run a line either side of the mast and presumably either side of the cockpit. Our jack lines are on either side of the boat. We always walk on the high side of the deck when heeling over.

Safety: Unless it is very calm, we let each other know when we are on deck and when we return to the cockpit, even if the other is asleep (yes, that means waking them up). Usually a call out of 'I'm going on deck' or 'I'm back' is enough for our sleepy bodies to absorb. If the conditions are not ideal we do sail adjustments together.

The best safety idea for harnesses is never to fall overboard! Prevention is better than cure. Test your jack line set up in calm water before tackling lump seas, and readjust as necessary. *(See MOB in Boat Handling section.)*

Short story We know two separate couples who have stories of going overboard while harnessed on. One couple were on deck together, she was washed over with one wave and the very next wave washed her right back onto the deck! With the second couple, the female went over and her partner leant down and pulled her straight back on board with superhuman strength (no doubt fear driven). They were all harnessed on.

Jerry Jugs/Water Containers

<u>Black is best</u>: Water containers and any plastics exposed to the sun will deteriorate unless covered or painted. Black containers last longer, they do not absorb as much UV and therefore do not deteriorate as fast.

<u>Chafing</u>: If your water containers are lashed on deck, check them frequently when underway for chafing. *(See 'Stowing' in the Voyage Preparation section for more ideas.)*

<u>Keep it simple</u>: Keep your smaller water containers for ferrying water to your boat if necessary (when on anchor or mooring). It is much easier and less of a chore with ten litre containers as opposed to straining with twenty litre containers.

Knots & Splicing

<u>Know your knots</u>: Everyone on board should know the fundamental knots, especially the Bowline (a Bowline is a reasonably secure knot, however, no matter how tight it becomes the Bowline is easy to undo). Purchase a good knot book and practice when underway. We have had to tie knots in emergency situations, very quickly. Learn some basic, useful knots by heart, as you may not have time to look in a book. Books with photos tend to provide better visual clues.

<u>Resources</u>: RYA Knot, Splices and Ropework Handbook by Gordon Perry & Steve Judkins.

<u>Safety</u>: Knots reduce the strength of a line by around 50% (depending on the type of knot). Splicing reduces the strength by around 20%. *(See 'Knots' in the Boat Handling section.)*

For online learning, Animated Knots by Grog is brilliant for knot tying and lots of other useful information. http://www.animatedknots.com/indexboating.php

Lamps

<u>Kerosene lamps</u>: are delightful to use in port. Under the lampshade use tin foil to reflect the light, or paint the underside white for a brighter light.

<u>Ventilation</u>: Lamps and non-electric heaters produce carbon monoxide which is a silent, odourless killer. Ensure your boat is thoroughly ventilated if using a lamp or a fuel heating system. *(See 'Heating' in the Health & Well-being section.)*

<u>Secure your lamp</u>: Use elastic cord with good quality hooks to tether your lamp in place from the base of the lamp to the top of your table, (we have a permanent ring on our table that lies flush when not in use). Alternatively, use two cords attached to the base of a lamp, stretching out to the edges of your table at about forty-five degrees apart. If you are on a catamaran, fill a small canvas bag with clean sand, tie one end of the cord to the lamp, the other to the bag that sits on your table, this will dampen the lamp's movement. *(See our set up on Pyewacket in the picture under 'Sewing Machine' further on in this section.)*

Lead Line

Keep a lead line in the dinghy for use when you are in places where the charted depth is only noted for the main channel and you want to anchor off channel. *(See short story below.)*

<u>Our lead line</u>: is a lump of lead on the end of twine, marked every metre. Sound the bottom of a potential anchor spot while in the dinghy and remember to sound the entire turning circle of your vessel.

<u>Find the seabed properties</u>: A lead weight with a concave bottom can be used for determining the seabed type. Press in some animal fat or peanut butter and sound the seabed, what sticks to the bottom will reveal what sort of seabed you have. (We have not tried to determine the seabed with any of these items, but friends have with various degrees of success. We'd love to hear about your results!)

Short story The Great Loop charts that include the Intracoastal Waterways of America do not contain depth information off the main channel. So when coming off the channel to anchor we had to sound the bottom ourselves. Also, when we circumnavigated Tahiti, we wanted to anchor in shallower water, the charts charted only deeper depths (twenty metres plus), so we took it in turns to jump in the dinghy to sound a good anchorage – great fun! (Keep your outboard in neutral when swinging the lead to avoid the line snagging on the spinning prop!)

Life Jackets

<u>Harness included and comfort</u>: If you purchase inflatable jackets that lie flat you will be more inclined to wear them when out on deck. Our life jackets inflate by a gas cylinder when we pull a cord. They are very flat and include a harness. You can purchase self-inflating jackets that inflate automatically when immersed in water.

<u>Safety</u>: We wear our jackets when we are alone on watch (and in rough weather) as we can utilise the in-built harness to clip on. *(See 'Jack Lines' earlier in this section. Also, see picture in Health & Well-being (under 'Heating'). If you look carefully you'll see that while Jackie is writing she is also clipped on - note the bikes too!)*

If you have visitors on board you must have enough life jackets for everyone. Check the safety regulations of the country you are visiting to avoid hefty fines. For example, in Australia life jackets must be worn when crossing a bar.

Short story Our previous life jackets inflated when wet. These are good if you are knocked out before falling overboard. However, mine inflated in the rain one day and we both came close to having a heart attack when it happened! (They go 'POP' then 'WHOOSH' very loudly.)

<u>Additional equipment</u>: Your jackets should have lights and whistles attached. Not all jackets are sold with these attachments. Check their operation regularly and carry spare life jacket gas bottles.

Personal EPIRBS are now another great option *(see 'EPIRBs' above)*.

Life-Rafts

<u>Servicing and care</u>: Life-rafts should be serviced on a regular basis and by an approved centre. Most rafts are stowed on deck and exposed to extremes of temperature, weather and sea conditions. On Mariah and Pyewacket, our life-raft was covered with an additional canvas cover. Trained personnel have confirmed that this extra protection helps maintain the raft for longer. Moisture can hasten deterioration and possibly reduce reliability.

At each service the raft will be unpacked (by inflating as you would in an emergency), cleaned and dried thoroughly (checking material). The inflation system will be fully charged and the valve checked to ensure it is in good condition. The survival equipment inside the raft will be checked to ensure it is in good condition and any out of date items can be replaced.

Check the expiry date for the life-raft you have on board. The time it takes to service a life-raft depends on how much work it needs and its size. For reference, a four-to-six person raft is usually serviced in about 4-6 hours.

Watch, learn and adding items: Watch your raft being inflated, especially if you have not completed a sea survival course (highly recommended). At this point, you can usually add additional items into the life-raft supplies. We added an old pair of prescription glasses, space blankets, extra water, seasick tablets, a hat each, a t-shirt each and sunglasses.

Safety: A life-raft that is too large is just as unsafe as one that is too small. A six-man raft with two people inside is liable to be tossed over too easily in seas. If you do have a large life-raft for just a few people (and should the unimaginable occur), try to weigh the raft down with some heavy items, such as full water containers.

Lights
Night vision: When on watch at night we use red LED lights for reading, chart work and manoeuvring around the boat. Red lights help you maintain your night vision. It is useful to have several different torches scattered in handy places throughout the boat, so they can be reached quickly if necessary.

Keep it simple: We have a small headlamp each (LED) that has white and red bulbs. These also allow hands-free work for tricky jobs or holding on when reading on watch.

Lines/Ropes
Maintenance and care: Your lines on board are integral. Keep plenty of spares, even halyards of the right length. Never drag your lines across the ground; they pick up dirt and grit which will gradually cause internal damage.

Wash salt-sprayed lines with fresh water and allow them to dry in a ventilated area before furling properly. Stow your lines out of the sun when possible. The sun and salt air shortens their life.

Lines will chafe whether at anchor or tied to a dock. Halyards can chafe while underway, so regular checks are imperative. For extra protection when using dock and anchor lines, run your lines through fire hose where the line passes through the fairleads (or any potential chafing point). Rags, foam and plastic hose can also be used.

'Freshening the nip' just means letting out or bringing in a little of the line to change the part that is beginning to chafe, it is a quick, temporary fix, but not prevention.

LEDs
Tri-colour/anchor light: Replace regular light bulbs with LEDs, they are a great power saver. Ensure you check polarity. On regular bulbs it does not matter which wire is positive or negative, on LEDs it does. The LED will not function if the polarity is reversed. This characteristic of LED can be used to your advantage, e.g. installing an anchor light above your tricolour. You can use the same single duplex wire used on the tri-colour. All you need to do is install a polarity-reversing switch at your control panel. One way turns on the tricolour, the other way turns on the anchor light.

(See 'Anchoring' in the Boat Handling section for an alternative (and safer) location for your anchor light.)

Power consumption: We replaced our masthead light with LEDs. This is an important power saving idea if you are not generating power at night. The typical incandescent bulb in a masthead light is 25 watts. That's 2 amps per hour, plus all that resistance travelling the length of the mast. Get rid of it. These days there is no excuse for turning off navigation lights or anchor lights to conserve power!

Non-Slip Mats
Non-slip mats are very useful at sea, especially in the galley or under the laptop and anything you want to keep in one place. They are useful too, for packing up and protecting delicate items.

Plastic Containers
Spares: Keep jars and cartons that have lids and wash them thoroughly. If you do not have a need for them immediately, at some point you will, whether it is for dried food storage, or unplanned oil or diesel spills that need collecting and disposing of properly.

Dinghy bailer: A large plastic vinegar bottle with a good lid makes a great dinghy bailer. Cut off the bottom, keeping the handle. The soft plastic will fit right into the bottom of your dinghy. Attach a lanyard to the handle so you do not lose it overboard.

Noel bailing out after a large rainfall in Moruya, NSW Australia.

Quality: Not all plastic cartons are strong enough. Some milk cartons are made with very thin plastic. Use only sturdy plastic for storing items or they may split, spilling the messiest of ingredients everywhere. Use the thin plastic for a dinghy bailer. For cooking oil, use good quality containers.

Recommended Safety Equipment
Short story As mentioned in the introduction of this book. When Noel introduced me to cruising I asked him what it would cost; his reply was 'everything we've got'. Sceptical at the time, I can now see the truth in what he said. The equipment available to purchase for your boat is limitless and purchases only stop when you decide to stop buying!

Here's the minimum we had:
- EPIRB
- MOB equipment
- Radios (2 x VHF radios and one SSB (HF) radio)
- Compressed air horn or foghorn
- Whistles
- Life Jackets
- Life-raft
- Fire extinguishers, including an auto/remote suppression system in engine room
- Flares
- Additional signalling devices e.g. mirrors
- Radar
- GPS/Plotter
- Grab Bag
- Medical kits
- Sea anchor

Additional necessary equipment:
- Paper charts (and associated equipment - parallel rulers, divider, 2B or 4B pencils, plotting protractor, pencil compass, rubber, pencil sharpener)
- GPS (at least two) and/or Plotters
- Binoculars
- Sextant (plus, at minimum, a five year Almanac/Celestial Navigation book; this should provide all the information you need to navigate with a Sextant) and/or a Merlin calculator
- Hand-bearing compass
- Storm sails
- Drogue

Of course, equipment on board must be appropriate for the type and size of your vessel and number of people on board. There are endless items of safety equipment available.

AIS: Many of our friends have AIS (Automated Identity System). When cruising again, this is a piece of equipment we would certainly purchase. Be aware that although some commercial vessels are required to carry this equipment, fishing vessels are NOT required to. Like all electronic aids, they are just that - aids. They are not to be relied upon completely, remember a human has to operate it! *(See the Navigation section for more information on AIS.)*

Care and maintenance: A boat (and its equipment) is exposed to the elements of the weather and salt, so regular checks and maintenance are imperative. Simply cleaning radio plug connections regularly can make a big difference to reception quality.

Store your equipment properly. Take equipment below decks when not in use or cover it with a canvas cover, this will help prolong its life.

Read the manual: Understanding how your equipment works is important for everyone on board. It is pointless having it if you don't know how to use it.

Sea Anchor
There are many different types of sea anchors available; the best advice here is to ensure you have one on board. Good seamanship includes being prepared. (*Recommended Reading: Heavy Weather Tactics by Earl Hinz and Storm Tactics Handbook by Lin and Larry Pardey.*)

Self Steering

Aries: We like the Aries, Monitor and Fleming wind vanes and have used the Aries for tens of thousands of miles. Mount an electronic steering ram onto the Aries for light air conditions. *(See article 'Electronic Compass Control' further on.)*

Take care of your gear: If your auto/self steering gear is working too hard (electric gear using too much power, or wind vane tiller or rudder with over extended movement) then you should reef down immediately, you have too much sail up (usually too much main sail).

Safety: We steer by hand when necessary, for example, when leaving or entering port (until docked, moored or anchored), in close quarters situations, in fog and when adjustments are necessary.

Good quality and reliable self steering is very important. If your gear fails in the first few days you may end up hand steering for weeks. This is when fatigue occurs, creating dangerous situations. When at sea for days or weeks, you do not want to hand steer. Self steering allows you to take time to plot your position, carry out regular checks around the vessel, make tea and have a pee! You can't do these things with your hands on the wheel or tiller.

ARTICLE: Published in Australia by Cruising Helmsman.

Electric Compass Control
by Noel & Jackie Parry

'Wander' the trim tab style wind vane was the creator of 'Killer Tiller.' When using the home made steering gear we purchased with Mariah II, we wandered side-to-side, so much so that the tiller took on an ankle breaking swing, side swiping anything that dare get in its path. The tiller took up a lot of the cockpit - these were dangerous times.

Enter 'God', 'hero' or 'our saviour', more commonly known as stainless steel bracket made from bits and bobs. This bracket has steered us around the world in all weather; metres of rolling swells, opposing waves, washing machine conditions and howling gales; this little bracket has become a revered part of our boat. Well, let's be sensible, the added attachment of our beloved Aries wind vane and its phenomenal steering power was quite a help too.

Nature's power
Wind vanes for steering your boat are a brilliant idea. They use the power of the water and the direction of the wind to steer your floating home. With a good sailing breeze these clever devices are reliable and can provide a good course, usually varying between 10°- 20°, maybe closer if the equipment is set up well and the conditions are ideal. More often than not, though, 15°-20° variations occur and sometimes more.

It is all pleasant enough if you are beam on or closer to the wind, the performance is not affected too greatly, however as you come off the wind, apparent wind speed and performance of the vane gear drops. Wandering side to side can have the boat losing both direction and speed. All of which is still far better, we think, than steering shorthanded around the clock. We hitch up our self steering on leaving port and usually do not touch the tiller again until entering the next port.

Improving the marvellous
An adaptation to the reliance on wind is to connect the tiller pilot ram (Autohelm) to the wind vane. Thus the enormous rudder loads that can happen are driven by the water powered vane, but the reliance on the sometimes fickle wind for direction is eliminated and a more reasonable 5°-10° variation is achieved. Electric power consumption is kept to a minimum as the tiller pilot has an almost nonexistent load as it moves in and out. All the energy controlling the rudder is taken by the vane's apparatus of levers, gears and swivels.

Temp to Perm
On our circumnavigation we fitted the tiller pilot to the vane, thinking, 'well at least it will be nice for going down Brisbane River.' 45,000 miles later we now think it is marvellous all the time. Actually, on exceptionally narrow rivers (we like flat water) we set the tiller pilot directly to the tiller for pinpoint accuracy; the rest of the time, in any seas, the bracket, Autohelm tiller and wind vane teamwork in harmony all the time.

Working Reliance
Mariah II's aft hung rudder is like a barn door, wave loading can be high and an autopilot ram directly mounted to the tiller would have to work hard. Most boats that we met along the way, that had their autopilots connected to any other part of their steering, had failures. Quadrant mounted servos have to be enormous and use too much electricity, even wheel mounted pilots failed, they spend too much time over-compensating and thus working hard and using more power.

With our sails balanced, our tiller would be moving 50mm side-to-side. It is hard to do that in 'in the groove' sailing, even by hand. It's remarkable to watch as you're sailing along at six knots in three metre seas, the wind on the quarter and the tiller barely moving. Even better is the fact that we barely waver off course, we all know that with two boats in one ocean it means a race, with our steering gear and course precision our odds for a smug win have improved!

What's needed (if steering by tiller)

1) A good wind vane, Aries, Monitor, Fleming etc.
2) An electric tiller pilot with a remote control box.
3) A mounting bracket, e.g. 'L' shaped bracket bolted to the aft rail with a hole in it.
4) A universal joint acting in three dimensions, this connects the pilot to the vane. Swivel and plate to connect the push-pull end to the 'in place of the sheet of ply wind vane.'

If that makes sense skip the following, if not bear with me - it sounds more complicated than it is.

Mariah's set up. We use an Autohelm 4000, but a 1000 would be just as good as the loads are minimal.

Wind vanes have two vanes, the top wind vane and the bottom water vane. The top wind vane which is removable and when in use is pointed into the wind, acts with two arcs of movement. One arc is the most obvious and rotates about the almost horizontal axle on the frame. The second arc, smaller and not readily noticed, rotates the vane on the vertical axis. So you don't need to worry what all that means if the idea of a double acting universal joint is accepted. I finally did and it saved me a lot of staring into space.

So what is a double acting universal joint, besides something that may be found in Holland? All it is, is two U- shaped brackets with two bolts, one bolt in the vertical and one in the horizontal.

The vertical bolt goes through the open parts of the first 'U' bracket and bolts through a hole drilled into the end of the pushy-pully thingy, the second bolt goes through holes drilled in the bottoms of the two U brackets. The second U bracket bolts directly and firmly onto a plate that replaces the ply wind vane!! Got it??

Another thing, the length of the plate needs to be correct. The electric tiller pilot arm has a certain length of travel. The wind vane frame has a certain range of travel. With the tiller pilot fully extended or retracted, the wind vane should not hit its inbuilt stops otherwise you are trying to bend the whole expensive and much loved apparatus.

It all sounds complicated, but rest assured it is not. Just look at your wind vane, dig out all your stainless steel bits and bobs, nuts and bolts, washers and lock nuts and have a go. On board Mariah we have used bits and pieces that were lurking in the bilge for years and the system has worked faultlessly for eight years. I think I spent in total, two hours cutting and drilling (once I had figured out exactly what I needed, which can take forever) and like I said I thought it'd be good going down the Brisbane River. It really has been one of the best two hours used for long-term gain, peace of mind and general well-being. The other time was when I got married, both are working just fine and come to think of it, I wouldn't be able to have one without the other!

Mariah II

ADDENDUM: On Mariah, with her aft cockpit, we lived with the Autohelm and were alert to its requirements. On Pyewacket, with a centre cockpit, the Autohelm, (on three occasions crossing the Pacific Ocean), spent too much time fully extended and the shear pin inside would break.

We hope this article inspires you to use your resources on board to improve the working characteristics of your boat.

Sewing Machine

A sewing machine is a great investment. Not only for sail repairs and canvas constructing, but also for making courtesy flags. Having the facility for both electric and hand cranking is a good idea.

Jackie on board Pyewacket.

Sail-maker's palm: Alternatively, invest in a good quality sail-maker's palm. A sail-maker's palm is just a bit of leather and steel to help work the needle through all the layers of sails. Sooner or later most cruisers have to sew up sails. Have a supply of good quality UV twine and stick-on sail material for back up in an emergency.

Snubbers

Snubbers absorb shock loading due to their elasticity and strength. Using nylon line with built in elasticity works better than the chandlery purchased black rubber snubbers. These tend to suffer in the sun quicker and eventually break.

Speakers

If you are installing speakers, ensure they are not too near your boat compass as the magnets in the speakers will affect the compass. Install them at least one metre from your compass or the recommended distance provided by the manufacturer. If using head/ear phones do not hang them near the compass for the same reason.

Spinnaker Poles

Practice the set up in port. Noel and I are both capable of setting up and lowering our six metre spinnaker pole alone. In less than ideal conditions we do it together.

We rarely flew a spinnaker, preferring to avoid the concentration required. When we did deploy our spinnaker, invariably the wind would pick up another 5-7 knots and over power the sail, then we would have to take down the entire sail.

We preferred to pole out our Genoa to windward, (which we could easily furl with the pole still in its place) and raise the mainsail and staysail to leeward. Occasionally we found benefit in poling out the staysail to leeward as well. To fill the gap between the luff of the Genoa and the staysail we would fly our jib to leeward off the bow - held only by the head tack and clew (the single forestay used by the Genoa). Flying the jib definitely added power to the rig, but this was the first sail we had to haul-down quickly in a rising wind.

We have a tried and tested method that has worked on our cutter rigged sloops.

Step by step: how we put our spinnaker pole up (alone):
1. Taking it slow is the key.
2. Our pole was always lashed to the deck (horizontally). We'd clip-on the topping lift first, before untying, so the pole was always attached to the boat.
3. Carefully manoeuvre the pole to the desired side of the boat.
4. Tie off the end, nearest the bow, on top of the stanchions. Position to allow easy manoeuvring of the other end of the pole (that is near the mast). Slide the Genoa sheet into the beak of the pole (the Genoa sheet should not be too tight).
5. Attach the foreguy and cleat off. (With experience, the approximate length of the foreguy is known.)
6. Lift the end nearest the mast and clip onto the mast track, raise the track, (if the pole is not already at desired height).
7. Unlash the end on the stanchions (ensuring the sheet is still in the beak) and raise the pole via the topping lift. Both ends are attached as well as the topping lift and foreguy (albeit loose), so the pole should be quite secure.
8. Then go back to the cockpit to unfurl the Genoa.
9. Set pole height to give a ninety degree angle off the mast.
10. Tension or release foreguy to desired clew position and state of furling.
11. Foreguy, topping lift and sheet should be snug and prevent movement of the clew.
12. Enjoy the power surge from your poled out Genoa.

Splicing
See 'Knots' earlier in this section for a recommended animated website for knots and splicing. If you know someone who can splice, take a few lessons, it is far easier than working from a book.

String/Rope
You can never have too much. Collect odds and ends and rolls when you can. We have used lots of string to lash down the canvas and for jury rigging along the way.

Stripping
Strip down old equipment before you throw it out. Keep saddles, screws, wire and anything that is removable. You can be sure you will use it somewhere.

Short story One day a boat on anchor near us threw a salt-seized bronze winch overboard. Noel still mutters about the waste, most winches can be rebuilt and there are lots of useful parts within a winch.

Vice
If you do not have enough room for a permanently mounted vice, find a place where you can install one temporarily. They need just four nuts and bolts to put up and take down. It's one of the most useful tools on a boat.

Windlass/Capstan
A windlass (anchor winch) is the type where the gypsy turns on the horizontal. A capstan gypsy turns on the vertical. The gypsy (or wildcat) is the wheel that handles the chain.

Horizontal windlasses: operate via a horizontal shaft, which allows them to carry an additional wheel - a warping drum (wheel for rope) on the opposite side to the gypsy (wheel for chain).

However, the gypsy and warping drum must be correctly aligned with the bow rollers. Some of these windlasses have a disadvantage as the chain does not occupy much of the wheel on the gypsy and therefore it has less grip.

Vertical capstans: do not have two separate wheels, only the gypsy. Chain has better grip as it usually runs around the gypsy. However this advantage means that the chain must be matched perfectly to the gypsy, as any difference is heightened by the number of links engaged at any one time.

For detailed winch information take a look at:
http://www.maxwellmarine.com/gen_which_winch.php

Wind Vane
We used an Aries wind vane on both our vessels. They are nothing short of fantastic. The second Aries steered Pyewacket (51ft) with no trouble at all, despite several cruisers' doubts. *(See 'Self Steering' above.)*

Care and maintenance: Cover any equipment that is mounted outside (e.g. a wind vane) when not in use, it prolongs the time between having to rebuild and free-up gears and bearings.

BOAT HANDLING & ASSOCIATED EQUIPMENT

Anchoring & Anchoring Equipment

<u>Weakest link</u>: Your rode (chain, rope or combination of both) is only as good as the weakest link. Invest in good quality anchoring equipment; your anchor is not an ornament, it is an insurance policy.

At minimum, your anchor should be heavy enough to hold your boat in up to sixty knots of winds.

In Ecuador we re-galvanised our chain for a very fair price.

The man in the picture is showing us the frame the chain is hooked onto and bit by bit, hand-dipped into the small basin of melted zinc.

<u>Our favourites</u>: Our personal favourites (through use) are the Bruce (used on Pyewacket) and the CQR (plough anchor), which we used on Mariah. At least two different types of anchors for different seabeds (weed and mud/sand) would be ideal. No single anchor is capable in all seabeds. Deployment ability and stowing are important considerations too.

<u>Considerations</u>: Use the manufacturer's recommendations as a starting point only. Anchor manufacturers provide size recommendations based on boat length. Anchor loads are far more dependent on weight and windage; if you are anchoring in an exposed area you will need a bigger anchor. If your boat is heavier than other boats of the same length, or if it has a high above-the-water profile (more windage), you will need a heavier anchor than the recommendation.

As a rule of thumb, a minimum of 1.25lbs of anchor weight per foot of boat length. Or 1.8 kilos of anchor weight per metre of boat length. Anchors do not drag because they are too big; they drag because they are not big enough.

For example: 35 foot boat = a 45lb anchor
11 metre boat = a 20 kilo anchor

Carry a spare anchor that is ready to go at a moment's notice.

Chain: We use all chain on our main anchor, adding important weight. It also helps keep the anchor stock parallel to the seabed and therefore the anchor is not lifted out. Chain is better for strength and weight. However, chain can still be cut through by coral if left swinging long enough on coral heads. Rope will certainly part on coral, is not as strong as chain and chafes quickly. *(See 'Floating your chain' later on in this section.)*

Short story Our good sailing buddies purchased new galvanised chain from a reputable store, accompanied by all the testing guarantees. Not many weeks into regular usage, they hauled up the chain to find a weld on one link completely broken! It was only pure luck that the chain had not parted completely. They took the chain back and it was replaced.

Rope: If you are using rope, Nylon is light, easy to handle and strong. It also has some elasticity which is important for increased comfort (not snatching) and for reducing stress on equipment. Braided line is more flexible and easier to handle, but with minimum elasticity. Three stranded laid line has great elasticity, which stops the snatching impact-loads on the anchor and boat.

As a guide, use one-eighth of an inch of rope diameter for every three metres of boat length. Small diameter rope is hard to grip, and large diameter rope loses its elasticity.

Set up: An anchor bend can be used to tie the rope to the chain in an emergency. It is better to have your equipment already set up, the end of the line should be eye spliced around a thimble and shackled to the chain. It is better to have at least a few metres of chain between the anchor and anchor rope to add extra weight and keep the anchor stock parallel.

Shackles should be a size larger than the chain, wire ('mouse') the pin to prevent the pin from working loose.

Anchor rode: Anchor rode is all the components that join your anchor to your vessel, e.g. chain, rope, shackles and pins.

Scope: Scope is the ratio of length of rode:height of bow roller above the seabed. E.g. 4:1 scope means the rode is 4 times longer than the height of your bow above the seabed.

In calm anchorages we would sometimes raft-up.

Check the weather first, there's nothing worse than having to part in the dark hours.

Here with our Canadian friends Rolande and Angus on board SV Periclees, in Noumea, New Caledonia.

31

The amount of scope you lay out relates to different factors. Take into account the height between the surface of the water and your bow roller, plus the true depth of water from where your anchor sits on the seabed to the surface (not where your boat sits).

Depth considerations: When finding an anchor spot, consider the distance from your depth sounder to the bottom of your keel (if your depth sounder is not right on the bottom of your keel or adjusted for the difference). Do not forget the height of tide, so you know what the minimum and maximum depths will be.

The greater the scope the more horizontal the pull on the anchor, and the better it will hold.

Scope	Holding Power
10:1	100%
7:1	91%
6:1	85%
5:1	77%
4:1	67%
3:1	53%
2:1	35%

A new type of anchor? Consider the seabed (noted on your charts). This weed was very heavy to lift.

Step by step: how to anchor:

1. Two-way radios are a good way to communicate easily. We use clear and simple hand signals between the windlass operator and helmsman. It's pointless shouting instructions at each other, as the wind will carry your voice away.

2. When anchoring, complete a three-sixty degree circle to ensure there is enough swinging room depth, then return to anchor in the middle of the circle. Stem the wind or current, whichever is the strongest to allow your vessel to go astern naturally.

3. To determine whether the wind or current is stronger, look at other boats that are similar to yours to see which way they are facing. If you are not sure, or there are no other boats around, put your boat in neutral and see how she behaves. (This is a good idea prior to docking too.)

4. The helmsman holds up some fingers in relation to the depth in metres. Usually we are together when turning the circle we wish to anchor within, so whoever operates the windlass knows the depth.

5. Let go the anchor when stationary or making way slowly astern. Once the anchor is on the seabed, if the boat is not already moving astern herself, use astern propulsion to gently lay the chain out on the seabed. You do not want the chain in one big heap. The person operating the windlass should point to the stern if astern propulsion is required.

6. Just before the desired amount has been let out, put the engine in neutral, allowing the momentum to carry your boat back (ensure the windlass brake is applied). This gentle slowing will help the anchor dig in.

7. Allow the anchor to settle for a while, and then apply astern propulsion. Once the chain pulls up, look at buildings or trees abeam, one in the foreground and one in the background, i.e. objects in transit (like leads when you come into port, i.e. one behind the other in a line). If there is no discernible movement between the two objects this means the boat has not moved. Lay your hand on the chain (do not grip) while applying astern propulsion; usually you can feel if it's dragging.

8. If the anchor is dragging, the signal is similar to the 'anchor stuck' signal *(see 'hauling in' further on)*, but the fist works back towards the body to mimic the dragging/jumping motion of the anchor.

9. A quick way to check any movement once you are dug in is to take bearings of conspicuous buildings onshore, one on port and one on starboard. Take hand compass bearings and note them down. Ensure everyone on board is aware of which buildings/markers you have used. *(See 'Bearings' in the Navigation section.)*

10. Running a bridle strop (line with elasticity, e.g. three-strand nylon) from cleats at the port and starboard bow to the chain prevents the chain snatching and also gives the rode a better angle. The chain lies lower and makes it harder for the anchor to pull free; this prevents the windlass equipment taking the load.

11. Set your GPS anchor alarm to detect dragging at night. Sit in the cockpit on anchor-watch in extreme conditions. If the anchor area is small, you have very little time if you drag.

12. Regularly swap roles from windlass operator to helmsman, in order to maintain various skills. In emergency conditions whoever is the better windlass operator or helmsman, takes that responsibility.

(See 'Anchor Etiquette' further on in this section for more information on allowing suitable swing room.)

In the Marquesas Mariah dragged anchor.

It was slow and eventually she stopped, a little way from the fleet, but then the anchor dug in and we were safe.

The extra dinghy ride was not an issue and we had plenty of room if the weather had turned.

Hauling in:
- While pulling up the anchor we point with all fingers (closed together) in the direction of the anchor so the helmsman knows where to steer the boat. Do not use your windlass to pull the boat forward, you want to preserve your equipment and keep it running for as long as possible. To prevent overriding the anchor, indicate you want the motor in neutral by putting your hand out horizontally and complete a sweeping motion from left to right.

- If the boat's momentum carries you over the anchor, point to where the anchor is and wait until the chain is slack before starting to winch it in again. (So the helmsman knows what is happening). When the anchor is off the seabed put one thumb up; when the anchor is fully on board, two thumbs up.

- If the anchor is stuck, we make a fist and jerk the hand back two or three times, mimicking a caught anchor. To pull the anchor out of the seabed we use the boat, i.e. propel over the anchor to help lift it from the mud. After showing the 'anchor stuck' signal, we point in the direction to steer to enable the helmsman to drive the boat over the anchor, using this motion to lift the anchor slowly. Tie the chain off to a cleat first, so the force is not directly on the windlass.

Short story At anchor in Portugal we experienced a huge continuous swell wrapping around the headland and coming at our stern. We also had twenty to thirty knot winds on the bow. Mariah would override the anchor with the swell, then ping back with the wind. The anchor gear, when fully extended, would groan and creak. Then we would catapult forward again. At 3 a.m. we decided that it was easier to up anchor and get sailing, the relief was immense. Any number of problems could have arisen with that motion: broken equipment, dragging anchor, etc.

We keep our boat ready for sea when at anchor. If you have to make an emergency escape, there will be no time to stow gear. More than once we have upped anchor in the middle of the night during a severe wind shift. This applies especially in large bays open to the sea (aka 'open road anchorages').

Weather watching on anchor is just as important as when at sea.

Picture taken in the Caribbean on board Mariah.

Short story Seconds to spare: A wind shift creating a lee shore accompanied by thousands of miles of swell is an ideal recipe for dragging anchor, which we did with just seconds to spare before disaster. At 3 a.m. off the east coast of Barbados in an 'open road' anchorage, we dragged anchor. The wind had shifted at about 2.45 a.m. and we were instantly awake, feeling the boat move differently. Suddenly we had a lee shore, twenty knot winds and several other boats around us to consider. We were holding at this time but didn't like our chances, especially as we watched a nearby boat drag up onto the coral reef (shouting and horns by all other vessels failed to wake the occupants). At that moment Noel said 'I'll put our engine on, just in case' and as he did, we dragged and had only a few metres and seconds to spare until we collided with another vessel. By this time our bow was pounding three metres up and down in the swell that had grown over thousands of miles of ocean. On the helm, Noel kept us steady. I sat on my bottom, looping one arm around a stanchion and pressed the anchor windlass button with my left hand, there was no way I could stand up. We had enough moonlight for hand signals and for me to know when the chain was slack enough to haul in. I didn't want to pull against the chain when it had become bar-taut and I had to wait until the bow pounded down to create enough slack to pull some chain in. Fortunately, Noel and I make an excellent team; we don't panic and just get the job done. I felt like I was riding a bucking bronco, but never felt under pressure to rush. Taking time to get the job done right meant no injuries or broken equipment. We were soon in deeper water, which was much calmer. We puttered a few miles south to a better anchorage. One boat ended up on the coral shelf, by some miracle only suffering superficial damage. However, it took two days and the services of the Bridgetown Tug Company to pull the stricken vessel over fifty metres of coral to get the boat back into deeper water. Note: In order to support the enormous loads for this tow, a strong 38mm line was wrapped around the gunwale line of the stricken vessel. The tow line was then tied to this 'girdle'. The gunwale laid rope was held in place by a web of lines over the deck and under the boat to keep it in position - it worked.

Seabed properties: If depth, clarity and conditions allow, take a swim to check that your anchor has set properly, as this aids peaceful sleep.

In most places you will find the seabed characteristics from your chart.

Cl.	Clay
Co.	Coral
G.	Gravel
Grs.	Grass
M.	Mud
Rk.	Rock
S.	Sand
Sh.	Shells
rky.	Rocky

Two anchors: are good for winds of a consistent direction, for example, at anchor with a big blow for a few hours without the tide changing. In shifting winds and currents the lines can twist together. Monitor your gear regularly and if there is any doubt, do not leave the boat unattended.

For tidal water and conditions with strong wind over tide, try anchoring with two anchors off the one chain. This requires three elements:

1) Your vessel's primary anchor and rode.
2) The second anchor and approximately one boat length of chain.
3) A shackle and mousing wire.

Step by step: how to deploy two anchors:
1) Anchor facing the stream or wind (whichever is the strongest force influencing your vessel).
2) Dig your primary anchor in as per your usual method.
3) Once you are satisfied that the first anchor has dug in, pull in the primary rode leaving approximately 2:1 scope.

4) Have your second anchor ready at the stern.
5) Shackle and mouse approximately one boat length of chain from the second anchor to your primary rode.
6) Ensure that the chain is not behind the shrouds, stanchions or sheets.
7) Throw the second anchor over.
8) Now pay out your primary anchor rode to your desired scope.
9) The more you let out, the better (if you have enough swinging room).
10) You should now be hanging off your primary anchor and rode.
11) You must wait for the tide to change (i.e. facing the other way) in order to check that the second anchor has dug in.
12) This method ensures that you have a steady pull on at least one anchor and neither of them will need to re-set themselves.

This may sound like a lot of hard work, but it is far simpler than dragging anchor at midnight or untwisting two anchor rodes that are hung off the bow.

If using two anchors off the bow with two separate rodes, place the anchors off the bow at an angle of about forty-five degrees from each other. Take a look at this website for more information: http://www.boattraining.com/waterways/issues/ww_00-spring/technique_anchor.html

Anchor Collision Regulations: If another vessel hits your boat on anchor and you are not showing the appropriate 'at anchor' signs (day or night), the captain of your boat will be held partly responsible for any injury or damage. The International Collision Regulations state (you should have a copy of these regulations on board to check full details): *Night-time, show anchor light. 'A vessel at anchor shall exhibit where it can best be seen: A vessel of less than 50 metres in length shall exhibit an all-round white light where it can best be seen.' Daytime show black ball, 'Vessels at anchor shall hoist a ball shape forward where it can best be seen'. (Black balls should be 0.6m in diameter).*

We hang our black ball from a halyard on the fore deck, quite high. Many people ask 'what is that for?'

Rafted up with our great buddies, Den and 'Tash on board SV Frodo. Anchored in the Intracoastal Waterways of America.

You can clearly see our black ball.

Two short stories Devastating Deaths, are you responsible? An Australian sailor was anchored in the Brisbane River. One night, two lads in a speed boat hit her boat and were killed instantly. Investigation proved that she was carrying her anchor light and therefore absolved from any responsibility.

Two jet-ski riders in the USA ran over an anchor chain of a boat on anchor during the day. They were too close, hit the chain and both died. The skipper of the boat on anchor was held partly responsible for their deaths, as he did not have the black ball hoisted.

It seems little effort for a lot of insurance. It is not your problem if others do not understand what these signals mean. Make sure you are doing the right thing.

Anchor light location: Our anchor light was mounted on the forepeak, at about head height. Masthead anchor lights can be difficult to see when they are on the top of the mast. Generally when entering an anchor area at night, most people do not look up. If your anchor light is lower down, it will be in most people's line of sight and light up part of your deck, leaving no doubt as to where you are and what you are signalling.

Anchor light: Turn on your anchor light when going ashore; you never know if you are going to be delayed until after nightfall.

Homemade Black Ball: Make a black ball out of a sturdy black plastic bag, roll it in a ball and stuff with material (or foam) if necessary. Lash on a line and hoist. Alternatively, use a black round buoy, which is a perfect anchor ball, but takes more stowage space. You can purchase flat plastic pieces that slide together to create a black ball, this is much easier to stow. Don't forget to take your black ball down when lifting anchor.

Floating your chain

If you are anchoring in coral, try to locate a sandy patch if visibility allows, then float your anchor chain, even in low-lying coral. In shifting winds the chain can catch on coral heads and prevent you from swinging in the same way as other boats, potentially creating a close-quarters situation.

When your chain is snatching and rubbing on coral, it will be rubbing the galvanisation off and adding an unnecessary load on your entire equipment. The snatching on the chain occurs because you no longer have the graceful and soft catenary curve in your rode.

Step by step: how to float your chain (using buoys):
1. If possible, dive on the anchor first to estimate where the buoy needs to be situated. You do not want the buoy too near the anchor to affect the angle of the chain, i.e. not to pull the anchor up.

2. Sometimes we use two buoys, one above the other, to help float the heavy chain. The unseen buoy below the water is highlighted by another that is on the water, i.e. visible. If you do not have buoys, fenders work just as well.

3. Tie a loop on the top or side of the buoy (or fender) to enable you to pick it up easily with the boat hook as you pull in the anchor. You need to keep the line away from your propeller. The line can become difficult to reach under the buoys.

4. Have at least two spare boat hooks on board.

Safety: When anchoring there are a lot of forces occurring, especially in windy conditions. You can replace equipment but not lost fingers! Take care and take your time in all conditions.

Remove the mainsail cover and have the mainsail ready to haul prior to lifting the anchor. This is a good backup in case the anchor comes up and your engine stops.

If you are leaving your boat on anchor, make sure the end of your anchor chain is tied off in the chain locker. If a big blow comes through and your boat is dragging, someone else may let out some more chain for you. They will naturally assume it is tied off. We recommend using a knot that can be released fairly easily and/or have a sharp knife handy. *(See 'Knots and Splicing' in the Boat Equipment section.)*

Anchor Buddy, Sentinel, Kellets: An anchor buddy is an additional weight suspended from the rode to help maintain a catenary in the chain and to lower the angle of the pull on the anchor. We run ours about three quarters of the length along the rode (nearest to the anchor). You can buy these from any marine shop or make your own. This website shows how they work: http://www.anchorbuddy.co.nz.

Noel's Anchor Buddy. The roller detached to allow us to put the chain between the weight and the roller. The weight could then roll down the chain. We kept control with the nylon line.

Moorea (near Tahiti).

Maintenance: End-for-end (the end that was shackled to your anchor, swapped to be tied in the anchor bucket on board) your chain regularly as the last few metres of chain left in the chain locker will rust and weld together. This gives you a great opportunity to check your chain. If any links have more than 10% wear, the chain should be replaced.

Each year when we end-for-end our anchor chain, we mark the chain every ten metres using wire ties. They do eventually come off, so check and replace regularly. I find that snipping off the ends (once affixed to the chain) keeps them there longer. One wire tie = 10 metres, two wire tires = 20 metres and so on. When anchoring or hauling up in calm conditions, keep spare wire ties at the ready to replace any that are lost. An alternative is to use paint to mark the chain at intervals. Each mark will denote five or ten metres, so you will have to keep count as the chain is coming in or out.

Caring for your equipment also means that the windlass should not take the strain of the boat pulling on anchor. Hook a line through a link of chain (or use a Devil's Claw) and cleat it off, this is the line that should take the strain (check your cleats!). Preserve your equipment, as you want it to last.

Regularly perform a complete inspection for rust, cracks and weakness. Give the chain a thorough fresh water clean regularly. A good time to do this is when the boat is slipped or on a marina that will allow you to put your chain on the wharf.

Trip line: In a rocky or coral anchorage we use a trip line on the anchor. With a line attached to the crown of the anchor, you can pull the anchor out backwards, i.e. 'trip' an anchor, which may be fouled. On the end of the trip line tie a buoy or fender. Tie an additional loop near the top or side of the fender, so you can easily pick it up with the boat hook when hauling in your anchor.

In more crowded areas we avoid this for fear of traffic running over the line/fender and pulling out the anchor, or mistaking it for a mooring buoy! Alternatively use a Dan Buoy as a trip float. On the flag write your boat's name and an anchor sign, people will see this better. You could get really technical and add a small solar light for night-time.

Anchoring etiquette: If there are any problems with space e.g. swinging too close, last in is first out. If you drag close to someone, it doesn't matter when you anchored: you drag, you move.

Allow more room than you think you need. Most people laugh at us when we anchor so far out from everyone; 'What's the weather like out there?' they ask. But we see boats that are anchored at a reasonable distance move differently (same design, just different displacements), and come very close in light winds. Also, with any wind shift creating a lee shore, boats close to shore will experience greater seas. Shallow water means bigger onshore waves. If this occurs and boats are tightly packed, it can become very dangerous.

When anchoring, think about the circle each boat makes when it swings. Are other boats using rope or chain? Are they on a mooring with less swinging room? How much rode do they have out?

If you drop your anchor near or on the beam of another boat with a different rode, expect to encroach. Drop your hook far enough away from the other boat's beam to ensure you have enough room when winds and currents shift, build or die. Better yet, drop your anchor behind other boats, ensuring better swing room.

Talk to other cruisers on anchor. Sometimes there just isn't enough swing room for everyone. If this is the case and you have squeezed into a tight spot, stay on board. Don't leave your boat and expect other people already there to do anchor watch alone. At the very least discuss the situation and work out a plan whereby everyone can go ashore at different times, while someone is always keeping an eye on the boats.

If space is at a premium or you are near another boat, dinghy over and pay a courtesy visit. Goodwill is important, and other boats, knowing you are aware of their position, will be a lot more comfortable and happy you have discussed the situation.

Short story Be ready: we thought we were safe in all weathers, in a very protected anchorage. One night, we were bashed for three hours by sixty knot, vortexing winds. We almost lost Pyewacket that night.

If you are not sure where other boats' anchors are (which is quite often, unless there is a reasonable breeze, boats can be displaced by light winds or changing winds and currents), a simple solution is to ask a boat to pull back (or pull back yourselves if you are already on anchor). It gives everyone an idea (and reminder) of where their anchor sits.

It is so much easier to move prior to it becoming a necessity; if we anchor and we are too close to other boats or reefs, or simply not comfortable, we up anchor straight away. When upping anchor to move, bring your anchor above the water line and bring the stock of the anchor into the roller. This stops the anchor swinging into your hull. Do not just raise the anchor above the seabed and drag it to your next anchor site, you may well pick up other anchors!

Look after your windlass, when they stop working it is highly inconvenient.

For some time on Mariah we had to use a halyard hooked onto the chain, running back to a winch on the mast to haul up . . . a very slow process.

<u>Mounting an anchor windlass and water ingress</u>: It is important to have your windlass mounted on a reinforced part of the deck; preferably through-bolted to an internal bulkhead or a similar strong point of the hull.

At sea, to avoid water running down the hawser pipe, cover the pipe opening with a plastic bag and duct tape.

Crossing A Bar
Complete a full engine check prior to committing to a bar crossing of any sort. Physically inspect the engine carefully, not just the dials. Also check both forward and astern propulsion.

Short story We were about to cross a bar into Morro Bay (south of San Francisco), just before it was closing for oncoming severe weather. On inspecting the engine I found two fuel return lines had split (Pyewacket was new to us then and they were not fuel graded lines!) and we had diesel spewing out over a hot engine (we'd been running the engine all through the night). Noel put his hands on the new fuel line immediately and made repairs in minutes. The entrance was very narrow and becoming dangerous, we just made it in before the entrance was closed – with a few more grey hairs!

Research the entrance/bar crossing thoroughly and check your tide programs are correct (with local information or another tide program). Gain local knowledge where possible. Secure all equipment, close hatches and don life jackets. Resources: http://www.wxtide32.com/

Always leave time for the tide to rise should you become grounded (i.e. if possible do not enter on a falling tide). Watch for wave patterns; monitor and take note of 'sets' coming in or the occasional huge swell. Take the time to assess the bar entrance. Once you start crossing you will be committed, it can be very dangerous to attempt to turn around.

Lee Shore & Windward
The most dangerous place to be in heavy weather is off a lee shore. The term refers to a shore that is in the lee (downwind) of the boat. Wind and waves can quickly push the boat sidewards towards the shore. This is a real problem if at anchor and the anchor site is open to a possible lee shore if the wind shifts *(see 'Anchoring' above).*

The opposite is windward or weather shore, where the land is windward and therefore protecting the seas from becoming stirred up.

Leaving The Boat
When living on board we go ashore only when we are certain that a wind shift is not forecast (that could put us on a lee shore). On Mariah we turned off every seacock each time we went ashore. On Pyewacket there were far too many seacocks to do this. We did ensure both bilge pumps were functioning, the gas was off at two places and the pressurized (fresh) water pumps were off. If we were leaving Pyewacket for more than twenty-four hours, then we did turn all the seacocks off.

We always turned our LED anchor light on when we left the boat, no matter the time, in case we were delayed. *(See 'Leaving The Boat' in the Voyage Preparation section for more details.)*

Manoeuvring
Every boat handles differently. Full keel boats are difficult to manoeuvre; fin-keeled boats are a lot easier. Understand your vessel's design and research ways to help you manoeuvre out of tight spots. *(See 'Paddle Wheel/Transverse Thrust' and 'Springing Off' later in this section.)*

We traversed the inland waterways of The Great Loop in America and Canada; and the French canals. After hundreds of locks and anchoring each day for over a year our boat handling was much improved.

Over time you will naturally feel what effect the wind and current have on your vessel. Use these to your advantage.

Man Overboard (MOB)

Short story We have seen shocking video footage of a young fit man who had been sailing all his life, being flipped overboard. A flapping sail that he went forward to adjust tossed him over like a piece of cotton and instantly he was lost . . . it was daylight and in calm seas. Several boats searched for hours, but he was never seen again. (See 'Jack Lines' in the Boat Equipment section.)

Seamanship books are an excellent resource to start planning what to do in a Man Overboard situation. We like Capt. Dick Gandy's Australian Boat Manual. You will need to adapt a strategy that is sympathetic to the conditions it takes place in and within your boat's and your own capabilities. Here's our advice:

- We always wear a harness when alone on deck or in the cockpit, especially if it is an exposed cockpit. We are well versed in what to do, should our worst nightmare occur. Regularly we discuss different conditions and what would be the best process to retrieve a person in those conditions. We can both handle every aspect of the vessel and we change roles frequently to ensure our skills are kept up to date.

- If you see someone go overboard and there are other people on board, yell at the top of your voice, 'MAN OVERBOARD' and don't take your eyes off the person in the water for one moment. Keep pointing to the person in the water so the helmsman knows which direction they are in.

- This scenario is okay if there are more than two of you on board. If there is just you left on board, hit the GPS man overboard button, this will record the position where they fell over (if you saw where and when it happened).Throw life-rings or whatever you have handy for the person to get hold of, this also gives you a larger target to search for. People easily disappear within waves.

- Depending on the conditions, I would put the vessel on a beam reach, start the engine, furl Genoa, drop the staysail and go about (tack) to come back on a reciprocal course (beam reach), hopefully slightly downwind of MOB. Come up and luff into the wind, take the engine out of gear and drop the main sail. Then pick up MOB (see below). But there are so many variables here, depending on your vessel and conditions. The best solution is to know how your boat handles and operates and have the ability to manage your boat single-handed.

- If you are using your engine to manoeuvre, ensure you put the engine in neutral as you approach the person; propellers and soft limbs do not mix!

- I would use a halyard to help haul Noel up. Running a spare halyard (from the mast) forward to our windlass is possible, making winching easier. *(See 'Mast Climbing' in the Maintenance & Repairs section.)*

- If you have lost someone overboard and are not sure when it happened, i.e. it happened while you were asleep, the only thing you can do is back track. You will need to take into account set and drift. If the weather is severe, chances of locating the person and recovery are extremely low. Best tip here is prevention - stay attached to the boat! *(See 'Set & Drift' in the Navigation section.)*

Short story At least once every trip, Noel will be on watch and I wake up to find he has gone from the cockpit. Momentarily I panic, thinking he has gone overboard. He is usually just ducking behind something or in the head!

Paddle Wheel Effect/Transverse Thrust
A right-handed propeller turns clockwise (think of yourself as standing behind the propeller, looking forward). This means your vessel's transverse thrust will be turning the bow to port (and stern to starboard) when applying forward propulsion. When holding a course, we naturally compensate for any transverse thrust, but it can be useful when docking.

With a right-handed propeller, a quick spurt forward and the bow will go to port (stern to starboard). A quick spurt in astern, the bow will go to starboard (stern to port). There are influencing factors such as the prop size and speed, so test this theory in calm, flat water (with no current) and feel how your boat responds.

Traversing the Panama Canal, our crew had a job holding Mariah in the lock while the large boat in front used his props to keep his boat in the right place.

Reefing The Mainsail

It is important for us to be able to reef our mainsail on any point of sailing, including downwind. Turning into the wind to reef can be highly dangerous and incredibly difficult. You could be reefing down when the wind is too strong and therefore there are large waves. Turning into the weather is stressful for the crew and for the boat.

Rig reefing lines through all your reefing cringles so that you can haul down (using a winch) on the luff and leech as conditions dictate. This is known as Jiffy or Slab reefing and works, even if the sail is full of wind. Reef down early; our theory is: it is easier to shake out the main if the wind does not develop, rather than trying to reef in strong winds. You can only sail at hull speed, excessive heel just slows you down.

Rudder

If you have lost your rudder, first make sure that the boat is not leaking through the rudder stock stuffing box and/or hull connections. What you do next depends on where you are and the conditions you are in.

By adjusting the main and jib sheets, you can balance your boat to sail on a particular course without the use of a rudder. While monitoring the sails, this may give you time to jury rig a rudder. *(For emergency steering ideas turn to 'Emergencies' in the Maintenance & Repairs section.)*

Preparation is important. Remember that if using a temporary rudder, it is very important to trim your sails correctly to ensure there is minimal strain on the repairs.

Running Aground

If it is a gentle running aground and you are on sand (your chart will tell you what the seabed is) apply astern propulsion as soon as possible. Be aware of how much sand/mud you are kicking up, as this may end up in your water intake. (*See some relevant chart symbols in 'Anchoring' at the beginning of this section.*)

Considerations: If this does not work there are other options, depending on the circumstances. Is the tide going in or out? If it is a rising tide, you could simply wait until the boat is lifted off the ground (ensure you know which way to go to avoid doing it again). Is the tide going out? Then you had better move quickly, the situation will only get worse.

Short story While cruising the Intracoastal Waterways of America with my mum and dad on board, we ran aground. Fortunately it was gently and on mud. We pushed our long boom right out to the opposite side of the grounding and my dad and I shimmied along to the end to add more weight. Meanwhile my mum hopped from one foot to another worrying about us! The boat heeled over enough and off we went. Obviously this was carried out in enclosed water, with no waves.

Mum watching dad and I on the end of Mariah's boom.

Kedging off: Kedging off with your anchors is another way. Use the tender (dinghy) to run out your anchors in the direction you want to go. Using winches, pull on one, then the other to pull backwards. You can use these anchors in combination with your engine. Ensure all lines are kept clear of the propeller. Give some forethought to getting your anchor(s) back on board easily if you do not have an anchor permanently mounted astern (assuming you are pulling the boat backwards off the grounding).

Create a list or heeling over: If you are on rocks or coral then you could move weights from the area of the vessel that is stuck, altering the trim or creating a list. If you are on a sailboat, use your sails to heel over. You could also let out your boom to the side and add weights to create a list.

Another idea for listing: Our good friends Chris and Gilli on SV West Wind have used the following to create a list (the definition of a list is the angle from the upright caused by an uneven distribution of weights athwartships). They create a list and then use the anchor to pull them clear (kedging off):

Elements required: A strong dinghy with three very strong attachment points with lifting strops.

Method:
- Put the anchor out, using the dinghy, so once the boat is leaning over you can kedge off.
- Hold out the boom using preventer ropes, fore guy and topping lift.
- With the dinghy in the water, attach the mainsheet to the dinghy lifting strops.
- Fill the dinghy with water using a bucket.
- Pull on the mainsheet. If the dinghy doesn't come up, then the boom must come down.
- This pulls the boat over (creating a big list) and then the keel will be lifted off the seabed.
- Haul in the kedge rode and you are free to run aground another day!

Jettison weight: If it is a serious situation, you will have to consider jettisoning some weight to get off. There are legalities involved in dumping items in the water, unless there is danger of loss of life. *(See 'Environmental laws/MARPOL' in the Voyage Preparation section.)*

Assistance: If you are stuck fast, what is the next tide (is it high or low)? Should a tow be arranged now? Can you pull the mast over using another vessel? If you decide to heel your boat over using another vessel to pull your mast over, be cautious of down-flooding (i.e. pulling the vessel over too far so as to allow water ingress, creating further problems with stability and flooding). *(See short story below.)*

Lighter coloured water usually means shallower water. If you are unsure of the depth, go slowly or send out the tender first to sound the bottom. *(See 'Lead Line' in the Boat Equipment section.)*

Before the situation becomes serious, ask for help. If you are offering assistance, take care. Why has the other boat run aground? Can you get close enough to help without running aground too?

Short story While in the Intracoastal waterways of America (there is limited information of chart depths marked on the chart when off the main channel), we ran aground – admittedly we were too near a marker, but we were still in the main channel! The tide was racing out and Mariah started to lean precariously, it was not good. Fortunately, we were in company of our great friends, Den and 'Tash on board SV Frodo. We passed over a halyard from the top of our mast to Den, in their dinghy. This didn't work, so they used Frodo (their sailing vessel), and pulled us over (heeling) enough to get us off, with much relief.

Smelling The Bottom/Water Pressure Phenomena
Smelling the bottom happens when you are going too fast in shoal water. You can create a 'suction' effect, which can pull the boat towards the seabed and may cause you to run aground (usually only with flatter bottomed vessels).

'Sucking the bank' is when the bow is repelled and therefore the stern attracted. So take care in narrow waterways. Passing a vessel too close can also create a repelling/sucking effect. Give other boats a wide berth and slow down.

Springing Off
Springing off is a handy manoeuvre in order to leave a wharf when boats are tightly packed or when the wind and/or current is pushing you onto the wharf.

Firstly, let's clarify the names of the all important spring lines.

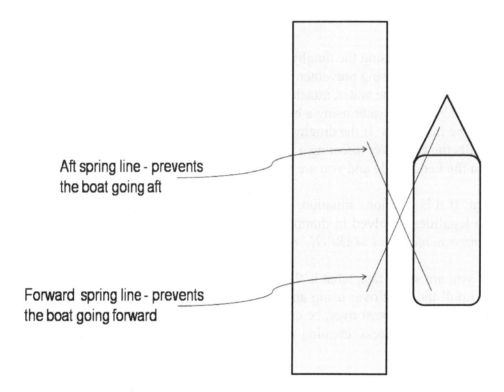

Aft spring line - prevents the boat going aft

Forward spring line - prevents the boat going forward

<u>How to remember which line is which</u>: The **aft** spring line is on the **aft** part of your boat, preventing the boat going **aft**. The **forward** spring line is on the **forward** part of your boat, preventing the boat going **forward.**

<u>Step by step: how to spring off your stern</u>:
1. Cast off all lines except the forward springer.
2. Rig the forward springer so you can release it from the wharf as you depart (e.g. looped around the cleat on the dock, so you can just pull it through when leaving).
3. Power very gently forward with the forward springer tied off, and turn your wheel towards the dock. This will 'spring' your stern away from the dock (i.e. your stern will come away from the dock without your boat going forward very much).
4. You may need a fender strategically placed near the bow.
5. Once your stern is at an angle to allow you to go backwards, stop engines, release the forward springer and apply astern propulsion until you are completely clear.

Do the reverse for springing the bow out. Just use the aft springer and gently apply astern propulsion first. Once your bow is clear of all obstructions and you have enough room to manoeuvre, stop engines, then release the aft springer and power forward and away. (As you are springing off, watch your stern carefully as well as the bow.)
See http://boatsafe.com/nauticalknowhow/docking.htm for a graphic demonstration.

<u>Tying fenders</u>: When tying fenders or a dinghy to the boat, tie the line at the base of the stanchion; it is stronger there. The best knots to use are the Clove Hitch or Rolling Hitch as they are easy to adjust quickly.

Storm Preparation
Obtain weather forecasts and track the storm's position and movement. Try not to rely on one source of information. Wear a life jacket and issue one to all on board, making sure they put them on. Work out the best track to sail (the safe/dangerous semi-circle - see below). Get some sleep before the storm arrives, if you can.

If you are cruising in a cyclone area during cyclone season, ensure you understand the usual behaviour of the storm within your location. Analyse the best track to sail should you be caught in a cyclone. Note that in the northeast of Australia, cyclones generally move in a south-westerly direction before curving towards the south or southeast (but there are no guarantees).

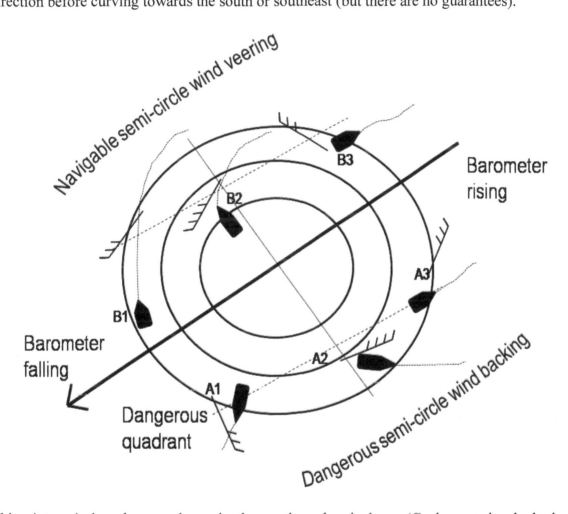

This picture is based on cyclones in the southern hemisphere. (Cyclones spin clockwise in the southern hemisphere, anti-clockwise in the northern hemisphere.) Therefore, the dangerous semi-circle of a cyclone is to the right of an approaching cyclone path. This area has the strongest winds and it is the direction the cyclone is expected to move.

<u>To evade a cyclone</u>: In the southern hemisphere, if you are in the navigable semi-circle, keep the wind on your port quarter and manoeuvre away from the cyclone. If you are in the dangerous semi-circle, keep the wind on your port bow and try to manoeuvre away from the vortex.

Remember, no part of a cyclone is safe. It is just that in the navigable sectors you have a better chance of escaping the path of the vortex.

In the diagram above, vessels at B1, B2 and B3 have a chance to run away from the vortex. Vessels at A1, A2 and A3 are in a perilous situation: if they run they will be sucked into the vortex. Therefore, they have to keep the wind on the port bow to try to get away from the vortex. Conditions will improve, believe it or not, by A3. From here keep heading NE until the cyclone dies out. *(Note from Noel: 'Then I'd run aground somewhere, climb a tree and never go back to sea!')*

Basic preparation:
Anchoring or in a Marina:
- Are there good hurricane holes that are reachable quickly? Is there enough room? You won't be the only boat there.
- Keep topped up with fuel and water.
- On a warning, proceed to your selected hurricane hole early.
- Does your boat insurance cover damage you may do to other boats? Think about boats in the same hurricane hole or next to you in a marina, will they be covered for damage they may inflict on you?
- Take pictures of your boat and all the expensive equipment and keep these pictures with your insurance policy in a safe place like your grab bag.
- Prior to the hurricane season starting, find out where to get information.

When a cyclone warning is issued:
- Prepare for the worst.
- If you have time, strip the exterior of your boat: sails*, dodger, canvas awnings, solar panels, wind generators, lines, BBQs, anchors and as many non-permanent items you can. (*You may need your main, so leave it on, but lash it down very securely.)
- Stow your dinghy and outboards below.
- Tie, lash and fix everything else left outside.
- Ensure all lines (snubbers on anchor or lines in a marina) have spring (elasticity) in them. Rig up additional lines.
- Use rags, pipes, leather or foam on all possible chafing points.
- If you are on anchor and have time, dive on your anchor and check its setting. Ask other boats to do the same.
- If you are leaving your boat, remove all your personal items, specifically your personal and boat documentation and let someone know where you are.
- Turn on your navigation lights.
- Note your position in your log and on your chart.
- Let someone else know where you are, preferably someone onshore.
- Prepare several meals and hot liquids in a flask/thermos.
- Eat and feed everyone on board a hot meal.
- Get as much sleep as possible.
- Hand out seasickness pills (take them prior to the storm, you are going to experience horrendous conditions; it is better to be ready for becoming seasick, even if you have never suffered previously).
- Check every corner to ensure everything is stowed properly down below.

Personal preparation:
- Take seasickness medication early.
- Have torches and head lamps ready.

- Have snorkel gear (dive goggles) ready for going outside if necessary.
- Have wet weather gear and harnesses easily accessible.

Detailed preparation:
Above Decks:
- Remove/lash down anything loose, stowing below is best.
- Remove the anchor and chain and secure in a low spot below deck.
- Lash the spinnaker pole.
- Secure spare halyards.
- Prepare storm sails.
- Turn off the wind generator, lash down the blades or remove them.
- Check the self-steering gear, vane and paddle.
- Secure all vents.
- Remove winch handles from mast.
- Fit storm boards on portholes.
- Ensure propane tanks are secure using additional lashing.
- If you have an inflatable dinghy on deck, deflate and store below.
- Additional lashings on hard dinghy.
- Remove all sails and lines where possible and stow below.
- Find extra lines to tie down solar panels; in extreme conditions you may consider cutting the wires and taking panels below.
- Stow jerry cans below where possible.
- Ensure swim ladder is in.

Cockpit:
- Remove anything loose.
- Remove biminis/dodgers and any canvas where possible.

Below decks:
- Ensure all hatches are closed and dogged firmly.
- Stow any loose items.
- Have extra bungs and hammer at the ready.
- Lock all lockers and drawers and oven door.
- Go through the entire boat, checking everything is secure.
- Rig up your lee cloths with additional lines to help keep you in the bunk.
- Double check your grab bag. *(See 'Grab/Ditch Bag' in the Boat Equipment section.)*
- Lash your full water jerry cans together in readiness in case you abandon ship (they will float, saltwater is denser than fresh).
- Review life-raft procedure and check all emergency equipment, flares etc.
- Clear navigation station of all plotting instruments.
- Test all bilge pumps.
- Test radios, if possible.
- Move heavy objects to the lowest part of your vessel and lash.
- Remove any food wanted before covering cupboards with sails and other equipment stowed below.
- Stow computer away properly and all other equipment.

Safety:
- If you are on board and dragging towards shore and cannot stop it, try to stay on board for as long as possible.

- If you hit the shore, try and step ashore if it is safe to do so. Take your grab bag, which will hold all your documentation. This is obviously dependent on conditions, as it may be too dangerous to try.

Storm surge:
- You may not be in the full force of the storm, but storm surge can be felt hundreds of miles away.
- In a marina, double up your lines and ensure they have elasticity.

Remember: whatever preparation you have done and however smart you are, what about the guy anchored just in front of you? Can you be sure that he has done the same amount of preparation?

Short story In Portugal we knew of a storm far enough away not to affect us directly, but the swell did affect us in the marina. We spent hours fitting our most elastic lines and where some of the lines weren't elastic enough, we helped them with metres of shock cord. In the morning, after a terrible night, the marina looked like a battle ground, only one or two boats (us included) came away unscathed. The docks were covered in broken and snapped lines and many boats had suffered damage by crashing into other boats and the dock.

Tropical Revolving Storms, Cyclones, Hurricanes & Typhoons
The USA uses the Saffir-Simpson Hurricane Scale, but Australia uses a different scale for their cyclones, which are issued by BOM (Bureau of Meteorology). Both have category one as the weakest wind speed, increasing up to category five (strongest wind speed).

Saffir-Simpson Scale
1	74-95 mph	Minimal
2	96-110 mph	Moderate
3	111-130 mph	Major
4	131-155 mph	Extensive
5	> 155 mph	Catastrophic

Australian Scale
1	63-88 km/h	
2	89-117 km/h	
3	118-159 km/h	Severe
4	160-199 km/h	Severe
5	> 200 km/h	Severe

To convert mph into km/h multiply by 1.6.
To convert km/h into mph divide by 1.6.

Whatever the distinction between Cyclones, Hurricanes, etc, being caught in one of these extraordinary systems would be a nightmare. If you want to cruise in the areas where these storms occur, carry out your research with books, the Internet, local authorities for anchorage locations and have a plan. Read your insurance documentation carefully, as it may well state which latitudes you should avoid at specific times of the year.

Short story True hit? Noel and I have read numerous articles and books on hurricane weather. It has always been our decision not to play with Mother Nature and never be in a hurricane area when they can develop. Some of the accounts we have read are not direct hits. They quote forty, fifty, sixty knot winds and are elated they 'survived a hurricane'. Whilst these winds are awfully scary and take clear thinking, preparation and knowledge to deal with – they are not a true hit. Hurricane winds can be in excess of 100 knots, that's real food for thought in your preparation.

Towing
If it's necessary to tow another vessel, consider the different dynamics of the boats involved and how they will behave in big seas. For example, due to their dynamics, in some conditions sailboats can try to overtake a motor vessel that is towing them. To prevent this happening use a drogue, a steel bucket, or anything that is sturdy enough to be tied off the back of the sailboat to slow it down.

Equipment and set up: If you are being towed, avoid tying the towline to your anchor windlass. A bridle on two cleats (port and starboard) is the correct method.

Carry a good heaving line with a monkey's fist on the end (to add weight for control). Even in calm weather, boats move a significant amount, three dimensionally. Coming close enough to throw a line is very risky and tricky to do. A heaving line is a light line that is easy to throw. Once the heaving line is on board the other vessel, they should haul it in quickly, taking up the heavier line that is attached to the lighter line. Time is of the essence as the boats are drifting, but remember you can fix a boat but not a hand quite so easily, so take care.

An alternative to throwing a line is to drag a line in the water with a fender attached. This helps the line float and streams it across the bow of the vessel that requires towing. They can then pick up the line with a boat hook. This is not as easy as it sounds, especially in large seas.

Considerations: There are many things to consider when towing, dependent on conditions and the vessels involved, here's a few suggestions to think about:

- Plan the tow before starting. Good communication is critical before, during and after hook-up. Ensure everyone on both boats knows and understands the process. Select a VHF channel to converse on (whilst maintaining watch on ch16).

- When approaching the vessel to be towed, think about wind and current, and ensure you can manoeuvre your vessel away should the boats start coming together due to swell and surge (and they usually do). We come along side at an angle, almost diagonally across the distressed vessel's bow, allowing us to move away with a spurt of power. At the last minute we turn to the same direction as the boat about to be towed. This allows us to be facing the same way but just in front, making it easier to take up the tow carefully.

- Once lines are in place, take up the tow slowly, propel forward, and as the line is taking up try to come out of gear for a few beats, then power on gradually. The line should maintain a catenary (dip in the line), it should never be bar-taut. Dipping the line in the water is a good way to add weight.

- The length of the towing line should be at least three times the towing vessel's length.

- Maintain a steady speed, too much speed puts excessive strain on the vessels and the towing equipment. In protected waters, shorten the towline or bring the vessel alongside. Take care when manoeuvring the vessels, as they will slow down at different rates.

Towing with a dinghy: A dinghy (with an outboard) can propel a much larger boat. Ensure that the stern of the vessel supplying the power is behind the stern of the vessel being 'pushed'. It is useless having a dinghy out in front, as it will simply lose steerage and be pulled back. The larger vessel uses their rudder to steer, the dinghy is just pushing.

Safety: When you are towing someone, assign one person to watch the towed vessel and lines at all times.

Err on the side of caution. Close quarters manoeuvring at sea is not easy and can be very dangerous. If you are in any doubt, don't do it. A good option is to stay with the distressed vessel until conditions improve, or another vessel arrives that is better equipped for the task.

Do not stand in line with the towline, stand well off to the side in case the line parts.

We all have an obligation to render assistance at sea, but only if it does not place our own vessel and/or crew in any danger. Some considerations:

Do you have the power to tow that particular vessel?
Do you have enough fuel?
Do the conditions allow a safe hook-up?
Do you have the correct/strong enough equipment?

Avoid knots that cinch tight. Consider a weak link (sacrificial line) that will break before other parts of the rig. At the very least have a knife nearby. Think what might happen if one of the vessels sinks and you cannot untie the line quick enough!

A Towing Hitch is a good knot to know. It is also known as a Bollard Hitch or a Lighterman's Hitch. To tie, take several turns around a single post, then bring the bight of the line under the standing part and drop the bight over the post.

Turning Around & Returning To Port
We consider this a safety issue. If you are going to weather and it is getting worse, consider turning around or changing your destination. Remember it is not just you that is under strain, so is everything on your boat. It is not cowardice to turn around and try again on a better day, it is good sense.

Wing On Wing
We often haul an additional foresail next to our furler jib when going down wind. The leech of the sail is not within a track or on a forestay; it is simply tied at the head and the clew, and poled out with a second (lighter) pole. This is the first sail to come down if the wind picks up. *(See the picture of Mariah 'wing on wing, at the end of the Navigation section.)*

Boat handling is not always on the water. Here, Mariah (with us on board) is on the Big Chute in Canada. The Big Chute is a Marine Railway boat lift lock of the Trent-Severn Waterway in Ontario. This construction was built to deal with a change of height of about 18 metres and to keep two waterways separate. The separation was important for control of biological contamination. The Chute works on an inclined plane to carry boats in individual cradles over the change of height. It is the only marine railway (or canal inclined plane) of its kind in North America still in use.

CLEANING

Part of maintaining a seaworthy vessel is to have a clean vessel. You would think that as your boat is smaller than your house (for most people) it would be easier to keep it clean. But if you live aboard, you will see that plenty of dust accumulates. Add to that the natural elements, salt and wind blowing in the dust and, hey presto, much more cleaning.

I spent fifteen minutes (on a 51 foot boat with two very messy people) a day doing a quick dust, wipe down and sweep. This meant the housework didn't build up and I didn't end up using a whole day to catch up. This also keeps the boat clean for unexpected (but always welcome) visitors and it is ship-shape should we have to make an emergency move.

When cleaning, I cast my eyes over everything to ensure there are no leaks or deterioration/corrosion occurring. I like an orderly boat, I relax better when it is clean, and therefore I am happy, which means a happy husband and happy boat!

Jackie on board Pyewacket. Cleaning in those 'hard to reach' spots is better left until in port!

Canvas

Check the manufacturer's instructions for cleaning or use a mild soap/detergent and fresh water (do a small test patch first). The best life preserver for canvas is to keep it clean and dry.

Wipe and brush off any loose dirt. Hose down with fresh water if possible, or use a cloth or sponge and fresh water. Rinse thoroughly and do not let the soap dry on the material.

Do not put it in a washing machine or dry clean, as this will disrupt waterproofing and UV inhibitors.

In high humidity, mildew grows on Sunbrella material. Mix fifty/fifty water and vinegar and spray or wipe onto the undersides of the canvas to help kill the mildew.

Look after your canvas and it will look after you. Noel in Pyewacket's cockpit.

Cleaning For Port Arrival

The day before arriving in a new port (or on the day we are arriving, if we have all day to get there) we arrange our time so I can have a couple of hours to clean up. Not only am I able to rest properly once we are in port, but if the officials come aboard, they are impressed with the neatness and cleanliness of our boat. This tends to help smooth the checking in process, especially if there is a possible question of fumigation.

Clear Vinyl

Ensure all dirt and grit is rinsed off thoroughly or it will scratch. Carefully use your hand to check for leftover grit and remove any remaining dirt. Use a non-abrasive cloth (sponge) and a non-abrasive cleaner. If you like to use diluted bleach, note that if it gets on the stitching, it will negatively affect the thread (depending how much you use). I would recommend using a proprietary cleaner.

Cockroaches

The most effective way to keep them at bay in the tropics is by mixing borax with water, sugar and flour. Mix into a paste and create little balls to sit on your stringers or dark places in your boat. This will keep working for months on end. As with all baits/poisons, place in locations where pets and children cannot reach. The cockroaches eat the borax and die. Other cockroaches eat the poisoned cockroach and they die too. Borax can be purchased from most pharmacies.

Short story Gliding across the ocean towards Easter Island, we had a lot of rain, which wasn't draining down the scuppers in the cockpit very quickly. I was in the galley not knowing what Noel was up to. He turned on the deck-wash hose (which has a lot of pressure) and put the hose down the cockpit scuppers. Noel was very pleased with himself when a plastic packet came up and cleared the scuppers. However, the scuppers were plumbed into the galley plumbing and all the gunk that had gathered over the years flew up into the sink. As we heeled over, all the revolting, filthy, smelly water slopped over the edge onto the floor – all this at seven knots in bouncy seas!

57

Drains
To clean drains, pour a hot solution of saltwater down the drain. Unclog and clean a drain by pouring half a cup of baking soda down the drain, then slowly pour half to one cup of white vinegar after it. Let it sit for five minutes while it bubbles up. Follow up with some boiling water.

Exterior Cleaning
Cleaning off barnacles and weed: As well as a snorkel and/or breathing apparatus (e.g. dive hookah or tank), use a glass suction pad (for carrying glass) or a plumber's mate. The suction part will 'stick' onto your hull and you can hold the handle, keeping you in place. Dive belts with added weights help too.

Cleaning the topsides: Hanging on in the dinghy and cleaning at the same time is arm achingly difficult. Noel and I try and organise ourselves to do this together. One of us can hang on and clean the easy bits while the other is free to reach the harder areas. (Use of a deck-wash pump makes life easier.) We use environmentally friendly proprietary products.

Both the hull and the deck are usually washed in saltwater and followed up with a fresh water rinse (unless we are in a marina, where we take advantage of all the fresh water). Be aware of environmental laws and use the correct environmentally friendly products. *(See 'MARPOL/Environmental laws' in the Voyage Preparation section.)*

Jackie cleaning Mariah's topsides.

Galley
Keeping your galley clean is not just about having a smart boat; you also want to avoid attracting bugs and bacteria too. Carefully manage your rubbish. *(See 'Garbage management' in the Galley section for hints on keeping rubbish quantities to a minimum.)*

Oil and grease spills? Sprinkle baking soda on the spot and scrub with a wet brush.

Cleaning your grills and burners can become hard and heavy on water usage. When you have finished cooking and have a particularly stubborn stain, wet a paper towel and lay the wet towel on the area to clean. While it is cooling it will soak up a lot of the grease and loosen tenacious bits of food. Baking soda neutralizes fatty acids and grease.

General Cleaning Tips
• Do not buy steel wool wire scrubbers for on board, they rust and make a mess.

- Use newspaper to clean windows and mirrors to avoid streaks. Use vinegar if you have plenty of elbow grease!

- Keep a supply of newspaper to cover the workbench for when you are cleaning an oily item, such as a winch. It will protect the workbench without using up your entire supply of rags in one go.

- Clean windows and glass with coffee filters when you're out of newspaper towels. Coffee filters leave no lint or other residue.

- When you pack away your travel bags for some time, place a laundry dryer sheet or a bar of soap in the bag to keep it fresh.

- Clean stainless steel with a soft cloth and four tablespoons of baking soda dissolved in half a litre of water. Wipe dry with a clean cloth.

- To clean solar panels, use a non-abrasive soap, e.g. washing up liquid, diluted well. Spray this onto your panels and use a soft sponge to clean. Rinse with fresh water and leave to dry. (Tie up your wind generators if they are close by!)

Jackie cleaning the solar panels on board Pyewacket in Bahia de Caráquez, Ecuador.

Hand Cleaner
Make a paste of oatmeal and water and use this to scrub very dirty hands. Lime juice will rid hands of smells (such as raw onion). Or while soaping your hands add some salt or sugar for a good scrub.

Prior to tackling any dirty job, scrape soap under your fingernails, it makes clean up easier.

Inside
Use WD-40 to remove sap, tar, adhesives, labels and tape from surfaces without damaging existing paint. It's also an effective cleaner for tools and equipment. See http://www.wd40.com/files/pdf/wd-40_2042538679.pdf for the numerous uses of WD40.

We sweep the floor at least once a day; it is incredible what collects there. Keeping the floor clean helps prevent small items making their way to the bilge and potentially blocking the bilge pump!

A simple way to clean the inside of the boat is to use a tiny amount of laundry powder in water and wipe down the timber or fibreglass. One of our friends uses just a few drops of bleach in water and cleans the inside of their vessel that way, including all timber. Whichever method you prefer, always do a test patch first, as some chemicals can affect the colour of the varnish. It is always best to immediately wipe each section with a dry cloth to prevent the timber absorbing moisture.

To maintain its lustre, varnished wood should be waxed or polished. The process of cleaning can dull the shine (do not polish timber steps, they will become slippery). For fibreglass, a mild diluted soap will also work, or use a proprietary cleaner.

If you have carpet on board, remove it when you can, especially if it has become damp and let it dry in the sun to prevent mildew. Only leave it in the sun long enough for it to dry, the sun may eventually affect the colour.

Mould
With enough ventilation in your vessel you should avoid mould, but sometimes it is not that easy within a high moisture atmosphere.

If you find some mould, wipe it with vinegar (plain white, cheap vinegar). This will clean it off and help prevent it growing again.

Oil/Diesel Spill
A problem with the engine can cause fuel and/or oil to leak. Having an emergency set of soak up pads will help you clean up quickly and in an environmentally friendly manner. Baby's nappies (diapers) are great for this.

Cleaning under the engine after an oil change on Pyewacket is a good opportunity to have a thorough inspection.

Odours

Bicarbonate of soda is supposed to absorb smells, but the best remedy is to get rid of the smell by finding the problem and sorting it out.

Eliminate odours: Vanilla essence eliminates smells. Wipe a small amount around a container, fridge interior and any offensive smelling surface and rinse if desired. For a narrow lidded container that doesn't allow you to wipe inside, put a few drops inside the rinsed container, close the lid, shake the essence around vigorously and leave for ten to twenty minutes, then rinse and dry.

Smelly pipes and hoses: Head pipes and hoses can eventually start to smell, but only if they are really old. As long as the head is used regularly, flushed plenty of times and kept clean there should be no problems. Your marine head should be flushed more than you think, especially manual toilets. Do around twenty pumps for a pee. This means the urine does not sit in your pipes and create an odour.

Plenty of pumps will mean less smell. The pamphlets that come with new toilets recommend the amount of pumps to use. Our new manual toilet required at least seven pumps per metre of hose.

To check if a pipe or hose has an odour, wrap a rag that has been soaked in hot water around the hose at its lowest point. Once the rag has cooled off, smell the rag. If the unpleasant smell has transferred to the rag, it's time to change the hoses.

Breakdown of formations and cleaning: Once in a while pour vinegar in the head and flush it through to your holding tank. Vinegar will help breakdown the hard formations that build up over time, keeping your pipes clean and fresh.

Short story Some of the pipes on Pyewacket's loos were old and we replaced them. Some looked okay, but however many times I cleaned I could still smell a faint, but noticeable smell. It was driving me a bit batty (Noel couldn't smell it!) and I was about to replace all the pipes when I received this little gem from a cruising buddy: wrap aluminium foil around the old pipes. There was only a small section to do. I also put more aluminium foil around the holes where the pipes went through the floor behind the toilet - hey presto - no smell. (This was a temporary fix until we installed new pipes.)

We regularly clean our pipes with half a cup of baking soda, followed by vinegar. Flush through to pipes and leave for about thirty minutes, then flush out.

If you are laying up your boat, flush out all the saltwater and replace it with fresh water, right throughout the plumbing. This will avoid nasty smells created by the build up of micro-organisms that give off that rotten odour when the toilet is flushed after being left for some time.

Products

Mix bicarbonate of soda and vinegar (cheap white) together and use as cleaner. I use a ratio of two parts vinegar to one part bicarbonate. It is environmentally considerate, contains no chemicals and cleans well.

Use olive oil and lemon to polish your timber, it has no harsh chemicals (not on steps, it can be slippery). I make up one cup with approximately one quarter of a cup of lemon juice and the rest of the cup is oil.

Stains

Spilt red wine on your clothes? Immediately rub in plenty of salt to absorb the liquid then wash as normal.

Lemon juice will clean tea and rust stains from clothes - apply lemon juice to the stain and leave the garment in the sun for few hours, then wash normally.

Time Saving

Keep a bottle of cleaner in each head and cabin for a quick wipe over when necessary. Keep face cloths or flannels dotted about; they are great for just grabbing and wiping up spills around sinks. I've found this simple action has made life a lot easier.

If you have a 'wet room' (shower in your head), before showering spray the head with cleaner and simply wipe down after your shower. You have to wipe everything down after a shower anyway, this way it has had a clean too. Caution: never mix different cleaners. Vinegar is a cleaner and should not be used with other cleaning chemicals. Different cleaning chemicals can create lethal gases if mixed.

Vacuum

A 12-volt car vacuum is ideal for keeping the bilges clean if they are dry and not too deep.

Washing Up

At sea we do the dishes in saltwater and rinse only cups in fresh. If you prefer to use fresh, it is possible to use cold water (unless particularly greasy food has been consumed). The trick is to buy good quality detergent. I usually wipe greasy items with a paper towel first, and use hot water for really greasy items only.

Windows

Clean both windows and curtains regularly to prevent corrosion and deterioration. Our stainless steel portholes and fitted mosquito nets are excellent dirt catchers and need regular cleaning. (I use mild soapy water on a soft cloth, rinsing with clean, fresh water.)

COMMUNICATIONS

Communicate

Communications is not just about radio and Internet equipment. Chat to other cruisers in your area to say g'day or when you need help. We needed a new dinghy in Alabama, but there wasn't anywhere within 100 miles that sold them. Chatting to another cruiser, he was delighted to get rid of his dinghy and gave it to us for nothing. It was perfect!

Our new (gifted) dinghy was perfect for us.

Ahe atoll, in the Tuamotus (French Polynesia).

Communications & Staying In Touch

No one should leave shore without a VHF Radio (Very High Frequency), which is used for short distances (works at a distance of antenna to antenna in line of sight). For long distance, a HF Radio (High Frequency) is highly recommended, for both safety and seeking information. *(See 'Radios' and article 'Breaking the Ice with a Net' at the end of this section.)*

HF/SSB (Single Side Band) radios can be used to download free weather via Weatherfax. *(See Voyage Planning section.)*

Unless you have a Ham Licence, Internet on board will involve some cost. We simply let our family know that we will be out of touch until the next port. Internet connections are now available at 99% of global locations.

Internet is available in most places. Turtle Bay in Mexico; sitting outside a closed cafe I found an Internet connection.

That's some office!

Short story We do not have Internet on board when underway. Part of the reason we sail is to escape and having a break from the Internet is part of the escape. We let our friends and family know approximately when we will be leaving, how long we are sailing for and our next intended destination. Every time we do this, we add on several days or even weeks longer than it should take and always remind them that this is only a guess-timate. We always arrive and get in touch a good few days/weeks before they expect to hear from us.

Short story Many people have email on board 'to keep in constant contact with friends and family at home and stop them worrying.' My mum is a professional worrier (in the nicest possible way!) and I asked her if she would prefer to be in contact with us all the time, bearing in mind that if we have an electrical or equipment problem on board, we may suddenly become out of touch and she will not know why. She has confirmed that the arrangement of not hearing from us for a quoted amount of time, is just fine. Being in touch at sea and suddenly disappearing (should there be a problem with equipment) would cause her a huge amount of worry. Our family are aware of EPIRB technology and know they will be one of the first to know if there is a problem.

Note: Many cruisers opt for a satellite phone instead of (or as well as) an EPIRB. It is a personal choice and needs much research depending on your budget, wants and needs.

Email Addresses
Take a hard copy of all your contact email addresses, as they can be lost. When we send an email to all of our contacts (or most), I simply copy and paste the addresses into a word document, save it and print it out from time to time.

Internet
Connections: Almost every port has reasonable Internet cafes or Wi-Fi connections available with a credit card payment. For an even better deal, find out if there is a library nearby, usually they have free Internet for a period of time. Don't forget to show them your passport; because you are a visitor you may receive priority treatment if there is a queue.

Ensure you check for a hotspot when on anchor or mooring, you never know your luck. But be aware of security, I wouldn't send any personal information when using an unsecure hotspot.

Save time and money: If there are a lot of emails to catch up on after a lengthy voyage, in order to help keep connection time to a minimum, we copy and paste all our emails into Word and save them on a thumb drive for reading later. We type replies on Word and only go on the Internet when all the replies are ready to send.

Resources: The Wi-Fi free spot directory http://www.wififreespot.com/

Short story The availability of Internet has changed the cruising world since our last adventures. We have noticed that most cruisers spend their time ashore on the Internet and not socialising. We are just as bad. In Ecuador we found that every day we would spend at least one hour a night, before showers, on the Internet. It seemed to be addictive. We rationed ourselves to every other day, unless on a specific task that required research/communication. That's why we like a complete break from the Internet when we are sailing.

Mobile Phones & Cell Phones
In many countries you can pick up a cheap mobile phone and/or SIM card for cheap calls just for the duration of your stay. This is exceptionally helpful if arranging work/parts for the boat.

Phonetic Alphabet
Write the phonetic name of your boat near the radio for those who cannot remember it and for use in the event of an emergency. It is important to know your phonetic alphabet for clear radio communications.

Letter	Phonetic
A	Alpha
B	Bravo
C	Charlie
D	Delta
E	Echo
F	Foxtrot
G	Golf
H	Hotel
I	India
J	Juliet
K	Kilo
L	Lima
M	Mike
N	November
O	Oscar
P	Papa
Q	Quebec
R	Romeo
S	Sierra
T	Tango
U	Uniform
V	Victor
W	Whiskey
X	X-Ray
Y	Yankee
Z	Zulu

Important numbers are:
9 - say 'niner'
0 - say 'zero'

Radios & Radio Schedules Or Nets

VHF (Very High Frequency): radios are excellent for short-range communications. Their range is 'line of sight', that is a transmitting antenna is within sight of the receiving antenna. So you may or may not see the vessel you are talking to, depending how high the antenna is.

Channel 16: The international hailing (calling up) channel is 16. Once you have made contact you must immediately switch to a working channel.

SSB (Single Side Band) or HF (High Frequency) Scheds: These radios are long-range (can be several thousand miles). A receiver is less expensive and useful for listening in, however you also need a transmitter to transmit. An SSB transceiver transmits and receives. This is a highly useful tool when following the trades and becoming involved in a 'Net' or 'Sched' with other cruisers. (A radio 'Sched' is a radio Schedule and a radio 'Net' is a radio Network.) These are organised radio communications between boats with SSB transceivers. A time and frequency is chosen and when traversing an ocean, you can listen in, respond and have people to talk to other than your crew. Help, advice and assistance is always available. Those cruisers several days in front of you can pass back priceless information about checking in, anchoring and weather etc. *(See 'Responsibility or Involved' in Kids On Board section.)*

Radios are great for breaking the ice and creating new friendships. When arriving in port you often find several boats you have already spoken with for some time. *(See 'Breaking the Ice with a Net' article at the end of this section.)*

Scheds can grow and take much time. We have earphones with a long cable that allows us to listen in as we are sailing and keeping watch from the cockpit.

You can use your SSB to:
- Receive/download Weatherfax, a fantastic, free worldwide service. *(See 'Weather' in the Voyage Preparation section.)*
- Download emails (free to Ham licence holders via Winlink or purchase additional equipment/access via SailMail - www.sailmail.com

Short story The first third of the Red Sea heading north was a dream run; the rest was a tough beat. There are many anchorages to duck into that we made good use of. The boats on this trip organised a great Sched and it worked wonderfully. Those boats a few days in front of the next group of boats would report their conditions. Those behind always knew exactly what weather was heading their way.

Radio Fun

Listen to commercial radio when underway on your SSB (HF) radio. For news and interesting discussion topics look up the shortwave frequency for the area you are in. The BBC broadcasts worldwide: http://www.bbc.co.uk/worldservice/schedules/frequencies/

Radio Reception

If you have solar panels and also use an SSB, fit an isolation switch to turn the solar panels off when transmitting and receiving. If our solar panels are left on when receiving, the incoming charge interferes with transmissions. Our switch is in-line on the positive wire between the solar panel array and the circuit breaker, and makes a big difference to transmitting and receiving quality.

Some radios, especially SSB (HF), are easily distorted by other equipment that is running at the same time. If you have interference while transmitting/receiving, turn off *all* your appliances, including wind generators, fridges and inverters.

Antenna improvement: Using your rigging as an antenna is a good way of lengthening the range and strength of transmitting/receiving. Ensure no one is holding the rigging while transmitting! Much to our amazement, a radio guru recommended we make our entire rig an aerial. It tested and worked brilliantly.

From the ATU (automatic tuning unit), connect your aerial wire to a backstay or shroud that is not insulated.

Safety: Ensure you carry a spare aerial in case you lose your rigging, you still want to be able to transmit if an emergency occurs! And don't forget to ensure everyone on board knows when you are transmitting as the entire rig will be live!

Frequencies: For SSB radio (HF), the higher the sun, the higher the frequency needed.

Radio Licensing
Different countries have different requirements. Some foreign ports may ask to see your radio licence (one such example is Chile). Be sure to research qualifications/licences necessary for your next port.

Radio Safety & Distress
Silent period: Australia is one of the few countries that still observes the period of three minutes silence on the hour and on the half hour. This is to provide a vessel in distress a period of quiet to try and transmit their message if their signal is weak.

Etiquette and procedure: Always listen before transmitting, and talk slowly and clearly. Be brief and know your phonetic alphabet. I remind myself to speak 'slow and low'. High-pitched voices do not carry well. Always acknowledge you have heard what the other person has said. For example, if they ask you to 'Stand by', acknowledge with 'Standing by'. Or if they say 'Go to channel 68' acknowledge with 'Going 68' or 'Going up' (if switching upwards, or 'Going down' if switching down).

Before sending emails via the SSB, ensure that no one is using the frequency. We find that email signal interruption is becoming more and more frequent (and annoying).

Tuning: When using SSB (HF) make sure you auto-tune your radio slightly off the frequency that is in use, especially if you are late joining the Sched. When using automatic tuning on the frequency that is being used, it blanks out all noise (including speech) for two to three seconds. You do not have to be right on the Sched frequency to tune, just close to it. Once you have tuned, then just turn the dial that last bit, to get on the right frequency.

Short story Remember that if your transmit button is pushed, everything on board will be heard. Obvious, we know, however . . . In Oman, we had friends on board, a social evening was arranged with other boats and our friends used our VHF to help organise events. When not in use the microphone had to be hooked at an angle, or else the button was depressed. Our friends didn't know this, we didn't tell them, and we didn't check the radio. We all went on board another boat for some fun. In the morning, about 10 am, we heard a shout from a nearby boat, 'hey, Mariah II, we are all loving your morning chatter, but it is getting dull now, please turn off your mic!' Oops. We had a quick rehash of all we had said and done, thankfully it was all very benign!

Jackie using the VHF on board Mariah.

Snail Mail

We try to write and mail letters or postcards - a practice that is disappearing. Everyone still loves receiving a letter you can physically hold and cherish.

In the Galapagos one of the islands is called Post Office Island.

Trading ships left their mail here in the hope the next ship would collect it and make delivery.

We left a signed message for sailors and postcards for our families. In exchange we mailed two postcards (to Japan and America) for others. We added our email address to the postcards we were mailing and received a thank you email from Japan some months later.

Short story During our circumnavigation on Mariah, we sent postcards to family from every port we possibly could. Our family in England put a world map on a wall, with hand-written dates of our arrival/departure. Scattered around these locations they displayed all our postcards. They are now a fantastic memento.

ARTICLE: Published in Australia by Cruising Helmsman and in the UK by Yachting World.

Breaking the Ice with a Net
by Jackie Parry

On the ocean our radio is almost like a telephone (power permitting). Now, back in Australia we have used our HF (SSB) to speak to buddies in New Zealand. The crackle and buzz moving us to melancholy; we remember how great the radio was on our travels. There's the one time we realised ignorance is bliss and the other time the radio proved its potential to save lives.

'Net' or 'Sched' example
'Good morning, this is the East Atlantic Safety and Security Net on Friday 26th December. This is Jackie and Noel on board Mariah II. Could I have a radio check please?'
The sun is still sleeping, it is 5 a.m.; a scratchy voice looms eerily into the darkness, someone can hear us, so I continue, 'Are there any emergency or priority calls?'
(I wait one minute, silently praying that the radio stays quiet.)
'Nothing heard, does anyone have weather details they can share with the Net?' *(someone always knows something, if not I translate our Weatherfax picture).*
'Now we'll proceed with the vessels under way, Frodo, Frodo, come now with your report please.'
The yacht 'Frodo' responds, 'we are at…' *giving position, heading, wind direction and wind speed, boat speed and confirms all is well. Then I continue with the boats on my list that have already joined the Net.*
'Are there any other boats who would like to join the Net?' *(underway or in port).*
'Any news for the Net?' *(This could be funny, informative).*
'I'll close the Net now and open up the frequency for boat to boat traffic.'

Noel and I shared the responsibility of Net Controller as it grew.

It took over an hour each morning to get through all the boats!

During our Atlantic crossing the Net list grew to over thirty yachts, spread right across the vast ocean. Our American friend Carol on the yacht 'Star Cruiser', who started the Net, divided the list into eastern and western Atlantic and recruited us to lend a hand. In our logbook we noted every single detail, including how many on board and names. In the latter part of the Net, vessels in port are given the opportunity to impart information if they wish. As Net Controller it is presumed that you know the answers to all sorts of obscure questions. It's here you become adept at fielding off the batted queries, someone, somewhere always has some sort of answer. At the end, the Net has to be officially closed and then opened for boat-to-boat traffic. It is courteous to call up your buddies on the frequency that was used, then immediately select an alternative frequency, and 'meet' them there for a chat.

Responsibilities both ways

On the oceans you are not alone. During our last few years of cruising we were often Net Controllers and this creates its own responsibilities. Being able to log umpteen boats' positions (given in a plethora of accents and transceiver qualities) can be hard while hanging on, but if a boat that is on your list doesn't 'come up' one day, as Net Controller you are responsible for following up that boat's whereabouts. This could be as simple as asking the rest of the group to look out for the boat (you will have a description from the details you obtained when they joined the Net) and informing authorities on making port. Looking at it the other way, there is also some onus on the boats taking part: if you join in, you MUST 'come up' each day. Of course, if you no longer want to continue, that is fine, but you must inform the Net Controller or somehow pass a message along.

I'd rather not have known that!

During the Indian Ocean crossing, the radio Net, which we maintained twice a day with ten other yachts, was a good break from routine (and speaking to each other!). It also made the ocean seem a bit more friendly and not as empty or frightening. All was well with the world until we were two days out from Oman. A pirate attack was reported; automatic rifle fired through the rigging, knife at the wife's throat, ransacked boat, lots stolen, but fortunately no casualties. After hearing this shocking news we had stepped on deck. On the horizon sat a fishing boat which took on sinister tones and instead of the usual wave or quiet contemplation, they received the view of Mariah's stern. We demanded full speed ahead from our poor Yanmar. It took two hours to leave the fishing boat on the horizon. It felt like two days. We still had 400 miles to the area of attack, so we thought we had better calm down and reduce the revs from the red line on the tachometer.

Dummy Infantry

The Net continued, information was collated, we plotted the attack on our chart. It happened off the coast of Yemen. From Oman, we would pass the coast of Yemen in order to reach the Red Sea. Cape Town was sounding like a good place by this stage. Nerves were fraught. At Salalah in Oman, a meeting was planned. In the meantime we spent solitary hours designing camouflage nets, grenade launchers and dummy infantry to stand on deck. The meeting was to take place at the local ex-pats' clubhouse and chaired by one of the more apparently knowledgeable yachties. He's American, our friend who goes by the name of Ed, on board 'Dream On'. Ed's served time as a marine or so the whispers went. There were various ideas put forward, such as, 'can the French Navy form an escort?'. Apparently they were sympathetic to the ongoing problem, but they could not help. All private vessels enter these waters at their own risk. There were some radio distress frequencies we could use. These were for the U.S. Navy, the French Navy and the Yemen Maritime rescue services. However, none of these stations would guarantee a response, and if they did it was unlikely that they could have reached us in time to be of any assistance during an attack. 'Marvellous,' Noel murmured. 'If the cavalry arrives they can help sift through the wreckage!'

Those with guns on board had been discussing whether to open fire on sight or only if they had to. Most of the Yanks wanted to start firing as soon as they left port. Then, presumably, not stop firing until they reached New York and that was only to re-load. The trouble with guns, is that you need good ones. The reports we had received was that the pirates had automatics and approached the boats firing into the rigging. Do you open fire in return to save your radio and hidden American dollars? By this time Noel was wondering where we could buy Navy Bofors, find a place to mount the critters and join the Yanks heading to New York. The pirates, we were informed, travel in high powered speedboats and carry radio-monitoring equipment. Using this gear is apparently how they have located yachts that talk between themselves on VHF. Personally, we thought Ed should be given a carton of Rum, armed with a few Uzi machine guns and let loose. The final plan was for everyone to maintain close quarters to each other under sail, which was interesting as there were *no two boats the same, maintain strict VHF silence and only use the HF (with too many frequencies to detect) on set contact frequencies that were not divulged to anyone else. This was the great plan. 'What happens if a boat is boarded?' Noel asked. 'Do we ram the culprits, if it's a matter of someone's life at stake?' This was greeted with silence as everyone, including myself, pondered the reality of such a scene. Do we ram or observe; or head for the horizon, blocking out the sounds of mayhem behind? The meeting ended. We were stunned with real and imagined horrors. We adjourned to the Bar. Two weeks later, despite having a tense nine-day sail, we experienced no troubles.*

Crazy consultation across continents

Again, in the Indian Ocean, the daily Net's value was successfully tested. It was Noel's first attempt at Net Controller. We remember it vividly, because in the part where you pray no one answers ('any emergency or priority calls?') the radio crackled into life with a distress call. For a second we looked at each other in stunned silence. Pulling himself together, Noel took down the details. The caller in distress was a crew member, his skipper's head had had a run in with the boom. He had lost all feeling down one side and the crew were understandably worried. The fleet leapt into action. Within what seemed like just a few minutes, via satellite phone we had the Australian Air Sea and Rescue on standby. 'Just give us the ok and we are on our way'. An American Doctor in the group gave a number of a New York specialist to another boat with a satellite phone. Imagine - in the middle of the ocean, we couldn't even see these other boats and there was a New York specialist 'treating' a patient over the sat phone and then via radio! The injured skipper was lucky, suffering only bruising on the brain and made a complete recovery. As for the rest of us, we felt like commandoes, flying into action. After the adrenaline had calmed we realised the unparalleled value of daily communication.

Licences & equipment

Noel and I have our commercial radio licence for our equipment on board and anyone can join a Net (and run one if they desire) if they have a radio call sign, providing they are not HAM Nets where you would need a HAM Licence. The volume of information received over our radio is staggering. Indeed, we would have missed out on Borneo if we had not heard the exultant experiences of fellow boaties who were already there. All you need is a radio that can transmit and receive. Of course, it has to be long distance (HF SSB). At times you can find yourself skipping through several frequencies, so it is a good idea to become completely familiar with your set.

Who's out there?

It can be daunting, but rewarding and good fun once you get over the nervousness of realising your voice is booming into several dozen boats. The reasons for the Net are obvious: if you go missing, someone has your last position within twenty-four hours; if you need help, a fellow sailor maybe just over the horizon. While observing radio etiquette you can still have fun. To have the day brightened with stories of a boat's head breaking in mid use or hearing about ferocious eagles tearing at birds and fish, leaving dead heads and entrails all over a yacht sailed by vegetarians, is amusing (for the listeners!). The most rewarding outcome is making friends with people from all over the world. The usual shyness of being the new kid at the anchorage is overcome, as often there are boats there we have already spoken with. The ice is broken; it's like opening a jar of coffee, instant friends.

Radio Networks

There are literally hundreds of radio Nets all over the world, the following list contains but a few. Ensure you listen first to identify the format and to see if you can join. If they are HAM, you will need a licence, many are amateur and anyone can join in, some are professional and require a nominal fee. Most Nets provide comprehensive weather.

Remember that Nets constantly come and go and change frequencies/times. The best source for current radio Nets is chatting to other sailors. (This was last updated in 2013.)

NAME	TIME	FREQUENCY	AREA COVERED
Sonrisa Net	0730 hrs (PDT)	3.968 MHz	Sea of Cortez
Russell Radio New Zealand	1800 hrs (NZ) 1830 hrs (NZ) 1900 hrs (NZ)	6.516MHz 4.445 MHz 4.417MHz	South Pacific
New Zealand Wx Net	2000 hrs (Z)	7.080	New Zealand
Med M/M Net	0700 hrs (Z)	7.085 MHz	Mediterranean
Comedy Net	2040 hrs (Z)	7.087MHz	Australia, South West Pacific (very informal – multipurpose)
Harry's Net	2000 hrs (Z)	7.095 MHz	W & S Pacific
Baja California M/M Net	1530 hrs (Z)	7.238 MHz	Coastal Baja & California
Caribbean M/M Net. Saint Croix	1100 hrs (Z)	7.241 MHz	Caribbean
Chubasco Net	1445 hrs (Z)	7.192 MHz	Mexico West coast
The Namba Net	0815 hrs local time Vanuatu (Z + 11)	8.101 MHz	Operates May to October, sister Net to Sheila Net
Radio 'Peri-Peri' E. Africa	0500 hrs (Z) & 1500 hrs (Z)	8.101 MHz then, 12.353 MHz (after weather)	Indian Ocean & South Atlantic (both times, both frequencies)
Caribbean Safety & Security Net	1215 hrs (Z)	8.104 MHz	Safety & Security issues in the Caribbean
Panama Canal Connection Net	1330 hrs (Z)	8.107 MHz	Pacific from Mexico to Galapagos, Atlantic from Belize to Colombia (emphasis on SW Caribbean)
Panama Pacific Net	1400 hrs(Z)	8.143 MHz (Alternatives: 8.137, 8.155,6230)	Panama to Galapagos (depending on propagation – Southern Mexico to Ecuador too)
Cruiseheimer's Net	1330 hrs(Z)	8.152 MHz	US East Coast & through Eastern Caribbean
Sheila Net	2200 hrs (Z)	8.161 MHz	NE Australia, New Guinea, Louisiade Archipelago, Solomon Islands, Vanuatu and Noumea
Rag of the Air Net	1900 hrs (Z)	8.173 MHz	SW Pacific
Northwest Caribbean Cruisers Net	1400 hrs (Z)	8.188 MHz	Mexico to San Andres Island, Colombia
Coconut Breakfast Net	1730 hrs(Z)	8.188 MHz	French Polynesia
Coconut Breakfast Net	1830 hrs (Z)	12.353 MHz	West of French Polynesia
Herb Hilgenberg's Southbound II Net	1930 hrs (Z)	12.359 MHz	Atlantic & Caribbean (reaches into Pacific later in the broadcast)

NAME	TIME	FREQUENCY	AREA COVERED
French Net	0300 hrs(NZ)	13.940 MHz	French
'Le Reseau Du Capitaine' Net Montreal, Canada. Bi-lingual operators	0700 hrs Montreal time 1830 hrs Montreal time (emergency traffic & weather)	14.118 MHz	Atlantic, Caribbean and Pacific
Mississauga Net	1245 hrs (Z)	14.122.5 MHz	Europe, Med, Atlantic, Caribbean & Central America
European M/M Net (Italian and English)	2000 hrs (Z) (1900 hrs (Z) between 30/3 & 20/10)	14.297 MHz	Weather for E & N Atlantic & S Atlantic between Africa & Brazil
M/M Service Net	1700 hrs (Z) during winter 1600-0200 hrs (Z) in summer	14.300 MHz	Atlantic from Cape Town to Greenland, the Eastern Pacific & Gulf of Mexico
UK M/M Net	0800 hrs (Z) & 1800 hrs (Z)	14.303 MHz	UK, Med and Atlantic
Confusion Net	1900 hrs(Z)	14.305 MHz	Pacific
Pacific Seafarers Net	0300 hrs (Z)	14.300 MHz	Pacific (HAM)
Robby's Net, Australia	1000 hrs (Z) & 2300 hrs (Z)	14.315 MHz	Australian waters
Tony's Net New Zealand	2100 hrs (Z)	14.315 MHz	South Pacific, Australia Area HAM Net
Pacific Inter Island Net	0800 hrs (Z)	14.315 MHz	Micronesia to Hawaii
Tony's Net, Kenya	0500 hrs(Z)	14.316 MHZ	Indian Ocean and Red Sea
South Africa M/M Net	0630 hrs (Z) & 1130 hrs (Z)	14.316 MHz	Indian Ocean & South Atlantic
Arnold's Net (South Pacific)	0400 hrs(Z)	14.318 MHz	South Pacific
SE Asia M/M Net	0025 hrs (Z) 0055 hrs(Z)	14.323 MHz	SE Asia
California Hawaii Net	1600 hrs(Z)	14.340 MHz	Pacific E, NW and Hawaii
Manana M/M Net	1900 hrs (Z)	14.340 MHz	US West Coast to Hawaii
Trans Atlantic Net	1300 hrs (Z)	21.400 MHz	Med, N & S Atlantic & Caribbean

Zulu (Z) = Greenwich Mean Time
M/M= Maritime Mobile

Some basic Do's and Don'ts
DO:

- ✓ obtain a Marine Operators Licence (see your local telecoms authority)
- ✓ register your vessel as a maritime station (see telecoms authority-SSB only)
- ✓ listen first, wait until any traffic is finished before talking
- ✓ identify yourself with name of vessel (authorities will require your call sign)
- ✓ ensure all crew familiarise themselves with the radio and how to call for help
- ✓ tune your radio off frequency (so you are not interrupting station)
- ✓ say 'over' when you have finished your bit and want the other party to respond
- ✓ be brief and clear
- ✓ keep your radio in working order, your safety may depend on it
- ✓ be considerate of others, they may want to use the channel
- ✓ keep a log of all details of any distress calls you may hear
- ✓ listen in if it is a 'Net' you cannot join (e.g. Ham Net if you are not licensed), they have useful information
- ✓ enjoy!

DON'T

- ✗ operate radio in an electrical storm
- ✗ talk-over people (if working channel is in use, go back to calling channel and pick another)
- ✗ keep talking on a frequency when an established 'Net' is about to start
- ✗ assume all channels can be used
- ✗ wait until you have cast off to set up and use the radio
- ✗ be afraid to ask
- ✗ use profane or obscene language
- ✗ transmit fraudulent messages

Setting up your own Net
1. Be confident your radio is up to the task (receives/transmits well)
2. Check there is not a Net already running
3. Select a marine frequency, check it is free and there is good propagation at the time you choose
4. Double check with authorities and locals that selected frequencies are free
5. Pick a suitable time, bearing in mind crossing time zones/nightshifts
6. Decide format, keeping it informal and friendly
7. Ask for volunteers straight away, your Net will grow and can become lengthy and tough on your batteries
8. If you need to change times/frequency mid journey, give everyone a few days notice - always check into the old frequency
9. Spread the word
10. Have fun and enjoy meeting new people

Propagation
Use 2 MHz frequencies when within close range (50-100 miles daytime, a greater range can be expected on all frequencies at night).

Use 4 MHz frequencies as the normal daytime frequency for distances greater than 50 to 60 miles and for night-time communication.

Use 6, 8, 12, 16 and 22 MHz for daytime and night-time communication when distance or propagation prevents satisfactory operation on 4 MHz.

Generally, the higher the sun and greater the distance, the higher frequency you need.

Try to use the lowest frequency possible for communication.

We hope this article shows you the wonderful benefits of a good radio system. Satellite phones work well but you miss out on the social bonding that the radio fosters.

ELECTRICAL

Alternator

When tensioning the alternator v-belt, always adjust the adjustment bolt *and* the pivot bolt. Failure to do both may result in alternator twist and vibration. This could lead to undercharging and/or premature belt wear. *(See 'Engine Care' in Maintenance & Repairs section for more tips on belts.)*

Batteries

All batteries self-discharge when not in use.

Batteries in series:
- Batteries should be the same make, model and age.
- Connect positive on first battery to negative on second battery.
- This will increase volts, but the amp hours (Ah) will remain the same.
- For example, connect two six volt 230 Ah batteries in Series; you will get 12 volts and 230 Ah.

Batteries in parallel:
- Connect the positive on first battery to the positive on another.
- This will increase Ah, but the voltage will remain the same.
- For example, connect two six volt 230 Ah batteries in Parallel; you will have six volts and 460 Ah.

Battery types: Use deep cycle batteries to withstand cycles of long continuous discharge and repeated charging. Battery life is a function of the number of cycles and the depth of cycling. Batteries continually discharged to 70% then recharged will last longer than batteries discharged to 40% capacity before recharge.

When purchasing batteries, if you have a choice of plastic or rubber battery casings, choose rubber as it is more durable and resilient to knocks and vibrations.

Battery storage: Batteries should be stored high enough to avoid being flooded if you take on water and low enough to avoid adversely affecting the vessel's stability, i.e. raising the vessel's centre of gravity.

Battery safety: Batteries should be well ventilated; when charging they produce hydrogen gas, which is explosive when mixed with oxygen. A spark or a flame can ignite it. Always use an electric light to check the electrolyte level, as a flame could ignite any gases present.

When disconnecting batteries, always remove the ground cable (black) first. This eliminates any chance of creating sparks. When connecting a battery connect the positive cable (red) first.

The electrolyte in a battery is sulphuric acid. It is weaker when the battery is discharged, but could still cause burns. It is capable of eating holes in skin and clothes and severely damaging eyes if splashed. When working with batteries, take off any jewellery and watches to prevent an accidental short circuit. Ideally you should wear rubber gloves and eye protection.

Neutralize electrolyte spills with a solution of baking soda and water. Do not use saltwater; saltwater mixed with the electrolyte generates chlorine gas.

Carry batteries by the handles if they are provided.

Our deep cycle batteries are incredibly heavy. When we purchased new batteries we rigged up a system of ropes and tackle to lift them in and out; the equipment took the weight, not our backs.

Battery maintenance: Terminals should be kept clean. Contact surfaces should be bright metal and connected dry (free of oil, dirt & Vaseline). Once connected and tightened the overall surface of the terminal connections benefit from a thin smear of Vaseline to prevent corrosion and verdigris (green gunk formed by acid reacting with copper alloys, such as brass terminal connections).

We neutralise build up of battery acid on our terminals by using baking soda (bi-carb soda) in a solution with water (two teaspoons of baking soda in a third of a cup of fresh water). Caution: use a small amount only.

Top batteries up with distilled or deionised water, rainwater is acceptable. Levels should be checked monthly. Water made by an onboard Watermaker is the perfect source for distilled water for filling lead acid batteries. As above, never use saltwater as it reacts with the acid to form chlorine gas.

Battery charging and plate sulphation: Charging your batteries as soon as possible after discharge helps prevent sulphation. Sulphation (or sulfation) is the chemical reaction that takes place during discharge, this causes loss of capacity by increasing internal resistance. Sulphur can also build up and short circuit the batteries killing them dead, instantly. Providing some charging is taking place, even a trickle, then sulphation will not occur.

If you have limited charging capability, turn off unnecessary appliances to provide maximum charge to your batteries. However, without a Smart Charger it is usually better to leave some appliances on, so that the regulator doesn't cut in at a high voltage peak on the battery. The batteries may not be fully charged even though it reads a high voltage. Using a Smart Charger to regulate voltage will help you get the most out of your batteries.

Power management: We have two battery banks: one for the engine only and one for the 'household', e.g. lights, TV, laptops etc. All batteries are constantly receiving a charge from solar or wind power.

Charge levels

Charge level	Specific Gravity
100%	1.250
90%	1.235
80%	1.220
70%	1.205
60%	1.190
50%	1.175
40%	1.160
30%	1.145
20%	1.130
10%	1.115
0%	1.100

Note: The tropics and cold temperatures can alter the specific gravity readings.

On board we do not get too scientific about calculating which item draws how much power. If we need an electrical appliance, we ensure it is connected into the circuit which shows up on the power amps (drawn) meter. We could then compare amps consumed by the appliance to amps coming in (from our solar panels and/or wind generators).

Battery backup: AA batteries are very useful as a backup for the handheld GPS and also for torches and other small appliances. We use rechargeable batteries, as they last longer and in the long run work out much cheaper.

Electrical Wires

Make sure stowed items will not chafe wires. Check all wires throughout your boat to ensure they cannot move when underway. Wires must be bound and secured at least every 300mm.

Do not connect ground wires to metal hulls or through-hull fittings that are metal, as you will cause electrolytic corrosion problems. Connect all your metal hull fittings together by common bonding to a ground plate *(see 'Dissimilar Metals' in the Maintenance & Repairs section)*.

General systems:
12 volt: use for 12 volt items such as hand held GPS.
240 volt Australia and England, 110 volt in America.

Inverters

As most boats are wired with a 12 volt system you will need an inverter (or inverters) to run some appliances. To make use of an inverter you need a good supply of battery power. An inverter works by converting the 12 volt DC current from the battery to 240 volt AC or 110 volt AC mains current.

Sizes of inverters vary and size will depend on what kind of electrical appliances you wish to run. Small inverters are usually fine for televisions and computers. Use Sine Wave inverters on sound systems, e.g. TVs. Continue to monitor your batteries regularly when using your inverters.

Generators

Small portable generators are relatively quiet, but will only power smaller appliances for a short time. Larger generators are obviously heavier and thirstier and at a quiet anchorage can annoy your fellow cruisers. Be aware of your surroundings and the time you are using your generator.

It is important to understand the basics of your electrical system on board. We decided that solar panels and wind generators would supply us with all the power we needed (for the majority of the time). The initial expense and effort is worth it in the long run. Generators (gensets) are noisy, take space, create more heat and are an additional expense with fuel and maintenance.

Lightning

Your oven (or microwave) is a good temporary 'Faraday cage' for protecting equipment during a lightning storm. (Faraday cages shield their contents from static electric fields.) During a lightning storm ensure you disconnect your equipment, flicking off a circuit breaker is not enough if you are hit. If you have put your equipment in the oven, don't forget to remove it before next using the oven or microwave!

In a serious electrical storm, the following is recommended:
- Stay below decks (bear in mind to keep a good watch if at sea; the regulations state that *'Every vessel shall at all times maintain a proper lookout by sight and hearing as well as by all available means appropriate in the prevailing circumstances and conditions so as to make a full appraisal of the situation and of the risk of collision'*).

- Stay away from the mast, boom, shrouds, chainplates, the mast compression post and mast below decks.
- Plot your position and turn off all your electronic equipment.
- Be aware of the set and drift so you can do a DR (deduced reckoning) if you have to. *(See Navigation section.)*
- Do not operate radios unless in an extreme emergency.
- Lightning storms are usually short lived.

If you suffer a strike:
- Check your through-hulls (if they are metal) for any discoloration in the fibreglass or other signs of damage associated with the strike.
- Check for electrical damage and check your rigging. Double check your compass, it may have been affected.

Protection: There are lightning protection devices which some people like and others do not. Research your circumstances and see what suits your situation and set up best.

Indirect hit: A lot of damage can be suffered from an indirect hit; a nearby boat or buoy could be hit and the charge can transfer through the water to other vessels.

No GPS or Radio: It will pay to be able to navigate by chart and deduced reckoning; you may have no electronics and no way to radio for help.

Insurance: If you are insured, after a lightning strike call your insurance company at the first opportunity and follow instructions. It will probably mean a haul out and/or inspection.

Multimeter
A multimeter is an important piece of equipment to have on board. It is a measuring instrument and combines several functions:
- Ammeter: measures current
- Voltmeter: measures voltage (the potential difference between two points)
- Ohmmeter: measures resistance

Voltmeter:

12.6 volts or more	=	100% charged
12.3 volts	=	75% charged
12.2 volts	=	50% charged

To measure current, the circuit must be broken to allow the ammeter to be connected in series.

(AC/DC): DC is direct current, where current flow is always in the same direction. AC is alternating current where current flows first one way then the other (the current reverses or alternates in direction).

Power
Unless you want to run your main engine or a generator all the time, you will need the help of Mother Nature for power. It is important not just for running equipment, but also for maintaining healthy batteries. If you are running a fridge together with your navigation equipment and laptops/TVs, you will need a lot of power and good batteries.

Start with good batteries and then consider what you are running, e.g. an autopilot takes power so use a wind vane instead.

Do you need a fridge? It is surprisingly easy to live without one. *(See the Galley section for ideas.)*

Lighting: LEDs are incredible power savers. Consider also using kerosene lamps in port.

Jackie fitting a new LED masthead light on Pyewacket.

Mariah had just one 80W solar panel; the boat was smaller and far simpler than Pyewacket (we did not have a fridge on Mariah, but used the laptop and watched movies regularly). On board Pyewacket, we had two solar panels and two wind generators. Having both wind and sun power meant we could run our fridge, TV and laptops most of the time.

Turn off what you are not using!: Alternative power = a disciplined lifestyle. On Pyewacket we turned off our fridge at night to prevent our batteries going below 75%, giving the batteries a longer life.

In comparison with living on land, you have to adjust your behaviour as far as power is concerned. You may not be able to watch that movie tonight, so find some other entertainment. *(See the Fun, Games & Pleasure section.)*

When running the engine, plug in and charge your laptop and any other devices that have their own battery and need charging.

The quoted output of your batteries is from tests completed in ideal laboratory conditions, you probably won't achieve the same results.

Short story My 'live aboard' training of saving power and water often bleeds back into land life. I will still turn off all lights and power sockets and anything not in use to conserve power. I use very little water when washing up (doing the dishes). However, needs and wants change. On board Mariah, we were quite content with an open cockpit, cold showers and no radar or fridge. But on board Pyewacket and several years older, we felt we would have struggled without our hot shower, enclosed cockpit (I've always wanted to sail in my slippers), radar and fridge!

Solar Panels

Solar panels are great. Once installed the only maintenance required is periodic cleaning, as there are no moving parts to maintain (except perhaps a frame to tilt them towards the sun). It is not always possible, but if you can, mount the panels so they pivot to follow the sun. This definitely helps. Locate the panels in a position where they are least affected by other equipment causing shadows.

Clean your solar panels (with a soft cloth, do not scour) as they can become covered in town grime at anchor, or have bird poo on them at sea and become less effective.

Wind Generators

In our opinion, solar panels are the best option if deciding between wind generators and solar panels. However, if installed correctly, wind generators can be a great advantage on cloudy days and at night. If you really rely on your wind generators, carry spare blades.

We strongly recommend buying quiet running wind generators.

Safety: Constantly monitor your lines on your boat to ensure they cannot go near your wind generators (it happens).

Ensure they are installed high enough to avoid injuries from the spinning blades if you are reaching up to other equipment that is nearby.

Resources: The 12 Volt Bible For Boats by Ed Sherman.

FUN, GAMES & PLEASURE

Board Games
Board games and a pack of cards are a fun way to spend evenings with others, especially by kerosene lamplight. You can have good fun and use no power. *(See 'Games' further on for more ideas.)*

Be Happy!
This is it! We only get one chance. *(See 'This Is It' article at the end of this section.)*

In Ecuador the 'sweet treats' are about ten cents each; bunches of flowers are not much more. Indulge in the simple things in life.

Bahía de Caráquez, a place very close to our hearts.

Boatie Banquet Or Pot Luck
Some of the best times are when cruisers get together. Everyone agrees on a place and time to meet, usually a beach or park. Each of us brings along a dish that will feed the number of people that are on our boat and everyone takes along their preferred drink. Prepare yourselves for a fabulous banquet!

Christmas
We often find ourselves without family and friends at Christmas and try to get together with other boaties that are in the same position to hold an extra special 'Boatie Banquet'.

Christmas presents: We are constantly on a budget, but we enjoy Christmas. Each year (and you can do this for birthdays too), we set a ridiculous budget, such as $5 per person. Recycle shops or local craft stalls are sought and rummaged through. The gift has to be as useful and meaningful as possible. It is great fun sourcing good presents with such a small budget and it is surprising what you can come up with.

If you are in a location where there are no charity/recycle shops or local craft shops, then make a gift. You'll be amazed at the creativity this task produces. *(See 'Gifts' section for ideas.)*

At Christmas boatie banquets with other cruisers, we usually agree on an amount (anywhere between $1-$5) for gifts. Everyone buys one gift, no nametags or identification necessary. After eating, sit in a circle and put the presents in the middle, then decide who starts (oldest? youngest?). They select a gift, sit back down and unwrap it immediately. Go clockwise, the next person can either take a gift that is open already or select a new one to open immediately. The game ends when everyone has a gift, they are all open and the swapping (arguing) is finished! (This game usually works better with larger numbers and creates lots of laughs.)

Short story I'll never forget Rob, on board SV Magic Carpet and I having a battle for a coveted gift. He had opened a present of a plastic water pistol. When my turn came, I didn't take from the centre pile of unwrapped gifts, but took Rob's pistol. The game continued around again and soon it was Rob's turn again. He took the pistol back. The nature of the game has it going around the group several times. During this time the pistol had become full of water. I think Rob won in the end!

Short story At a Christmas celebration in Thailand all the cruisers got together. We had all purchased (or made) gifts for less than US$4 and we took turns in picking one each out of Santa's hat. Our Irish friend Jaime on board SV Breakaway, had painted a wonderful picture. We picked it out in the Christmas Gift Game. It was an Orangutan, and the picture meant a lot to us as we had spent some time in Borneo with Jamie and his family playing with these wonderful creatures. It's a truly treasured gift that still has pride of place in our home.

Christmas Decorations
String coloured (or plain) popcorn around the boat for swift and cheap homemade decorations.

Coloured popcorn
1 tablespoon vegetable oil
¼ cup of popcorn kernels
½ - 1 cup of sugar
½ cup water
½ teaspoon of food colouring

Heat a little oil in a large saucepan with a lid. Add the popcorn, cover and cook, shaking occasionally, until the popping stops. Set aside.

Put the sugar, water and food colouring in a saucepan and heat, stirring, until the sugar has dissolved. Boil for about 15 minutes or until a teaspoonful of the mixture sets when dropped into cold water. This is your caramel.

Pour the caramel over the popcorn and stir until all the popcorn is coated.

Spread the covered popcorn on a plate or baking tray and allow to cool. Separate into bits and serve. Alternatively, leave it out overnight (or for a few hours) and the popcorn will soften - then you can string it.

Stripy Popcorn
To get 'stripy' coloured popcorn with less processed sugar, put one tablespoon of oil in a pan with two tablespoons of honey and add one quarter of a cup of corn kernels, plus half a teaspoon of your colouring. Heat up until the mixture boils, keep it boiling (not too hard) and eventually the popcorn will pop. You need to shake the pan vigorously for about five minutes to spread the dye all through the corn. You will end up with some corn completely coloured but most will be a sort of funky stripy colouring.

Serving Suggestion

If you just want to eat the popcorn and not decorate with it, add colour another way by cutting out large circles in coloured paper, fold the circles in half and bring the curved ends together to make a cone. Secure them with sticky tape and/or sit the cones in a glass or cup. Serve the popcorn in the cones.

Decorative Knots

Buy a good knot book that details decorative knots. They make great gifts and give you something different to do on watch. *(See 'Gifts' in this section.)*

Resources: The Book of Decorative Knots by Peter Owen.

Short story We met Jenny and Randy on board SV Mystic in San Diego. We were thrilled to meet them again in Mexico and then at different islands across the Pacific Ocean the following year. In Mexico, Jenny had made some rope pulls (the little tags you need to help undo things like pelican clips) and she gave us some for our boat. She had made them herself and they were a treasured gift. After much sun and several years of use, most perished, but we kept one hooked on a button in the galley. We always thought of Mystic when we touched this button. Homemade gifts are always treasured.

Entertainment

There is always a lot of work, repair, maintenance or upkeep on a boat; it's time for some fun!

Dinghy racing: Arrange a dinghy race (oars only), within the anchorage, followed up with a boatie banquet. To add a twist, the oarsman can be blindfolded and a partner in the dinghy has to provide the directions verbally.

Group game: At a banquet, party games always go down well. String, nails and empty beer bottles are all you need. Fashion a belt with another piece of string hanging to just below the knees on the back of the belt. Contestants tie this string belt around their waist with one part dangling down behind, like a tail. On the end of the string tie a large nail (or similar narrow, long object). Line empty bottles (beer/wine) up a distance away, and have four to six contestants ready to go. As a race together they run backwards to the bottles and squat down to try and get the nail in the bottle, first one in wins!

Having fun is about going with the flow. Midway through the Panama Canal, anchored in Gatun Lake, the crew took advantage of the fresh water lake. At 9 p.m. we had a lovely swim with crocodiles lurking nearby!

Noel, Jackie and Jackie's dad (Roy), were crew on board SV Theta with our lovely friends Judy and Barry. (A practice run before taking Mariah through.)

Swinging the lead: Boat fun for kids and adults: learn how Mark Twain got his name and what fun he had doing it. There is some skill involved, watch out for the propeller! *(See 'Lead Line' in the Boat Equipment section.)*

Sarongs: Arrange a sarong tying party. Research the various ways to tie a sarong (there are many more than you think) and share your knowledge. *(See Health & Well-being for sarong tying ideas from 1WORLDSARONGS at www.1worldsarongs.com)*

Music jamming: bring spoons, buckets, voices and any other instruments.

Dancing: Teach or learn local dance moves. *(See short story below.)*

On Palmerston Island, Noel and his handmade drum.

Short story In Suwarrow* (pronounced sue-arhh-row) with about eight other boats on anchor, we had many potlucks and other entertainment. One fun evening stands out. A family on board SV Grommet had spent a year in Huahine (French Polynesia) and the two beautiful daughters had learned the local dancing moves. They wowed us with their swinging hips, then patiently taught us to tie our sarongs (also called páreus or pareos) different ways and taught the women some dance moves (much to the laughter of our partners). They managed to teach us a whole segment, which we thoroughly enjoyed. All this happened on an atoll in the middle of the ocean.

(*Suwarrow is also called Suvorov, Suvarou or Suvarov. It is a low coral atoll in the Cook Islands in the Pacific Ocean. It is about 1,300km south of the equator and 930km NNW of Rarotonga.)

Sharing skills: Teach or learn a new skill. *(See short story below.)*

Short story At Suwarrow again (one of our all time favourite places), a creative afternoon was organised. You could learn how to weave palm fronds, make jewellery with beading, paint and draw. All this came from other cruisers, some whom had only just learned the skill themselves that very morning!

Beading: many women enjoy beading as a hobby and they sometimes make some pocket money by selling pretty bead-jewellery.

Short story A young girl on a Canadian vessel created professional bead-jewellery and made some great money selling items when the cruise ships came to town.

Arrange a cooking display: using local foods and a favourite recipe. (See short story below), yes, it's at Suwarrow again!

Short story As you can imagine, coconuts are in abundance on Pacific islands. Angus from SV Periclees makes a wonderful Thai noodle dish with coconut milk and offered to perform a demonstration. Anyone else wishing to create a dish using coconuts could join in, the remaining cruisers brought along nibbles and drinks and their taste buds. The caretakers at Suwarrow arranged a coconut peeling, creaming, shredding and tasting demonstration, which was fabulous. Coconuts are amazing! Four different coconut orientated dishes were cooked in the Yacht Club and a great afternoon experienced by all.

Meet new people: Experience local culture.

On the island of Moorea (near Tahiti) we joined in with the Puddle Jumpers for fantastic entertainment and fun.

Latitude 38 Magazine (USA) organises the Puddle Jump Rally each year. This is a great way to make lots of new friends and experience French Polynesian culture to the full.
http://www.pacificpuddlejump.com/

Fishing

Do not rely on feeding yourself with caught fish.

Killing fish: If you are lucky enough to have a good catch, an easy way to kill fish instantly is by pouring a little alcohol in their gills - what a way to go! We have a very cheap bottle of rum for this purpose. Friends use methylated spirits in a pump spray to kill fish quickly. Alternatively, keep a small baton handy for a quick knock on the head.

A great catch in the Pacific on Pyewacket

Set up: We use simple round, plastic reels and an assortment of lures. The reel is on the deck, low down and the line hitched onto a stanchion. We use some elastic with hooks either end. Attach one hook to something secure on the boat and the other in the loop you have made a few feet down the line. This works well as you don't lose the reel or more line and know when a fish is on the line with the elastic stretching and thinning out.

Catching birds: Twice we have had birds entangled in our line. Both times we carefully hauled them on board and put a large towel over their heads (this pacifies them). We managed to free both birds. They were a bit startled, but fine. Leaving them quietly on deck to recover from the shock, they both fluffed their feathers and after a while flew off.

Lures: We use regular lures. We have heard (and tried without success) that a silver spoon is good, especially if dipped in WD40 (which has fish oil as an ingredient).

Make your own fishing lures:
- Strips from an aluminium can or toothpaste tubes.
- Use the inside of bungee cord, for 'squid' type lure.
- Strips of white garbage/rubbish bag.

Friends
When cruising you will make lifelong friends.

Years later and thousands of miles apart, 'Tash (from SV Frodo) is still one of my greatest friends.

Games
Select some photos and crop them down to show only a small segment of the picture. Save that segment in a separate file on your laptop. Show one picture at a time, everyone has a guess where it was taken, either in turn or first answer wins! You could make this an educational game with trips onshore/boat parts/animals, etc. (Remember to save the cropped photo with a different name, so you retain the original photo in its original shape and size.)

Remember game: Put eight objects on a tray and cover them with a tea towel. Let the crew look at the objects for thirty seconds and try to remember as many as possible. See who can list them all.

Run out of games? Try something different. The TV on deck on a calm, balmy night is a unique treat.

In the Great Loop in America on Mariah, in very protected waters.

Guess who I am game: One person at a time selects a famous person, writes the chosen name down and keeps the piece of paper it is written on. Everyone takes turns at asking him/her a question that can only be answered with a yes or no. Keep going until someone guesses who they are.

Theme nights: Create a theme night and dress up (and behave) as characters from your favourite movie. If you are playing with younger children, choose characters from their favourite story or animals.

Short story Table Celebrations: Our great friends Andrea and Clive on SV Rainbird were integral in helping us build a new table on Mariah. As a carpenter, it had taken Noel nine years to build the promised table on board. The big celebration was held one evening with the sponsors of the timber and they helped create the celebratory atmosphere. Here Andrea is sporting the nautical look of a unique rope and clip necklace. Clive has gone the more debonair route with his bow tie and t-shirt!

Our lovely cruising buddies Andrea and Clive (from SV Rainbird), on board Mariah.

Gifts
The best gifts are handcrafted gifts.
- Decorative knots are a nice idea, see: http://www.boondoggleman.com for gift ideas *(see Decorative Knots above).*
- Bake a cake.
- Sew up some squares of material for oven mittens.

Unique food: As a creative alternative, find a tin or jar of food you have on board that is unavailable in your current port and make that your gift. *(See short story below.)*

Short story We were in Thailand and hadn't seen proper mayonnaise for months. For my birthday, I received a jar from another cruiser's supply, an ingenious gift!

Homemade: Relish or bread, or anything 'homemade' is always greatly appreciated as a gift.

Presentation: Small shells make ideal casings for homemade chocolates. With a ribbon, this makes a grand looking present.

We gave this local girl (in San Blas Islands, near Panama) an old magazine. She was so excited. As soon as she saw the pictures only her eyes moved - she was utterly absorbed.

Perfume: Small, sample bottles of perfume, soap, and lip gloss are always nice to receive (if a woman). Giving perfume to a guy is okay too, especially if he is sailing the South Pacific, as perfume is a great trading item with the locals. *(See 'Trading' further on in this section.)*

Flowers: Wild flowers are a real treat on board. When visiting a boat or giving a gift, a small bunch of flowers tied with a ribbon is beautiful and appreciated.

Recycle: If you are given a gift, keep the wrapping paper and ribbons and reuse them.

Guest Book
They are a great item to have on board and to look back on.

Short story In Ecuador we met a Canadian couple on board SV Alcheringa. We chatted with them on and off over a few weeks and it transpired we were in the Caribbean, at St Martin Island, at about the same time (a good few years ago). Benita looked at their log book and saw that we had actually all met before on another boat. We had a good laugh, as we didn't remember them and they didn't remember us!

Mementoes
Beach combing turns up some great mementoes (provided you aren't prohibited to take shells or other items).

Short story One of our favourite mementoes is from Cuba. We were stuck in port waiting for the right weather to leave, as the pass was being pounded by surf. While waiting, we went beach combing and found a very old Cuban oar. It is now bolted to our guest cottage veranda at home.

Purchase local music from each country to bring back instant and vivid memories.

This was our contribution to the Suwarrow Yacht Club. It was made from an old life jacket we carried on board. Suwarrow is one of our all time favourite places. We had tears in our eyes when we left.

Photography

Equipment: If possible, experiment with different types of cameras prior to buying one, in order to gain a full understanding of what you will need. We find digital cameras that are waterproof and drop proof are the best, and they provide excellent quality pictures.

Be prepared: Don't go anywhere without your camera; a magic moment that you want to capture may come when you least expect it. That's another reason we prefer the digital camera, as it is small and light.

Carry spare batteries with you, there's nothing more annoying than having them run out at prime opportunities.

Filing: I file my pictures on the laptop by location and date. They are always easy to find and I have at least one backup of my collection (preferably on a separate hard drive).

I take hundreds of pictures and when viewing them, I immediately delete any that are out of focus, meaningless or repetitive. I then select the top ten to twenty best pictures of that destination. These are for magazine articles and/or for a slide show for friends.

Composition: Experiment with the camera's settings to gain the best composition. Don't be afraid to experiment with different perspectives and colours.

Don't overlook mundane subjects for your pictures; a foreign menu, shop sign or building will evoke your memories.

If taking pictures for magazines, think about what is in the picture. I took some lovely snaps of a winch in pieces, all clean and shiny. The winch was sitting on newspaper and a large man's head, printed on the newspaper, appeared in the shot. It made the picture look very strange.

Taking pictures of the ocean and conditions has a foreshortening effect (distorted perspective) which means the pictures will show the conditions as only half as bad as they really are.

When you're taking a close-up, soften the brightness by placing a coffee filter over the flash.

Editing: If taking pictures for a magazine, do not edit them using your software, leave them be. The editing (if necessary) will be done by the magazine. If you change them yourself, you may well reduce their quality and usability.

Take the largest size pictures (more pixels) you can for best quality. Before emailing sample pictures reduce their size on the computer, BUT ensure you save the originals as they are and the reduced pictures separately. I label my reduced pictures with the same name as the large ones, but with an 'r' at the end (to note they are reduced in size). If your article and pictures are accepted by the magazine, you can then send the full size pictures.

Another good use: When taking an item apart, take pictures of the progression as well as written and labelled instructions. This is useful to look back on to see which way around that left handed doodad went when putting it all back together!

Take a picture of the item you want to replace to help you find it on land and to get the right match, without lugging the actual item to shore.

Backup: From time to time, send copies of your photos home to family or friends so they can keep a backup copy for you.

Photos (as well as the mandatory photocopies) of all your important documents are a great backup too.

Take pictures of your equipment and serial numbers to aid insurance claims.

Swaps
You will accumulate gear you will not use. Arrange a 'swap meet' or a 'boat mart' with fellow cruisers.

Sweet Treats
Buy your favourite treats in excess (whenever you find them). Divide them up into sensibly sized portions and hide them in various places around the boat. Put them in cupboards you rarely go to, as well as in more regularly used spaces. Put them at the bottom or corners of cupboards, so you won't see them for ages, unless you are digging. These are a nice surprise, especially when doing long ocean legs.

Short story I have a very sweet tooth. The best way to curb my chocolate intake is to have Noel manage it. He hides my treats in the workshop; admittedly I know where they are, but I rarely pinch anything. He knows how much is in there and rations it out to me as and when it is needed. Having someone else know how much I eat and be in charge of it, helps curb chocolate binge attacks (mostly)!

Tours
Organised tours can be a great way to experience different cultures, but what type of tour are you going on? Will you need sunscreen and mosquito spray, or boots and socks? For trips around

industrial areas, such as a beer factory, you will need to have your feet covered. When arranging excursions, ask if anything in particular is required *(see short story below)*.

Short story With a group of seven, we visited a beer making company in Apia, Samoa. We all wore three-quarter length pants or shorts, t-shirts and sandals. When we arrived, they told us that we all had to wear boots. Thirty minutes went by as staff frantically searched the building for boots to fit. We had no socks and some of the boots were new and others weren't. I was glad mine were new until the backs of my legs, above the heel, rubbed to a degree that I could hardly walk. Several weeks later I still had scarring. (The excursion was great fun though!)

Trading
Before you leave your home port, find a bargain shop (recycle or cheapie shop) and buy items to trade.

Over the years we've traded sweets/candy/lollies in exchange for fruit; pens and crayons for kids to watch over our dinghy; t-shirts and playing cards for fish; perfume for wooden carvings and cola for hand woven items.

Sweet treats stored on Pyewacket for trading and gifting. There may have been one or two less after I'd stowed them!

In addition, we have printed out photos for islanders (who almost went hysterical with delight to see themselves) and we gave out little items such as balloons and coins (of local currency) to the kids, who also shared the delight.

Trading is not just for different cultures you are visiting: you trade between other boats. Our friends gave us a generous container filled with hummus, which I traded for homemade muffins.

At the Marquesas, the local women went mad over perfume, even half a bottle that had been sitting on the boat for six years! We received a beautifully carved wooden bowl in exchange.

Fun Resources:
Fun and Games - try your luck at http://www.funny-games.biz/captain-chaos.html
Free Boat Clipart plus Ship Animations and Gifts http://www.fg-a.com/stgifs7.htm

In the Tuamotus, these girls were delighted to help us in exchange for some sweets/candy and pens.

Local ladies in the San Blas Islands were happy to trade their Molas (beautiful sewn fabric) for cans of cola.

ARTICLE: Published in Australia by Cruising Helmsman.

This Is It
by Jackie and Noel Parry

What do Michael Jackson and sailing have in common? Not much you say, but concepts from each make us happy.

I never thought Michael Jackson would inspire us. 'This Is It', the recent MJ movie exposed him as the creative genius he was. His dancers extolled their excitement of up and coming live performances. Michael softly reminded them 'this is it' - life's happening right now, enjoy this moment.

On board our new boat (new to us, at least), this is our mantra. Steadily, the hands of time click by, each second adds up to one less moment to enjoy in the long run. We are living a great life, but installing a new head, fixing an oil leak and all those 'not so pleasant' jobs to complete before ocean miles, can be hard, frustrating and rather disagreeable. This concept may seem obvious to some, dumb to others, but for us this works. We are enjoying everything we are doing. Which is pretty lucky, as at times I think I am about to lose my mind. It's been rather an extraordinary time lately.

We purchased Pyewacket II in America. Our plan was to go adventuring, not race home to sell her on. What we wanted was the lifestyle back. We had lived on board our cutter rigged sloop Mariah II for nearly nine years. Then we spent three years on terra firma and finally the pull back to the ocean was too strong to ignore any longer, so we upped anchor.

The idea of buying in the States was to give us another opportunity to explore the bejewelled Pacific Ocean; last time we saw just a smattering of its diamonds. We weren't that interested in doing the Panama Canal again, and we'd already explored much of the East coast and the inland waterways of America (including Great Lakes, Ohio River, Mississippi).

What were we looking for in a boat? Primarily, a longer water line than Mariah, which meant a bigger boat. It was time to try something different. Our aim was a waterline of around twelve metres, which lets the length of the vessel dictate itself. (Longer water line means higher hull speed and increased comfort). Neither of us were interested in steel, timber was okay, but we seemed to be steering a course to fibreglass - again, for something different. Other specifications included:

- *6 ft draft (not missing out on shallow anchorages)*
- *Two cabins*
- *Two heads*
- *Lead keel (encapsulated, no chance of corrosion)*
- *Full keel with protected prop (help protect from fouling ropes)*
- *Double spreaders (strength)*
- *Double back stay (strength)*
- *Centre cockpit (something different)*

Really, that list could go on and on. We avoided balsa cored hulls and teak decks. Teak decks look fantastic, however, we viewed eight teak decked boats and they all leaked to varying degrees. Mariah was, what I call, a dry boat. This was important, as there is nothing more demoralising than getting wet down below.

The idea of two cabins is to accommodate all our visitors. We have a lot of sailing friends keen to do a leg with us or just come and sit on anchor. We like that idea and two heads means a little extra comfort for us all.

We landed in San Francisco in mid October. We arrived with the clothes on our backs and one bag each stuffed with handheld GPSs, Nav equipment, sextant, handheld radios, hand Watermaker, a clean set of undies and a huge dollop of determination. We were already exhausted. Our impossible timeline between finishing work and flying out meant we had to perform miracles to organise our house and affairs in Greenwell Point, NSW, Australia. We are lucky to have great friends renting the house, so when I simply could not pack up the last items of the kitchen (kettle and toaster), as the plane would not wait, I didn't have to worry too much.

San Francisco is a buzzing, colourful city, crammed with characters. We have two marvellous sailing friends that live there, who kindly provided a base and put us up (or put up with us) for two weeks, while we found our feet. The first amazing concept in boat hunting in this part of the world is that most boat brokers are not the slightest bit interested in selling boats. We were staggered at the lack of interest in our enquiries. In desperation, Noel wrote an email to one broker stating 'we are from Australia, we have cash, we have jet lag and a desperate stare in our eyes. In short we are mugs ready to be led down the path of nautical slavery, if you can't sell us a boat there is something very wrong.' Perhaps they just don't get the Aussie humour.

In the suburb of Sausalito we approached a broker who worked in a long narrow office. He sat at the back and shouted at us from his chair, some twenty metres away. We were asking to view a boat he had advertised and all he kept saying was 'I need twenty-four hours notice', we tried to give him that notice, but got tired of shouting. The first broker that we pried from his chair was out of a Hollywood movie, not because of the glamour, but because he was unbelievable. 'Jed' wore plastic thongs (flip-flops), Hawaiian shorts and t-shirt, and a smoking fag hung perpetually from his mouth. The boats we viewed were on the hard. He would smash the ladder onto the topsides with a crunch that made us cringe. He did this with a shrug at our horror and sat in the cockpit puffing like a steam train, while we looked at the generally beaten up boats. Another broker yelled 'Buy!! Sell!!' down his mobile phone while we were all crammed into a tiny aft cabin. We were close to Hollywood, but this was getting ridiculous.

During this fiasco, we commenced discussions to view a boat we literally stumbled across. At this point we had only been in the States for two weeks. It felt like two years. We quickly became disillusioned with what we saw, which was primarily rot, delaminating decks, blisters and mould. It sounds like a dream to hop on a plane and spend each day viewing boats, but the reality is quite different. Our budget meant we had clean motel rooms, but that was all you could say about them.

We found hiring a car in the States extremely expensive due to insurance costs. Our desires were also difficult to fulfil, as centre cockpit boats seemed few and far between. We toyed with going to Seattle, where we had just missed out on an Olympic Adventurer, but there were other boats that sparked interest. Ted Brewer designs caught our eye.

How did we find Pyewacket? As I said, during the bothersome brokers' debacle we were arranging to view a boat we accidentally found. On our first boat viewing we spied Pyewacket II a few docks down. The boat we had arranged to see was not for us. We stepped on deck, saw the teak and a cockpit only two children could possibly squeeze into with the aid of a crowbar and told the broker to forget it. With our buddies Roy and Chris, we wandered down the dock to a proud, large monohull. 'Wow, look at the rigging' was the first comment. She had two backstays, running backstays and wider diameter rig than was necessary - a good start. While Chris, Noel and I, oohhed and aahhed, Roy disappeared. A few moments later he returned accompanied with a big smug grin. 'It's for sale and here's the owners number!' Detective Roy had made enquiries in a fishing shop next door (which sold the most spectacular Clam Chowder).

Noel rang and Ed (Pyewacket's owner) explained that she was for sale, but he was tired of dealing with brokers, he was selling her privately for just a little more than we could afford. He told us that he had just dropped his price significantly (for the third time). I was already ahead of everyone, working out the finances. I sharply reminded myself with a stab of doubt that history dictated I'd be disappointed once below decks.

We inspected Pyewacket several times, in between the fiasco with brokers. I was not disappointed. Over the next few weeks, buyers and seller became friends. Ed let us view Pyewacket over and again and he took us for a test sail (motor sailing on a calm day). We were impressed and found it hard to believe that we were actually sailing on San Francisco harbour, gliding past the famous Golden Gate Bridge.

Ironically, with all of our complaining about a lack of suitable boats, while negotiating for Pyewacket we were also in discussions with a broker for another boat. We were honest with both sellers, as they were with us and other buyers. Funnily enough 'Escapade' was on the books with a broker named Don from Heritage Yacht Sales, Newport Beach. Don could not have been more helpful, a true lover of all things nautical and he bent over backwards in the negotiations. He even offered to take a small cut in the commission to try and seal the deal. However, it was not to be and now we are glad it wasn't. 'Escapade' was very close to what we wanted, a fine boat, but a smaller cockpit and an enormous generator to lug around (in addition to the main engine) was not ideal for our purposes.

The negotiations were hard, we seemed to be increasing our offers but the sellers were not coming down. Finally frustration hit its maximum and we booked flights to Florida. 'We'll find our boat there,' we said, in an ever so grown up way!

The day before flying out (to more sailing friends) to commence our search on the east coast, we were back with Roy and Chris. One evening Noel said to our hosts, 'We've managed to stop ourselves calling Ed fifty-four times today!' Finally, Noel looked at me and said 'I'm going to call Ed one more time'. I was annoyed as I had already booked tickets, but couldn't hide the spark of excitement that twitched on my lips. We didn't speak to Ed until we were driving to the movies to see 'This Is It' with Roy and Chris. We increased our offer, taking us over our budget. While watching the movie, Ed gave the dollars some thought.

We came out of the movie inspired to enjoy every waking minute of what we were doing, and the phone rang. I'm not usually the negotiator, but I felt motivated and launched into a deep conversation with Ed. The first time I stepped on Pyewacket, I knew she was our boat and I wanted her. After ten minutes of more negotiations and a little more money for us and a little less for Ed we reached an agreement - I was ecstatic. As I put the phone down, Roy, Chris and Noel gave me a round of applause and Roy offered me a job, 'My goodness, you can negotiate!' he said.

So, here we sit on board Pyewacket II in Ecuador. We've owned Pyewacket for six months. During that time, we've hauled out, completed a survey, antifouled, changed anodes, fitted filters, fan belts and freed up the spinnaker pole and seacocks. We have fixed hanks, hosing and housing, cleaned, wiped, scrubbed and washed everything within an inch of its life. We've balanced, built, bodged and bought tonnes of gear. On board are the builders' notes that we have read, absorbed and regurgitated. We have also polished her hull, moved on board, sealed the deal and sailed several thousand miles south. It's no wonder we are tired. But we realise how lucky we are, we found what we were looking for incredibly quickly.

And Pyewacket? She successfully meets 99% of our requirements and this glorious old girl will be our home for some time. Don't forget 'this is it'!

Advice

We knew this would not be easy, but it was much harder than we imagined. We spent almost two years carrying out Internet research prior to leaving. There are thousands of boats for sale, but most we saw had major problems.

- Have a very clear idea of what you are looking for and where you will/will not make any compromises.
- There will be at least one compromise you have to make.
- Budget 50% more than you think for expenses and for the boat.
- A lot of boats have a survey of varying age. If you ask, the brokers may let you read them - some reports are staggering and will save you wasting your time.
- Ask chandleries for a discount. Many give discounts if you have just purchased a boat or you spend enough - if you don't ask, you don't get.
- Hire a document agent - be aware of fraud, check and compare engraved numbers to document numbers and use an insured and certified document agent.
- Research, research, research. We joined several 'chat rooms' on the Internet for lots of different builds of boat. This led to a day out sailing on a Pan Oceanic 43 on Sydney Harbour!
- Ensure you extract the construction of the boat from the broker before viewing. One broker avoided this question for nearly a year - just before flying to Mexico we found out it was fibreglass/ferro boat, a build we did not want.

Costs (in US dollars)

- Car hire $320 per week (including all/any discounts I could find).
- Value Motel rooms $70-$100 a night (with discount coupon).
- Food.
- Fuel.
- Mobile phone (you simply can't operate this task without one) - you are billed when you make calls AND receive them in America.
- We took our laptop, as most places have free Wi-Fi.
- Document Agent - $500 minimum.
- Surveyor - $500 minimum.
- Hauling costs for surveyor (organise antifouling then too) - $250 haul out/in +$102 per day.
- Import tax: 15% + of value of vessel when returning to Australia (plus possible fumigation costs). If you are not returning for some time, they may require the vessel to be re-valued in Australia. They will also take into account any work you have had done since the purchase. Full payment is required on return into Australian waters.
- Inspiring movies!

We hope you enjoyed this article. We are all inspired by different things!

GALLEY
Includes: Cookers & Stoves, Cooking, Eating Out, On Board & Underway, Preserving, Shopping/Victualling & Stowing, Other Ideas & Tips

COOKERS & STOVES
Galley stoves have to be able to operate at different angles. The pots and pans must be prevented from being able to move (or at least slide off) by utilising pot holders. These are either brackets or clamped on 'bars' that enclose the pots and pans and stop them moving. Lids should fit well.

Oven doors should have the facility to lock to prevent being forced open when the boat heels over. All controls should be at the front of the stove, you do not want to lean over a stove that is moving!

Gas Safety
Gas cookers (LPG) are a popular choice and are clean and easy to use. However, gas is highly flammable. This is its one disadvantage when comparing with other cooking fuels *(see advantage/disadvantage comparisons below)*.

If a gas leak occurs it will sink into your bilges, as gas is heavier than air (LPG is liquid form in the bottle and burned as a gas). Thereafter the slightest spark will create an explosion, so we suggest having the following safety systems in play:

- Fit a solenoid valve to remotely turn the gas off at the bottle.
- Fit a thermal switch near the flame to stop the gas flow if the gas blows out.
- Fit a bubble leak detector (a requirement in some countries).
- Set up the system so it allows you to have two places where you turn off the gas when you are finished.
- When leaving your boat, you should always turn the gas off at the bottle.
- Empty the gas line of gas after each use by turning off the solenoid before turning off the oven button.
- Fit a gas alarm for additional peace of mind.
- Never use a match to detect a leak. To locate where the leak is, put some washing up liquid (detergent) in a little water, wipe this along the gas line and connections. Where the bubbles get bigger, that is where your leak is.
- To check the gas flame in the oven has not gone out without opening the oven door, fix a reflector or mirror behind the flame (and a touch lower). This allows you to look under the stove and see in the mirror whether the flame is still going without losing some heat as you would if you opened the door. (You will need a gap under your gimballed stove that allows you to do this.)
- Gas cylinders should be stored upright with the valve at the top.
- Ensure the cylinder is completely secured.
- If your gas bottles are stored in a cupboard, the cupboard should be completely sealed with a vent positioned at the lowest point. The vent must not drain into your boat, but over the side. Ensure that any drain holes, for a potential gas leak, cannot be covered by the wake of your vessel!
- Never leave your stove unattended. If you have to change sails, go up on deck or leave the galley for any reason, turn everything off. (This applies for all types of stoves and fuel.)

Gimballed Or Not Gimballed?

Gimballed: A gimballed stove pivots backwards and forwards, so when the boat heels, the stove top remains level and prevents the pots and pans from moving in most seas. In a violent motion, the pots can still slide unless they are fixed into place with pot holders.

We had gimballed stoves on our boats and never experienced a problem. Whether gimballed or not, problems can occur. Opening a gimballed oven door has to be done carefully to compensate for the change in the centre of gravity. With good shelves (that prevent your oven trays from sliding), this isn't a problem. A pot on the top will only be a problem if it is not clamped in or is overfilled. A gimballed stove should have the facility to lock when in port.

Fixed: A fixed stove maybe better and easier when using the oven, but if boiling liquid is spilled on the top and the boat heels - guess where that liquid is going. Friends have a stove which is not gimballed. They use sturdy pot holders to keep the pots in one place, and use larger pots so nothing spills when they are heeling over. They are very happy with this set up.

Athwartships mounted: An athwartships mounted stove is another idea. An athwartships stove is mounted with its back facing directly forward or aft of the vessel, as opposed to port and starboard. Therefore, if it were gimballed, it would move more when the boat is pitching and be more secure when the boat is rolling. We have never used a stove that is mounted athwartships and have seen only one boat with the oven this way. Our friends have their stove athwartships and gimballed and are quite content with this set up. We have heard of some cruisers having an athwartships mounted stove that is not gimballed - again the user is perfectly happy. However, I can envisage the same problems if the stove does not have good clamps to keep the pots from moving. It seems that we all get used to what we have.

Either way, gimballed or not - they both have their pros and cons. It is like everything - there is inherent danger in sailing. You just need to know your limits and the limits of your equipment.

Our gimballed (gas) stove on Mariah was a simple caravan stove with a very useful grill.

Cooking Fuels
1. Propane (LPG)
This is probably the most common fuel used on boats.

Advantages: Inexpensive, clean and readily available. Good for cooking in extreme conditions as it lights instantly and it is simple to regulate the flame. Tanks are easy to remove and it cooks efficiently.

Disadvantages: Requires maintenance (or at least regular checking) to ensure no leaks. Propane is heavier than air and settles in areas low down in the boat, which presents a risk of explosion.
We use propane. On average, a nine kilo bottle lasts us three months. We do a lot of cooking on board, including baking bread regularly.

2. Diesel
Advantages: Hot burning fuel, it heats up the cabin in a cooler climate and is safer than gas (less flammable).

Disadvantages: Requires exhaust chimney as they can be sooty. Lighting them can be difficult and it heats up the cabin when in the tropics!

3. Electric
Electric cookers are for people taking short voyages and/or who have a separate generator just for running electrical items (not propel the boat). They are safer than gas, but it means you have to carry around another engine and maintain it.

Advantages: Safe and no fuel to handle (except the fuel for the generator).

Disadvantages: Expensive in power and diesel. Running a generator for a cup of tea!

4. Alcohol & Methylated Spirits
These are very similar fuels.
Advantages: Safer than propane (LPG), when it is liquid it does not explode. It can be extinguished with water.

Disadvantages: Low heat content, can be smelly if not burning correctly. Needs priming.

Older alcohol stoves use pressurised tanks. The burners must be pre-heated with liquid alcohol to obtain the right heat in order to vaporize the fuel and make it burn effectively. This can be tricky and must be done properly to prevent a flare up. Many fires have been caused by these flare ups and therefore these types of stoves (with pressurised burners) are used less often.

Modern alcohol stoves store the liquid fuel in absorbent material and therefore do not have pressurised burners. A burner creates a draft to intensify the gentle flame. Priming is unnecessary and therefore these stoves are safer than the older alcohol stoves.

5. Solid Fuel
Advantages: Safer than propane, hot burning.

Disadvantages: Takes lots of storage space, difficult to regulate and requires an exhaust chimney.

6. Paraffin/Kerosene
Advantages: Hot flame, safer than propane.

Disadvantages: Can be smelly and produce soot if not burning correctly. It can be difficult to light, as it needs priming. Sometimes it is difficult to source.

Lighters
Keep additional lighters for your stove and even a supply of matches. We prefer using the butane BBQ lighters, as they are easy to use and safe.

Oven/Cooker Maintenance
If your gas oven (or burners) won't light, try this (this method worked brilliantly on our old stove):

- Use an emery board, followed by fine sand paper to clean the tip of the thermocouple.

- Clean the orifices of the burners, take the burner cap off burner and remove air basket and the orifice from the burner. Soak the orifice in alcohol and scrub it with a toothbrush. Do not poke metal into the hole, use a wooden toothpick instead.

- Clean the fuel line by pushing a pipe cleaner into the hole in the middle of the burner. Prior to assembling, turn the fuel on just a little, to blow out any carbon.

Buying A New Oven
Ensure you view the oven with the heat dispersion pan inside to ensure the pan is not too high and taking up half the space. Take your bread tin with you when searching to check for ample space; double check that the dimensions reflect the actual space available to use, including all parts (trays, heat dispersion pan).

Other Cooking Equipment
Pressure cookers: They can save time and money. Cooking time is reduced and therefore the amount of fuel you use is less. Be sure to read the safety instructions carefully, especially on attaching the lid securely, reducing steam pressure and opening the pot. If you want to purchase a second hand pressure cooker, check the seals very carefully. Timing is important when using a pressure cooker; it is easy to overcook vegetables. Buy a timer to avoid timing mishaps.

Avoid aluminium - our aluminium pressure cooker was thrown out when the aluminium started to leach into the food!

Microwave: We had a microwave on Pyewacket, which I used to store the laundry powder! We do not have the power, need or inclination to use it as a microwave, but it makes a good cupboard.

Pot holders, crash bars and straps: Your stove should have pot holders (clamps or bars) to stop the pots from sliding. Crash bars are positioned in front of the stove so if you are thrown against the stove, both the stove and you are protected.

A seat-belt type strap installed in the galley can be a good idea to hold you firm if the weather is really bad. Fiddles around the stove are there to stop the pots sliding off. They need to be a good height so pots cannot topple over them.

COOKING
Baking
When baking one loaf of bread, add a tray of muffins to make efficient use of all that generated heat.

Boiling
When boiling up potatoes, add carrots and other vegetables to the same pot to save gas and water.
Steaming: You can put cabbage, zucchini or any vegetables on top of the boiling potatoes in a colander. Place a lid on the colander and the vegetables will steam. Do not pour the water down the sink, save it for a vegetable stock or add a few drops of soy sauce and drink it! It makes a very healthy, tasty drink.

I love making bread and tried many different recipes until I found one that worked for me and my oven.

A very basic bread recipe, rising once, worked on Mariah. On Pyewacket's oven I used a 'French Bread' recipe, which worked very well. *(See Reading & Resources section for recommended galley books.)*

Bread
For years I made loaves of bread while on watch (normally during the graveyard shift, giving Noel fresh bread at dawn when he started his shift). I kept a large, heavy-duty paper bag for storing the bread, it lasted for up to six or seven days.

Stowing: Friends say they buy regular bread in a supermarket and freeze a couple of loaves. They keep this frozen bread in the bottom of their fridge and the rest unfrozen. If you don't have a freezer, the supermarket may freeze some bread for you. Alternatively some fridges are almost freezer temperature at the bottom, making this a good place to store bread.

Cooking With Seawater
The only time we used seawater for cooking was when we boiled eggs. However, many of our friends use seawater more often. Here are some of their recommendations:

- Boiling potatoes: Half fresh water, half saltwater.

- Pasta: Two thirds fresh, one third seawater.
- Vegetables: Half fresh, half seawater (use only fresh if you want to make stock from the water).

The quantity by which you dilute the saltwater is a personal preference, but remember it is best to be a number of miles offshore to collect the cleanest water.

Simple Meals
We always make more than we need for one sitting and store the extra food carefully to last a few days. Lunch and dinner can be as easy as a spoonful of coleslaw, cold lentil burgers and a slice of tomato - ready in thirty seconds.

Special Occasions
If you plan to cook something special with several different ingredients and have many hungry crew on board, mark the specific ingredients to be used with a black marker pen. Train all on board to know that it must not be touched!

Cooking our catch at the Cayman Islands, on Mariah's stove.

Three bits of rolled up bread on the line snagged us three fish!

EATING OUT, ON BOARD & UNDERWAY
Eating On Board
Budget cruising means lots of meals on board. This can sound fun or easy, but the reality can become quite different. It does mean work. For two of us, that is six meals a day in total. Including the purchasing of food and the clearing up afterwards, it can feel like a full time job.

Share & prepare: We share the cooking so neither of us gets too bogged down. When one of us feels in a cooking mood we have a big cook up. Noel is great at stews, coleslaw and a fabulous tomato sauce. I roll my sleeves up and get into lentil burgers, yoghurt, cereal, muffins and bread. If you have an urge to cook at sea, cook plenty of variety, as you never know when the weather will turn or your next cooking urge may come!

Have fun: We do go out occasionally and forget about the budget - we think this is healthy and try not to dwell on it too much - after all 'This Is It' *(see article 'This Is It' in the Fun section).*

Balance: How you eat on board is a four-way balance between food availability, your palate, effort and budget. The more effort you put into sourcing reasonably priced supplies and cooking on board for the majority of time, then the less you will spend.

Eating Out

Enjoy the outdoors: If you are out for the day, it does not always mean you have to eat in a restaurant or cafe for lunch. We often buy fresh rolls at the bakery, a couple of bananas and an avocado, and find a nice bench to sit on. More often than not, we have our own water bottles with us and can find a park to enjoy our lunch in.

Tools: A small knife carried in the backpack is always useful. Noel carries his multi-tool (Leatherman), which is perfect. I usually carry tissues and/or wet wipes with me to make clean up is easy.

Leftovers: When eating in a restaurant, we always take our leftovers home. I never feel embarrassed about this, it is my meal and I have paid for it. The people in the restaurant are always delighted that we have enjoyed the food so much we want to take it home.

Eating out can mean making use of park facilities. In Australia, public BBQs are often scattered along the foreshores and make a great treat with friends.

Angus (left) from SV Periclees and Noel are the chefs.

Location, location, location: In a foreign port, eat where the locals eat, not the tourists. It's usually cheaper and better! Avoid the main street and venture further in to the back streets. Where large portions are the norm (such as the USA), we will often share a main course; the restaurant/cafes are always happy to oblige with extra plates and cutlery.

Short story Arriving to Galapagos for the first time was thrilling. On Mariah we did not have a fridge, so we were both keen for some meat (and, of course, a beer). Tired from the journey, we walked into one of the first cafes we saw. Although it was very nice, it was aimed at the tourist trade - and so were the prices! Just two streets back you could buy a three course meal, with a fresh fruit drink for $2-$2.50 (US dollars). They did not have menus, you simply had their 'special' each time. The food was delicious and as the supermarkets in Galapagos were not stocked well, we ate out a lot-our excuse was to preserve our supplies!

Eating While Underway

We tend to eat little and often when underway. Eating is considered 'fuel' more than an 'event'. That said, we take care to create good meals that we enjoy. The food on board can be closely linked with morale.

Make life easy: If the seas are very bouncy, reef down the sail for a while and turn to go with the seas. This will help make the motion smoother. Once the meal is cooked and eaten, you can carry

105

on beating into the seas. If bad weather is forecast, prepare some meals while you can and eat something before the weather deteriorates.

Hasty-tasty: Always have in mind a 'hasty tasty' to prepare, whether it be tinned food or packaged. Sometimes at sea, both Noel and I simply cannot be bothered to make anything that takes time and effort.

Be inventive: If you are in the mood, have fun and be a little creative:

- We bought a run-of-the-mill packaged cake mix as a backup. Noel baked it for my birthday and found a packet of colourful M&M sweets and stuck them all over the cake. When I woke up, I had a lovely, colourful and yummy surprise, right in the middle of the Atlantic Ocean.

- A lot of meals are dictated by what needs using up. Use anything soft right away and make up a mock pizza: fry any leftovers, add whisked eggs (like an omelette) and pretend it is a real pizza!

- Soup in a cup is a quick, warm, easy to hold meal.

- Pita bread, as a pocket for a sandwich.

- Try holding a sandwich in a circular coffee filter, for less mess when underway (and less washing up).

If only fishing were so easy.

These fish were on Palmerston Island, caught by the locals and generously shared with the visiting cruisers.

Take Outs

Always budget conscious, when in port and desiring a takeaway, we sometimes buy the main meal, e.g. some dim sims and then cook the rice and maybe onions on board. Sharing the cooking and expense!

PRESERVING

Cheese

Feta cheese can be kept for months. Cut it into approximately one inch cubes (dependent on the size of your jar), fill the jar loosely, add herbs and spices to taste and fill up the remaining space in the jar with olive oil.

To ensure the cheese does not float up and become exposed to the air (it will go mouldy), cut a piece of plastic from an ice-cream carton, big enough so that when you push it in through the neck of the container/jar, it opens up to fit the shoulders of your container. The shoulders will keep the plastic down ensuring that the cheese is kept below the oil level.

Cheeses covered with red or yellow wax seem to keep very well.

We enjoy feta, but also tried the preservation idea with a local cheese in Ecuador, which while less crumbly and quite soft, worked wonderfully.

Short story I also tried this oil preservation idea with a cheese from Panama that looked exactly the same as the cheese in Ecuador. However, it went VERY off. If you cannot find true feta, do a test run with the cheese you would like to preserve first.

At times you will not be able to buy mature cheese. To 'mature' your own cheese, wipe down your un-waxed cheese with vinegar, wrap it in a muslin or cheese cloth (cotton, breathable), store in a cool dark place and ensure it cannot move, as it will bruise. Check it regularly and slice off what you want, when you want it. If there is any mould, cut that off and wipe the cut edge again with vinegar. This is not recommended for soft cheese, as any mould can burrow deeper into the cheese.

Chillies

If you like chillies, chop some up and cover with oil and a little lemon juice - they will last for years! Then, to add a quick zing to your cooking, you simply use the chilli or just add a drop or two of the oil.

Fruit & Vegetables

Long-life fruit and vegetables like pumpkin, cabbage, onions, garlic, potatoes, oranges and lemons are good to stock up on. Store in well ventilated areas; nets are great for this.

Small baskets within the nets help with ventilation and therefore longevity. Ensure they are not near a window, or make sure the window has a curtain to shade the items.

Purchase fresh foods that are not bruised and damaged.

Ginger

Ginger lasts a long time as it is, but over time it will dry out. Peel, slice and keep it in vinegar for many months of fresh ginger. Alternatively, freeze it if you can, then just grate as needed.

Mayonnaise

If supermarket purchased mayonnaise is not contaminated by other food stuffs or fingers, it will keep indefinitely in or out of the fridge. Purchase the squeeze bottles of mayonnaise to help avoid contamination. Just ensure you wipe with a clean cloth before closing the lid, not your finger or tongue!

Preserving Foods - Tinning & Canning

We do not can food ourselves as I am a sloppy cook and fearful of botulism, but many of our cruising friends do. We also enjoy the healthier diet of eating less meat while at sea. There are different ways to carry out canning. Research the best way for you on the Internet or even better, find a cruiser to recommend a recipe.

I do can acid foods that are less problematic, a particular favourite being 'Sweet Cucumber Relish'. This is very simple, relatively quick and yummy. With our preserved cheese this is a big hit at sea. You can research via the Internet for many recipes for relish, I just picked the simplest method that suited me.

SHOPPING/VICTUALLING & STOWING

Don't fret over food. In the remotest places, if there are people living there (or nearby), you will survive; they have to eat too.

Find out where and when the locals shop. In the Marquesas the local fresh market was fantastic if you got there at 5 a.m.

Cost comparison: I always compare the weight of the item with the cost, and then calculate an approximate cost per 500 grams (or whatever works) to facilitate price comparisons. I have noticed things change every few years. It used to be that the largest items, such as large instant coffee jars, were the most economical. However, at the time of writing the mid-size coffee jars are more economical. When you compare meat, how much fat and bone are you paying for?

<u>Don't miss out</u>: I always walk up and down every aisle in the supermarket, just in case I spot an item I have neglected to list or I find something new to try.

<u>Enjoy!</u>: When you are ashore in a foreign port, you may find smaller shops, a different weight system, different names, and even names and items you do not recognise. Most locals shop as part of their daily routine, especially for fresh produce. It then becomes a social event. For a foreigner, this can be fun and exciting. People are always happy to help. We cannot know every language, but pointing, gesticulating, miming and drawing can ensure you get what you want. That is the beauty of travelling: meeting new people, experiencing different cultures, understanding how they live, and trying new foods. We always had good fun when shopping in a new port. *(See Measurements & Conversions.)*

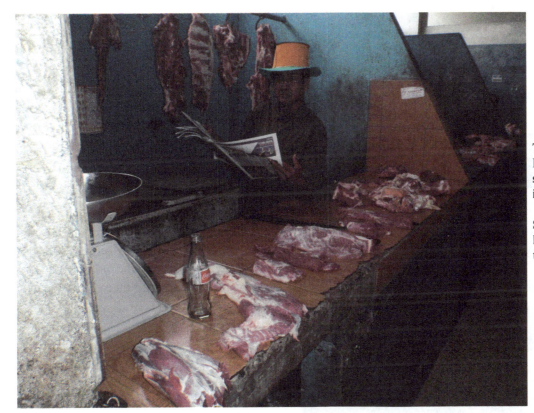

The markets in Ecuador turned a shopping chore into an adventure.

Sometimes you have to be brave though!

<u>Garbage management</u>: If you are on anchor/mooring, throw away all that extra packaging before returning to your boat. Some people like to use a marker pen to write expiry dates on the remaining packaging, but we never bothered, as it never stayed on board that long! Ensure, at the minimum, all cardboard is thrown away immediately; cockroaches like to lay eggs in cardboard.

<u>Make life easy</u>: When you go shopping, take spare bags and egg cartons. We have a trolley that carries two large bags full of groceries. It has two wheels and an extending handle, ideal for stocking up if the walk is reasonably close. Otherwise, we hire a taxi. When we do a huge shop a taxi fare is just part of the cost.

Dress as the locals do when shopping, as scantily or offensive dress sense can irritate certain folk. Always go for the more conservative look.

Make life easy. If the shop is in walking distance, borrow the trolley. In the Cayman Islands we gave my dad (Roy) the job of ferrying the goodies.

We cleared the shelves of baked beans. We had not seen just plain baked beans for over a year and when we found them again, it was very exciting!

(Make sure you return the trolley!)

We have pushbikes on board. They are extremely useful and we found space on both Mariah and Pyewacket to stow them fairly easily. They are very handy if you have purchased quite a load, as the bike can take the weight of the shopping, even if you just end up pushing the bike while you walk (loop shopping bags on the handle bars, sit the bags in baskets or even strap them to the seat).

In the Gambier Islands, fruit was for the picking.

We found a tree loaded with mangoes, falling off and rotting. We had to traverse thick forest and fallen trees (that were rotten and broke when we stepped on them). It was hard work, but great galloping fun and we hauled in a bounty!

Member's card: When visiting any supermarket, ask for a member's card. Quite often they will give you one straightaway and you can take advantage of discounted goods.

Quantities: We buy enough food for the duration of the trip, plus at least 50% more. Some people log what they eat over a period of time and use that as a guide. We just made a list a week or two before we left (and kept adding to it until we shopped, just before departure). We also carried copious quantities of lentils, rice, pasta and tinned food as backups.

Short story You will be surprised at how naturally expert you are with the quantities you need, and it becomes easier and easier. When we stocked up in Panama for the second Pacific Ocean crossing, we were aware that many of the islands had limited items and/or were expensive. We focused on dried foods, tinned food, and alcohol for 'long-term' food. We purchased enormous quantities of onions and potatoes that kept for months and basically stocked up so well, we still had food/alcohol on board from Panama a year later. We purchased meat and fresh produce at the islands.

Que?: Translation programmes on the Internet can help with a tricky word and can even pronounce it for you. As a backup, you could translate certain items you really want to find and have this with you when shopping. If you own a camera with a large screen on the back, you can take a picture of an item to show shopkeepers.

Supermarket selection: On arrival to a new port, take time to look at the different shops and work out which ones to visit. Ask other cruisers who have been there before you, they will be a great source of information. Ensure you keep in mind your own tastes, some people like different kinds of shops. Some cruisers we have met would go out of their way for 'western style' supermarkets, whilst Noel and I are usually happier to shop where the locals shop.

Spend time in different supermarkets researching items. Not my favourite task, but when I make great savings I am glad I made the effort.

Short story We love homemade chocolate chip muffins for trips, especially to have as a treat during the night with a cup of tea. In Tahiti, where we got back to large supermarkets, I could buy a tiny packet (about one handful) of choc chips for US$6. Or, I could buy a large packet of choc chip cookies (brownies), for US$1.20! Delicious.

Share the burden: Noel and I both go shopping prior to a voyage. Neither of us feels it is fair for the other to be burdened with the enormous and important task of stocking the boat. It can be a huge task, resulting in umpteen trolley loads of food. If an item has not been listed or thought about, one of us will usually spot it on a shelf.

In Cuba, shopping together became a fun highlight with the locals.

<u>Short cuts</u>: I like to buy condensed soup, as you get more for your money (just add water) and they make great pasta sauces when I am not feeling very creative.

Individual noodle packets were a big hit on board Pyewacket. They are very simple to prepare and are a plain food to have in your tummy if you are feeling a little seasick. You can jazz them up a bit by adding an egg (one per person). Simply let it cook in the juices or add extra water, herbs and plenty of lemon (be careful not to overcook the noodles), for a quick, light and refreshing soup.

Cake mixes, noodles, ready-made meals and soups in a cup are all very handy for when you have bad weather, or when you simply cannot be bothered to put on your chef's hat.

<u>Try before you buy</u>: If you are stocking up at a foreign port, try the tinned/canned food prior to buying large quantities. The contents may surprise you, even if you can read the label. The list of ingredients on tinned food is listed with the most predominant first. This also applies to packaged foods with unfamiliar brands. Try them first; coffee, cocoa, sugar, cheese etc, can have very different flavours.

'No name' or generic supermarket brands can be just as nice and sometimes better than the more expensive branded types.

<u>Variety is the spice of life</u>: When shopping in home supermarkets or somewhere with lots of choice, purchase a variety of ingredients - think international: Japanese, Chinese, Thai, Indian, all the different cultural flavours. This is the time to stock up on these items, as fish, meat, rice, pasta etc, are available at most places. It is the flavouring and some specific items (e.g. dried mushrooms) that can make all the difference and compel you to create a themed night with your meals.

Harvested mussels can be transformed into most international dishes.

To Stockpile Or Not To Stockpile?

I often hear from others that stockpiling rice, lentils etc, is unnecessary because you can buy food everywhere. This is correct, of course, although I do not really follow this advice. For me to have a good stock (sometimes two enormous bags of rice and lentils) on board is very satisfying, but that is not the only reason. The main reasons are:

1. Journeys can turn out to be much longer than anticipated.
2. You may arrive in a foreign port and there may have been a political problem or natural disaster and food could be short.

3. Recently in Ecuador we could purchase dried foods, but they were comparatively more expensive, found in much smaller quantities, and appeared to be quite old. Therefore, I tend to stock up in places where high quality dried foods are available in bulk at good prices. I have never had a problem with these foods going off, indeed from Mexico to Ecuador our year old lentils looked far 'fresher' than the locally sold lentils.
4. If I have the luxury of a borrowed or hired car and a bargain, I grab the opportunity to buy in bulk.
5. You may stay much longer at a remote anchorage that has no shops (it happens) and what a sad reason to have to leave a place.

Sundowner Supplies
We stock up on alcohol when it is priced reasonably. Most islands in the Pacific sell alcohol at high prices. For example, before leaving Panama to cross the Pacific Ocean, every nook and cranny on board was filled with beer, wine and spirits. Watch for import/export quantities allowed by Customs though.

Taxis
When hiring a taxi, always negotiate and agree on the fare BEFORE getting in the taxi. There are many places where the taxis do not have meters.

Stowing food
Food shelf life: Check your fresh items daily to find those that are going soft. You can then decide to use or throw (depending on how bad they are), and thereby ensure they do not contaminate the rest of the produce.

The freshness of your purchases will determine how long it takes for them to deteriorate. Some really fresh produce can last for weeks. Avoid bruised fruit and vegetables, as they will rot much quicker.

Stowing fruit and vegetables: Some fruits and vegetables emit a natural gas called ethylene (listed below). This helps them ripen. Generally, fruits emit more ethylene than vegetables. To avoid your fruits and vegetables ripening too quickly, stow them separately where possible.

Ethylene emitting fruits: bananas, tomatoes, avocados, peaches, pears, nectarines, cantaloupes, honeydews, lemons, kiwi fruit, mangoes, apricots, plums and pawpaw.

Ethylene emitting vegetables: carrots, apples, broccoli, potatoes, green beans, salad greens, zucchini, cucumbers, eggplant (aubergine) and asparagus.

Refrigeration: If you purchase fruit or vegetables that have been refrigerated in the shop, then their longevity will rely on continued refrigeration on board. Not all fruit and vegetables need to go in the fridge. Just try to buy fresh stuff (local markets are the best) that has just been picked and remains unrefrigerated prior to purchase.

Stowing location: Secure baskets, bowls and other storage containers to ensure the produce does not move around too much. Good ventilation and dark, cool places are best.

Test various spaces on board to find the best place. One day Noel had put some tomatoes where the onions and potatoes were kept (cupboard under the cooker). I did not know about them and he forgot about them, yet they were quite happy there for a couple of weeks.

Potatoes and onions: The cupboard where we store our potatoes and onions is very dark and cool. Unwashed potatoes and onions with their skin on last longest. Check them daily and remove (or use) any soft produce to avoid tainting the remainder. There is nothing worse than the smell of a rotting potato or onion! We know cruisers who will not store potatoes with onions. We have never had any trouble storing these items together, and indeed, when really fresh we have had both potatoes and onions (together) lasting for months. (Perhaps potatoes don't emit that much ethylene).

Potatoes: If you buy potatoes that have not been washed and keep them in a dark cool place that is well ventilated, they can last for many weeks. The dirt helps them stay fresh. (Caution: when entering a new country; places like Australia will not want to see mud on your boat from another country.)

Apples: Friends wrap their apples in newspaper for longevity.

Lettuce, green beans and carrots: Wrap fairly tightly in a plastic bag and keep in the fridge. Cabbage, we store in a cool, dark spot.

Tomatoes: If we have a good supply of tomatoes at sea, we store them in the boxes they come in (like large egg cartons without a lid), in a cool dark area. This means they are secure, separated and unable to roll. We buy red and green tomatoes, and try to keep them separate. This works well for limes and lemons too.

Carrots: Some cruisers swear by wrapping carrots individually in aluminium foil to preserve them for longer. I have tried this once and I think the carrots had too much moisture in them, or were not completely dry as they all rotted away very quickly. We find carrots last a long time in a cool, dark, well-ventilated area, or in the fridge (unwrapped).

Remember to inspect and turn all produce daily.

Stocking up and preparing for a voyage.

This case of precious beer got wet in the dinghy. Noel lovingly wiped off the saltwater with fresh, before drying and stowing.

Mushrooms: Store them in paper bags. They will last a lot longer, especially in a cool and dark place.

Bananas: Dunk the bunch of bananas in seawater for one minute to ensure all bugs and spiders are dead. Separate the bananas and place in different cool and dark areas around the boat. Keep them away from other fresh foods, as they promote ripeness of other produce. We buy ripe bananas and some very green bananas. We keep the green ones dark and cool, taking out a couple every few days into the sun for ripening. If they ripen too quickly, use them to make muffins.

Eggs: They should last for two to three weeks at sea. We've successfully tried the general advice of turning the eggs every other day to help lengthen their life. I have never refrigerated eggs. Some cruisers paint their eggs in Vaseline to help them last longer (I could not stand them being slippery!).

Fruit and vegetables: Ensure fruit and vegetables are completely dry before stowing.

Stowing dried foods: Sturdy plastic containers with screw lids suit us best. If the container is too small to allow the contents to be scooped out with a cup, or too large to pour directly, I use the scoops that come in laundry powder boxes. They are a very useful size, but remember to clean them thoroughly first!

A good place for bananas if space is short.

Stowing meat: Pork is usually good quality in most places, although there are places I'd never buy meat from again. The best way to stow meat for any length of time is out of the plastic, in a metal or ceramic bowl, covered with aluminium foil and in the fridge or the coolest part of the boat. Marinating in oil, spices and herbs may also improve longevity, not to mention taste.

Stowing canned and tinned food: Do not buy canned products that are dented, leaking or bulging, or those that show any signs of tampering. Check the expiry date on the label to be assured of freshness. Store canned food in a cool, dry place and avoid cabinets over the stove and under the sink. If storing cans low in the boat, label the contents on the lid of the tin to make finding what you want easier. It is also a good idea to clean the top of the container before you open it. If the container spurts liquid or foam when you open it, do not eat it.

Stocking up Pyewacket in Panama for crossing the Pacific Ocean.

This was only one of many shops and we did buy more food than wine at times!

Two years later, we still had four cartons of wine left.

Trim: Once you have stowed all your supplies for the voyage, you should check your boat's waterline to ensure the vessel is trimmed correctly. Just hop in the dinghy and take a look.

OTHER IDEAS & TIPS
Apples
Don't throw them out if they are old, but stew them and have as a dessert, on your cereal, or with pork chops.

Bananas
Fry bananas that no longer look appealing. Add some brown sugar and lime juice. Yum!

Use really black bananas to mash into your muffin mix.

Mix soft bananas with homemade yoghurt, add milk to taste and voila! A banana milkshake.

Banana Sap
If you have bought a stalk of bananas, the stalk can sometimes drip sap. Ensure this cannot reach your gel-coat as it can cause damage and be very hard to clean up.

Barbecues
Ensure they are fitted securely, so they cannot be knocked over. A lid is an excellent idea for further safety and retaining heat. Ensure you always have a fire extinguisher at hand. If there is a 51ft boat downwind of you called Pyewacket, either invite them on board or refrain from letting the yummy smells drift down to them!

Short story While moored in the smart marina called 'Moodys' on the south coast of England, we stood out like a sore thumb. Most of the other boats there were probably used once a month, but polished once a day – whereas we looked like we had sailed halfway around the world (because we had). A neighbour was preparing to sail some ocean miles and one day invited us for sausages on his new BBQ. He came around to Mariah, and I was sitting in the cockpit. He said 'well, you look like you have done a lot of miles', and for a brief second I thought he was being rude to me! We had a lovely evening on board, he owned a restaurant, but certainly was not a cook. The sausages were burnt to a crisp outside and raw in the middle, but it was a wonderful, memorable evening.

Bean Sprouts
Sprout mung beans and lentils for fresh, 'home grown' vegetables. For brown/green lentils, wash in fresh water first and place in warm water for six hours. Keep in a dark, cool place (a good place is the oven when not in use). Twice a day rinse with water and drain. In just a few days they will be sprouting. Leave for four days (repeating the watering), then on the last day leave them in the sun for a few hours to green up.

Bicarbonate Of Soda & Baking Powder
Bicarbonate of soda and baking powder are leavening agents. Bicarbonate of soda needs to be mixed with moisture and an acidic ingredient for the necessary chemical reaction to take place to make food rise, because it needs an acid to create the rising quality. Use in recipes where there is already an acidic ingredient present, such as lemon juice, chocolate, buttermilk or honey. Baking powder contains bicarbonate of soda and comes pre-mixed with the acidic ingredient. Therefore you only need to add the moisture. Use in recipes that have neutral tasting ingredients, e.g. milk.

To make your own self-raising flour, add one teaspoon of baking powder to every cup of plain flour. It saves having to stock different flours.

Bicarbonate of soda is a great cleaning agent and odour absorber. *(See the Cleaning section.)*

Baking powder is almost identical to the powder in dry chemical fire extinguishers. So think of this as an option for putting out small fires if there is not an extinguisher handy. Scatter the powder by hand to 'suffocate' the fire making sure that the fire has gone out entirely before clean up, as a blast of oxygen can cause the fire to reignite. It is a great emergency item in the galley near the stove, but a fire blanket or extinguisher is better. *(See 'Fire' in the Boat Equipment section.)*

Bread Crumbs
Use dry/savoury biscuits, the type you would ordinarily put a slice of cheese on. Put them in a plastic bag and crush them with a rolling pin. (Our rolling pin is a wine bottle.)

Budgeting - a taste of money saving ideas
Good meat is expensive in most places. Save your cash by reducing how much meat you eat and enjoy the added benefit of a healthier diet.

Short story We lived on board Mariah for almost nine years without a fridge and we ate far less meat. Nowadays, meat is so much easier to keep as it is so well preserved (vacuum packed items and salami as examples). With a fridge on Pyewacket we carried more, however we carried more weight too – both on the boat and on our bellies!

Short story In New Caledonia we found that vacuum packed sliced ham was very expensive. But digging around in the shelves nearby, there were 'end cuts' of the same meat, vacuum packed and priced at a third less than the sliced items. The only difference was the way it was cut.

Buy meat that delivers a lot of flavour for not much cash. A couple of slices of salami or bacon will add a lot of flavour to salads, pasta, egg dishes and potato meals.

Bulk up meat dishes by adding a cup of lentils or a tin of beans (kidney or butter beans).

Short story In French Polynesia, frozen chickens are subsidised and therefore cheap. In Europe, pork was the cheapest meat (in most places). We are happy to change our diet to suit our wallet and destination. That's the purpose of travelling, experiencing the entire culture as a whole, including food.

Cabbage
Never cut cabbage, it lasts so much longer if you remove only the number of leaves you need for the meal.

If your cabbage is becoming less crunchy, when you have broken off the leaves you want to use, give them a fresh water bath for a few moments. It will help restore some crunchiness.

Cheese
For extra thin (small) slices use the potato peeler.

Chocolate Fix
If you have run out of chocolate and need a fix: mix powdered milk and drinking chocolate powder together and a little water to make a paste. Spread on bread. (You need a good quality, sweetened cocoa powder.)

Chopping & Dicing
Chopping herbs: At sea, put fresh herbs (if you are lucky enough to have some still) into the bottom of a straight-sided cup. Use a pair of scissors in the cup to chop up the herbs.

Chopping almonds: Buying whole almonds is cheaper than buying them sliced or slivered. To chop (for salads or granola) simply squash each almond with the flat part of the knife, as you do garlic. The almond starts to crumble, then just chop the rest to the size required.

Chopping olives: If you have olives that are not pitted, simply flatten them with the flat side of a knife. The seed pops out easily and you can continue to chop.

Vegetables: If you are dicing a large batch of vegetables, keep those you've already diced in a plastic container with a lid and put aside while you do the next batch, especially on a rolling sea.

Cleaning & Preserving
The acid in lemons is strong enough to kill most bacteria. *(See the Cleaning section.)*
Every so often we clean our wooden chopping board with a lemon and let it sit in the sun.

Stains: As well as sanitising your chopping block, you can remove food stains from light coloured timber and plastic chopping boards by simply squeezing lemon over the stain and letting it sit for fifteen to thirty minutes. Then just wipe it off. *(See the Cleaning section for more ideas.)*

Vinegar preserves food because the acid kills bacteria that could spoil it. *(See the Preserving section.)* Lemon juice prevents sliced fruit browning.

Coffee
Percolated coffee: Percolators take a lot of power, so it's not always possible to use one unless you are using shore power. However, we still use our percolator at sea. Simply load the filter and coffee as normal then boil the kettle and slowly pour the water into the filter.

Coffee filters: Use the filters to strain wine from a bottle with a broken cork. Serve snacks, like popcorn, the filters act as disposable bowls.

Coffee grinder
A coffee grinder is not just for coffee. After a good clean (remove strong coffee smells with drops of vanilla essence, *(see the Cleaning section)*:

- Make bread crumbs from toast or stale bread
- Grind up fresh spices
- Create chilli pepper flakes for your pizza
- Make your own flour from grain
- Make very fine sugar for baking

Cress
Friends grow cress on damp toilet paper. You just need to keep the paper damp at all times.

Crumbs
To break up biscuits for cake or pie crust, fill a Ziploc bag with the biscuits and roll over them with a rolling pin.

Cucumber
After peeling a cucumber, we use the inside of the peelings to wipe on our faces. It is very cooling on a hot day and good for the skin. *(See 'Beauty on a Budget' in the Health & Well-being section.)*

Cups
Each person on board should have his or her own cup and/or glass. It is then their responsibility to wash, wipe and put away their cup. This saves an enormous amount of washing up!

Dinner Party
Sharing the load: Whenever we are invited to a boat that is hosting many cruisers and feeding us all, we take plates, knives, forks and glasses. It makes the host's life so much easier. We simply put all the gear in a carrier bag and take it home at the end of the night, so our host has not been left with piles of washing up.

Whatever the size of the group, we always take our preferred drinks. Most people are on a budget while cruising so we like to contribute to the evening. We always contribute something towards the meal as well, whether it is cheese and biscuits with drinks, or a dessert. Separately and together, Noel and I have done this all our lives, whether on boats or land. I couldn't imagine turning up to someone's house or boat and not bringing a thing! If someone has the grace to play host and prepare and clear up after us, the very least we can do is contribute.

<u>Creativity</u>: Dinner parties, lunches, or inviting friends round for coffee can be made to feel extra special if you take care over the presentation. You don't need to be elaborate: cruising on a budget may not mean the finest fare, but use what you have already - creativity. Sandwiches cut with petite cookie cutters into various shapes can make something spectacular. If you do not have cookie cutters, use a cup or a hole-saw part from the workshop (clean it thoroughly first!). This is something we might do for a special occasion.

<u>Colour</u>: On a nice plate, make a display with red grapes and freshly picked flowers. A sprinkle of herbs, a garnish of petals, any flash of colour - makes for a gourmet appearance.

<u>Garnish</u>: Raw onions that have been sliced and soaked in vinegar for ten minutes make a great accompaniment for cheese. If you soak red onions (Spanish onions) for a while longer, the vinegar turns pink and the white of the onion turns pink. These make a great garnish on any plate.

Drinks
If you find a supply of your favourite tipple that is reasonably priced, stock up. If you are low on mixers, create your own. Our favourite is used with gin or vodka:

- Juice from four limes.
- 1 very heaped teaspoon of brown sugar, stir well.
- Now add equal (at minimum) quantity of water.
- Add required alcohol to taste.
- We keep a supply of fresh water in the fridge to use in the drinks.

We never drink alcohol when underway. We do not have the desire and it makes us sleepy, which is not good when you are supposed to be on watch. Also I am also constantly thirsty at sea and do not need to heighten my dehydration further.

Egg Cartons
Keep some empties. Some countries do not sell eggs in cartons, but in plastic bags - it is quite a challenge to get these home in one piece.

Spray the bottom of empty cartons with cockroach spray and leave them for as long as possible before putting your eggs in them. Eggs are porous and could absorb the chemicals.
(See 'Personal Equipment' on how to rescue broken eggs using a stocking!)

Finding Food
Every few weeks, rummage at the back of your food stores. Find those items that have wheedled their way into hiding, dig them out and use them to inspire you to create a new/different meal.

Food Poisoning
If food smells funny or is discoloured, do not eat it. It sounds obvious, but think about how many times you have thought 'that tastes a bit funny, but not too bad' and have continued eating! Food that is incorrectly packaged and stored can be a source of botulism. Ensure that foods you purchase are packaged correctly and that the packing is intact.

Eggs are bad if they can float. To ensure that your cooking is not spoiled, break each egg, one at a time into a cup, prior to adding it to the rest of the ingredients. If I have a couple of eggs left and add new ones to the carton, I write on them with a felt tip pen - 'use 1st'.

Finding food can be easy, hard or plain funny. Noel is the intrepid hunter on Palmerston Island!

Freezer

We like the idea of having a freezer, but they are hungry for power. Also, if you have stocked up and then have a power problem you could lose a lot of your food, especially at sea. However, we have met some cruisers who would not go cruising without a freezer.

If you have a freezer, fill up Ziploc bags with homemade soup, then lay them flat in the freezer. When the bags of soup freeze flat, you will be able to pile them up like stacked books for easy, space-saving storage.

Cleaning the freezer: Spray cooking oil onto the cooling unit when cool (not frozen). When it freezes it will protect the surface of the unit. When you defrost the unit simply wipe off and it will be nice and clean. This also helps prevent corrosion.

Galley Organisation

An organised and functional galley is very important. Before leaving port, ensure everything you need is at hand. For example, decant bulk rice into smaller, manageable containers.

Stow properly so when you open the cupboard everything does not topple out. We use non-slip rubber mats over all surfaces in the galley that, together with the fiddles, work well. Pockets that attach to the walls are handy, as are hanging nets.

Keep your galley clean and clear. If you start feeling queasy, step outside for five minutes before continuing (or better still, swap roles). For bad weather you should have meals pre-prepared and if they run out, have snacks to grab. Granola bars, dry biscuits, chocolate, sweet biscuits, dried fruit - anything will do if you can just grab it, unwrap it and eat it.

Galley Equipment

Cookware should be multi-use. We have two different sized oven tins, both can fit on one shelf in the oven. We have five different sizes of saucepans, tiny up to large (which double as a large mixing bowl). They are all utilised.

I use a large plastic (square) container for mixing large quantities of bread dough. It has a lid so I can let it rise in the container. It helps keep the flour in the bowl and not on the counter top (I am a messy cook).

Insect Control In Food

I use the old favourite: bay leaves in the flour. Other people zap foods in the microwave for a few seconds. Using cloves instead of bay leaves is another option. Otherwise allow the item to sit in the sun for an afternoon and let the critters cook in their own juices!

Kitchen Roll & Paper Towels

Tear off only half a square; nine out of ten times this is all you will need.

Lentils

Lentils provide fibre and iron, but they can take a long time to cook. A pressure cooker is a big help, but if you do not have one, another way to shorten cooking time is to bring raw lentils to the boil and cook for ten minutes, then leave them in the saucepan with the lid on (wrapping the saucepan in a towel for an hour or two helps). By dinner time they only need a few more minutes on the boil and they are ready.

As an alternative to potatoes, we sometimes have a portion of lentils with a touch of chilli sauce on top. (They are cheap, healthy and filling.) We add lentils to spaghetti bolognaise, as they seem to 'disappear' in the mixture and bulk it out a great deal. They can be added to homemade burgers too.

Limes

Limes are not just for eating. Use limes for heat rash, mosquito bites and as a disinfectant - just rub it on. *(See the Health & Well-being section.)*

Milk

On Mariah we used powdered milk at sea. On Pyewacket we used long-life cartons. The cartons last for a long time and we refrigerated them once opened. Buy smaller cartons (we use one litre) if you do not have a fridge. We still keep a supply of powdered milk as it is useful in an emergency and for making sauces or cooking.

Non-Perishable Foods

If you spot a bargain, and/or have additional space, buy extra non-perishable foods. It is never a waste.

Olive Oil

Use a small spray bottle filled with olive oil and spray on bread/toast as an alternative to butter. We use just a little and have never had to worry about refrigerating butter (olive oil should not be refrigerated). Extra virgin olive oil is considered to be far healthier than most processed butter, as it contains only 33% saturated fat while butter is composed of 66% saturated fat. Olive oil has no cholesterol.

Pipe Frosting

A Ziploc bag can be used as a piping bag. Just snip off a tiny corner opposite the zip edge.

Plenty Of Potatoes

Cook extra potatoes and vegetables. The next breakfast (or lunch or dinner) we mash the leftovers together, stir in an egg and fry up burger-sized potato cakes. This is a great 'hasty tasty'.

Don't peel potatoes; wash them well in saltwater and cook with the skins on. Not only is it a new flavour, but the skins and what lies just beneath them is good for you.

Parry Potatoes - one of our favourite ways to eat potato is to boil carrot, parsnip and potato together in one pot and mash. This is a meal in itself in rough weather and is delicious.

Porridge

Do not discount the simple stuff. We often have porridge when we want something warm and plain, with just a little brown sugar or honey. It is perfect to warm you up, without upsetting your stomach. If you make too much, use it the following day. Simply add water or milk, mash it together gently and reheat.

Preparation

We generally prepare a meal before we leave port. Our first twenty-four hours at sea are always tinged with some anxiety and therefore a little queasiness. You can warm up a prepared meal quickly and keep something in your tummy, which is also good for combating seasickness.

Remember when preparing a meal to always make up more than necessary and have the leftovers the following day. Creating three meals a day on your boat for weeks on end can become a chore, so shortening the time in the galley is a bonus.

Refrigeration

If you are installing/buying a fridge, ensure it is top loading so the cold does not 'fall out' as you open the door. It is also easier to use when heeling over and allows better use of space. Try to only refrigerate items you buy from the refrigeration section in the supermarket, otherwise you will use more power to maintain the fridge's optimum temperature as it refrigerates warmer items (that were not already cooled). You will also unnecessarily fill up your fridge. We follow the rule that if it is not refrigerated in the supermarket, we don't refrigerate it on board.

If you do not have a fridge, store items that need to be kept cool below the waterline on board. This should keep them close to sea temperature, which is usually cooler than the air temperature.

Fridge organisation: Most fridges on board are deep and open from the top. Storing food can be tricky if there are no built-in trays and with just a gaping hole to lose food in. We purchased small plastic box containers (depending on size of fridge) and strategically placed them in the fridge. Stuff stored at the bottom is easily accessible by simply lifting out the plastic boxes. Also, if there is a leak it is contained within one spot.

Rolling Pin

Use a wine bottle. When not in use for baking, clean the bottle and pour your cask wine into it to take along when visiting friends.

Rubber/Elastic Bands
Keep in a Ziploc bag with a little corn starch or flour. The powder will soak up the moisture and help prevent your bands perishing in the harsh elements.

Salt
A good quality salt grinder with good seals helps prevent the salt soaking up moisture for longer.

Cooking salt should be kept in an airtight container. It is very irritating when you want to use it and it has become rock hard!

Add a pinch of salt before beating eggs or whipped cream to make them whip up faster. Rub salt into the cavity of a chicken or turkey before cooking to keep it moist. Sprinkle salt on zucchini or eggplant before cooking. It prevents the meal becoming too watery.

Ship's Cook
Someone has to do it! You will not have everything you desire to cook with when underway and cannot nip out and buy it, so make do. You will be amazed with what you come up with.

Short story I met a sailor one day (at a Marine Swap Meet) who put it perfectly, saying, 'I am not a cook, but in the galley I am serviceable. I came up with some marvellous concoctions on board. We loved them, not sure what other people thought, but I don't care!' If you're hungry enough, you'll eat it!

Sink
The galley sink becomes your friend. When mixing batter or anything sloppy, keep the bowl in the sink in case of sudden heeling!

Place the juice jug in the sink while searching for glasses/cups.

Measuring jugs organisation: With twin sinks, measuring jugs can be hooked over the edge of one sink to create a good holding place for cutlery, cups and other small items, preventing them sliding around your sink when at sea.

Spices
We love trying new spices in foreign ports. When using local spices to make lentil burgers, we name them according to where we are, such as 'Ecuadorian Burgers'.

Substitutes
If you do not have the exact ingredient for a recipe, substitute.
- If you have run out of lemons, use vinegar in its place. Use half the quantity e.g. for one tablespoon of lemon juice, use half a tablespoon of vinegar.
- When making sweet chilli sauce for the first time, I didn't have any sweet paprika so I used a spice that looked the same and had a similar taste (no idea what is was as I had purchased it in Ecuador) and in another recipe, instead of fish sauce I used soy. Both substitutes worked a treat.

Tableware
Horses for courses, some people like pewter, ceramic, even plastic. Friends have a 'dog bowl' for eating while at sea, as the bowl has a large rim and you can hold them with one hand. We prefer

ceramic plates. We have lost one or two over the years, but we still choose to eat off ceramic. A deep bowl or dish is easier to eat from when underway.

Tin Opener
A good quality tin opener is very important. In some destinations, a well-made tin opener can be very hard to find. Have at least two on board.

Toaster
Electric toasters use a lot of power and not all stoves have a grill. Buy a camping toaster, or you can easily make your own toaster with metal gauze and wire. Affix stainless steel metal gauze on to a wire frame (to fit comfortably on your burner). The next 'level' of the frame should be about 32 mm from the flame for even 'grilling'. Place the gauze on to the flame and sit the bread on top of the frame.

Tinned Food
When you are low on fresh food and have mostly tinned food left, add some ginger and/or garlic to help eliminate that 'canned' taste.

Tinned food is not just for passages. When you feel uninspired, open a can of soup or baked beans and have some toast. If you have some fresh herbs, whack a few in to freshen the brew up and hey presto!, an easy meal.

Adding a tin of tomatoes and a diced onion transforms this type of tinned food. Adding some lemon or lime also helps. A teaspoon of brown sugar in tinned tomatoes boosts their texture and taste.

Buy a treat in a tin, like hot chocolate sponge or cream for those times when goodies are low.

Our tinned food is stowed low in the boat and securely. Prior to a trip we move a good selection of tins into a more accessible place.

Washing Up
Wash up in seawater to save your fresh water. We found it does not leave a layer of salt crystals on the kitchenware. We do not rinse most items, only cups usually, but if you want to, just use a fresh damp cloth to keep use of fresh water to a minimum.

Ziploc Bag
Store prepared bread dough in loaf size portions in the fridge, ready to use. Keep yeast that is not sold in jars in a Ziploc bag to maintain freshness. (*See 'Personal Equipment' for more uses.*)

Store leftovers in Ziploc bags to avoid spills.

HEALTH & WELL-BEING

ARTICLE: I thought I'd start this section with an article I wrote for Cruising Helmsman magazine.

The Beginning of the End Reality Reflections
by Jackie Parry

I didn't talk to my husband for two days. His peculiar answers to my naïve nautical questions stung my bewildered ears. Back then, as a mere fledgling to sailing, my raw researching met brutal honesty. With travel and freedom gnawing at our vitals we sought a sailboat and home. I tried to intuit the invisible, like financials and what, exactly, was I letting myself in for.

'How much does it cost to buy and then maintain a boat?' Coming from the corporate world I was gearing up to write in-depth budget plans. I was scuppered when Noel gave me a look that would stale a baguette and replied, 'It'll take every penny we have.'

'Oh right, well, what's so great about sailing?', I asked, expecting to be assailed with vivid pictures of slicing splendidly through clear, flat water, palm trees etched on the sky line and white sandy beaches supplying a dreamlike backdrop. This image shattered as Noel's ruthless reply tore through my reverie: 'Getting to port and the local bar.' Eight years and over 40,000 miles later, I can see the wisdom in his answers.

Jackie 'chillin' in the dinghy, anchored within the atoll of Tahanea (Tuamotus in French Polynesia).

Enduring the Escapade
Long-term cruising is an incredible adventure. It's also hard work. Arriving in a new country or town, our thoughts steer to: How do we check in? Where do we get fuel and potable water? How much is it? The men talk amps and engines; the girls talk laundry and supermarkets. So aside from reflecting on our magnificent voyage, I thought a few ludicrous 'learnings' deserve a mention.

First, let's be positive. Our escapade divorces and insulates us from the world's day-to-day problems. We are not ashamed to bury our heads in the sand and enjoy, while we can, the 'ignorance is bliss' scenario. While landlubbers, we found that the TV news never changed; it was sad and depressing today and tomorrow. While cruising we frequently meet like-minded people, of all nationalities, where age is no friendship barrier. Hooking up with similar sized boats and sharing the ocean brings the comfort of companionship and the joy in sharing the dolphins that play on our bow during those perfect sailing days.

Mostly, cruising provides the freedom to live simply. We have no letterbox where small bits of paper with large numbers intrude into our sanctuary, sucking dry the bank account to allow landlubber luxuries. And yes, there is the odd G & T (Vodka for me please) while watching spectacular sunsets, performing an anchor pirouette, savouring the sedate, shifting views as we would fine wine.

Secrets of the initiated

Over the years, advice, hints and tips have deluged our salt saturated minds, but there is always more to learn. Here are some little gems that we learned along the way:

*(1) **Constipation** - the most fluid of us struggle on long trips. That comfy cockpit seat will become well acquainted with your behind when you're on watch, causing, what we refer to as, 'the cork affect'.*

*(2) **Seasickness** - the toughest of us will become seasick. After corkscrewing down unrelenting waves for forty-eight hours, your tummy will give up all hope of hanging onto anything. Most of us unwillingly feed the fish at some point. It is like puberty, you just have to get through it. Despite suicidal thoughts during the worst bouts of seasickness, once you have reached the sanctuary of a good anchorage and spent a few days in flat water, going back out into lumpy seas suddenly becomes a good idea again. On the plus side it is a great diet!*

*(3) **Toilet tantrums** - at some point most marine toilets will block. If you have not been allocated the repair task, leave the boat while it is being fixed. Build up of pressure while trying to pump it clear will create the most spectacular explosion. Becoming AWOL at this time will help avoid a good dose of (5).*

*(4) **Landlubbers** - your farewell from home will be tearful, exciting and filled with unfulfilled promises from friends and family, who assure you they will keep you up to date on home happenings. After two years you will be grateful for an email once every six months from your bestest buddies, all of which think you spend your entire life sitting on the aft deck sipping G & T.*

*(5) **Arguments** - the closest relationship will suffer at times. Falling out with your spouse is inevitable especially when you are woken three and a half minutes before you are due on watch at 3 a.m. Learn to talk about it and laugh, it can get damn lonely otherwise and create a yearning for (4).*

*(6) **Moon-fright** - the moon is a crafty bugger. You know it is due up but as you next scan the horizon for boats there is a luminous light that assumes the shape of an approaching aircraft carrier. This will be the moon, strategically cloaked with black cloud to form heart-stopping shapes. However, the moon will become your buddy, especially if dealing with number (5).*

*(7) **Cravings** - two days into a long haul sail you will desperately desire all those things you haven't got: roast chicken, ice cream, ...*

*(8) **Spiders** - having an abhorrence to the skittering critters my husband assured me that life on board meant no spiders. This seemed reasonable, after all we are away from land a lot of the time. The reality of the situation is that our skin-crawling friends love dark hidey holes in the boat. I am sure we have been responsible for inter-breeding crawly critters from different countries, probably creating a whole new weird and wonderful breed.*

*(9) **Time** - boat maintenance is a full time job in addition to washing, cleaning and sourcing supplies. If you are fortunate to momentarily catch up, item (3) will fill the gaps. At the end of each day you'll just have time to read a page or two of that book you've always wanted to read, before you're fast asleep.*

*(10) **Fishing** - you will fish once per trip. After you have battled and heaved the huge Dolphin fish on board and it has thrashed itself to death, splattering blood over the clean, white cockpit and your battle weary body, the fishing gear will gather salt in the Lazarette (or any small compartment) for the rest of the journey. By the next trip, you will have forgotten all about this sticky mess and you will merrily break out the fishing lines once again.*

(11) **Sinking** - *on your watch, typically in the graveyard hours, you'll do a routine check of the bilge for the last time before the welcome warmth of bed and the bilge will be full of water. Instantaneously you are wide-awake and have no problem in screeching at your partner who is obviously having their best ever sleep. Turning the mains off is not an option and two hours later you will find the problem is something as simple as lack of grease in the stern gland. Finally, you'll crawl into bed and the stampeding adrenaline will keep you awake until twenty minutes before you are due back on watch.*

(12) **Plip-plop** - *you will lose something overboard. Deal with it, it is gone.*

(13) **Fitness**-*sailing will not make you super fit. Although you do become trim, see (2).*

(14) **Turning back** - *face facts that the storm you can no longer punch into has beaten you. It is not a failure to turn back, it is common sense and above all the boat's and your safety - also helps relieve item (2).*

(15) **On a long passage** - *if you are like us (without a fridge), then once the fresh food has all gone you will need to resort to tinned food. After a week all tinned food will taste the same. It will have an unmistakable metallic flavour (tinny flavouring assists number (2)).*

(16) **Dust** *will collect with intensity, especially in those tiny, 'boat shape', awkward places. Adds to (9).*

(17) **Company** - *your partner is only ten feet away sleeping below, at that time when you are on watch, it is the same as single-handing. It can be lonely - maybe a good thing if dealing with (1), (2) or (5)!*

(18) **Plunging** - *on moonless nights you plunge into thick darkness, with any vision coming to a shocking end at the bow of your boat. It's best not to dwell on this too much.*

(19) **Meteorites** - *the dark nights are abundant with shooting stars, but watch for the big ones. Without notice a spot light will beam down on you while you sit quietly in the cockpit minding your own business. You'll imagine a huge ship bearing down on you before you realise it's just an enormous, bright meteorite. This will cause you to lose another few million heartbeats.*

(20) **Advice** - *some will be good and some, well, let's just say, will be totally fictitious. You will meet some gold medal winning know-it-alls. For example this article: is it fact or fiction? The best way is to get out there and find out for yourself!*

I hope you enjoyed this article, I wrote this after finding a particularly large spider on board Mariah in Canada. This made me reflect on all the things I didn't expect to find when cruising.

Advice

It comes thick and fast. Bear in mind, while most of it is very useful, there will be some that you can disregard. Don't forget that views come through various shades of lenses.

Have confidence in your own decisions; you've done your research after all. What works for others may not work for you and vice versa.

Puttering through Chicago, on board Mariah II, during our Great Loop adventure in 2004.

We met a cruiser prior to this trip who said we'd never be able to do it!

You do not have time to act on everyone else's opinions. It's <u>your</u> cruise.

Baby Wipes/Wet Wipes

Keep a few baby wipes in a Ziploc bag when venturing ashore. They are good for wiping hands before and after a meal.

They are also great for a quick wash at sea. Put them in a Ziploc bag in the fridge for a cool wash.

They can be used to remove small stains on clothes (test garment first).

Beauty On A Budget

While cruising, 'fashion' is not really a factor. Your clothes, your hair, your style is your own. But I also like to take care and treat myself to a few essential beauty ingredients.

<u>Protection</u>: Sunscreen is imperative on a boat, even on cloudy days. We purchase more expensive brands for our face, brands that do not sting your eyes and are easy to apply. For our bodies we buy cheaper brands, they all work. (Don't forget hats and cool loose cotton clothes to keep the sun off your skin. You only have to look at what the sun does to plastic, material and your sails to understand how damaging it is.) *(See Sunscreen & Protection later in this section.)*

In George Town, USA, 'Tash (SV Frodo) and I were invited on board a charter boat. We enjoyed the ride without the responsibility.

Health and well-being is not just about products, it's about enjoying life and seizing every opportunity.

Short story Sunscreen can be expensive. However, it pays to search around. In Panama City we found a 'cheapie' shop where you could buy almost anything. We purchased some face flannels (for extra rags around the boat) and also found sunscreen that was at least one quarter the normal price. It came in a slightly larger than average bottle too. It worked fantastically, didn't sting our eyes and was easy to apply (i.e. not thick and gloopy).

Skin conditioning: Gently rub Vaseline on your eyelashes at night; it is a great conditioner. During the evening, I use Vaseline on my lips to make them look healthy and shiny. Warning: do not put Vaseline on your skin (including lips) if you are going out in the sun - it will intensify the sun on your skin and you will burn very quickly!

Skin repair: For sunburn use cold tea to help reduce the redness and pain, it will help repair and cool your skin. It also reduces puffy eyes. The inside of cucumber skin (or slices) is also great for cooling hot skin and reducing puffy eyes. Yoghurt, too, can help. (See the section on yoghurt further on.)

If you are doing a job that requires you to wear gloves (painting etc), rub some Vaseline into your hands and around your fingernails first, put on a pair of rubber or plastic gloves under the main protective gloves you are wearing and set to work. The heat generated while working will allow the Vaseline to dissolve into your skin, making your hands smooth.

Olive oil is a good skin conditioner (do not use in the sun - you will burn very quickly!). At night after a warm face wash, while your skin is still warm, rub in a little oil and allow it to penetrate.

Wind burns as much as sun. Give your skin a break and seek some shelter. If we have been in the wind during our watch, we apply Vaseline to our skin off watch. (A reminder: do not have Vaseline on your skin when in the sun, it will burn). The Vaseline helps replenish the skin while we are sleeping.

It sounds obvious, but if you drink plenty of water, it helps your body naturally moisturise your skin. I do not need to use moisturising lotion if my body is hydrated properly (it's very hard to maintain proper hydration at sea). A squeeze of lemon or lime in drinking water is refreshing and entices you to drink more and remain hydrated. I use sunscreen as a moisturiser during the day. *(See 'Dehydration' further on in this section.)*

If you use eggs when cooking, once you have cracked open the eggs, keep the shells. When you have a few spare minutes (and before the liquid in the shell dries), apply the leftover white that is in the shell to your face. Let it dry for a few minutes, it will feel a little tight. Lie back and take ten minutes just to sit and let the natural ingredients do their job. Gently wash off the egg and your face will feel fresh and soft.

Health and well-being fun: When in port, arrange a 'health' afternoon get-together with other cruisers. Everyone brings an idea: massage, moisturiser, etc. I am not a trained hairdresser, but have cut many heads of hair as a favour - all have been miraculously happy with the results! I also cut my own hair and Noel's. *(See 'hair' in this section.)*

Health and wellness: Yoghurt has a whole host of uses: it's more than just a yummy breakfast. It is very easy to make your own, then to use part of the homemade yoghurt to make more yoghurt.

>   To make:
>   - Slowly heat a litre of milk.
>   - When milk feels like a 'hot day' temperature, take off the heat and gently stir in three tablespoons of yoghurt.
>   - Wrap well (keep warm) for eight to twelve hours (or pour into a flask).
>   - Sometimes the yoghurt separates, I pour off the thin liquid if I want firmer yoghurt, or mix it all together and I don't worry about it being a bit runny. It still tastes good.

- Yoghurt can enhance your immune system and help prevent gastrointestinal infections. The 'good bacteria' helps restore natural intestinal cultures.

- Yoghurt is a good treatment for yeast infections: it can help to restore the normal bacteria in the digestive tract and in vaginal yeast infections. It can also help prevent urinary tract infections. Eating yoghurt is the obvious method, but I have heard of women putting yoghurt on a tampon (sanitary product) and inserting it into their vagina, for one hour only, to treat yeast infections. (I personally have not tried this and would recommend you seek advice before trying this out.)

- Use yoghurt on your face and neck to help cleanse your skin and even out skin tone. Clean your face first, apply yoghurt and sit back for twenty minutes. It is good for highly sensitive skin.

- Eating yoghurt twice a day can relieve canker sores (mouth sores). Yoghurt can also sooth sunburn: leave on your skin for twenty minutes and rinse.

- Eat unsweetened yoghurt and do not add sugar, it will cancel out the good stuff. If you need something to make it sweeter, add honey.

Deodorant: Dusting baking soda under your arms will help to absorb body sweat.

Salty skin: When at sea, clean saltwater off your face - and other parts where it may gather - daily. Just a soft cloth dampened with fresh water will suffice, and then apply moisturiser.

<u>Mini makeover</u>: Take time to moisturise your body, as the elements are very harsh on our skin. During calm days at sea I enjoy spending some time (when I am on watch in the cockpit) having a DIY pedicure and manicure.

Moisturise your cuticles with olive oil.

<u>One for the ladies</u>: When buying lip balm with SPF factor, choose one with some added colour or gloss, it looks good and it will be protecting you all at once.

<u>One for the tea drinkers</u>: Save your used teabags. When the used bags have cooled, rub them gently on your face for a highly refreshing wash. Tea leaves contain a healing quality for your skin.

<u>Make-up</u>: If you use make-up, store it in the fridge or in a cool part of the boat (cupboard located below the water line) as it can melt.

Remove eye makeup with a small amount of olive oil.

<u>Exfoliate</u>: Regularly exfoliate your skin. Wash your face, then apply a soft paste made of three parts baking soda and one part water. Massage gently with a circular motion, avoiding the eye area. Rinse and clean. Or you can exfoliate with sugar or salt. Mix with oil or honey, or press some salt or sugar into your soap. Don't forget to thoroughly wash all the oil off before going in the sun. Walking barefoot on the beach is a great way to exfoliate your feet.

<u>Teeth</u>: For extra white teeth, brush using a paste of baking soda and water. Mixing a little toothpaste in as well makes it a bit easier on the palate.

<u>Shaving</u>: Use olive oil when you run out of shaving cream.

Looking after yourself is not all about what to 'apply' to your skin, but protecting it too. I am wearing overalls and a facemask as I'm sanding; goggles and gloves too at times. Antifouling paint is highly toxic (Alabama, USA).

Bruises
Expect many bruises when first on board. In time your body will become accustomed to the shape of the boat and movement, and bruises become fewer. Relieve your bruises by first cooling the skin, and then applying Comfrey ointment. (Comfrey is a herb and Comfrey ointment is available at most

pharmacies or health shops. As with all medications and treatments, follow the application instructions carefully.)

Chinese Whispers - Relax & Take Rumours With a Pinch of Salt
People love to tell horror stories. We try not to get caught up in rumours until we have done our research. If there is a serious issue, we do our research (for example political unrest or sailboats unwelcome). Otherwise we take things as they come, nearly every time the rumour is untrue or hyped. Everything always turns out a lot easier than envisaged.

Short story Prior to traversing a narrow waterway in The Great Loop (USA/Canada inland waterways), we heard someone say that the narrowest part was only three feet deep. This caused us some concern as we had a draught of five feet! Double checking the chart, it confirmed that there was about six feet of water, which was correct.

Climbing On Board
When on anchor or a mooring buoy, we prefer not to have a permanent boarding ladder mounted on the boat to allow us to climb on board from swimming or the dinghy. In foreign ports, we have experienced unsavoury characters attempting to board us during the night. Without easy access to get on board, anyone trying to do so will make noise, which you are likely to hear. This may give you a chance at fending them off.

That said, ensuring you can climb back on board should you fall in when at anchor is important. *(See 'Safety' further on for more ideas on how to climb back on board.)*

Cushions
Cockpit cushions: Many cruisers recommend closed cell foam, as they are okay to sit on in hot weather because they do not cause you to sweat/stick to them. Also, they do not absorb liquid.

We have vinyl-covered cushions and are lucky enough to have an enclosed cockpit, so we just put a towel or colourful sarong over the cushion, to sit on, if it is a hot day.

Cushion care: Check underneath your cushions regularly, moisture can gather here. Turn cushions over or stand them up to air out.

Saloon cushions: These have a propensity to fall over when your boat is heeling. To keep them in their place, using complementary colours, sew two vertical straps along the front of your cushion. At the top of the strap sew on a piece of elastic. Near the top of the cushion, on a solid part of the boat, fit cup hooks, so you can loop the elastic over the hooks. This will look neat and is far easier than trying to line up Velcro.

Compromise
Compromise is a good word when buying a boat and with living on board too.

While cruising is fantastic fun and a marvellous freedom, don't forget you will be leaving your regular friends and family behind. You will have fewer luxuries, private time can be harder to come by and there is always less space than your land home.

However, the rewards will be amazing...

Noel at Suwarrow Atoll, Pacific Ocean.

Constipation
On watches you may find yourself sitting for a long time. This happens to me if I am feeling lazy and tired, especially during the first few days of a voyage, or if I'm deeply involved in a great book! This can lead to constipation. Lentils are great roughage to help combat constipation. They also spread meals further, like spaghetti bolognaise and homemade burgers. *(See the Galley section for more ideas.)*

Don't forget to keep hydrated too *(see article, The Beginning Of The End Reality Reflections at the start of this section).* I also do some simple exercises - which can help - if the passage is calm enough *(see 'Exercise' later in this section).*

Cool Engine Room, Warm Feet
An engine room extractor fan is a good idea to help keep the engine room from becoming too hot.

Run ducting from the extractor fan to carry the warm air out of the engine room. You can position the flow of warm air either outside via a porthole (in good weather), or into your cockpit to warm your feet (in cool weather).

Coping In The Tropics
Hatches and canvas: If you are planning on an extended cruise, most trade routes will mean following the dry season in the tropics and summers in the higher latitudes. Hatches are important for airflow and canvas to shade your decks is imperative to help keep your decks and therefore your boat cooler.

Keep cool: A small spray bottle of water can help when it becomes unbearably hot. Fill it with water and keep it in the shade to spray on your face and neck every so often.

Reflect the heat out: A car windscreen sun reflector can be purchased with little expense. Cut this into the shape of your portholes for when the sun is beating in. It will reflect the heat away.

Let the breeze in: If you are away from an area that has bugs, take down your mosquito nets to allow more breeze in.

Thousands of tiny black bugs cover Mariah's bowsprit and anchor: they may not be mosquitoes, but bugs in America bite too.

Scoop in extra air: A wind scoop aids airflow. The material and frame from an umbrella can be fashioned into a makeshift scoop. Adjust the frame to fit your hatch, (a halyard on the top may help to hold it up) or just lash-on a sturdy golfing umbrella. *(See 'Umbrellas' further on in this section.)*

Decisions
Whilst the cruising life is filled with kindred spirits, you will always receive conflicting opinions on where you should go and how to do it. Some people like to sail around the world slowly; some like to keep moving; some have no desire to circumnavigate. It just doesn't matter. Do what suits your time, budget and most importantly - desires. It is impossible to go everywhere and see everything.

Dehydration
This can become serious very quickly, especially if you are suffering with seasickness. Being at sea causes me to dehydrate much quicker than I would when on land or in port.

To stay on top of my fluid levels, every time I go for a pee, I drink a cup of water straight away. I find this routine really helps. I also keep a bottle of water in the cockpit at all times, so I can take regular sips.

When in port we keep a jug of water (with juice of two limes) and two cups on the saloon table. This seems to motivate us to drink more than going to the tap!

Dieting
Living on board is the best diet and health regime I can think of. While sailing won't give you a perfect physique, you will benefit from the fact that you are always moving.

In port, carrying water, gas bottles and shopping keeps you fit. Rowing is great exercise and when at sea, for us, food becomes a fuel not an event. (Although interesting and yummy meals are an important motivation for some; at times, when it is calm, we take the time to prepare something more exotic.) We tend to eat four or five small meals a day at sea, which is much kinder to our digestive system.

At each port we swim as much as possible, but only where there are no crocodiles, no strong currents and hopefully no sharks!

Disappointment
We find it a bit dismaying when some cruisers remark about other cruisers' choices in their destinations, how long they stay and whether they take part in excursions, etc. We all want, need and desire different things. We all have different budgets and energy reserves. Not everyone has the funds to spend years cruising. What matters is that we have taken the step to go! We met a young couple who had just two years of time and money to see and do what they could before plunging into careers. They decided to get as far as they could around the world. How disheartening it would be for them to hear that they should slow down. We'd prefer to congratulate them on getting out there and doing it! So, if another cruiser expresses disappointment in your choices, try not to take it on board. Likewise don't be too quick to judge others!

Doctors & Medical Examiners
Do not neglect your regular and important health checks, no matter where you are. *(For medical supplies and first aid, etc, see the Voyage Preparation section.)*

Short story Pleasantly Surprised: While in Ecuador I was due a regular test that is important for women. I found the doctor (recommended by a local woman) to be the most professional doctor I had ever attended in any country.

Don't Sweat The Small Stuff
Niggles, small frustrations and insignificant whinges drain your energy. Save the worry until you really need it!

We arrived into Panama on Pyewacket on New Year's Eve. Delays in checking-in meant a few beers and a dance with the locals outside the Customs office!

Drugs
Do not be tempted to carry any illegal drugs on board and be aware of everything your guests/crew bring on board.

Make unbreakable rules about ALL drugs. If a guest has drugs on board and one speck of powder is dropped, years later that speck of powder could still be detected.

Short story Friends were crewing on a boat. This boat was used many years previously for a New Year's party. While our friends were crewing, drug-dogs came on board and found a minute particle of a used drug. The forensics suggested it had been on board for years! This is now a 'marked' boat.

Ear Plugs

Ear plugs are a good item to have on board if the engine is driving you mad, or if a crew member is snoring. If they help you get some sleep - use them, remember fatigue at sea is a real safety issue.

Environmentally Friendly

Try to practice environmentally friendly techniques in all you do:

- Always practice clean fuelling techniques and organise a container and rags to catch drips. Use kitty litter, shavings or nappies (diapers) to soak up any spills immediately.

- Carefully read your fuel gauges and sound the tanks to calculate how much fuel you need, so it does not overflow if the automatic stop does not work.

- Be aware of fire hazards, no smoking while refuelling!

- Recycle your rubbish/trash ashore.

- Use bio-friendly cleaners and products. *(See 'Cleaning' in the Maintenance & Repairs section.)*

- Pump out properly. *(See 'MARPOL' in the Voyage Preparation section.)*

- Pick up that plastic bag that is floating past or from the shoreline.

- At a place where you have been staying for some time, organise a clean up day with the other boats on anchor. This could become a kids' project, followed up with a 'reward' BBQ.

- Follow environmental practices when hauling your boat out of the water by collecting the strips of antifoul paint *(see 'Stripping Paint' in the Maintenance & Repairs section).*

- Clean up barnacles as per the regulations for the country and port you are visiting. Some countries require you to dispose of them in a certain bin/receptacle, rather than putting them back into the water. This makes an interesting challenge when scraping off barnacles when in the water! (In Australia, if scraping the hull when the boat is in the water, we have to collect barnacles in a bag to dispose of appropriately)!

- For sanding and painting, use screens to capture dust.

- Abide by working hours for use of noisy tools and if possible, rig up screens to reduce noise.

Exercise

Gentle exercise aboard is possible when underway. Even though it is a challenge to convince my limbs to move when on watch (especially at night), I try to exercise at least once during each watch (conditions permitting).

- Basic leg lifts: Lying on your side, bottom leg bent, top leg stretched out in line with your body, head is supported with your hand, elbow on the floor. Complete twenty lifts per leg (keeping the lifted leg straight but knee soft and pushing through heel). The foot of the lifted leg starts about two feet in the air and only lift it another one to one-and-a-half feet up and then back down. Repeat.

- To increase intensity, as you lift, point your toes on one lift and flex the foot on the next and repeat.

- For even more intensity, change from a simple lift to a circular movement, clockwise then anti-clockwise for ten.

- Stomach crunches: Lie on your back, knees bent, lift your head and shoulders (supporting neck/head with hands) and squeeze the stomach muscles together.

- For arms: I furl ropes a few times on each arm.

- Stretch before and after exercise.

At sea it can be physically demanding for days on end. The environment can be cold, wet, dark and noisy, with plenty of stress for you and your vessel. Your lifestyle dictates that you will be reasonably fit, carrying water, gas bottles, walking or cycling to the shops and swimming; however, having a strong back, good general body strength, stamina and flexibility, good food, good rest and hydration is all important. Avoiding injuries and illness at sea is paramount.

Short story Two, fit healthy friends went sailing recently. He contracted a kidney infection and hit his head accidentally. Both incidents were serious and on reading their first aid manual, the couple had to discuss the possibility of drilling a hole in the guy's head to relieve pressure, fitting a make shift catheter (so he could pee) and they even discussed what to do in the event of him dying. Fortunately, it wasn't necessary to perform any of these procedures and they returned to port after two weeks and received medical attention. Both are fit and healthy now (see 'First Aid & Medication' in the Voyage Preparation section).

Fatigue
The first few days on passage are when we are most tired. Generally after three days, we become accustomed to the watches.

Our motto is: three hours, three days, three weeks. It takes about three hours after leaving port to get the boat and crew settled; three days to get the body used to the 3D movement of the boat and (two to) three weeks to *really* enjoy living on board at sea. And three years to set the boat up just how you like it. After thirty years you will still be learning!

At sea your body is constantly moving and hanging on, even during sleep sometimes, so you will probably feel more tired.

Constant awareness of your fatigue is important, before it becomes a serious safety issue. We discuss our sleep patterns and feelings regularly when underway, and make adjustments to our watches where necessary.

Feet

We have found that as we are bare footed most of the time on board, over the years feet will spread, so avoid taking any shoes that are too narrow to start with! (I am not sure if my feet 'spread' because they were no longer squished into shoes every day or the different movement on the boat meant I used different muscles which altered the shape of my feet slightly, or even whether it was a middle age phenomenon (which I read about somewhere)!

Bare footed and using a pumice stone = healthy, happy feet. However, care must be taken when walking around the deck. In bumpy weather soft shoes to protect your feet are a good idea.

Dressy shoes are not ideal on a boat, although having one good pair is a good idea for a special occasion *(see 'Clothes' in the Personal Equipment section).*

Exfoliating is really important when living on board, as split heels can become a problem in this environment. A little exfoliation every few days is enough and a pumice stone on board is a must. *(See 'Beauty On A Budget' earlier on in this section.)*

Flowers

A small simple bunch of flowers freshens and brightens the saloon on any boat. If there are acres of wild flowers onshore, pick a few for the table. *(See 'Gifts' in the Fun section.)*

Forgive

Anger usually stems from fear. Fear is a frequent emotion on a boat. If your partner is shouting at you, try to remember it is probably fear driven - and forgive. If you are the one doing the shouting it helps to think about this too. Try to remember that you are both working towards the same goals.

Noel and I are lucky (or silly) enough to avoid most friction on board. Unless in a very serious situation, we normally end up in fits of giggles! We have great harmony on board.

Short story Our first enormous lock in the French Canals made us giggle like naughty children. We had been told that there would be buoys to tie up to in the locks. As we puttered in, we could see nothing but walls and water. The doors clanged shut behind us and the lock started to fill and we had nothing to tie up to, except each other! We started laughing, but it wasn't funny. As we puttered deeper into our grave-like hole, we noticed that there were cut-outs in the wall that cunningly housed floating buoys. Noel was at the helm slowly puttering forward, he put the aft line on a buoy and continued slowly forward so I could reach the next buoy for the bow line. He was running out of line and I had not yet reached the forward buoy. We stopped laughing and got on with the job. Noel frantically steered the boat with one foot, tied another line onto the end of his disappearing line and only just completed the knot in time. We reached the forward buoy where I simply slipped my line over without a problem. We soon learned to put the fore and aft lines around just one buoy located near the middle of the boat! The point being, you will sort it out, just don't shout your fears at each other, get on with what needs to be done. Blame does not live well on board.

From Little Things, Big Things Grow

To avoid becoming overwhelmed or daunted, avoid looking at the big picture. When we made the decision to leave Australia for England, the thought terrified us. We calmed down by taking the journey a step at a time. When going from Darwin to Ashmore Reef we only thought of that journey and not the miles thereafter. At Ashmore Reef we prepared and thought about Bali. Of course, there is some fore-thought required about supplies that will be needed down the line.

Hot Bunking

It is quite normal to share one bunk when at sea. We do, especially if the boat is heeling. When it is hot, the bunk is easy to air if you use cotton sheets. Each of us uses our own pillow.

When it is chilly at night, there is nothing nicer than hopping into a warm bunk. Before jumping in your bunk, wipe off the salt from your skin, so it doesn't collect and become clammy in the bunk.

Glass

I like drinking wine from a wine glass. It is something I enjoy. Noel hates having glass on board for obvious reasons. Pewter is a good alternative.

Short story I am fairly clumsy and regularly break things. One day I broke a glass in the cockpit and spent a long time cleaning it up carefully. Months later, we were sailing along at 3 a.m. and we were both on watch as Pyewacket was in the middle of a large squall with thirty-five knot winds. It was raining and rather unpleasant. I stood up in the cockpit and yelped, thinking something had bitten me. A shard of glass, standing on its end, about one inch high, had gone straight into the ball of my foot. It was very painful and I couldn't believe after all that time a piece of glass was still right where I trod! (It was easily identifiable as the wine glass I broke a long time before.) Despite this we still have glass on board!

Goodbyes

Cruising life can be like a lifetime of goodbyes. Meeting new people and then parting - we all have different ideas, destinations, wants and needs. The great thing about cruisers is that they will stay friends for a lifetime, even if they are the other side of the world.

When I had uttered that I found the constant goodbyes sad, a good friend told us, 'Don't say goodbye, just don't say it.'

Hair

If water is limited and/or you are in a hurry with not enough time to wash your hair, use a tiny amount of talcum powder to soak up oil (use a small amount and add more, little by little rather than use too much - otherwise you will look grey haired)!

When leave-in conditioner is unavailable, I use a little 'wash-out' conditioner just on the ends of my hair and leave that in.

If you have a preferred type of shampoo, stock up with it when you see it, it may not be available at your next destination.

<u>Safety</u>: When working on the engine or any moving equipment, ensure your hair is properly tied up and/or covered. If your hair is caught in moving parts, it can rip your scalp off or drag you into machinery!

Haircut/Cutting Hair

I usually cut Noel's hair with clippers, as they are cheap and easy to use. I trim the edges with good quality hair scissors. If we are away from the boat (and power) I use the scissors and comb. With a little practice, cutting hair into simple styles is fairly easy.

With scissors and comb, I use the thickness of my fingers as the length and I keep going over Noel's hair until it is all the same length - it looks neat enough.

For me, I find long hair easier to manage and cut. I can divide it into two, bring each length over my shoulder and cut. Once I have cut the longest part, I comb my hair straight down. I then cut up the sides (shorter as it gets nearer the top, similar to layered), just by holding a piece straight down between two fingers, bit by bit. Comb again and check each side. Noel checks the back for straightness and/or any missed bits.

If you prefer to go to a hairdresser, but are reluctant as they speak a different language, simply take a photo of you with your hair how you like it, back and front. Give this to the hairdresser and they will be able to see what you want.

Hatch UP!

If you lift up a hatch or floorboard that is going to stay up for a while, ensure everyone on board knows you have. Usually we shout 'Hatch UP!' and continue to do so until the other acknowledges that they have heard the call. This will help avoid nasty accidents.

Health

The people we have met that embrace the cruising lifestyle look far younger than their land based counterparts. Long-term cruisers wear their journey on their skin. I'm not talking brown and sun-wrinkly; most cruisers know the power of the sun and the necessity of good sunscreen and hats. What I am referring to is health. We meet cruisers well into their sixties, seventies and eighties with the most amazing skin. They are fresh, alive and youthful. Their bodies retain general fitness from constant movement, work and effort to maintain this life.

Heating

If you're going to be living on a boat in a cold climate, then heating is going to be particularly important. If you're not prepared, it will make boat living an almost unbearable experience.

There are many different types of heaters you can buy that use different types of fuel. The fuel you already use for other things, such as cooking, may influence your choice.

The diesel heater on Pyewacket worked fabulously and used little fuel. Friends who had the same diesel heater installed a small fan that blew across their diesel heater chimney to help circulate the warm air.

On board Mariah on a chilly day. Wedged in I can still write!

Mariah had a small potbelly type stove. Cutting timber for fuel was always fun in unusual ports. (It was rarely used at sea but fantastic in port.)

We can recommend both types of heaters, though the diesel heater takes a little less work. For a quick, temporary heater, you can place a fired clay plant plot (not enamelled) over a gas flame on the stove, this heats up and in turn heats the boat.

The main issue with any heater is to ensure it is installed firmly and not able to fall over. Ventilation is imperative, especially when using flame-producing devices. Carbon monoxide is colourless, odourless and tasteless, it is non-irritating and very difficult to detect and it is deadly. It is a product of incomplete combustion of organic matter with insufficient oxygen, to enable to complete oxidation to carbon dioxide.

Do not use flame-producing devices in non-ventilated areas, such as:

- Propane heaters
- Petrol/Gasoline lamps
- Oil lamps
- Grills
- Alcohol heaters
- Diesel heaters
- Charcoal stoves
- Engine exhaust

If oxygen levels drop in an enclosed space, blue flames will become yellow and smoky.

We have heard some awful horror stories of people dying without realising they are being poisoned. At the very least, purchase a reliable carbon monoxide alarm, but complete ventilation is the key. Not just one hatch - a proper through breeze.

Hoarding

Limit the hoarding of knick-knacks and clothes and stuff you just don't need. On a boat you need to hoard spare parts. Not just of the conventional kind, but the unconventional kind, pieces of stainless steel, lead, pieces of timber. You never know what you are going to need in the middle of the ocean.

Homemade Medication

I find porridge a great tummy settler and very comforting. We use rolled oats. For two, one third of a cup of oats covered with water (half-an-inch above the oats), bring to the boil and simmer. Sprinkle with a bit of brown sugar or honey.

Chamomile tea is a good tummy-soother too.

Hygiene

Purchase pocket sized hand cleaners/sanitizers that do not require water and keep one with you at all times. Not all places you visit will have soap!

Alternatively, if lemons or limes are served up, rub these on to your hands for a makeshift wash. Using limes this way will also get rid of any fish or onion smells that linger on your fingers.

Hypothermia

Hypothermia can occur very quickly and surprisingly easily. Simply sitting at the helm in a cool breeze can allow hypothermia to creep in. See the resources list at the end of this book to find books written by medical professionals who provide medical advice to diagnose and treat hypothermia.

Shivering is your body's automatic defence against cold temperature, as an attempt to warm itself. Constant shivering is a key sign of hypothermia. Signs and symptoms of moderate to severe hypothermia include:
- Shivering
- Clumsiness or lack of co-ordination
- Slurred speech or mumbling
- Stumbling
- Confusion or difficulty thinking
- Poor decision making, such as trying to remove warm clothes
- Drowsiness or very low energy
- Apathy or lack of concern about one's condition
- Progressive loss of consciousness
- Weak pulse
- Slow, shallow breathing

The symptoms of hypothermia begin gradually, so a person with hypothermia is usually not aware of their condition. Coupled with confusion that is associated with the condition, this prevents self awareness of the problem.

As hypothermia progresses, the shivering will stop as the body is trying to conserve energy; the patient may actually be getting worse if they stop shivering.

Laugh

Learn to laugh at yourself. Laughter promotes laughter and therefore promotes happy people and longer life. The real challenge in cruising is keeping your sense of humour, and it makes the journey far more enjoyable when you are well acquainted with it!

Laugh and be positive, it has been proven in tests that people in a life-raft with a positive attitude are likely to survive longer.

Laundry

I have never found it necessary to do laundry at sea. Mostly we were in tropical weather and didn't wear much. Our water is too precious to use for laundry while away from land.

Powder or liquid: If you prefer using powder and you find a laundrette that only allows you to use liquid detergent, simply mix your powder with some warm water until dissolved. Most machines do not get hot enough to dissolve the powder completely, so diluting it first is a good idea anyway.

Use minimal detergent, the water need only feel slippery. This eliminates the necessity of excessive rinsing. I am always pleasantly surprised at how clean everything turns out.

Do you need to rinse?: (Thanks to Lis Brown on My Little Bus, a motor-home traveller in Australia, for this great tip). Wool Wash is for washing woollens and you are not meant to rinse, as the eucalyptus oil component is meant to replace or sustain the oil in the natural wool. Most people that are using this product (that I know), do not rinse their washing. If you do prefer to rinse, it rinses very easily, therefore only a light rinse is necessary.

- Use it for everything: clothes, body, hair, dishes, dogs and for everything else where you would normally find a few soap suds.
- Not having to buy any other cleaning products (except for a little bleach, some vinegar and baking soda) I save a lot of money.
- More importantly, I save a lot of space and I do not have on board, or use, any chemical based products.
- Wool Wash contains no added sulphates which is the product in soap and soap products that leave scum in your bath and shower recess etc, (when it mixes with body oils).
- If you are using Wool Wash frequently, a good rinse is recommended from time to time.

Hand washing: I hand wash our clothes 99% of the time as I generally find the public laundrettes (in a marina or not) harvest everyone's dirt. I always seem to get back that extra bit of 'fluffy-dirt' on a favourite shirt or linen. Unless we have an enormous quantity of washing or other major projects that are taking priority, I am happy to sit in the cockpit and play with water while washing clothes. It is sometimes nice to have a simple, non-thinking job.

There are plenty of benefits of hand washing. Our clothes aren't mixed with strangers' dirt and it saves money. At smaller ports, there might be a tap available for cruisers to gather to do their laundry (or even a well, which is what we used in the Maldives). These can often be most enjoyable social times.

Alternative ideas: Friends put their laundry in a large black plastic bag (reinforced/tough type), add fresh water and detergent. Knot the top of the bag and leave in the dinghy, which is tied off at the stern of the boat. The black bag helps heat the water in the sun and the laundry becomes agitated with the movement of the dinghy. You could also have a ride around in the dinghy to agitate further, then rinse and hang out.

In Las Perlas (just south of Balboa in Panama), there was a fresh water stream in the shade.

It was ideal for a morning of playing in water and doing the laundry.

Hand laundry doesn't have to be hard work:
- Use four buckets (two soapy and two with just fresh water for rinsing) to keep several processes going at once.
- Use a sink plunger to agitate the wash for a few minutes.
- Let it sit for a few minutes and repeat. Then use the next bucket for rinsing.
- To wring out, I put my foot on one end and use both hands to twist the item - it works a treat.

Mostly you are just washing off a little sweat, but for extra dirty items I give the item two washes. Or soak for longer. Sometimes I soak washing in a bucket throughout the day. Every time I walk past the bucket, I give it a bit of a swish and by the end of the morning, or day, it only needs a few minutes wash before it is clean enough to rinse and hang. As an added bonus, the water has warmed up in the sun.

Agitators: I have seen two homemade agitators: one is a plumber's mate, the ones that are made to unblock a sink drain (this is what I use); the other was a large funnel with holes drilled into the flared section. A wooden rod is attached to the narrow end by screw or glue and used as a handle.

Tough stains: For really tough stains, I put extra laundry powder directly on the stain and scrub with a stiff brush.

Water supply: In countries where you have to purchase bottled drinking water, use the local tap supply for laundry. At times, you may have to carry the laundry water to your boat. When in the Gambier Islands we could gather water from the village tap, but not do our laundry next to the tap, as the locals did not allow it.

I've never been a fan of washing clothes in saltwater and rinsing in fresh, it takes far too much fresh water to remove all the salt. But I'd be interested to hear from you if you've tried this.

Drying: To dry, hang the laundry on the lifelines or rig up another line between the rigging. Always wipe down the lifelines first.

Suwarrow Atoll, (Pacific Ocean) the luxury of long lines.

Pegging: Use wooden pegs as they last longer and are not environmentally damaging if they accidently drop overboard.

Place the clothes over the line and peg the clothes together beneath the line, they seem to stay on better this way. As an added precaution if it is very windy, button-up the shirts, shorts etc, around the lifeline. Knickers can be taken around the line and looped back through themselves. I've seen plenty of clothes blown away.

Learning
When cruising, you never stop learning. All cruisers have knowledge to impart that you can learn from, whether they are just starting out or an old salty.

Even where friendships are not developing, we take care to listen to others; their advice and knowledge may be very pertinent one day at sea.

Maintaining Your Sanity
No matter what length, boats are still relatively small inside. If you have any sharp timber angles or edges that can catch your ankle or head, file them down or round them off. It is very demoralising to continually hurt yourself on the same thing.

Take your time moving around your boat, even in an emergency. Remember you can usually repair a boat, but not lost or damaged body parts.

Hitting your head and banging your shins and other sensitive parts of your body is part and parcel of living on board, especially at the start. It's something I find very frustrating. The best remedy is to remind myself to slow down!

Protect exposed brackets in your cockpit that are mounted at head height (the type that usually hold things such as your radio or plotter screen when underway). This equipment (plotter, GPS, etc) should be stowed below decks when in port. To avoid a painful meeting of head and bracket, use a tennis ball with a small split in it on each bracket edge. This helps to maintain sanity.

Having a sort-out on Mariah - life on board can be cramped, especially when sorting out cupboards. This was a great test of patience for me!

Memorable Moments
Enjoying the simple things in life = health and well-being. *(See short story below.)*

Short story In Martinique we had just shopped for fresh baguettes and French wine (delicious and ridiculously cheap). On the walk home, the heavens opened and we searched for a cafe to take refuge in. Everywhere was shut. We found a closed cafe with outside seating (seats left outside) which were undercover. We sat down, opened our wine (pushed the cork through) and broke up the bread. It was one of the most delightful times, simplicity at its best.

Mariah II anchored at Martinique in the Caribbean.

Refuge in the rain with bread and wine.

Mistakes

You do not make mistakes unless you are trying to do something worthwhile and useful.

Mosquito Bites

Prevention is better than cure. Apparently, mosquitoes are attracted to blue, so avoid wearing too many blue items. Lavender oil is a repellent and does not contain nasty chemicals.

Personally, I prefer to use any repellent available rather than being bitten. The thought of a needle snout of a creature that has buried this snout in other skin; then burrowing into mine, makes me feel physically ill! That said, bites are unavoidable at times.

To relieve the itch if you are away from home, put a little spit on your fingers and wipe on your bites. Wait a few moments and the itch will ease.

Neat vinegar, directly onto the bite will help stop the itching too.

Mosquito Nets

Netting and Velcro are a necessity on board. To create nets to go over deck hatches, sew a material pocket around the edges of the netting. Thread an old piece of rope into this pocket or place clean sand in the pocket to keep the net weighted down.

Velcro around your companionway hatches is a simple solution, or make up an aluminium frame (from any hardware store) - these can be stored under your saloon seat cushions when not in use. Heavy rope can be sewn straight onto the edges of netting for weight.

Necessities

Think 'what do we need' rather than 'what do we want'.

New Year's Resolutions

Short story Someone once told me that they had stopped making New Year's Resolution lists, as they tended to break the resolutions and feel bad. Instead, now they make a list of all their achievements during the past year. I think this is a great idea and it can be done on the boat. Don't just have a list of what you have to do, keep a list of what you have achieved. It will startle you!

Neighbours - Respect Thy Neighbour

When entertaining in the cockpit into the wee hours, bear in mind that sound carries well across the water.

Talking over your outboard when in your dinghy means your conversation can easily be heard by other boats.

Tie up flapping halyards, especially if you have an aluminium mast. *(See 'Halyards' in the Boat Equipment section.)*

Keep the generator running for shorter periods and not late into the night or at first light.

Possessions

Moisture does not mix well with treasured items unless you take great care. On board you will only have space for a few 'nice to haves', so be selective. Enjoy not being bogged down with hoards of possessions, it is very liberating.

Problem Solving

If possible, give yourself time to think through problems you may be having on board. Other cruisers (whether in port or on the radio, underway) are a great source of information and may help you look at the bigger picture or point out something that you haven't thought of.

Noel's great saying of 'something will happen' is a great calmer for me!

Most envisaged problems melt away with time. You never have to look far for support:

Short story Noel had a fever in Ecuador. He spent twenty-four hours on a drip in the 'hospital'. This hospital did not take credit cards, so I had to organise a cash payment (it wasn't very much at all). Noel spent the day in his air-conditioned room, with TV and the rehydrating drip. I went back to the boat (fifteen minute walk) to collect Noel's credit card to take to the bank to withdraw money. I never use my card, so I had forgotten the number. I always use Noel's card. I had used Noel's card last and I had put it in a safe place (he wasn't with me at the time so it didn't go back in his wallet). I tore the boat apart looking for his card. Then I panicked, thinking it must have been stolen! I went back to shore (we were on anchor) and on Skype I cancelled Noel's card. As soon as I cancelled the card, I remembered where I put it, in my camera case! I rang back the credit card company and they would not let me reinstate the card! I had no other way of getting money. I went back to the hospital and Noel had to ring the bank. He couldn't ring from his room. We had to walk him down the road (in his hospital gown with his bottom peeking out!) and carrying his drip. We found an Internet connection in a gym of all places. The computer itself was practically on the kerb. Noel sat there thoroughly embarrassed while he rang the credit card company to reinstate his card, while I took photos! What a nightmare. When I told our neighbouring friends on anchor about the dramas I had encountered all day, they were really upset with me for not asking them for help!

Rain
We fabricated tarps for the entire boat to help keep it cool, but also smaller tarps to go over the hatches, enabling us have open hatches when it's raining. *(See 'Water' in the Voyage Preparation section for tips on catching rain.)*

Reaching The End Of Your List
Forget it, it will never happen. As long as your vessel is seaworthy, then be comfortable with your ability and go.

While you are cruising you will work at maintaining and repairing your boat. A boat is never finished. If you wait until your list (or every job) is complete, you will never leave.

Relationships
Noel is my best buddy, which helps make cruising together work. Anger and stress are usually borne from fear and the best remedy is to eliminate that fear. Communication on board is imperative for a well-run ship and for your relationship.

Communicate: Learning to listen to fears as well as being brave enough to air them will help smooth any bumpy path.

Equal partners: Being equal partners on board is important to us both. We both like to sleep well when off watch. This was hard to do until we were both completely competent on board. Being in command of the boat is a very serious deal; I have Noel's life in my hands when he is asleep and he has my life in his when I am off watch.

Independence: Being able to manage the dinghy, lower it overboard, start the motor and fault find is important for me. Actually, being able to do everything on board is important to me, to maintain my sanity. We both think it is a good idea to be able to single-hand the vessel, as illness or an accident could make this situation very real. Needing help all the time to do things around the boat would send me a bit mad.

Personal space: Noel and I instinctively know when each of us has to allow the other some space. Even on Mariah, which was a smaller boat, we managed by crawling into the v-birth quietly with a book, lying in the cockpit or taking a cushion out on deck.

In port, occasionally one of us might spend more time in town, either because we need the time, or to give the other some space on board.

Being in tune with each other helps; to be able to understand that no matter how much you love someone, you still need your own time is a great gift.

We had two dinghies that we could use separately. However, we also had kayaks, which were easy for one person to launch and haul back on deck. These provided a simple solution to independence on board.

On a voyage with two on board, it was a bit like a tag team match. We often only had a few hours at dinner time together. One of us was always on watch, the other catching up with sleep or doing a job. So in reality, although together, we had plenty of personal space.

Rescue-a-relationship: Going cruising to 'rescue' a relationship is something I would not recommend (I am happy to be proven wrong though). If you are intending to cruise with your partner - a solid relationship is an important basis for safe and enjoyable cruising.

Noel and I laugh at most things, especially ourselves!

Years later memories of a near disaster, fumbling moments, or our own stupidity can bring tears of mirth to our eyes.

Safety

Have a game plan for getting back on board if you fall overboard whilst in port, in a marina or on anchor. In these situations people have been known to drown from panic and hypothermia. A rope ladder that is lying on deck with a lanyard hanging down to enable you to haul the ladder down the side of the hull, from the water, is a good plan. *(See 'Man Overboard' in the Boat Handling section and 'Dog Overboard' in the Pets On Board section.)*

Always have one hand for you and one for the boat (use one hand to steady yourself and one hand to work on the boat).

When helping someone on and off the boat, offering them a hand is very nice, but wrist-to-wrist is far more secure and stronger.

Ensure your stanchions and lifelines around the vessel will keep you in. We are always surprised when cruisers say 'don't hold them, they are not strong enough'. I couldn't imagine being at sea without that extra security.

At sea, when folding a sail that you have just taken down, try to avoid sitting or standing on that sail to prevent it from filling with wind while it is on deck. Crew have been lost overboard when the wind has caught the sail and the sail has then flicked them straight over the side.

Sarongs

Sarongs are a very versatile piece of clothing. They are also known as Páreus, Pareos and Lava-lava in the Pacific Islands. Read on for fabulous sarong ideas from 1World Sarongs (www.1worldsarongs.com).

Short Deep V-Cut Dress

Short and sexy, great bikini cover up.
Chose a tie dye print and be stunning!
http://www.1worldsarongs.com/
tiedyesarongs.html

Step 1: Wrap sarong lengthwise behind you.

Step 2: Tie the sarong ends behind neck.

Step3: Pick up sarong along the skirt or desired length and tie ends around waist.

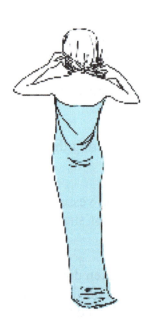

Elegant Dress

Turn a casual afternoon into an elegant evening without the extra wardrobe! This two piece dress is all you need to look classy anywhere anytime.

Step 1: Fold sarong to adjust to desired length.

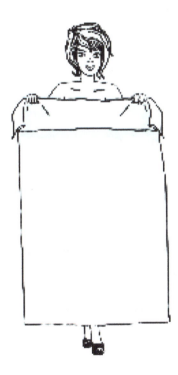

Step 2: Tie sarong in the front then slide the sarong to hide knot in the back.

Step 3: Hold the second sarong lengthwise behind you, bring to the front under your arms and tie behind the neck.

It's just not right when your man looks better in a skirt than you do!

Noel, very handsome, in his Lava-lava in Samoa.

Young or old, male or female, most Samoans wear a Lava-lava.

Shampoo

If taking a saltwater shower, use shampoo in lieu of soap, it will lather up better.

When washing your hair, use only a small amount of shampoo and rub it together in your hands for about twenty seconds first, this will help it lather up and go further and cause less rinsing.

Shoes

Walking is a big part of the cruising life when in port, unless you hire a taxi all the time. There is no car to hop in to go shopping, so good walking shoes are a must.

Rub dry soap around the inside of new shoes and continue to do so until the shoes are completely worn in. This may help prevent 'rubbing points'.

Always take Band-Aids with you when out walking.

If your shoes end up getting wet in saltwater, ensure you wash-off any salt with fresh water before drying your shoes.

Soap

Bulkhead mounted liquid soap dispensers are much easier to use on a moving vessel.

Sunscreen & Protection

Keep covered: In our opinion, it is best to keep covered with light cotton shirts/pants in addition to using sunscreen.

The best sunscreen: Generally, we found the best sunscreens are the kids' bottles, they are not so thick, provide the highest protection and most will not sting your eyes.

Remember to apply sunscreen during cloudy days too. The water reflects the sun and even on cloudy days you can burn at sea very quickly.

Tanning and dangers: If you want a tan, you will still get some colour over time with sunscreen on. It will take longer, but will last longer and it will be safer. As the skin cancer adverts currently advertise on Australian TV 'there is nothing healthy about a tan'.

Don't forget: Apply sunscreen at the sides of your eyes, on your lips and on your ears. If you are swimming for a while, wear a t-shirt and don't forget to put cream on the back of your neck and around the tops of your thighs. Noel will often wear a sun hat too, in the water.

Additional protection: Polarized sunglasses are important to protect your eyes. The sun can cause permanent damage if you are not protected properly.

Use lip balm with a high SPF. Your lips are just as prone to damage as anywhere else.

Teamwork
Support each other. You will both be working hard at the jobs that fall into your lap. If your partner needs a rest and you feel like working, do not become resentful. Allow each other to rest when needed.

Things I Can't Do Without (Limited To Five)

(Jackie)
Noel
Good books (thrillers)
Chocolate
A good night's sleep
Comfortable bed

(Noel)
Jackie (correct answer!)
Novels
Tea
Coffee
Good toothbrush

Things I Can Do Without (Limited To Five)

(Jackie)
Wind at anchor
Too much wind at sea
Squalls on my watch
Too much sun
Too much rain

(Noel)
Big winds
Customs
Tired wife
Blocked toilet
Sunburn

Short story on the above: I thought these questions were a fun section to include. First, I thought about actual items that we cannot do without. You can see we are simple folk. The things we can do without turned out not to be physical items as such. We do not have many superfluous items on board.

Toilet Roll
You can never have too many toilet rolls. Stowing them is easy, you will always need soft items to stop rattles and clunks while under way and toilet rolls are perfect. In some countries they can be quite expensive, so stock up when you can.

To stop your toilet roll (or kitchen roll) from unravelling when at sea, simply flatten the whole roll slightly, so it can't spin.

Always take a supply when going ashore.

Towels

Microfibre towels are brilliant. Essentially they are a chamois-like cloth for the human body.

- It dries you in seconds.
- No matter how wet the towel gets, all you do is wring it out and keep on drying.
- As it's made from Microfibre, if you pack it away (if you are out walking) it won't get smelly or mouldy.
- It soaks up far more moisture from my long hair than regular towels do.

Transition & Change

We have made the transition from boat to land and land to boat several times. It is always harder than imagined (and remembered!) and takes time. The difficulty of leaving friends, family and stability is becoming easier with technology making long-distance communication part of everyday life. During the transition period, try to avoid forcing out plans, simply let them unfold. *(See 'From Boat To Land and Land To Boat' in the Voyage Preparation section.)*

Short story Recently returning to society after sailing the Pacific Ocean again, our first task was to purchase a mobile phone. As we were still together every day, sailing down the coast, we only bought one. We wanted a simple phone that just made and received phone calls. However, the plan that suited us best meant we had to choose a Smartphone. Well, for several weeks I became a phone widow while Noel was permanently stunned and amazed with all the capabilities of this little thing! The way technology leaves you behind when you are away for a relatively short time can be a little daunting.

Umbrella

A useful item for rain of course, but also handy when you are invited on board a boat that does not have any shade rigged. It's better than burning! You can also use an umbrella in your dinghy to protect you from spray. *(See 'Coping In The Tropics' in the Health & Well-being section for more umbrella ideas.)*

Rolande from SV Periclees ashore for an afternoon walk, armed with an umbrella for protection from the New Caledonian sun.

Ventilation

We installed several fans throughout Pyewacket. When motoring in tropical areas, we turned on all the fans to help keep the boat cool. Computer fans are small and can be quiet (test them first) and they use only one to two amps of power. (See *'Air Conditioning' in the Boat Equipment section.*)
Ventilation is important for many areas within the boat. Under our mattresses we have plastic lattice, which allows the air to flow. The timber that this lattice lies on has one inch diameter holes every six inches to allow more circulation.

Most of our cupboard doors have a section of timber lattice on the front with small air vents. These provide just enough ventilation. Our small clothes cupboard does not have the lattice; so every four months we air it out. Try to avoid cramming cupboards too full.

Wine

We enjoy wine and always search for good value alcohol. When we were first cruising on a very tight budget, we would buy quite cheap wines and find the one we liked best. It is amazing how your taste buds 'alter' to enjoy cheaper wine! *(See 'Budgeting & Money Matters' in the Voyage Preparation section.)*

If you are using mainly cask wine, keep an empty bottle or two and when visiting other yachts pour some of your cask wine into the bottle, it will look better and maybe even taste better!

If a small amount of wine has been left in the bottom of the bottle or cask for several days, set this aside for cooking.

Women On Board

We have met women (and men) who can't steer a boat, fix simple problems or have never dropped the anchor. We take the view that at any time, an accident or illness could occur and one of us has to manage the boat alone. I find that it makes sailing far more enjoyable to be a complete and integral part of the event. (It does happen: Noel contracted a nasty fever on a two day sail, he stayed in bed for most of that time and I managed alone).

On board, Noel and I share most of the jobs, (apart from electrics, which I just can't get my head around. Likewise don't ask Noel to peel a hardboiled egg or work with epoxy)!

Even in my best gear I like to 'have a go'.

This is the derrick used on the Island of Niue in the Pacific to haul out the dinghies when going ashore.

Short story It's a scary world when you know little about boats or the cruising life. I was horrified to find myself, at twenty-six, being catapulted into a new culture (I moved from the UK to Australia), new husband and an alien marine world. After being in control of my life, suddenly I was all at sea in more ways than one. Just a few years later I started to write articles for sailing magazines. Now I am teaching commercial maritime and writing books about it! The learning happens far quicker than you imagine and the support from other cruisers is unrivalled.

Many women cruisers wear cotton briefs, just like you would bikinis (with cotton t-shirt or shirt/blouse). Nylon knickers do not breathe as well and can cause infections, wearing cotton undies is more hygienic and comfortable.

For great resources, check out: www.womenandcruising.com

Worries

Landlubbers frequently ask us about sharks, sinking, drowning and pirates. Yes, they could all be a threat, but think about this. Drive a car at 80km per hour and hit another car doing 80km per hour, that is 160km per hour, what chance have you got?

If your boat sinks, you have a life-raft and an EPIRB (Emergency Position Indicating Radio Beacon) - a better chance I think, of getting out alive AND statistically, far less likelihood of it happening.

Pirates are just thieves on the water. Thievery happens on land, although we certainly understand the fears, as you are alone at sea.

Drowning is a fear of mine. Even though I can swim, the thought of being unable to take a breath gets my heart racing. I try not to think about it too much!

And sharks, well we rarely swim mid-ocean when on a voyage. We've done it once and took it in turns. We tied ourselves to the boat with rope! Imagine the wind picking up all of a sudden and the boat sailing away from you - now THAT is really scary!

We've swum with many reef sharks, which are usually more afraid of us than the other way around. I must admit, however, I was terrified during one pleasant swim when I looked behind me to find myself nose to nose with Jaws! (Well, okay, a 5 foot Black-Tip shark.)

Resources:
Travel health information - worldwide: www.nathnac.org/travel/index.htm
Centers for Disease control and prevention - travel information: http://wwwnc.cdc.gov/travel/
World Health Organisation - international travel and health: www.who.int/ith/en
The Travel Doctor: www.tmvc.com.au

ARTICLE: The last word on Health: Embrace every adventure . . . see my Whale story below, published in Australia by Cruising Helmsman magazine.

A Whale Sized Rush of Adrenaline
by Jackie Parry

As the sinister dark shadow came closer, we could clearly see the monster's tail propel his bulk through the water at an alarming speed. The three metre inflatable dinghy is overflowing with silence. The five passengers, of which I am one, sit still, stunned. The thump in my chest and the squeeze I feel in my eyes as they try to pop out, stir the silence. Looking around I note that my companions mirror these symptoms. The humpback whale has us in his sights and there is nothing we can do.

Neighbouring Tahiti, the island of Moorea is a comfortable anchorage where the green velvet sheer rock stretches up into the heavens shredding through the feathery clouds. Facing another day in paradise, friends collect Noel, his daughter Mel and me from Mariah II, for a trip to splash around with the friendly stingrays. Casting off, consumed in yachties babble, we drift for a few minutes, all vying for our say - until the words 'there's a whale heading our way' stops the gaggle of conversations.

The ominous silhouette moves towards us with speeding purpose. Some of us stand, some stay frozen on bottoms. With no wave, wake or drama the baby humpback slides beneath our grey island and there he stays.

'He's hurt, he's a baby,' the tourist boat skipper calls to us as we drift past. We are all perplexed that a whale would come into a narrow, windy channel (following the markers no less) and swim under our dinghy. 'I hope he's friendly,' my inner thoughts say aloud. The statuesque mountains that wear the vivid emeralds, pale into insignificance as we watch, helpless, while the magnificent humpback seeks sanctuary beneath us.

The seventeen foot long blue/black humpback hovers sedately, seemingly content to let us drift above him. One of us reaches to touch his soft, smooth skin, but does not linger, we know we should not be this close, let alone touch him. But what can we do? We study the tubby baby, chunks of fatty flesh hang across his solid body, but he obviously feels safe under our shadow.

'We're drifting and I can't start the outboard with the whale there,' stated Thor (the elected pilot), a little too coolly for my liking. As the men start to paddle with those Barbie sized oars that inflatable boat builders uselessly provide, we gently bump with the whale, shallower water bringing us closer together. Our friendly giant refuses to come out from his handkerchief safety cover. 'He's panicking,' someone calls, it may have been me. The whale, in his comfort zone, does not notice the water lose its depth. For us, our awareness of our surroundings is reaching red alert, even through our state of awe. The athletic men struggle bravely, but they cannot out row a whale! Suddenly our gentle giant friend flips his hefty, proud tail and elasticises his body, arching his solid back, doing that marvellous whale dance we have all seen on TV to ease his bulk back to deeper water. The fact that he has a rubber ducky on his back with five fearful passengers hanging on for dear life, does not seem to bother him. 'Hang on,' someone else calls as panicking faces search for the most stable part of the bucking dinghy. The comparatively small boat rises up out of the water and falls, balancing on the whale's curving back. A dip with our expensive camera becomes inevitable as I try to work out how to keep the pricey equipment above my head and dry. Sharp, unforgiving coral looms nearer and the seriousness of the moment starts banging around our heads in rhythm with the rocking dinghy. Worry lines carve patterns across the crew's tense faces.

Finally, the whale moves us all into deeper water and I remember to breathe. I do not think the paddle strokes that Noel and Thor managed helped at all. We all search for answers to why and how we could have avoided the situation. Luckily, we all survived unscathed, just losing a few thousand heartbeats each. For no rhyme or reason the whale moves havens and wallows under another dinghy that had helplessly stood by in the commotion.

Free of our clingy mate, we take the opportunity to race back to our mother ships and grab our snorkel gear. Noel, Thor and I want to experience his company in his world, besides there must be someone we can call to get him help, perhaps if we see how fit he is or how hurt, it will help. Speedily donning our masks and with our hearts thumping in our throats we jump in and slowly paddle up to the big guy. He's calm under the dinghy. His deep, chocolate, sad eyes watch us approach. We quietly allow him to get used to us being nearby, unthreatening, before swimming too close. Gradually, I inch to his left side and just hover in unison with his massive bulk, my wide eyes watchful of his huge fins that keep him balanced. Tears of gratitude sting my eyes, he is simply beautiful. To me, his wounds look superficial, like they are healing. He is quite fat and apart from scars, I'd say he was pretty healthy, although I am no marine vet.

We do not linger, and retreat after just a few priceless moments. A repeat of shallows and panicking whale/people is looming up again and we voice our warnings to the other dinghy. They manage to escape, carefully turning on their outboard, so not to cause the soft skin more damage. Cold and elated we return to our boats. We relish the incredible events of the last hour, but wonder how we can help the baby find mum.

After a hot shower and even hotter drinks, we peer outside at a small dive boat that anchors right by us. Climbing on deck to fend off and figure out just why they felt they had to be so close, we notice the whale right by Mariah II. On board the dive boat, a diver jumps in with the whale, grasping bulky photographic equipment. Urgently he snaps off film and a bright flash frightens our gentle friend. He seeks haven under our hull and I hope our small home offers the big guy a bit of protection, but another flash explodes in the water and the whale panics. With a huge flip of his immense tail he propels his bulk under our bow where he promptly snags himself between our two snubbers. He starts thrashing in his confined space and I can almost taste his fear as he becomes further entangled and trapped. For about two seconds, which feels longer, I watch, horrified. He thrashes to port and without conscious thought, I take the opportunity to release the slackened starboard rope. Our giant friend swims away like a bullet. Awe and sadness now sits in our boat. The gift of swimming with this glorious mammal is unforgettable. We hope he is strong enough to survive and finds mum along the way.

Postscript
The following day as friends approached Moorea, three adult whales were spotted together with a baby. Scars matching descriptions, we are sure that our friend found his mum. That's our hope anyway.

We hope this article touches your heart like this adventure touched ours. Sometimes you don't have to go in search of adventures, they find you!

KIDS ON BOARD

Noel and I are the only two kids on board our boats. Many of the tips here are from our great Dutch buddies Dennis and Natasha ('Tash), SV Frodo. They spent several years with their beautiful twin girls on a twenty-seven foot Contest. Other tips have been gratefully received from our Canadian friends Rolande and Angus on board SV Periclees, who also spent many years cruising with their children; and also the gorgeous Poms, Liz & Colin and their beautiful kids who spent several seasons in the Pacific Ocean on board their catamaran, Pacific Bliss. The rest of the tips are from the many families we were lucky to meet along the way. For ease of reading, I have put these tips as if the first person is speaking all the way through, even though that person changes!

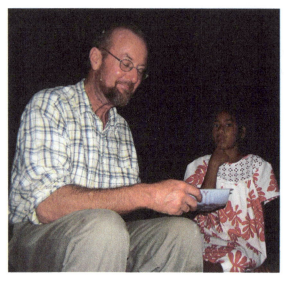

On the island of Ahe in the Tuamotus (French Polynesia), this little girl became enamoured with Noel and his food (especially his food!).

Avoiding Boredom
Give the younger crew interesting jobs to do; it will help avoid boredom and seasickness and help them feel part of making the adventure happen.

Geocaching: is fun for all ages; it gives everyone something to look forward to when making it into port. Geocaching is a real-world, outdoor treasure hunting game using GPS-enabled devices. Participants navigate to a specific set of GPS co-ordinates and then attempt to find the geocache (container) hidden at that location. http://www.geocaching.com/

Video games/DVD players: and the like, are great as backups to relieve boredom and in case of bad weather in port or at sea. The kids can just hunker down in front of a movie below decks. They are also doing something familiar from home, providing a little comfort.

Books: Good books are imperative for all on board.

There is endless fun at sea and in port: Beachcombing, dinghy handling, swimming, exploring, boat handling, fishing, practice on the helm, chart work, compass reading, hiking, nature walks identifying birds and plants, star spotting or looking out for satellites, snorkelling, etc. *(See resources list at end of this book for a Beachcombing website and other fun ideas.)*

Keep books on board to help you identify wildlife.

American Black Vultures, spotted while traversing the Great Loop.

Other amusing ideas:

- Store items for dress up, e.g. theme nights when watching a pirate film. Eye-patches, clip on earrings and bandannas take little space.

- You can't have enough pens/paper/crayons.

- Store kites on board for a new challenge on the beach.

- Find nautical related colouring books.

- Use carrots and capsicums for sculpting, they can be on the menu or as a dinner time decoration.

- Have a store of puzzles to stretch their minds into something different.

- Give them their own binoculars. It will encourage them to search and study their surrounds.

- Buy them their own camera and encourage them to create their own scrapbook with their pictures and mementoes. (Include a printer to print off pictures for their book.)

- Have some Play Doh on board.

- Before leaving, buy interesting and fun biscuit/cookie cutters to encourage cooking.

- Take some card making equipment (e.g. take glue to stick shells onto cards).

- Painting (water based paints are best for clean up). Take a bunch of white flags that can be designed, painted and hoisted.

- Painting is not just for flags and paper. When beachcombing look out for shells, rocks and driftwood for painting up interesting keepsakes.

Bunks

The kids' beds need to be small so they cannot roll around.

In the v-birth, rig up a net in front of the bed which cannot be opened from the inside. This will allow you some sleep, knowing the child can't climb out. 'It's something you don't want to think about, the idea that your kid can climb out of the bed while you are sleeping!'
The v-birth can double up as a playpen too.

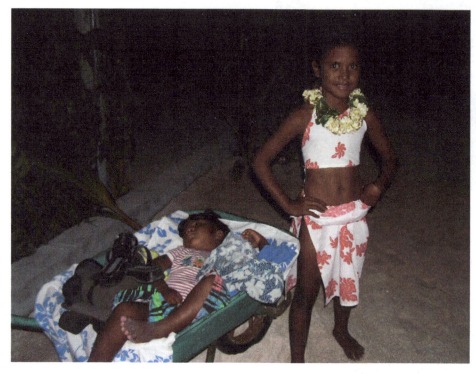

Ahe in the Tuamotu Islands, at a family gathering, kids sleep anywhere.

Cleaning & Tidy Up
Baking soda will erase crayon, pencil and ink from painted surfaces. Sprinkle the soda on a damp sponge, rub clean and rinse.

Organise stuffed toys: Make clean up fun AND save space! Attach a small piece of Velcro to the wall and its Velcro 'partner' to the stuffed animal (you may have to sew it on). They will enjoy velcroing the toys to the wall.

The smaller your boat the fewer 'things' your kids have. You soon learn that they have plenty without accumulating. There is no garage or large cupboard to store unused items.

Clear-out: Go through the store of toys regularly and throw out unused toys and games when there are new items to be had and not enough space for both. This extends to the galley, workshop and all cupboards on board.

Boat space is shared space. Being comfortable with your partner and/or children is something you will adjust to. Kids will soon learn that before they bring out another toy, the previous one has to be put away.

Creativity
Encourage thinking about alternative solutions to items you don't have, e.g. a pencil rubber. Dry bread can be used as you would a pencil rubber.

The inside of a toilet roll makes a great 'sight' to shoot 'dangerous' clouds with.

Create A Budget Challenge
Declare that for one week there will be no eating out and that everyone must contribute to galley duties, even if it is just meal ideas. New/inspired ideas win rewards at the end of the week. Save money and lead up to the end of the week with a special meal and awards night.

Cruising With Teenagers
Plan to visit places where activities excite them, e.g. scuba diving or windsurfing. They may still like the opportunity to go shopping and a stop at a major town with major shops could be a big hit.

Their own space/privacy is just as important as yours.

Keeping in touch with friends will be very important. Have the right equipment on board to enable regular communications, or plan stops where it will be possible to keep communication going that won't cost the earth.

Do not spring changes on them. Include them in discussions of possible destinations/changes.

Having their own responsibilities will be very important for their inclusion and enjoyment.

Don't Forget
Board games and a pack of cards don't use power and can be educational as well as fun.

On longer trips, remember that everyone needs a few days to settle into the routine.

Some of the nicest kids we meet are those who have spent much time on board a boat. They are well adjusted to life, content, happy, healthy and intelligent.

Fishing
Instigate a challenge to research the best time to fish, and carry out fishing at those times/moon phases to see which is more successful.

A quiet night at sea? Reflect a strong light straight down into the water, this will attract fish and other interesting sea life (ensure everyone is clipped on, with life jacket too).

Food
Kids will eat if they are hungry. I regularly give them porridge for breakfast; it gets calcium into them and keeps stowage to a minimum, as I use vacuum pack oats and milk powder.

Footwear
Crocs or Croc look-a-likes are great for kids and they are durable. They have grip, they are good for the beach and in the water. Also, they do not put marks on the deck.

Fun Night & Entertainment
Movie Night requires a laptop or TV, which most boats carry these days. Set up the saloon as best you can so everyone can view the screen. Prepare popcorn and treats just as you would have at the movies.

Kids can make entry tickets etc. You can also have ice-cream intermission (or a different treat if don't have a freezer).

Health & Well-Being

You need kids' sunscreen for kids. Protecting their skin is paramount, especially with the water reflecting the sun and strengthening it.

There are 'Sun-Suits' available for kids to protect them. They make life easier as it is just like putting regular clothes on them instead of rubbing sunscreen all over their bodies. The suits protect them well.

When at anchor, if you are swimming with the kids and you cannot touch the ground, always take something with you that floats (i.e. a buoy). If they panic, they then have something to hold onto instead of you!

Isolation

<u>Natasha and Den talk about Isolation</u>: To think that kids will be isolated on a boat is silly. Many people wanted to stop and chat more when we had Debby and Kim with us. Wherever we were, there were other kids waiting to be friends with our children. Debby and Kim benefited from the experience of being with different ages and cultures. We spent all our time together as a family, learning to work as a team and as one unit.

<u>Observation from Jackie</u>: While Noel and I do not have kids on board, my thirteen year old nephew came to visit in Ecuador for two weeks. After just one day he had made friends with a local boy and two Americans (one sailor and one lad on holiday). It was hard to separate them to take Kieran sightseeing!

Kieran at the helm in Ecuador.

There are plenty of responsibilities that are fun!

Keep In Mind
- Make time to be 'kids' with them.
- Ensure they have their own space.
- Factor in regular treats such as ice cream, chocolate, etc, especially when jobs and responsibilities are completed.
- Keep passages short to begin with.
- If someone's having a bad day, step outside, view your surrounds and remind yourselves how lucky you are.

Learning

Home schooling via correspondence schools provides all the information you need. But look at what else they are learning. Their lives at sea teach them so much about history, science, geography, and of course natural history. Swimming with two dozen Manta Rays went down a storm.

My own geography, history and practical knowledge in every subject imaginable has improved. What a great opportunity to learn new languages at a young age - the perfect time to do it.

Use the opportunity to embrace a language. We really like Linkword. It is definitely easier to pick up another language when travelling. (http://www.linkwordlanguages.com/)

Kids can grow up with an awareness of what is out there and learn that there are few limitations to what's achievable. They gain an understanding of the environment and learn to respect nature. They learn about the different currencies, how to work them out and how they change.

Take audio books and iPods. They are brilliant when you need to focus on sailing, plus it doesn't seem to make anyone feel seasick. Our son has listened and re-listened to all seven Harry Potter books about a thousand times. The only problem is, he will soon start speaking like Stephen Fry!

Home schooling can be frustrating. I found that the French have an incredibly structured system for home learning, which we thought was too time consuming at first. We have since changed our minds. The UK system was scant.

Parents often agree that a formal arrangement with a home schooling department that involves correspondence with a teacher has positive and recognisable benefits.

We recommend History Of The World by Susan Wise Bauer. It's the best history book in the world. We've met four families now who have used this range of books. All of these kids have loved the books and have retained so much information. At great expense we had them sent to Tahiti and it's been worth it. The kids love them and we are learning too. Even if we were not sailing, these books were a great resource for learning about history and geography.

Life Jackets & Harnesses (From Den And 'Tash)

Use a line of about one metre and connect it to their backs. Connecting to their backs is safer; if they fall overboard, they will be dragged backwards through the water.

Clip them on the lifeline with a special safety snap so they cannot undo it themselves.

Buy marine grade, strong plastic clips to clip them to the lifelines, so they do not damage the deck and it is not so noisy when they run around.

We found that most life jackets were too big for them at this stage (under two). When they were more than two years old, they had a life jacket.

When the weather was bad they stayed in the cockpit, on the short life line, in the car seats, or inside. *(See 'Safety' further on in this section.)*

Short story Natasha recounts fearful moments. 'Never take your kid in the dinghy without a life jacket on, even for a few seconds. Debby fell in the water twice! Fortunately, she had a jacket on. We have heard awful stories where the kid didn't have a jacket on for a short trip, fell in and slowly sank to the bottom – the water was apparently clear and the child was retrieved.'

They are never too young to learn cruising fundamentals.

The gorgeous Debby and Kim from SV Frodo.

Medical
We've not had any real illnesses. Stuff for treating stings is the main thing we use for jelly fish, wasps, mosquitoes, etc.

We like old fashion calamine and witch-hazel, as well as Second Skin spray and/or tape. It really sticks and keeps the wound clean for days.

We took a vast array of medications with us to cover every conceivable eventuality, but you always find the right thing for the right insect when you get to the islands.

Liquid medication is easier for kids to swallow, rather than tablets.

Responsibility Or Involved
Many cruisers with kids that we spoke to reiterated that kids like to have responsibilities. Think of easy but responsible jobs, like checking off the voyage preparation list, stowing specific items, even checking the oil and water in the engine - whatever suits your child and their character and age.

Just being involved helps, like servicing the life jackets (testing the whistle and light) or counting how many onions are left. Include them in sailing events such as turning winches, operating the GPS, dock-lines, etc.

Kids love water. When cleaning the deck, hand out extra brushes, it will be like a game.

Short story (and how to run a VHF Radio Network): Where boats gather at anchor(and or mooring buoy/marina) it is very useful to have a local VHF Net. In Panama at 8 a.m. the Net had many boats listening and offering advice and information. At times the kids would be Net Controller and always did a fine job. At Moorea (near Tahiti), there were so many families that the kids organised and hosted their own 'Net'. Usual format includes: Intro (who is Net Controller), any emergency or priority traffic, anyone listening (all boats just say their name), weather - if available (or request if anyone has it), help wanted (where to buy), buy/sell/trade (be careful here, in some countries you are not allowed to sell your items, simply announce you will take 'three coconuts' for the item and negotiate privately!), social events, any other items. You can add any category you wish. *(See 'Radio' in the Communications section.)*

Local VHF Radio Nets can be run by kids. Create a 'kids only' Net, or encourage them to have a stint as Net controller. Kids have hosted some of the best Nets we have heard.

The best tip we received is that all kids are different and what they do and don't do is very dependent on their maturity and character, not just their age.

Safety
Rig a safety line from the stern when swimming.

Rig up a strong, gimballed baby seat to hang within the companionway/entrance. In rough weather, use elastic straps to avoid the seat swinging too violently.

If you let them pick out their own life jackets, they are more likely to wear and take care of them.

Hammocks are a good idea for smaller kids; tempered with some elastic shock cord in bumpier waters.

To and from the boat: Use a wrap-around baby carrier. Prams and strollers take up too much room, so purchase a good front carrier.

Toddlers: For toddlers, create an area down below and in the cockpit where you can bolt down car seats. These are easy to use and super safe. They enable you to have your hands free while the kids can look around. When you have to anchor or tie up, you can rest assured that they are safely strapped in, while you are concentrating on tying up lines or dropping the anchor.

When the kids are around one and a half years old and not yet steady on their legs, use a safety harness and life jacket (vest) for them. The reach of the harness/vest should not exceed the edges of the cockpit and/or be short enough so they cannot fall over the side. The vest must keep their head out of the water. Use this equipment from the start so it becomes second nature.

If they see you wearing the same equipment they will be happier wearing it too.

Resources: Safety netting for boats http://www.ondecksports.com/Products/Sports-Netting

Things We Wished We Had
More books about the animals and sea life that we came into contact with, especially whales/dolphins/rays and sharks, plus good fish identification books. Also more books about the way the body works, vitamins and minerals, etc.

Useful Items To Include On Board:
- Small scoop nets for rock pooling.
- Frisbees.
- Volleyball net and ball.
- Books for identifying birds and fish.
- Encyclopaedias.
- Extra supplies of snorkels and masks.
- Boogie boards.
- Lots of beads and cord for making jewellery and other craft items such as ribbon.
- Modern decorative wall stickers are a good way to personalize a cabin.
- Solar night lights.
- Extra flip flops/crocs and always a pair of shoes they can walk in; plus the next size up.
- Rash tops (sun protective tops).
- Lego, Lego and more Lego.
- Books such as Where's Wally? by Martin Handford, and sailing stories Swallows and Amazons series by Arthur Ransome, and Tommy Tiller and His Dog Rudder by John Martin.

Words Of Wisdom
You may meet a lot of resistance from land based family when you announce you are taking your kids sailing. You will have to put their minds at rest.

Just read a newspaper or watch the news and add up all the muggings and murders in a large city. Compare them with worldwide muggings and murders on a boat.

Sailing an average of 5-6 knots, often without any other traffic must be safer than driving at 100km per hour.

Let your kids view the vessel as an adventure, as that is what it is. Respect for the ship and equipment will come naturally.

Cruising with kids can often be a wonderful ticket to meet folk.

And Finally . . .
Our Dutch friends tell us that their toddlers Kim and Debby were often naked on board, as they were mostly in the tropics (sunscreen /protection taken into account as above).

'To help potty train we kept the potty in an easy place for them to retrieve it. For them it was always fun to use.'

Follow a family on board at http://www.weliveonaboat.com/ (This family have now 'swallowed the anchor' however there is still a lot of good stuff to read on their website.)

MAINTENANCE & REPAIRS

Anodes (Sacrificial)
The anodes your boat comes with should be the recommended quantity and size from the boat builder and designer and should be checked regularly. *(See 'Dissimilar Metals' further on in this section.)*

Replace your vessel's anodes during the annual lift out. If they have been eaten too quickly, there is a problem: they are working too hard. If they are not eaten at all, there is a problem: they are not working hard enough.

If you think they are not behaving as they should, seek professional advice. Over a year they should be about half 'sacrificed'.

Antifoul
Preserve by very gently rubbing the growth off your vessel's bottom regularly. Use a soft cloth, a baby's nappy (diaper) or a very soft brush, otherwise you will scrape off your antifoul or even damage the gel coat (if GRP).

We could clean Mariah's hull wearing snorkels, as her draught was just five feet. On Pyewacket, we used a dive hookah, as she was deeper and we are older and cannot hold our breath as long!

Barnacles
The removal of barnacles is an incessant obligation. These formidable creatures affix themselves to your hull whether you are moving or not.

You get what you pay for with antifoul paint. Do not cheat on quality or quantity.

In port, at anchor, cleaning barnacles off the boat is a good idea. However, check local laws. In most places this is acceptable practice, however, Australian laws state that you should have a bag to catch the barnacles in and that you should dispose of them somewhere else other than in the water! *(See the Cleaning section.)*

This huge barnacle was one of the thousands on our anchor line in Ecuador.

Gooseneck barnacles gather on your hull as you sail the Atlantic or Pacific. These critters attach themselves at speed. Wait for a few days at anchor and with luck, most will simply fall off.

Pay particular attention when anchored in a river, even for a short spell. The nutrients in a river mean your propeller can rapidly become encrusted with barnacles. In previous years we've used a hammer to bash off the 'football' knot of barnacles. The barnacles will seriously affect the propeller and it may not provide any propulsion at all.

Bilge
If you do not have a fridge (or the fridge is full), there are lots of cool spaces in your bilge, which is a good way to store items you would usually refrigerate. *(See 'Refrigeration' in this section and 'Stowing' in the Galley section.)*

Keep your bilges clean. Debris will find its way to your bilge pumps, and the tiniest foreign body can jam and stop the impellers of your bilge pump.

If you have a through-deck mast, there will be a gap around the floor where anything you drop will inevitably fall. Find a length of rope to wrap around the bottom of the mast and sew the ends together. It will look nautical and help keep the bilge clean. *(See Article, 'Pelagic People' at the end of this section.)*

Boat Building Materials - Pros & Cons
When looking for a boat, if you are undecided on which hull material you would like, ask yourself what you would like working on best.

Timber
Pros: Light, strong, attractive
Cons: Rot, dents easily

Ferro
Pros: Cheap
Cons: Undetected terminal damage a possibility, poor resale

Fibreglass
Pros: Strong, light
Cons: Osmosis, UV deterioration

Aluminium
Pros: Best strength to weight ratio
Cons: Electrolysis: constant monitoring of electrolysis is required (e.g. earth leakages in power circuit). Galvanic Corrosion: don't drop a coin or sinker in the bilge, as it will corrode the aluminium

Steel
Pros: Strong, easy to repair
Cons: Maintenance, rust

Buying Parts & Supplies In Foreign Lands

If you still have the old part and it is not too large, take it with you when shopping for a new one. Alternatively, take the original package or wrapping of the part you need with you (especially in a non-English speaking country).

Take a photo of the part with a digital camera to show the part on screen. Write down the part and/or serial numbers.

Caring For Canvas & Vinyl

Handle clear vinyl carefully as it can scratch easily. Soapy water works well to wash the salt off (use fresh water and a mild detergent).

Proprietary cleaners are excellent and help with rain run-off (for example, Clearview applicators).

Never roll up wet canvas, as it will cause stains on the clear part and mould on the material part. Allow to dry fully if rolling up for any amount of time, or prior to long-term storage. Vinegar can be used to prevent mildew; use a spray bottle to administer the vinegar before drying.

Never yank up the canvas when unsnapping the buttons/poppers; hold the canvas near the buttons on both pieces of the fabric for support. Alternatively, use a lever between the button and base, e.g. a flat screwdriver.

Treat zippers with care, do not force them and if they start sticking use a little dry film lubricant such as RZ50 or WD40 if RZ50 is not on hand. If you do not use the zips regularly, ensure they are washed with fresh water and lubricated often.

Regularly check for chafe points.

Re-waterproof every three years (check manufacturer's recommendations). Always do a (hidden) test patch first for discolouration and follow instructions carefully.

From time to time, remove the canvas and clean the stainless steel frame. Rust and dirt on the frame will stain your canvas.

Corrosion & Material Damage

Rust & crevice corrosion

Rust does not just affect steel boats. The salty atmosphere is great at attracting moisture and dampness. In tropical climates, stainless steel will show cosmetic rust stains which can be easily cleaned. Stainless steel needs oxygen to prevent corrosion. Stainless steel fittings and fasteners which are bedded, can be affected by crevice corrosion if the bedding compound leaks moisture without allowing oxygen to refresh the anti-corrosive covering (that naturally protects stainless steel). It is a good idea to inspect fittings and fasteners like chain plates regularly for crevice corrosion.

Treat your engine, cooker (and boat, if steel) with proprietary protection.

For hand tools, ensure they are oiled after use and stored in protective canvas.

Rot
All boats can rot. Ventilation is the key, as well as avoiding fresh water pooling inside or out.

We kept a fine layer of salt in the bilges of our timber boat to prevent dry rot.

Fresh water in carpets can cause rotting; remove and dry in the sun.

Ultraviolet
It makes me cringe to see sails left out in the sun.

Sails should always be totally covered when not in use, unless you prefer dried and brittle sails! The darker the sail cover, the better protection your sails are getting. Navy blue is one of the best colours. *(See 'Sails' further on in this section.)* Your deck is the best protection, so put them away when they are not in use!

Osmosis
Osmosis is blistering, and occurs more often than not when fibreglass is not cured properly.

Most fibreglass boats will have some level of blistering and most blistering is not an issue, it is actually expected. As long as the blisters are either dry or have clear water in them, then there is no structural damage. If an acidic vinegar fluid appears, then it is probably more serious.

Wear protective eye equipment when puncturing larger blisters, as they may be under pressure.

If you are purchasing a fibreglass boat, slip the boat and complete a survey to check for blistering.

Friction
When underway check your running rigging regularly to seek and correct any chafing.

Adjust your blocks so the lines lead correctly.

Tightened sheets and halyards should be released and adjusted from time to time.

Salt encrusted gear will increase the danger of chafing.

When in port, wash everything down with fresh water.

On a particularly boisterous trip to Easter Island, our lines became salt encrusted with the continuous spray over the decks.

<u>In port</u>: Check your mooring lines often. At potential chafing points, run your lines through a plastic water hose, a length of fireman's hose, or at least place some rags to avoid wear.

Friction can occur anywhere. Know your boat and carry out regular checks of all moving parts.

<u>Shackles</u>: Never tighten up a permanent shackle without applying anti-seize grease first.

<u>Wear and tear - everything wears out</u>: The key to cruising on a budget is to check your equipment and to make good decisions about how much life it has left. It is tricky when money is tight, but we take time to think about potential purchases and put ourselves in the position of being at sea. If there is bad weather - that expensive item may seem very cheap all of a sudden.

For example, new sails are an expensive item, but well cut sails produce a lot more drive, which reduces how much time a passage will take. Thoughts of our old sails tearing during a 3,000 nautical mile voyage made the purchase a lot easier to swallow.

Check your mooring lines. Several months in Ecuador allowed barnacles to grow several inches deep.

It took a whole day of backbreaking work to clean the lines.

Tiny pieces of the shell would remain inside the strands, gradually wearing them away over time.

Cutting Grease

If you do not have any cutting grease to use while drilling holes or cutting metals (especially stainless), use Vaseline as an alternative.

Decks

In the tropics, decks can get exceptionally hot. This adds to discomfort below decks (and can scorch the bottom of your feet).

Paint decks with a light colour that will reflect the sun. We found light beige becomes very hot, but very light blue kept much cooler.

Use proper non-slip paint or purchase purified sand to mix in with the paint. Never pick up sand from the beach to use in the paint; it will cut you to shreds and the salt will adversely affect the paint curing. Cork particles work well as they are soft and they are readily available from most chandlery shops.

Mariah's cool blue, clean deck.

Diagrams

When taking apart equipment for repair, or even doing something as simple as changing your boat batteries, always draw a diagram to show their original place.

Alternatively, take pictures with a digital camera for viewing on your laptop.

We always think we can remember how things go back together, but jobs like these often go on for a lot longer than anticipated and the memory fades.

Dinghy Care

Inflatable dinghies should be covered at all times, as they perish in the sun very quickly. You don't have to be a seamstress to make one. Rectangular sections of material velcroed across the width of the inflated rubber will be enough to protect your dinghy (use marine glue to stick the Velcro on).

Do not make the rectangles too wide in order to ensure that the material can easily lay across the changing shape (coming to a point) of the dinghy. Also, do not make the rectangles too long; you do not want the material to drag in the water. Canvas is ideal, but cotton sheets, periodically changed (when sun damaged), will add years to your dinghy's life too.

Take time to ensure a good, tight fit. Loose material can have a scooping effect with the water.

This was taken at Newport Beach, California, before I had made the cover. *(See 'The Beginning of the End Reality Reflections' article in the Health & Well-being section for a picture of our dinghy cover.)*

Short story Friends purchased a near new dinghy and immediately made a cover with vivid floral cotton sheets. Their dinghy could be spotted several miles away, but it was never pinched! After several months you could see the sun bleaching and thinning the sheets. The rectangle pieces were simply cut from new material and replaced.

Noel cleaning our inflatable dinghy in Bahía de Caráquez, Ecuador. These tenacious barnacles accumulated during our daytime excursions.

On Pyewacket, we lifted the dinghy out of the water every night using the derrick, with a bridle on the stern and the main halyard on a bridle on the bow. (The 8hp motor stayed on.)

Lifting up the dinghy kept it clean (most things that tried to grow will die over night). It also helped prevent theft.

When storing your dinghy elevated and alongside your vessel at night, use additional lines to keep the bow down and tight into the hull in case the wind picks up. (A thirty knot gust of wind back-flipped our dinghy!)

Dissimilar Metals

There are two risks here: galvanic corrosion and electrolysis.

Galvanic corrosion: When using two dissimilar metals, precautions must be taken to prevent galvanic corrosion. When two different metals are in contact with one other and are subject to a corrosive or conductive environment (e.g. saltwater), a flow of current between them occurs. This flow of current causes the least corrosion-resistant (active-less noble) metal to corrode. It also decreases corrosion of the more corrosion-resistant (inactive-more noble metal). This form of corrosion is called 'galvanic' because current flow and dissimilar metals are involved. The transfer of mass occurs in the electrolyte, in this case water. This is not 'electrolysis' *(see 'Anodes' earlier in this section)*.

Electrolysis: This usually involves stray current in your boat. All through-hull metal fittings should be bonded together, so as to reduce electrical potential difference between metals. For example, stray current to one metal through-hull can cause an electrical potential difference to another metal e.g. your prop shaft. The less noble metal will breakdown (usually the bronze skin fitting). This process requires a source of direct current (DC), two metals (different nobility) and an electrolyte, such as seawater.

Electrolysis is an enormous field of study; there are books dedicated to the subject, and experts whose job it is to treat electrolysis.

Check the corrosion potential chart (nobility scale of metals) and avoid binding together materials that are far apart on the scale (i.e. brass and aluminium).

Do not place a small amount of active metal in contact with a large amount of inactive metal.

When connecting two pieces of the same material, use a fastener/bolt made of the same material. For example, use an aluminium fastener when connecting two pieces of aluminium. If the metals that are being fastened are structural, use a fastener/bolt of appropriate strength.

If you are using dissimilar metals, make a barrier with plastic. Ice cream containers, cut to shape, are ideal.

Duralac is an anti-corrosive jointing compound for dissimilar metals. Lanolin grease is good too. Thread Locker works well, but it does lock the threads and needs to be reapplied if the item is taken apart.

Nobility Scale of Metals

Active (less noble)-Anodic
most at risk - easy to corrode
most attractive for electrolysis

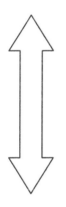

Magnesium
Zinc
Aluminium
Cadmium
Steel/Iron
Cast Iron
Lead
Nickel
Brass
Copper
Bronze
Stainless Steel (316 Marine Grade is best)
Silver
Gold
Graphite

Inactive (noble)-Cathodic
metals least at risk of
electrolysis/galvanic corrosion

The most common problem is stainless steel bolts on aluminium, e.g. SS fastenings to mast/boom. Use Duralac on the threads and shaft of the bolt and/or hard plastic under the head of the bolts and washers.

Drill Bits
Keep your drill bits sharp and ready to use, or have lots of spares if you cannot sharpen them.

If you are drilling stainless steel, buy one eighth of an inch drill bits by the dozen and buy a drill-sharpening machine before you start on your boat. It will pay for itself. Don't forget to use cutting compound to improve the drill performance. The compound helps by keeping the drill bit cool and lubricated; it also helps to maintain a sharp drill bit.

If you have room, buy a drill press and use cutting paste. A drill press saves drill bits from over-heating and the operator from sweating.

Emergencies

<u>Collision</u>: After a collision, the first priority is the watertight integrity of the vessel. Only then should you see to the injured. If you sink, no one will be able to help the injured.

<u>Loss of steering</u>: An emergency rudder can be rigged by running a drogue* aft. The set up of this system will depend on the configuration of your stern. The diagram below shows a vessel towing a drogue from the aft port winch. Along the towing line, another line is hitched on (using a Prusik Hitch, or use a steel ring, or shackle with three lines leading from it), that leads to the starboard winch. To steer in a straight line, the starboard winch must be utilised until the drogue is towing amidships. To turn to starboard, pull the starboard line tighter until the drogue is on the starboard side. To turn your vessel to port, loosen the starboard line and allow the drogue to hang off the port winch. (When a Prusik hitch is under tension it does not slip. It is also known as the Triple Sliding Hitch. *(See http://www.animatedknots.com/prusik/index.php)*

Emergency steering

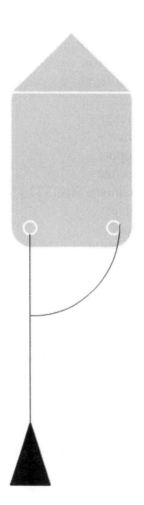

Drogue

Your drogue must have enough drag to counteract the force of the sails. This will require some working to achieve the correct balance. Changing sails or reefing may cause unbalance and the necessity of further adjustments.

*If you do not have an 'off the shelf' drogue, use a tyre (a tyre is a good alternative to purchasing a drogue), a steel bucket (holds better if tied through the holes in the bucket, rather than the handle) or even fenders will help. Perhaps even a mattress - anything to create drag. The trickiest part will be tying the chosen 'drogue' sufficiently well so it copes with the tremendous forces while being dragged through the water.

Broken boom: Use your spinnaker pole. Or 'loose foot' the sail: affix the tack (lower forward corner of sail) to the mast and clew (lower aft corner of sail) to any strong point aft. The main sail is needed to drive your vessel forward. Think ahead about the parts you may need, before any potential problems occur. The gooseneck connection (boom to the mast) is a weak point and can fail, e.g. if your vessel has gybed heavily. Ideally, the boom should be able to rotate at least ten degrees either way, be able to pivot up and down on the gooseneck and swing side to side. Freedom to move in three directions (i.e. up and down, side to side, rotate) will lessen the strain on your gooseneck fittings.

ENGINES
Engines - Care
Start up: Always check your engine's oil and water prior to starting up.

Short story Friends had an old motor which ran very well. They checked the oil and water every time they started up. The one time they did not check, the oil cooler had corroded and saltwater filled up their oil sump and made a real mess, which meant several days of repair and clean up. Luckily, they were in port at the time.

We enjoyed having a brand new engine on Mariah.

As an added precaution when we start our engine, we always crank the engine with the kill switch on, to see if the engine will turn over. This confirms that there is no water in the piston's chamber (water will not compress). Hydraulic lock can bend con rods and lead to all things horrible. Water in the engine can be caused by a failure of the cooling system, so check the anti-siphon valve in the raw water gooseneck for salt build up (as well as your regular maintenance checks). This valve can 'freeze' open, allowing back siphoning into the engine. A $10 part failure can destroy the engine. The valve is easily cleaned, but usually overlooked.

You can complete the same check by turning the engine over by hand cranking. This can be a bit of a chore, but it could save your engine.

Manual: Purchase the complete (mechanic's) service manual for your engine; you can't call a mechanic at sea.

Smooth rebuild: When dismantling parts, label everything, draw a diagram of the parts to assemble and take photos, so that the rebuild goes smoothly and you do not have parts leftover.

Short story Teaching maritime, you see some amusing stuff. During an MED (Marine Engine Driver) course, engines are taken down and re-built. One group had a small part leftover after the re-build was apparently complete. They signed their names on the part, noted the year of the course and bolted the part to an obvious place on the engine!

Engine room: If you install a new engine and you have an empty engine room for a few hours, clean and paint it white. It will make the room much brighter and easier to work in.

Inspections: Full engine inspection and maintenance is just something we all have to learn to do. Regular inspection of hoses is imperative. Just a visual inspection is not always enough, run your hand along the pipes to feel for leaks and cracks (prior to starting and definitely before the engine reaches its running temperature).

Impellers: Learn how to replace impellers in water pumps, and have plenty of spares.

Belts: Regularly check belts for tightness and wear. As a rule of thumb, to tighten engine belts (v-pulley belts): 12mm to 20mm of movement in the belt, between the pulleys. Check your manual. They should be tight enough not to slip, but not too tight.

If the belt is slipping, it won't turn related accessories properly (e.g. the alternator) and the belt could wear out and break prematurely. If the belt is too tight, it could accelerate wear on bearings and seals.

The belt is slipping or misaligned if you see fine belt dust (black smudge over engine) or the belt or pulley has signs of glazing.

Ensure each belt's profile correctly matches the pulley's profile over which it turns.

Belts should be even or stand slightly proud (less than one to two millimetres) above the top of the pulley wheels.

Heal a squeaking fan belt with a little spray of furniture polish (it's like a miracle)!

Continuous quality maintenance means you can venture just about anywhere with confidence.

Traversing The Dismal Swamp during The Great Loop adventure in America.

Engines - Spares

It's important to keep spares. These are the minimum you should have:

- Spare five litres of anti-freeze/anti-boil.
- Sufficient oil for at least one complete oil change on board and half-a-dozen engine oil filters (filters can be hard to source, ensure you keep a good supply on board).

- Fuel filters, impellers, hoses, hose clamps.

- An inline hand or electric fuel pump to make bleeding the fuel system easier and quicker *(see 'Spare Parts' further on in this section, for more ideas)*. The pump can be installed permanently on the diesel delivery line.

Engines - Work In Harbour

Safety: When working on the engine in a harbour while on anchor, mooring buoy or in a marina, take some additional safety precautions. Uncover the mainsail so it is ready to go. If an emergency occurs, you have the backup of hauling up your main (in case you drag anchor, for example).

Take the key out of the ignition and/or post a sign on the ignition. This is mandatory practice on commercial vessels and good practice on all engines.

Communication is imperative on board. Do not make assumptions that everyone knows and understands what you are doing; make sure. Have them repeat back essential points.

Short story Friends crossing the Pacific took on crew. The skipper was in the water carrying out some repairs near the propeller. A miscommunication took place and a crew member started the engine and put it in gear. The skipper had flesh stripped off his forearm and was lucky not to lose his arm; it was very nasty. It is worth taking extra safety precautions.

Engines - Fuel Filters

Homemade filter: A diesel fuel filling filter is sometimes required at foreign ports when filling up. You can purchase various models, e.g. the Baja filter is very common in the States. We use two or three layers of women's tights or stockings over a funnel. This works well and we have never encountered a dirty fuel problem. Obviously our homemade filter will not filter out water.

Filtering fuel: Be cautious if using this method as the length of the stocking hanging down in the narrow part of the funnel can cause the fuel to run through slower and overflow in the funnel. When buying tights or stockings be careful to check that they will fit over the funnel you are going to use, you may have to use a smaller funnel.

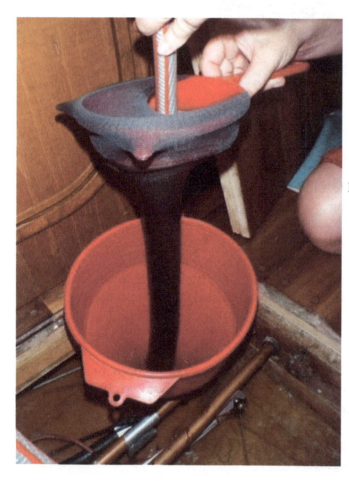

Filtering fuel on board Pyewacket.

These days fuel is generally good at most places. Letting a jerry can of fuel sit for a while will show what crud is in the fuel, if any. We've never encountered dirty fuel that our homemade filter could not cope with.

Diesel bug: The biggest problem with diesel is the dreaded diesel bug. A black sludgy growth that thrives at the level in your tank where there is fuel, oxygen and water, i.e. condensation on the insides of the tank. The best cure is to keep your tanks full as often as you can. There are treatments available, so seek professional advice.

<u>Emergency bypass</u>: If you have two inline filters plus the engine filter for fuel, set up the system so you can bypass the first filter using two stopcocks, i.e. stop the flow to the first filter inline. This is an excellent system, particularly if your fuel filter blocks while crossing a bar; you can instantly bypass the blocked filter and continue. You need the second stopcock to stop the dirty fuel being sucked out of the first filter.

The system on board Mariah II. Note the small hand priming pump bulb fitted in line (at the bottom). It makes bleeding the system easy.

Diesel engines run better and for longer if run under load.

Engines - Refuelling Safety
Turn off your engine and remove the keys from the ignition. Turn off all cooking, lighting and heating appliances, especially the pilot light on any gas appliances. Don't let anyone smoke nearby.

Measure fuel tanks first, carefully work out how much you need and then watch the fuel level indicator to avoid overfilling. Keep soak-up items on hand (rags, nappies, sponge, or purpose made products). Make sure any fuel spillage is thoroughly mopped up and that you allow time for the fumes to dissipate before starting up the engine or igniting any other naked flame.

Engines - Leak
If there is a puddle gathering under your engine that you think stems from the engine coolant system but you are not sure where exactly, sprinkle a bit of talcum powder over the suspected parts

(keep clear of the air intake), run the engine and the wet powder will clearly show the location of the leak.

Alternatively, place clean newspaper under the engine to spot whether the leak is fixed or not.

Searching for a small leak - note the talc and the silly person searching!

Engines - Oil Tray
Engines drip oil. Either when they are running and/or when the filters are changed etc. Keep your bilge clean by installing an oil tray. Some marinas and maritime governing bodies will check that you have an oil tray fitted. The tray is easy to clean if any oil is spilt and it helps you adhere to environmental laws. Keep an eye out for plastic or preferably stainless steel trays/containers that are large enough, to install under your engine.

If you do end up with oil in the bilge, try using disposable baby nappies (diapers) to clean up with. They are available worldwide and are very absorbent.

Short story In Minnie's second-hand marine store in Newport Beach, California, they had a weekly throw out pile that we loved to rummage through. One day, four fibreglass trays were left for the taking. One fitted perfectly under Pyewacket's engine.

Engines - Outboards & Fuel
It is important to drain the carburettor of fuel if the outboard is being stored for longer than a month. Old fuel and small engines don't mix. Old fuel gums up the vitals in the carburettor and then the motor won't start.

If the fuel has deteriorated badly you may have to pull the carburettor apart to clean it. However, sometimes in an emergency you can insert half a teaspoon of fuel into the throat of the carburettor and of course, change the old fuel for new; try and start the engine without the choke then repeat, you may be lucky. Remember you are playing with highly flammable fuels, so be aware of safety and no naked flames!

If you've had dirty fuel or your outboard won't idle, remove the carburettor and ensure all the plastic attachments are removed. Then put the carburettor in lime juice (bottled or fresh) or cola,

bring to the boil and simmer for fifteen to twenty minutes. This will clean it thoroughly. Alternatively, use a beading needle (used to make jewellery with beads) to push out and clean dirt from the carburettor jets.

To make general start up easier, give a couple of short tugs on the starter cord to get the piston to the firing position. You can feel when it gets harder to pull; it will then start easier when you do the 'start' pull at that point.

Engines - Raw Water Intake
Ensure you have a strainer over the raw water intake on the outside of the hull. A plastic bag can ruin your day!

If your engine temperature is increasing from its normal running temperature, the first thing to do is to slow the engine down. If a plastic bag or seaweed has been sucked in over the intake, slowing down may help release the obstruction.

Regularly check the inside raw water strainer and clean as necessary.

Impellers should also be checked, as well as the quantity of water pumped overboard from your exhaust. Each time you start the engine you should immediately check the gauges (oil pressure etc) and that water is pumping through the engine. Over time you will easily be able to judge whether the quantity of water pumped out has changed and therefore detect a problem before it becomes too serious.

Engines - Leaving Your Boat On The Hard
If leaving the boat on the hard (out of the water) for a long period of time in a hot climate, a good quality anti-corrosive anti-freeze with lubricant can be used to preserve impellers and rubber components. Just run the anti-freeze through the raw water cooling system just before stopping the engine. Remember to flush out and add correct quantities of water and anti-corrosive fluids before bringing the engine back into service.

Epoxy Thinners
If you've run out of thinners, use white vinegar to clean your brush and your hands, before the epoxy sets hard.

Filing Metal
When filing metal, use a draw card (similar to a wire brush but has short backwards facing wires) to clean your files. This will prevent burling, which is accumulated waste material balling up.

From Little Things, Big Things Grow
I've learned that all the jobs on board WILL eventually get done, even when there feels like an interminable list. Worrying about how much you have to do doesn't speed things up. Rushing only makes more work - you will get there!

Here we had just purchased Pyewacket. We listed all the work we wanted to do and then just tackled one job at a time without becoming daunted by the big picture.

Short story A good friend purchased a bare hull many years ago and he spent years fitting out the boat. When I talked to him about this book and how hard it is to keep going as the task is so enormous he said, 'Do you think I could complete this boat if I thought about everything I had to do at once? I did one bit at a time and thought of that part only before moving on.'

Give It A Good Coat Of Looking At!
Before tackling each job, step back and give it a 'good coat of looking at'. In other words don't just jump in:

- What tools do you need?
- How long will it take? (If you are at anchor, take into account the possibility that you may have to move quickly in a wind shift and lee shore).
- Consider safety (as mentioned above).

Jackie's dad (Roy) and Noel giving the Aries 'A good coat of looking at!'

On board Pyewacket II, in the lovely port of Newport Beach, California.

Glue

When using glue in a tube, wipe the lid and opening after you have finished. Then smear a little Vaseline on the threads of the tube before replacing the cap. This will prevent the cap sticking and makes it easy to open next time.

Hacksaw Blades

To choose the correct size blade, ensure you have at least three teeth touching the metal at any time. If you have thin metal, you need a lot more teeth (i.e. smaller and closer together). Cut slowly and use the full length of the blade.

Hauling Out

We haul out each year, mainly to apply antifoul, check through-hull fittings and do other jobs that are difficult or impossible to do while in the water. We almost always end up spending much more time and money than we originally envisage.

Mariah II in our home port, Greenwell Point, NSW.

- Haul the boat and power wash the bottom (hire a pressure washer and be careful not to take off too much antifoul) and scrape off barnacles.
- Inspect the hull and rudder for blisters, imperfections, or damage.
- Inspect rudder fittings, rudderstock and bearings.
- Inspect through-hulls for barnacles, integrity and corrosion.
- Inspect the rudder and operation.
- Check the propeller for any damage.
- Check the cutlass bearing by giving a good side-to-side shake of the prop shaft. Excessive play indicates that it's time for a new one.
- Replace anodes. (All anodes should have a certain amount of wear. If they still look brand new, they are not working. If they are nearly gone, there is another problem.) *(See 'Anodes' earlier in this section.)*
- Prepare the bottom for a new coat of paint (after scraping off the barnacles and removing anodes). Lightly sand with 80-grit paper, wearing a face mask and eye protection. Different colour paints can show where the most recent antifoul has come off. If you are changing paints, carefully check compatibility.
- I usually work on the hull preparation and painting, while Noel checks the integrity of the through-hull fittings and other moving parts (and has a little nap in the shade!).

Painting the hull with different colour antifoul helps you easily gauge how long it is lasting.

If time and money permits, we may do some cosmetic work on the freeboard, as this is easier to do on the hard.

Keep all relevant gear together in a project box or basket for the current job you are working on. You will take fewer trips up and down the ladder throughout the day and all your gear is together ready for the next day.

Head
Pour baby oil or used oil from the galley into the head to help keep it lubricated. Ensure it is pumped into your holding tank for proper disposal.

Some cruisers use fresh water to flush. If you are doing lengthy trips, this is not recommended. Raw (salt) water is in abundance!

If you are laying up your boat, flush out the saltwater and replace it with fresh to avoid lingering smells.

The pump on a manual toilet can become stiff as the seals dry out. To avoid this occurring, carefully wipe some baby oil on the shaft and let it trickle down. You'll have smooth operation and lubricated seals. If your head is not working to perfection, carry out maintenance and/or repair prior to departure; repairing a head at sea is the nightmare you imagine. Ensure you have suitable repair kits on board.

Hose Clamps
Always use two clamps together on any hoses you are connecting, especially below the water line. On board, keep a varied collection of hose clamps.

Hydraulic Steering

Spongy and/or notchy steering could indicate that you have air in the system. Top up the oil to the minimum fill mark and turn the wheel lock to lock; this action should bleed the air out of the system.

If your hydraulics are in need of repair, employ a certified hydraulics mechanic. Extraordinary pressure is created within hydraulics which, if handled incorrectly, can cause horrendous injury. Follow the manufacturer's maintenance guidelines.

Idle Equipment

If you are in port for some time, as we were in Ecuador, ensure all equipment on board is used from time to time. Equipment and moving parts tend to stop working if left idle. *(See 'Engine - Leaving Your Boat On The Hard' above.)*

Short story Showers onshore in Ecuador meant we had to carry less water to the boat. However, one day, fiddling in the head, I noticed the shower tap becoming stiff. From then on we showered on board every two weeks to keep it free (obviously utilising the onshore showers between these times!).

The same could happen to all moving parts. The knobs on the burners on your oven are another example; make sure they are all used from time to time. Even the TV, computers, radars, GPS; we have found that they all keep going longer if they are used regularly.

Short story Spending a year and a half in England with the boat on the hard, the equipment on board was rarely used. When we left, heading south for Spain, each week for several weeks a different piece of equipment would fail; and most of these problems were due to lack of use.

Inner Tube

If you have bikes and change a tyre, save the old inner tube. It will be useful for something, e.g. making gaskets for low pressure systems.

Inspections

Go up the mast prior to every passage to check rigging connections, lights and pulleys. Checking the top of the mast for chafing points and integrity of equipment is a must from time to time in port, especially prior to a lengthy voyage. Inspect sails, stitching and halyards before leaving port.

Instruction Manual

Where possible, keep or purchase the full instruction manual for every piece of equipment on board. If you do not have a manual, create your own. List the work done on the equipment, how it works, spare parts necessary and what you have learned from it, e.g. a seal that fails regularly. Carefully draw wiring diagrams and keep them with your manuals.

On board Pyewacket, we had the original owner's details on start up procedures, battery isolation, charging, etc. It was great for all on board and handy when certain equipment was not used often. We were also lucky enough to have the complete builders' notes.

Leather

Purchase an old leather jacket (or any leather clothing) from a recycling shop. You can cut this up and use it for sewing onto rope to prevent chafing or place between the cone plates on the windlass clutch (needs to be strong, thick rawhide). Use on canvas where there is chafing.

Maintenance

We divide the maintenance into three categories:

1. Preventative Maintenance, e.g. regular oil changes to ensure we don't promote our engine to 'necessary maintenance' category!

2. Routine Maintenance, e.g. re-aligning the prop shaft annually, running all systems regularly, cleaning.

3. Necessary Maintenance, e.g. when things break or stop working.

Mast

If you take your mast down for painting or repairs or for simply getting under low bridges *(see 'Short story' directly below)*, consider painting the top few feet a bright colour or covering with florescent vinyl. Generally white boats and dark blue boats are nearly impossible to see by rescue services in bad weather, even if the ship is large. A bright colour at the top of your mast means you will be easier to find.

Short story On Mariah, we took our mast down three times: once for traversing the French Canals (fabulous experience - not sure why I ever left there!), the second time for the Great Loop in America (the mast was lowered from New York to Alabama) and the third time was when we took Mariah to my parents' garden in North London. Each time the mast was thoroughly inspected. At least once we rubbed it back and re-painted the entire mast. We always put a dollar, pound or Euro under the mast before re-stepping it for good luck.

Mast Steps

If you have mast steps, your halyards are bound to get caught around them (unless you have in-mast halyards). Tie small diameter line on the outside of the steps, running vertically from top to bottom; this will help prevent the halyards catching between the steps.

Mast Climbing

On Mariah we had mast steps. Whoever was going up would climb using the steps and would also have the bosun's chair (plank of wood and ropes) kept tight under their bottom by the other person, using the manual winches.

On Pyewacket there are no mast steps. As the lightest, Jackie would go up more often.

We use a brand named Bosun's chair (which is excellent) and to begin with, Noel had quite a time winching me up as I couldn't help him at all by climbing. Now I send him up and I winch him using the windlass (anchor winch). The halyard is wrapped once around its usual winch on the mast and then leads forward to the windlass.

<u>Using a windlass to lift a person</u>: While the windlass is doing all the grunt work, I still have to operate this equipment very carefully. First, I either take the chain off the gypsy or isolate the gypsy from the warping drum. I wrap the halyard around the warping drum at least three times, otherwise it slips. I stand at an angle to the warping drum, as the entire line can slip off the drum very easily. For example, the halyard is wrapped from starboard to port, the bitter end coming off the drum on the port side. I stand slightly to starboard so the line cannot jump or slip off the warping drum. The line must be kept under tension at all times.

Once Noel is up top, keeping the tension, I cleat the line securely and stand well back (not under him in case anything is dropped or knocked off). Letting him down is controlled, using the warping drum. While operating the winch, not for one moment do I take my eyes away from the warping drum and Noel verbally gives me the signal of how he is going. I never release the tension off the line. Everything is slow and controlled. A second safety line should be utilised on a separate winch. Take it in turns to tension each line. I am super cautious, as we used this method on Mariah once and the line did slip off the warping drum. Luckily Noel had the steps to hang on to!

Short story Being in total control is addictive. When Noel is about a metre away from putting his feet on deck, I always stop the descent and take a few seconds to revel in complete control! He cannot get out of the chair and cannot reach the deck – I find this highly amusing, for some reason he does not. (Noel calls this my 'darling little habit' through clenched teeth!)

<u>Safety</u>: If someone has winched you up, make sure they move away from the bottom of the mast, but remain within earshot.

When up the mast, ensure all your tools are tied on with a lanyard (short line). Even the most careful of us can drop heavy items.

Short story Years ago I was doing some work at the top of Mariah's mast. Noel was standing at the bottom of the mast and I dropped a small shifter. From that distance it would have hurt – fortunately, it just missed him. We were both careless. The tool should have been tied on and Noel should not have been standing under me.

Mousing
Mousing is the tying up of the shackle pin to the shackle body. Shackle pins can unwind without mousing. If using wire ties, use the black ties, they are much better at withstanding the effects of ultraviolet light and therefore last longer. White ties will become brittle and split sooner.

Regular checking of the mousing is important, whichever method is employed. Wire should be of the same material as the shackle, especially underwater, to reduce galvanic corrosion. *(See information on Galvanic Corrosion earlier on in this section.)* Use two separate runs of wire for mousing shackles that are used on anchors and moorings.

Paint
Ensure that your paint and all chemicals are stowed properly. Some paints and chemicals are highly flammable and if spilt and mixed with other paints, can be extremely hazardous and create a fire or explosion.

Always read the label and follow stowage instructions (as well as usage instructions).

Climbing the mast is not just for regular checks. Here Noel is preparing to lower our mast (for the inland waterways in America).

It took a full day of preparation before we were ready to lower the mast using the small, hand operated wharf crane, completing the entire job ourselves. Wharf Crane courtesy of the Hudson River Sailing Club, New York.

If you open a tin of paint, especially expensive antifouling paint, and you find that water is laying on top, use a tampon (sanitary product) to carefully suck off the water. Your paint is ready to use without being tainted by water.

'Shall I include the tampon photo?' I asked Noel. 'Absolutely, it worked brilliantly.' (Demopolis, Alabama, USA).

The stirring attachment on the drill is a great way to reduce stirring time (and arm ache!).

Paint Brushes

Wrap cling film around your paintbrush when stopping for lunch, as it stops the bristles from drying out.

Painting

Overalls and work clothes are a necessity on board. You do not need to purchase expensive overalls, just visit a recycling shop. If there are no overalls available, buy some old jeans and t-shirts or long sleeved tops and keep these for work clothes only.

Paint Stripping

To strip the hull of flaking bottom paint, use good quality wood chisels. Run the chisel blade at a sharp angle to the hull and carefully peel off the paint. Have a selection of various sized blades; if you come to a tricky area, use a smaller width blade.

Keep a sharpening stone ready and regularly sharpen the blades. Longer shavings are easier to clear up than little chips - remember to be environmentally friendly in the clean up.

An old cotton shirt is sufficient in hot weather. Painting and varnishing is a regular job.

Problem Solving

Start with your manuals, they usually have some good problem solving ideas in the back. Go for simple solutions to start with, like checking the fuse in an electrical system.

If you're searching for a fault or if the piece of equipment is new to you, don't fret; just have a go. Take your time, have a methodical system, follow each step in the manual and do what seems logical.

Check each possible avenue for failure, one by one. More often than not you will fix the problem or at least identify which part you need. Ultimately, you may need to call in a professional, but have a go; it is very gratifying to make a repair. A big part of cruising is having the patience to increase your skills.

Other cruisers in port or on the radio when underway are a great source of information and always happy to help.

Rags
You can never have enough. Don't throw away old clothes, put them in the rag bag.

Refrigeration Maintenance
Evaporator: Defrost regularly. Chipping ice away can cause damage, so use warm water to aid defrosting.

Air condenser unit: Maintain good ventilation. Vacuum, brush and air blow the coils to keep them clean. Keep the fan clean and ensure no moving items can damage the unit when underway.

Cooling problems: Check the air condenser unit and fan to ensure they are clean. Is the raw water heat exchanger blocked?

Air cooled units work better in cooler climates and water cooled units work better (compared to air cooled units) in warmer climates.

Renew Or Repair
Short story Recently Noel's rucksack (backpack) looked decidedly sad. We would usually just buy another, but it was a particularly strong bag and apart from one or two patches, it was still strong. We weren't on the boat, as we were doing some land travel in South America. Investigating the cost to get the bag patched up was an eye opener. We could buy a new rucksack that was inferior quality for around US$30, or have the old one sewn up for US$10. It is much stronger now. I always keep spare material and good strong needles and a sail-maker's palm (and now a sewing machine!) on board so I carry out these repairs myself when on board. It doesn't need to be pretty (and more often than not, it isn't), but it is unique and functional!

Rigging
Replace all fittings and rigging that is worn, cracked or broken, before you leave. Remove and inspect chain plates (especially stainless steel) for crevice corrosion, under and in the deck area. *(See 'Corrosion & Material Damage' earlier in this section.)*

O-Ring Preservation
O-rings can perish in the harsh elements. Keep them in a sealed container or in a Ziploc bag with a little corn starch or baby powder (like talcum powder). Just a couple of teaspoons and the powder/flour will soak up the moisture. *(See the Galley section for more ideas.)*

Rust
For heavy duty rust, use an equal measure of brake fluid and acetone. Take care with brake fluid, however, as it can eat through paint.

Sails
Always cover your sails when you arrive in port.

These San Blas islanders could use some thread and patches!

UV Protection: Sun is very damaging to the sail; you will add years to the life of your sails if you look after them. Dark sail covers are better, as they prevent passage of light and therefore prevent damage more effectively than lighter coloured materials. Under the sail cover, a layer of space blanket material makes fantastic protection. At the very least, add an additional layer of heavy duty material to your sail cover. Sail-makers state that one layer of ordinary material is not enough for complete protection.

Wear and tear: If you are sailing in a light wind with some swell and your sails are 'slatting/snapping' hard each side, reef them down and turn the engine on (or be very patient). This will help keep the boat steady and give you a much more comfortable ride. It will also greatly reduce the slatting/snapping, which severely damages sails. The use of diesel will, in the long-term, be much cheaper than the amount of wear on your sails.

Preparation: Mount a separate sail track for your storm main. When a storm is predicted, prepare the storm sails while it is calm. Have your suite of storm sails in an easily accessible place at sea. In port, our storm sails live in the sail locker at the bow. When we are at sea we keep them under the saloon table, so we do not have to venture up to the end of the boat and rummage in a cupboard during violent seas.

Common sail problems: Baton pockets on sails are a major problem. If the batons have insufficient support they can chafe and damage the sail. Repairing sails due to baton damage is one of the largest sources of income for sail-makers. If you are buying or repairing sails, ensure this area is sturdy.

Chafing: Constantly monitor your sails. Pay particular attention to a partially furled jib in strong winds; the motion can cause chafing very quickly when the furling unit continuously moves, causing the sail to rub against itself.

Chafing can occur quickly, check your sails regularly.

Repair: Maintain a good supply of sail tape on board. This sticky tape (sail tape), together with sailcloth, is what makes repairs at sea possible. Sewing equipment like sail-maker's palms or sewing machines are a necessity.

New sails: If you can tear your sails by hand or poke your finger through the fabric, it is time for new sails.

Recut sails: If your sails are responding poorly when you tension the leech (aft edge of sail), they are overstretched. A mainsail that is stretched will not trim correctly. You may be able to have a sail recut if it is out of shape, but it is likely that the fabric at the seams would only allow an effective recut once.

Spare Parts, What To Keep & What To Throw Out?
You will need a lot of spare parts. Here are some ideas of spare parts to have on board.
Main Engine:
- Oil filters
- Fuel filters (six first inline filters, four second inline filters and two last inline at the engine)
- Gearbox oil
- Fuel injectors (at least one spare)
- Specific hoses moulded to suit specific equipment and design, plus lengths of spare hose and clamps
- Impellers and service kit (at least two spares)
- Gasket goo
- Gasket paper/material
- Anodes for raw water components (internal anodes)
- Spare propeller
- Fuel hose and clamps
- Spare pulley belts, two for each different size
- Air filter
- Stuffing box packing and suitable spanners for adjusting the packing gland
- Injector return line hose and clamps
- Thermostat

- Water pump
- Fuel lift pump
- Gaskets
- Regulator
- Alternator

Outboard:
- Shear pins
- Oil
- Filters, air, fuel and oil
- Propellers
- Spark plugs

Keep some tools in your dinghy (hidden), for changing a shear pin. If it is going to happen, it will be some distance from your boat and a long row home (don't forget to keep oars in your dinghy too).

At a fantastic anchorage in Tahiti, where few cruisers venture, we sheared the shear pin.

Fortunately we had spares in the dinghy (and the tools to carry out the repair).

Dinghy:
- Dinghy repair kit (in case of puncture)
- Oars and rowlocks
- Pump
- Wheels to help drag the dinghy up the shore, or two cylindrical fenders to use as rollers

Electrical:
- Wiring
- Connectors
- Multimeter
- Soldering iron, flux and solder
- Insulation tape, heat bonding and self bonding tape

Painting and cleaning:
- Varnish
- Paints
- Paint brushes
- Clean up chemicals
- Rags
- Containers with good lids for old paint and spilt oil etc.

Head and pump rebuild kits:
- Hose
- Clamps
- Impellers
- Bilge pump switches

Steering:
- Spare set of morse cables and relevant spares, e.g. hoses for hydraulics, fluids. *(See 'Engine Spares' earlier on in this section.)*

And
Nuts, bolts, screws, rebuild kits, blocks, tackles, lines, shackles, etc - buy in bulk. You cannot have too many, and a good selection of sizes and types is important. Sail tape, Leatherman, WD40, oils, hydraulic fluids, epoxy, resin, freeing goo, grease.

Spare plywood for repairs and/or to cover broken portholes. Appropriate wrenches, screwdrivers, hammers and bolt cutters. Check your socket set fits your engine and plumbing supplies.

Apart from the obvious fuel and oil filters, you will need pieces of timber, bits of metal, all sorts of doodads and thingymies. You will use 95% of everything on board. Remember, you have no one to call on when out in the ocean, you have to use what you have. Clothes and personal items take second place for space on board.

Most spare parts will be more expensive once you leave your country. Other countries may not have the type you need and shipping will add to the expense, monetary wise and time wise. Any surplus items you carry can be used for swaps.

Research common problems with your engine and major equipment on board; this will help you develop your spare part hoard.

Remember that hazardous items like certain paints, flares and fire extinguishers cannot be shipped to foreign destinations. Beware of import tax. *(See 'Import Tax' in the Voyage Preparation section.)*

Carry a magnet to test whether metal items are non-ferrous. 316 SS has no apparent magnetic attraction, so you can check if it is the real thing. If you haven't got a magnet, there is usually one to be found on board, e.g. in a radio speaker.

Strum Boxes

These are filters at the end of the bilge pump pipe in your bilge. They stop any large foreign matter clogging the strainer and your pumps.

If you have bilge pumps that sit deep in a well and it is a hard place to keep clean of foreign matter (remember only the slightest piece of plastic may stop the impeller spinning), fix some metal mesh to catch everything but water. They are easier to clean than some out of reach wells and will ensure the continuous running of the pump if necessary.

Speed Log & 'All Boats Want To Do Is Sink!'

All boats want to sink. *(See 'Short story' directly below.)*

Short story We clean our speed log by jumping in the water, i.e. externally. Previously, it was cleaned by removing the log from the inside, but I find this too terrifying! If you don't think that all boats want to do is sink, remove your speed log from the inside. Be prepared for the great geyser of water that shoots up!

Tools

Space may be at a premium on board, but ensure you have good tools that you know how to use. Take a course on maintenance and repair for your type of engine and your systems. You may not be at a place where someone else can fix problems. If you are, you may not want to pay the prices.

You may need a variety of the same tool, e.g., imperial and metric tools.

Manuals and 'How To' books are tools.

Toothbrush: When replacing your toothbrush, keep the old one. They are excellent for cleaning in fiddly places, or even as a paintbrush for a small epoxy job.

Noel installed two small hatches into Pyewacket's dodger en route to Isle de Cocos (Costa Rican Island)

It looks calm but there was still a swell running. Note he is harnessed on.

Varnish

Our advice on external varnish is to get rid of it. A preserving oil finish is far easier to keep. A green washing-up scrubber/scourer is ideal for a quick rub down of the timber, which you follow with preserving oil. Varnish initially looks better, but after a few knocks and scratches and persistent sun, it quickly looks worse.

Vaseline

Use Vaseline on the tracks of your mainsail and the furler luff groove; this will ensure smooth raising and lowering all the time. Vaseline is also good at lubricating threads and helps prevents corrosion; use it to assist the seal on the on-deck water and fuel caps.

Whipping

Care for your lines and whip the ends, it is easier than you think. *(See 'Knots & splicing' in the Boat Equipment section.)* Making up neat lines by your own hand is very satisfying.

Winches

Sticking winches? With time and patience, take them apart and give your winches a good clean, they may well work again. You can use a good quality detergent, degreaser or diesel with a stiff brush (toothbrush) and scourer. If they haven't been cleaned for some time and you need extra help, use penetrating oil and allow it to soak for a couple of days.

Wire ties

Don't open a packet of wire ties at the end. Make a slit in the middle (across the width) and pull the ties out by bending them at their middle. This will prevent them from falling out. To locate the slit easily, stick a small strip of coloured tape next to it.
Use darker colour ties, preferably black, as they last longer in the sun.

Zips

Even in a dry cupboard, metal zips will corrode. Treat zips on bags or any other item that you will not be using for some time.

Use an old toothbrush and a little water with detergent to clean the zipper head itself and the zip.
Allow to dry and then coat with a lubricant. A dry film lubricant without oil or silicon is best to ensure the zips do not corrode and become unusable, but Vaseline will work (it is just a little messy).

ARTICLE: Pelagic People
by Jackie Parry

It's one of those questions that is hard to articulate an answer to. 'What do you do all day?' It is tricky to know how to respond because no two days are the same, whether in port or at sea. Eventful, is the only recurring theme. We are never bored. In fact one boring day would be a little balm to our busy bodies. Those who are landlubbers or boat owners with vast vaults of money so someone else can take care of the vessel, may well ask. But for the majority of us, simply living on a boat is a full time job.

Today I had no fixed plans; Noel was looking forward to working with the Aries wind vane. If I wake up in the mood, I usually spend the first hour or two writing. I have non-nautical writing projects too. Related photos and paperwork takes time. I try to keep on top of the receipts, separating boat costs with writing costs for tax purposes. Preventing plagues of paperwork helps keep stress at bay and therefore a happy boat.

During the Aries/writing work, a fellow cruiser/neighbour rowed over to say 'hi' and could he borrow a tool. He sat with us for thirty minutes while we put the sailing world to rights. He noticed the pretty birds we had perched on the pulpit. I noticed copious plops of poo. After a cuppa, I dug out a bucket, tied it on, hauled up salty water and washed the offending material away. Ropes furled onto the stanchions had also been selected as a preferred toilet for the birds, so after washing with salty water, I then carefully rinsed the salt off with fresh. I have seen wire ties sticking up on top of stanchions to keep birds at bay, but you need a lot. I thought I'd try Vaseline. Smearing a thin layer on the top bar, I caught more than the odd glance in my direction from others on anchor. Within half an hour a couple of my feathered friends slipped and slid on my trap, but still stayed and pooped. I added more Vaseline in little peaks. Two hours later, not a feather or dropping has materialised. I must remember to wipe it off before we move tomorrow.

I had been contemplating a small job for a while and finally it was time to do, not think. The through deck mast has a small gap around it in the saloon floor, which is a magnet for anything

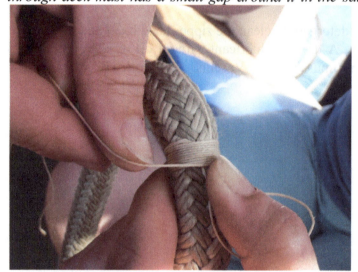

dropped. The deep cavern below the floorboards creates an interesting retrieval challenge. I found some old rope that was a wide enough diameter. Rummaging through the f'ward storage locker took some time and effort. I found the ideal piece, messed around on my knees a while to achieve the right length, then cut the critter. I had whipped the rope at the desired length first. Our makeshift hot knife works well, just a small gas bottle used to heat up a reasonably sharp paint scraper. Next, I sewed it in place, which was far less demanding than I thought.

Throughout this morning, Noel has been merrily working on adapting our emergency steering to connect up the Aries. Between our jobs, Noel and I call on each other to have 'hold that' 'what do you think about this?' and 'how about that?' type discussions. Noel's job was particularly complex;

there are stairs, hydraulic bypasses, hatches and life-rafts to think about, above and beyond the fixtures and fittings of the equipment itself. Today I came up with the idea of removing the pins from the hinges of the hatch to lift it over the emergency tiller stock, which simplified Noel's original idea. Noel had already helped me prior to this by saying it was better to make something to stop stuff falling down the hole next to the mast in the first place, rather than catch it, which was my initial idea.

We are both lucky that we can listen to each other, take different ideas on board, casting our own

out or amending them without worrying. I think it's called brainstorming; we are good at this, both not shy of outrageous idea. Often they are a bit quirky, but sometimes a real gem shines through. Either way we are often giggling.

After grappling with sewing under the table on my knees, I needed an upright job. We have sacks of rice and powdered milk purchased in cardboard containers and I had been saving plastic milk cartons for better storage. I washed them for a second time and dried them in the sun. A few drops of vanilla essence removes any lingering smells. Using an enormous and clumsy funnel, the dry ingredients were poured into the containers. At sea, these foods are now easily accessible and free of moisture. Generally a messy person, playing with flour means the galley looks like it has a light dusting of snow. Sweeping the floor is an almost daily event and I am constantly astonished at the dust collected in the dustpan. Fear of little doodads surreptitiously installing themselves in the bilge pumps motivates frequent use of the broom.

Last job for me today is some amendments to the newly made dinghy cover. It requires some touch up stitching and relocation of Velcro. Taking it off and putting it back on takes longer than the job itself. Noel has called the Police Dock to give them twenty-four hours' notice of our intended move tomorrow. There are strict limits to length of stay at anchor in San Diego and rules of notification.

Throughout the day we've monitored power levels and turned off/on equipment to keep our battery levels over 75%. It has been a sunny day, so there is plenty of power via the panels and just a small breeze - not enough to turn wind generators. In between these tasks, Noel and I take pictures for this article. In the evening I download the pictures and file them in appropriate files so they can be found easily. Noel is cooking dinner.

The day is stitched together with everyday chores, brekkie, lunch and dinner, washing up (shared by us both, whomever feels the more inclined) cleaning, dusting and putting things away (always ready to move in an emergency).

I didn't get to cleaning the wheels of the trolley (used for carrying water jerry jugs), treating it with WD40, and stowing or fitting the metal grates in the bilges to stop debris falling into the very lowest and difficult to reach part of the bilge. The canvas shade needs some work. That may be for tomorrow. However, the anchorage we are moving to tomorrow has Internet access. So some time will be spent on catching up with friends and family. Noel is keen to start on the deck wash pump, the latest piece of equipment to install on board. ('Tomorrow' became filled with a joint effort at an electrical job and laundry; maybe I'll get in that bilge during the next tomorrow!)

There is always something to fix, maintain, improve or add on. Once the boat is running smoothly, we try to do one main job a day, around the day-to-day chores. Then occasionally we can have a day off for sightseeing or simply enjoying swinging on anchor.

Life on board is like occupational therapy; as long as you accept it as such, it is mostly smooth sailing. You still have to live with your partner, and more pertinent but often not considered - you still have to live with yourself.

We hope this article provides you with an insight to life onboard. If you fear the cruising life will become boring, rest assured one of your great desires will be to have just one boring day!

ARTICLE: Published in Australia by Cruising Helmsman.

A Tender Moment in a House of Ill Repute
by Noel Parry

We made it across the Atlantic to Barbados, arriving just in time to celebrate New Year's Eve. Two weeks later, Den (my Dutch friend) and I are hard at it, every day, in a Bridgetown brothel. There's not much privacy either, we work at the rear of the establishment, in an open shed, exposed to the derisive laughter and unasked for advice from the local Cajuns.

'Hey mon, wat cha doo-in?'
'Well g'day, we're makin' a little dinghy.' Our laid back accents are almost vying for the horizontal.
'Oh, you makin' a little boat for the big boat, dat's good, hey mon, you gonna fibaglas dat ding?'

This is the basic conversation, repeated on the hour with each new smiling face.

As our cupboard-bred collection of materials begrudgingly transforms into an object of nautical symmetry, the laughter increases. What I look upon as fine lines, the locals view as a receptacle for ice and cold beer. If only we would 'fibaglas dat ding mon.'

The head honcho of the 'establishment' is very accommodating, has made us feel welcome and seems to run the joint at the command of the 'boss lady'. Mr Honcho stands 190cm (6ft 3 in the old money) is solid and has a flashy smile that should be fronting a toothpaste advert. Dripping gold from his wrists, neck, ears and even his mouth, I swear he's a walking dubloon. He makes me squint, and when he starts laughing, I slip on the sunnies. The red bandana on his cannonball head, the vivid shirt and baggy trousers, neatly round off the whole 'Pirates of Penzance' performance.

As he swaggers over he conspiratorially whispers, 'You don wanna laugh with dem Cajun's mon, all dey wanna do is steal yo' tools, rape yaw wife and den kill you!' As he is Cajun himself, I return to work wondering whether to laugh or take note.
'We're 'aving a party this Sat'day', our host continues, 'Celebrating a return to work for dis joint, we've been closed a year since dat murder dat night, you guys be finished by den, wontcha?'
At this point, I decide to take note.
'No worries' I reply, gazing at our two made up frames and sheets of furniture grade ply. 'We'll be out of 'ere Friday arvo.'

Deciding to build a replacement for our smashed dinghy 'Penguin Jack', sourcing materials and finding a building site, took a week. A week of bus rides complete with Bob Marley blasting through the speakers, pounding our ears. The driver dancing in his seat, chatting with his mates, while scattering pedestrians, all with his right foot firmly on the pedal. It took a week of relying on our good friends Den and 'Tash, from the mighty 'Frodo' to be our taxi to and from shore several times a day. It was 'Tash who bravely asked the woman, behind the three metre corrugated iron fence and barbed wire, whether we could use the shed 'out back'. Mrs Barkly was most accommodating, letting us leave our tools locked in her hallway. Mrs Barkly, as we soon found out, is 'The Madam'.

For three days we cut out frames, trying to bend Honduras Pine stringers into something resembling a boat frame. Honduras Pine looks like Radiata Pine without the knots, it has greater density and therefore more weight. Its oily feel, I thought, indicated longevity and resistance to rot. What I failed to notice, until much later, was its natural abhorrence to being bent.

On entering the yard one morning, I found one of 'the girls' all fifteen stone of her, sitting stark naked on a stool, all limbs akimbo and being hosed down by another woman, similarly clad. Not knowing where to look, I thought I would stare at one of the stencilled signs indicating that no credit is given and that guns are forbidden.

It was now Tuesday. Crossing the Atlantic only two weeks ago, I had images of coral sands, palm trees, scantily clad women and Pina Coladas. The images proved correct, except that instead of a deckchair and a cool drink, I have a workbench and a screwdriver. Cruising reality is a hot tin roof, sawdust, tramping miles carrying or looking for supplies and a shimmering crime-lord as custodian to all my worldly tools of trade. What went wrong?

We almost stayed on board that night, as the swell was swallowing the concrete jetty each time we tried to land. We were about to return for a rave up on Mariah II, i.e. a tinned meal and our favourite book, when our American friends, Roy and Chris from the catamaran, 'Solmates', suggested we tie up to their dinghy. 'It's anchored off as well as tied, so it'll be fine' they called. Their four metre, hard bottomed 'run-about' appeared to be sitting as comfortably as Mariah II out on anchor, so, 'what could go wrong?'

Successful cruising is a matter of continual awareness. This advice was not followed. Sitting at a beach bar, boasting about crossing oceans to the only people who care to listen (other cruisers) is not awareness. With my back firmly placed to the worrying scene of two dinghies porpoising in their attempts to ride the increasing swell, I figured the 'Ostrich Theory' would work. Could we not relax now, tonight of all nights? After all we have just crossed the Atlantic? We deserve a break, do we not? The result answers the questions. The concrete wharf rips the large, sturdy rib to shreds as if it is paper thin and its fifteen hp outboard drags what remains of the planning hull into the depths of swelling sands and coral sea. Our beloved servant from Aussie, 'Penguin Jack' aka 'PJ' is shattered, the remnants float off in the moonlight.

We stood on the jetty and with moist eyes wished each other an ironic 'Happy New Year'. We piled into our Dutch friends' dinghy, headed for 'Solmates' and dutifully awaited midnight. We soberly repeat our 'Happy New Years' and 'Goodnights'. Then I remember, PJ's gone, this begins the first of many pleas, 'Give us a lift, mate?'

Two weeks later on the promised 'Friday arvo', we launch 'PJ II' as the sun sets. It has been a frantic, albeit interesting time. 'PJ II' has been prime coated, but is barely dry. The next morning, our home Mariah II turns into a workshop. Jackie, my hard working wife and I, finish the work on our new dinghy.

'PJII', built in Barbados, in a brothel, by an Aussie and a Dutchman, is unique. As we putter along, people point, stare and the odd snort of laughter can be heard. We hear children say 'I want one', I think it's the green fenders that are cunningly made from swimming floats that turns their eye. But we have the last laugh. Each year many shiny, new dinghies are stolen in the Caribbean, which causes heartache and drama that we know too well. Providing the glue holds and the timber stays in one piece, 'PJ II' will see us home.

Dinghy costs
New, local fibreglass dinghy - from $1000
New inflatable dinghy - from $2000
Penguin Jack II - $200 and a bouquet of flowers for Madam Barkly.

This is one of my favourite articles. Just imagine the stories you will have when you get going!

MEASUREMENTS & CONVERSIONS

If you are planning on voyaging across oceans, then there is a good chance that at some point you will need to convert one form of measurement into another.

All conversions listed here are approximate and most are rounded to two decimal places. If you need a more exact conversion, there are some great 'conversion calculators' on the Internet.

Quick Conversions

At sea, distances are measured in nautical miles (rather than the statute mile that is used on land). Depths can be measured in metres, feet or fathoms, depending on the chart used (always check your charts carefully).

Nautical miles (nm) = statute miles x 0.87
Nautical miles = metres x 0.00054
1 nautical mile = 1,852 metres
1 nautical mile = 1.15 statute miles
e.g.   If you have a number of metres you want to convert to nautical miles,
         let's say 1,000 metres, the calculation is:
         1,000 metres x 0.00054 = 0.54 nautical miles

1 nautical mile = 10 cables
1 cable = 185.2 metres
1 cable = 202.6 yards
1 cable = 607.8 feet

Statute miles = nautical miles x 1.15
Statute miles = metres x 0.00062
Statute miles = yards x 0.00057
1 statute mile = 1,754 yards
1 statute mile = 5,262 feet
1 statute mile = 1,609 metres

Metres = nautical miles x 1,852
Metres = statute miles x 1,609
Metres = yards x 0.9144
Metres = fathoms x 1.828
Metres = feet x 0.305
1 metre = 3.28 feet
1 metre = 0.914 yards
1 metre = 0.547 fathoms

Feet = fathoms x 6
Fathoms = feet x 0.16667
Fathoms = metres x 0.5468
1 fathom = 6 feet
1 fathom = 2 yards
1 fathom = 1.83 metres
Yards = nautical miles x 0.00049
Yards = statute miles x 1,760

Yards = metres x 1.094
1 yard = 3 feet
1 yard = 0.914 metres
1 yard = 0.5 of a fathom

At a glance, seven nautical miles equals approximately eight statute miles.

Tonnes or Tons

1 Ton = 2,240 pounds (an imperial measurement)

1 Tonne = 1,000 kilograms (a metric measurement)

1,000 kilograms = 2,205 pounds. (It is a helpful coincidence that 2,240 pounds is near to 1,000 kilograms.)

1 kilo = 2.205 pounds

To confuse us further, in the American and English system, there is also what is known as the short ton or net ton, which equals 2,000 pounds.

The gross ton or the long ton is equal to 2,240 pounds.

So, if you are reading the word ton in the USA, you should assume this is the short ton (2,000 pounds) unless stated otherwise; whereas in England they use the long ton which is 2,240 pounds. This is why the metric system is better: it is what it is.

Imperial units are now officially abolished in the United Kingdom. The metric system was adopted in 1978. However, old hands (and many new ones) still talk in tons, pints and ounces.

For example a kilo relates to pure (fresh) water, so you can work out weights directly: one litre = one kilogram.

100mm x 100mm x 100mm = the volume of one litre.

In the metric system, the metric tonne is equal to 1,000 kilograms and is frequently spelled tonne, to distinguish it from the ton.

Therefore, a tank 1m x 1m x 1m = 1,000 litres of liquid; if this liquid is fresh water it will have a mass of 1 tonne.

Short story Why 2,240 pounds?

A ton is a unit of weight equal to 20 hundredweight (cwt*). In America and Canada, the hundredweight is 100 pounds and therefore 2,000 pounds is a ton. In the UK there are 112 pounds in the hundredweight (cwt), making 2,240 pounds to the ton. The terms 'long ton' (UK) and 'short ton' (USA) are used to help distinguish between the two.

(*Cwt is a British unit of weight equivalent to 112 pounds and a United States unit of weight of 100 pounds. It is also known as a hundredweight, long hundredweight, cental or quintal.)

The Imperial and USA systems have the same definition of the pound and the ounce.

But the Imperial system in the UK uses the 'stone'.
14lbs = 1 stone.

In the Imperial system, a hundredweight is equal to 8 stones, thus giving the weight of 112 pounds (14 pounds x 8 stones).

Common Measurements
The following tables show some of the more common measurements, and the conversion between larger and smaller units.

Metric Length

10 millimetres	=	1 centimetre
1,000 millimetres	=	1 metre
10 centimetres	=	1 decimetre
10 decimetres	=	1 metre
10 metres	=	1 decametre
10 decametres	=	1 hectometre
10 hectometres	=	1 kilometre (1,000 metres)

Imperial/USA Length

12 inches	=	1 foot
3 feet	=	1 yard
22 yards	=	1 chain
10 chains	=	1 furlong
8 furlongs	=	1 mile (5,280 feet)

Metric mass

1,000 grams	=	1 kilogram
1,000 kilograms	=	1 tonne

Imperial/USA weight

16 ounces	=	1 pound
14 pounds	=	1 stone (UK)
8 stones (UK)	=	1 hundredweight (UK) or 112 pounds (UK)
100 pounds	=	1 hundredweight (USA)
20 hundredweight (UK)	=	1 ton (UK)
	=	2,240 pounds
20 hundredweight (USA)	=	1 ton (USA)
	=	2,000 pounds

Liquid measurements
I tend not to get too caught up in these when cooking, as spoon and cup sizes vary so much. A good slurp is normally my measurement!

Short story Facts: Ounces, and therefore gills, have differences within the Imperial system and the USA version. The Imperial system has five fluid ounces to a gill and the USA system has four fluid ounces to a gill. Therefore, the Imperial version of the gill and its multiples are larger than the USA system.

The Imperial tablespoon in the UK is defined as five-eighths of a fluid ounce, and a teaspoon is 1/24 of a gill. But in other Imperial countries, the tablespoon is more often than not defined as half an ounce and the teaspoon as one third of a tablespoon. Listed below are the definitions in their simplistic value. Personally, as a messy 'cook' I chuck in what feels right and would probably never get a lumped or levelled spoon measurement right anyhow!

Metric Capacity
1,000 millilitres (mls) = 1 litre
1 teaspoon is approx. 10ml
1 metric cup = 250 ml

Imperial Liquid Capacity
2 teaspoons   =   1 dessertspoon
3 teaspoons   =   1 tablespoon
2 tablespoons   =   1 fluid ounce
5 fluid ounces   =   1gill
2 gills   =   1 cup
2 cups   =   1 pint or
                     20 fluid ounces
2 pints   =   1 quart
4 quarts   =   1 gallon

USA Liquid Capacity
3 teaspoons   =   1 tablespoon
2 tablespoons   =   1 fluid ounce
4 fluid ounces   =   1 gill
2 gills   =   1 cup
2 cups   =   1 pint or
                     16 fluid ounces
2 pints   =   1 quart
4 quarts   =   1 gallon

Thank goodness for the metric system!

Short story Clothing and sizes: Shoe sizes are measured differently for men, women and children. Likewise, clothing sizes. This is further complicated by different measurements from one country to another and different interpretations from one manufacturer to another. The following website has size guides, converters, size charts and conversion tables; clothing sizes for women, men and children; charts for dress sizes, suit sizes and shoe sizes. www.sizeguide.net/

Liquid conversions - important for fuelling up in different countries and calculating price conversions

1 litre = 1.76 UK pints
1 litre = 0.22 UK gallons
1 litre = 2.11 US pints
1 litre = 0.26 US gallons

1 US gallon = 3.79 litres
1 US gallon = 0.833 UK gallons

1 UK gallon = 4.55 litres
1 UK gallon = 1.2 US gallons

Lineal Conversions

Imperial/USA unit	Metric (SI) unit (SI stands for the International System of Units)
Inch	= 2.54 centimetres
Foot	= 30.48 centimetres
Yard	= 0.91 metres
Mile	= 1.61 kilometres

Metric (SI) unit	Imperial/USA unit
Centimetre	= 0.39 inches
Metre	= 3.28 feet
Metre	= 1.09 yards
Kilometre	= 0.62 miles

Weight (or mass) Conversions

Imperial/USA unit	Metric (SI) unit
Ounce (weight)	= 28.35 grams
Pound	= 0.45 kilograms
UK ton (2,240 pounds)	= 1.02 metric tonnes
US ton (2,000 pounds)	= 0.91 metric tonnes

Metric (SI) unit	Imperial/USA unit
Gram	= 0.035 ounces
Kilogram	= 2.21 pounds
Metric tonne (1,000 kg.)	= 0.98 UK tonnes
Metric tonne (1,000 kg.)	= 1.10 US tons

Mass vs. Weight

In the metric (SI) system, the term mass is used instead of weight. Weight is a measure of how heavy something is, whereas mass is a measure of the amount of matter. (SI stands for the International System of Units, and is the internationally recognised system for measurement.)

Short story Fact: Something that weighs sixty pounds on earth would only weigh about ten pounds on the moon (due to the lower gravity of the moon), whereas something that has a mass of sixty kilograms on earth would still have a mass of sixty kilograms on the moon (as the amount of matter is unchanged).

Temperature Conversions

The USA and Imperial systems measure temperature using the Fahrenheit system. The Metric (SI) system uses the Celsius temperature system (the Kelvin system is used for scientific purposes).

To convert between Celsius and Fahrenheit:

$$°C = (°F - 32) / 1.8$$

For example, what does 68°F equal in degrees Centigrade:

$$(68°F-32) / 1.8 = (36) / 1.8 = 20°C$$

Conversely:

$$°F = (°C \times 1.8) + 32$$

For example, what does 20°C equal in degrees Fahrenheit:

$$(20°C \times 1.8) + 32 = (36) + 32 = 68°F$$

The freezing point of water in Fahrenheit is 32 degrees, in Celsius it is 0 degrees.
The boiling point of water in Fahrenheit is 212 degrees, in Celsius it is 100 degrees.

Short story Fact: The difference between freezing and boiling is 180 degrees Fahrenheit (212-32) or 100 degrees Celsius (100-0). This means that 180 degrees change in Fahrenheit is equal to 100 degree change in Celsius, or 1.8 degrees Fahrenheit equals 1.0 degrees Celsius. Just add the 32° to get Fahrenheit and take off the same to get Celsius.

Examples:

Freezing = 0°C, 32°F
Room temperature = 20 °C, 68°F
Normal body temperature = 37 °C, 98.6°F
A very hot day = 40 °C, 104°F, e.g. (40°C x 1.8) + 32 = 104°F
Boiling point of water = 100 °C, 212°F, e.g. (212°F – 32) / 1.8 = 100°C

Area Conversions

There is no difference between USA and Imperial measures, except spelling!

Imperial/USA unit		Metric (SI) unit
Acre	=	0.40 hectare

Metric (SI) unit		Imperial/USA unit
Hectare	=	2.47 acres
Square centimetre	=	0.16 square inches
Square metres	=	1.20 square yards
Square kilometres	=	0.39 square miles

Oddities
A cord of wood is a pile 8 feet long, 4 feet wide and 4 feet high.
A perch of stone or brick is 16.5 feet long, 1.5 feet wide and 1 foot high.

How to convert

Length	Multiply by	To find
Inches	25.4	Millimetres
Inches	2.54	Centimetres
Feet	30.48	Centimetres
Yards	0.92	Metres
Miles	1.6	Kilometres
Feet	6	Fathoms

Area	Multiply by	To find
Square Inches	6.5	Square Centimetres
Square Feet	0.09	Square Metres
Square Yards	0.8	Square Metres
Square Miles	2.6	Square Kilometres

Mass	Multiply by	To find
Ounces	28	Grams
Pounds	0.45	Kilograms

Volume	Multiply by	To find
Fluid Ounces	30	Millilitres
Cups	0.24	Litres
Pints	0.47	Litres
Quarts	0.95	Litres
Gallons	3.8	Litres
Cubic Feet	0.03	Cubic Metres
Cubic Yards	0.76	Cubic Metres

Horse Power To Kilowatts
KW = HP x 0.746
HP = KW x 1.34

E.g. 100 HP motor is approximately equal to 75 KW.

Amps To Watts - multiply amps consumed, by the voltage = number of Watts or power.
Watts to Amps - divide the power (Watts) by your system voltage.

Watts = amps/volts
e.g. 2 amp consumption on a 12 volt system
        2 x 12 = 24 watts

Amps = watts x volts
e.g. A 20 watt bulb on a 12 volt system
        20 / 12 = 1.7 amps

Decimals Of An Hour *(for additional information see 'Latitude and Longitude' in the Navigation section).*

To convert minutes to decimals of an hour divide the minutes by 60
e.g. 20 minutes divided by 60 = 0.33 of an hour

Conversely, to convert decimals of an hour to minutes, multiply the decimal by 60
e.g. 0.33 x 60 = 20 minutes.

6 minutes   = 0.1 of an hour
12 minutes = 0.2 of an hour
18 minutes = 0.3 of an hour
24 minutes = 0.4 of an hour
30 minutes = 0.5 of an hour
36 minutes = 0.6 of an hour
42 minutes = 0.7 of an hour
48 minutes = 0.8 of an hour
54 minutes = 0.9 of an hour
60 minutes = 1 hour

NAVIGATION

AIS Automated Identification System

This is an automatic tracking system used on ships for communicating navigation information between AIS equipped vessels and to coastal authorities. Vessels with an AIS receiver can benefit by knowing the whereabouts and intentions of other ships with AIS. As well as location, the ships data can also be transmitted, which includes the name of the vessel, current position, speed, course and rate of turn (ROT), etc. This system provides a tool for improved safety and collision avoidance.

Resources: http://www.amsa.gov.au/publications/fact_sheets/aisa_fact.pdf

AIS is an additional aid to navigation. As with all aids to navigation, do not rely on it totally. AIS has been mandated by the IMO (International Maritime Organisation) for vessels of 300 gross tonnage and upwards engaged on international voyages, cargo ships of 500 gross tonnage and upwards not engaged on international voyages, as well as passenger ships (more than 12 passengers), irrespective of size. Note that fishing vessels are not included in this mandate. Fishing vessels will rarely have someone on constant watch. They are so well lit that they have very limited night-vision and the crew are often totally absorbed in working the deck. This means no one is on lookout all of the time! Therefore, even with AIS you still need to maintain a visual watch twenty-four hours a day.

Bearings

Three bearing fix: This is a great way to double check your position.

On your chart select three conspicuous landmarks to use, to avoid large errors when underway. Take a bearing with your hand compass of the landmark closest to your stern first, then closest to your bow, and finally, the one that is abeam (090° from your bow).

You must be 100% sure that you visually identify the correct landmarks and, ideally, the landmarks should be around sixty degrees apart.

You will need to apply Compass error (Variation), but no Deviation if using a hand held compass (Deviation is only applied if you are using the ship's compass and you know the Deviation).

Compass errors (Variation and Deviation): The difference between True North and Magnetic North is called Variation. The degree of Variation and its annual rate of change is indicated on nautical charts within the Compass Rose. Deviation is the deflection of the compass from its proper orientation. It is usually caused by magnetic materials on the boat (or indeed the boat itself). Deviation can be east or west, or zero, depending on the magnetic conditions on the vessel. The value will change with the boat's heading. *(See 'Compass: True to Compass' further on in this section.)*

Once you have converted the Compass bearing to a True bearing, plot the bearings on your chart. Where the three bearing lines cross, is your fix position. The time of the bearings taken is noted on the chart next to your fix position. This is very important, especially when using DR. *(See 'Position - DR' in this section - Ded Reckoning is actually 'Deduced Reckoning'.)*

Do not use navigation buoys for bearings, as they may have moved from the charted position.

You can take just two bearings, but they will not show any errors that may have occurred, as three bearings will.

With three bearings, you may end up with a cocked hat where the three bearing lines meet (usually looks like a witch's hat, see picture below). If it is not too big, mark your position in the cocked hat at the closest point to danger and have another go (in the example below, that position would be nearest to land). Cocked hats occur with errors (plotting, wrong identification of object, compass error incorrectly applied or unknown compass error), or this could occur with the imprecise reading of the compass or an unsteady hand when at sea.

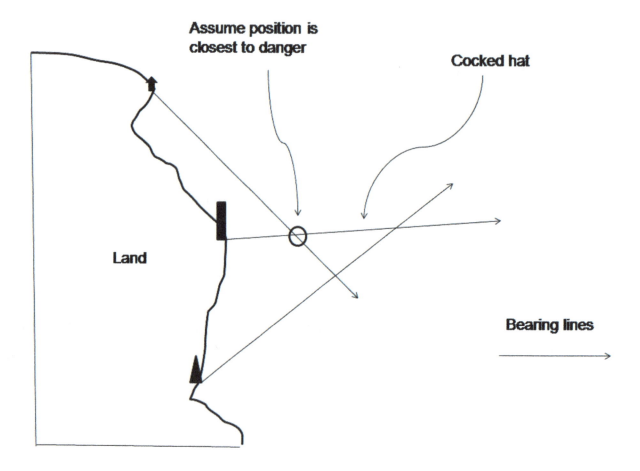

Assume position is closest to danger

Cocked hat

Land

Bearing lines

Radar bearings: These are not as accurate as radar ranges as the boat is often yawing, but it is good practice to use several methods to confirm your position (other than using the Global Positioning System).

The horizontal beam from radar produces a certain width (called the horizontal beam-width) and this will change the bearing by a few degrees. The wider the scanner, the narrower the beam-width and therefore the more accurate it is.

In Heads Up mode, simply use the EBL (Electronic Bearing Line) on your radar to obtain the Relative bearings on screen. Remember, only TRUE bearings can be drawn on your chart.

To convert the Relative bearing to a True bearing add your TRUE course to the Relative bearing. This is then the True bearing of the object or target and can be laid off on your chart.

True bearing (of object or target) = own ship heading (True), plus Relative bearing (of object or target).

Relative bearings: These mean they are Relative to the ship's head. Relative bearings are different from Red and Green bearings. Relative bearings range clockwise from 000° to 360°; Red and Green bearings range from 000° to 180° on either port (Red) or starboard (Green) side. Relative bearings are easier to convert to True.

Relative bearings: Looking straight over the bow = 000°, over the stern = 180°, port beam is 270°.

Red/Green Bearings: If a vessel is abeam on your starboard side, she is also '090° Relative' or '090° Green'. If a vessel is abeam your port side, she is also '270° Relative' or '090° Red'.

Convert Red and Green bearings to True (for chart work): If you have taken a Green bearing, add this to your ship's True heading. If you have taken a Red bearing, subtract this from your ship's True heading.

True bearing = Ship's heading (T) + Green bearing
True bearing = Ship's heading (T) – Red bearing

Note: If you end up with a negative number, just add 360, as we work within 360°.

E.g.
True bearing = Ship's Heading (T) – Red bearing
= 054° (T) - 085° (Red bearing) = -031°
= -31 + 360
True bearing = 329°(T)

(Of course, if you can see you will end up with a negative number, you can add on the 360 first if you wish.)

Notes on radar: Relative motion Course-Up (stabilised) or North-Up (stabilised)
With the addition of heading information from the vessel's electronic compass and/or GPS, the stabilised capable radar can provide True bearings. These True bearings can indicate the vessel's True course and the target's True bearing, and the effect of yawing is minimised on the screen.

Course-Up: display provides the more realistic view as the top of the screen is the direction of the ship's heading and so targets viewed on the right hand side of the screen are seen on the starboard side of the wheelhouse.

North-Up: display relates directly to the view of a chart that is read north up. It will have a different orientation to the view looking out of the wheelhouse.

(See 'Parallel Indexing' further on in this section for more information on radar set up.)

After circumnavigating the planet on Mariah, Noel and I completed the Master 5 course (commercial skippers up to twenty-four metres). We learned a great deal and now teach this ticket.

We went on to study the Master 4, Cert 4 (up to 80 metre vessels).

Here, Noel is studying Master 5 on board Mariah.

Charts

Chart catalogues: These show the different charts available. These are available to look at from most chart suppliers. Selecting and ordering charts takes time and effort, ensure you set aside at least one day for this exercise.

Storing charts: We store our charts, for the area we are traversing, in the chart table. This means they are folded in half. In pencil, we write the chart name and area (lat. and long.) on the reverse for easy identification (avoids having to open each chart) and place them in order of use.

Charts for other areas are stored separately, somewhere dry and ventilated. Storing them flat is ideal, rolling up charts is to be avoided if possible, as they take up more room and can easily be damaged.

Study your charts: Before setting off, study each chart, become familiar with the entire chart that you are using and find out what all the symbols mean. Highlight shallows and dangers with a highlighter pen. When you have your route plotted, check the charts thoroughly for information pertaining to your route. Do this prior to leaving, you could be in rough weather or suffer seasickness and be unable to read during the voyage.

Notices to Mariners: Keep your charts up to date with Notices to Mariners. These are issued free, available fortnightly (in Australia) through the Hydrographic office, or weekly from the National Geospatial-Intelligence Agency (NGA) in the USA.

Electronic charts: are fantastic, but can have errors. They are an aid to navigation and should not be completely relied upon. Use electronic charts in conjunction with paper charts. You could lose your electronic charts with a flat battery or lightning strike, but you won't lose your paper charts this way. It is good practice to zoom in and out (viewing different scales of the chart) regularly to ensure you can view all important navigation information. If you zoom out too much some pertinent information, such as offshore rocks, could be left off the screen!

Important data to note when using paper charts includes: The depth, is it in feet or metres? (Older charts may be in fathoms.) What warnings are included? What is the compass Variation? Are there compass anomalies noted? What do they say about tides and currents? What is the scale? (If you switch charts, check whether you are now using a different scale.) This important information should also be on your electronic charts, but can be hard to find and therefore easily overlooked.

Chart errors: If you are plotting on older charts you may find that the GPS co-ordinates put you on an island! In this case, the GPS is more accurate than the chart. All positions will need to be offset by the amount given in the title of the chart. Every modern chart will have a note stating whether the GPS co-ordinates can be plotted directly or an offset is to be followed. This is a good example that shows you must check all the information provided on the chart, very carefully. *(See 'GPS errors' later on in this section.)* Much older charts, prior to GPS, may have no information at all regarding GPS derived co-ordinates.

For example (1): Chart AUS 252 Whitsunday Group. Under the chart title it states:

SATELLITE DERIVED POSITIONS
Positions obtained from the Global Positioning System (GPS) in the WGS 1984 Datum can be plotted directly onto this chart.

Example 2: Chart AUS 802 Cape Liptrap to Cliffy Island, states:

Positions are related to the Australian Geodetic Datum (1966)
(see SATELLITE DERIVED POSITIONS Note).

Next to title it states:

SATELLITE DERIVED POSITIONS
Positions obtained from the Global Positioning System (GPS) in the WGS 1984 Datum must be moved 0.09 minutes SOUTHWARD and 0.08 minutes WESTWARD to agree with this chart.

Making the corrections: In the case of chart AUS 802 the correction would be as follows:

GPS (WGS 1984) position	39° 00.00' S	146° 15.00' E
	+ 0.09' S	- 0.08' W
	----------------	-----------------
	39° 00.09' S	146° 14.92' E

Corrections vary: Some South Pacific Island charts will note corrections that can be a nautical mile out!

Safety precaution: For an additional navigational safety precaution, learn how to Parallel Index using your radar. *(See Parallel Indexing later on in this section.)*

Measurements: A nautical mile is one minute of arc along a great circle of the earth, e.g. the equator. For chart work, we use Mercator projection. In Mercator projection, the correct scale for one nautical mile is one minute of latitude, measured off the latitude scale adjacent to the area you are working in.

Minutes are denoted by: ′   (60′ = 1 degree)
Seconds are denoted by: ″   (60″ = 1 minute)

<u>Fathoms</u>: 1 fathom = 6 feet (approx 1.83 metres). *(See the Measurements & Conversions section for a comprehensive list of measurements and conversion formulas.)*

<u>Chart symbols</u>: Carry an appropriate book on board to check what each of the symbols on your chart mean. We use Chart BA5011, as this book has all the symbols and abbreviations used on Admiralty charts. Here are some important examples:

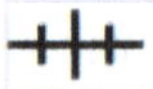 ┼┼┼	Wreck, least depth unknown but usually deeper than 20 metres.
 ⚓	Visible wreck.
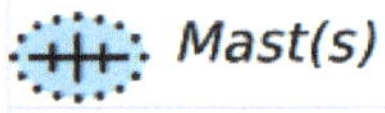 ⊞ Mast(s)	Wreck of which the mast(s) only are visible at chart datum.
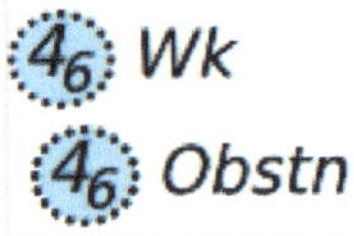 4₆ Wk 4₆ Obstn	Wreck or obstruction, least depth known obtained by sounding only.
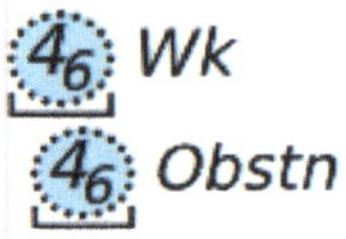 4₆ Wk 4₆ Obstn	Wreck or obstruction, least depth known, swept by wire drag or diver.
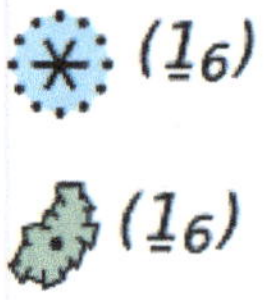 ✳ (1̲₆) (1̲₆)	Rock which covers and un-covers, height above chart datum. (In this example the rock is visible 1.6 metres <u>above</u> chart datum.)
 ⊞	Rock awash at the level of chart datum.
 ⊕	Underwater rock of unknown depth, dangerous to surface navigation.
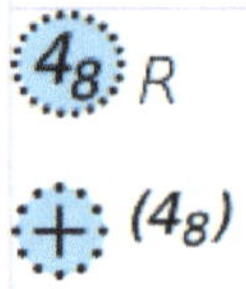 4₈ R ⊕ (4₈)	Underwater rock of known depth, dangerous to surface navigation.
 ♯	Remains of a wreck, or other foul area, non-dangerous to navigation but to be avoided by vessels anchoring, trawling etc.
 20	Wreck over which the exact depth is unknown, but considered to have a safe clearance to the depth shown.

Resource: Chart BA5011 Symbols & Abbreviations

The title block on a chart: Shows the official name of the chart, type of projection, scale, datum and unit of measurement. If you purchase charts by different providers (e.g. BA, AUS, NOAA, NZ, INT) the depths and scales could change from chart to chart. Check individual charts carefully prior to going to sea.

Hazards and symbols: Ensure you understand and identify rocks, wrecks, obstructions and any other hazards. Highlight them along your route. Learn about the given depths, tidal information, LAT (Lowest Astronomical Tide), MHWS and MLWS (Mean High Water Springs and Mean Low Water Springs), rips, eddies and currents, prohibited anchorages and traffic separation schemes.

The information contained on a chart is enormous and it is imperative to know, or at least be able to reference, what the symbols on the chart represent while on board. This subject is a book in itself; do not cut corners here. *(See 'Anchoring' in the Boat Handling section for some sample symbols on seabed properties.)*

Good navigation skills, good resources (e.g. charts) and perseverance will get you where you want to be.

Every landfall is a celebration of a successful voyage.

Arriving in the Galapagos Islands on Mariah.

Collision
If an approaching vessel is doing 26 knots (a large ship, for example) and you are doing 6 knots, that is a total approach speed of 32 knots. Check the speed, distance and time calculations later on in this section to see how quickly these boats will meet! *(Also see 'Alarms' in the Boat Equipment section.)*

If you have taken bearings of another vessel and each bearing does not appreciatively change whilst the range appears to be decreasing between you both, you are both heading for the same piece of water and a collision! Take bearings regularly; the time interval between bearings will depend on the range of the vessel, and the smaller the range the smaller the time interval between taking bearings.

Collision Regulations (Col Regs or Rules of the Road)
Ensure you have an understanding of the International Collision Regulations. Carry a copy of the regulations to refer to.

Resources: Capt. Dick Gandy's Australian Boating Manual
Chapman Piloting and Seamanship by Charles B. Husick (USA)

The Annapolis Book of Seamanship by John Rousmaniere (Illustrations by Mark Smith) (USA)

Compass
The compass functions as an indicator to Magnetic North. The magnetic bar in the compass aligns itself with the earth's magnetic field.

True North and Magnetic North: The difference between True North and Magnetic North is called Variation. The reason for this is that the Magnetic North Pole is not at the Geographic North Pole, around which the earth rotates. The degree of Variation and its annual rate of change is indicated on nautical charts within the compass rose *(see Variation further on in this section).*

Cardinal points and steering: North, east, south and west are called Cardinal points. You should instinctively know which way to turn to achieve the compass degrees you wish to steer. Learning to steer by compass is important - what if your electrics fail? It is easier to steer by compass if the compass card is dampened correctly and positioned directly in front of the helmsman.

Every boat should have a compass on board and everyone on board should know how to steer by compass. This sounds obvious and easy, but I was always surprised how many students would turn the wrong way if steering by compass.

If you want to steer from 010° to 020° you would turn the boat in a clockwise direction, i.e. to starboard. Apply the opposite for fewer degrees, e.g. going from 020° to 010° you would turn to port.

The other way to think of it is to turn the top of the wheel away from the number you want. For example, if you are steering 000° and want to turn to 090°, then turn away from 090° on the compass (top of the wheel to starboard). With a tiller you have to push it towards the desired number (i.e. course) on the compass card. This applies to a compass that is read from the front of the compass itself. Check with your compass layout.

Of course, knowing where north, east, south and west are in terms of where you are currently heading is natural for most of us, but for new crew it is something to be aware of - especially if the self-steering suddenly stops on a dark night in lumpy seas and in high density traffic. Remember that if you turn to port, the numbers on the compass will get lower. If you turn to starboard, the numbers will increase. (When you reach 359° the next number is 000° which would still be 'increasing' the number.)

Selecting a marker to look at and head for, is the easiest way to steer by compass. This is okay if you are coastal sailing (i.e. get on your compass course then look/line up a marker/headland). At sea, away from the coast, this is more difficult, but you can pick a star or even a cloud to temporarily aim for.

Points of a compass: Sometimes sailors indicate a direction to an object by using points of a compass, e.g. 'vessel two points off the starboard bow'. In navigation, a 'point' is 1/32 of a full circle. One point is 11.25 degrees. For example, four points to starboard = 045° to starboard.

True for chart work: All chart work must be in True because north on Mercator charts is Geographic North not Magnetic North. When using your boat compass you must convert Compass readings to True in order to lay off bearings or courses on your chart.

True to Compass (or Compass to True): If you have found the course to steer on your chart, that will be in True. The helmsman needs a Compass course to steer by, therefore you need to convert True to Compass.

If you use a hand-bearing compass, there will be no known Deviation. (Deviation is caused by magnetic material altering the compass point by so many degrees.) *(See 'Deviation' later in this section.)*

To convert Compass to True or True to Compass there are two useful memory aids to help you.

First write down the key points:

CAN	**C**ompass (your boat's compass)
DEAD	**D**eviation (from your boat's Deviation card, created by Compass Adjuster)
MEN	**M**agnetic (same as Compass but with Deviation applied)
VOTE	**V**ariation (found on your chart, always either east or west)
TWICE	**T**rue (all chart work must be in True)

(Or, **T**ele **V**ision **M**akes **D**ull **C**ompany, which are the above letters in reverse.)

Example - Compass to True: You have taken a bearing with your ship's compass of 100°C and on that heading you have a Deviation of 2° East (taken from your compass Deviation card or you have calculated Deviation yourself). *(See 'Deviation' further on in this section.)* Variation is 5° West (from the compass rose on your chart, nearest to the area you are in). First write down what you know:

C	100°	
D	2°	East
M		
V	5°	West
T		

There are two ways of calculating the answers:

1) Use the rhyme: Error East Compass least; error West Compass best

You have 100°, now apply 2° East, (error East Compass least which means C must be less than M) therefore M = 102°.

M = 102°, now apply 5° West (error West, Compass best), M (which is Compass with Deviation applied) must be more than True (T), therefore = 097° True.

C	100°	
D	2°	East
M	102°	
V	5°	West
T	097°	

You can now plot the bearing 097°T on your chart.

2) Write out the process using CADET. The word CADET tells you that from Compass to True you must ADD EAST (ADE).

C → AD E → T

Using this word and expanding the meaning gives you something easy to follow. Simply apply the opposite for True to Compass.

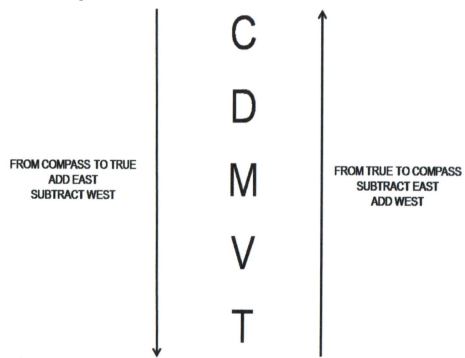

FROM COMPASS TO TRUE
ADD EAST
SUBTRACT WEST

FROM TRUE TO COMPASS
SUBTRACT EAST
ADD WEST

Above we have:
1) Written out CDMVT with arrows each side.
2) We know by using CADET, when going from Compass to True we ADD EAST (ADE). So draw a line pointing from C to T and write, next to this line 'Add East'. If you add east you must subtract west - write this on the same side.
3) On the other side of CDMVT, draw a line with an arrow going in the opposite direction from the first arrow on the other side.
4) The instructions for East and West are the exact opposite. Therefore write subtract East, add West.
5) Simply follow the directions.

As per our example, we have 100° Compass and you want to convert to True. Using the above, it states that from Compass to True (C → T) you have to add East and subtract West.

Therefore 100°C + 2° East = 102°M, then 102°M − 5° West = 097° True

You can now plot the bearing line of 100° Compass as 097° True on your chart.

Resources:
http://www.geomag.nrcan.gc.ca/apps/mdcal-eng.php - A magnetic declination calculator.
http://www.ritchienavigation.com/service/compensation.html for compass compensation.

**Good navigation will get you safely to where you want to go . . . fancy the San Blas Islands?
(East of the Panama Canal)**

Deviation: As a reminder, Deviation is the deflection of the compass needle from its proper orientation. It is usually caused by magnetic materials on the boat (or indeed the boat itself). Deviation can be East or West, or zero, depending on the magnetic conditions on the vessel. The value of Deviation changes with the boat's heading.

Deviation is usually calculated by a professional Compass Adjuster, however you can check Deviation errors yourself by lining up your vessel on a set of leads and noting your compass heading.

Calculating Deviation: Choose a set of leads and place yourself right on the leads with your bow facing them. On the chart, it will give you the True bearing of those leads. The boat should be stationary for this exercise. You can determine the Deviation on different headings (of the vessel) by rotating the boat in a fixed point and taking bearings of the leads.
In our example we will assume the bow is facing the leads:
1. Note your ship's compass heading.
2. Apply Variation for your area (noted on the compass rose on your chart.)
3. The difference between the Magnetic bearing (True with Variation applied) and your Compass reading (C) is your Deviation for that heading.

The Deviation is usually slightly different for each course the vessel is on. This is usually noted in multiples of 10° on a Deviation card.

Don't forget your charts will show the TRUE bearing.
- Use the Variation to work out the Magnetic bearing (M).
- Get your COMPASS heading
- Note the difference between Magnetic and Compass, *that* will be your Deviation - FOR <u>THAT</u> HEADING ONLY.

If you use your GPS to check your Deviation, ensure your GPS is set to TRUE. This only works if you do not have a tidal stream or leeway to account for. GPS gives your course over the ground, not through the water.

C	103°	
D	°	
M	098°	
V	2°	East
T	100°	

Above, you have:
1) The True bearing from the chart of a set of leads (100°), i.e. the line you are sitting on (on your boat).
2) Your Compass reading (103°) (pointing at the leads).
3) The Variation (from your chart) can be added in and now you have calculated Magnetic (error East, Compass least which is 2° in this example).
4) Now, you just need to calculate the Deviation (remember it is for that course only).

The difference between 103° and 098° is 5°. So the Deviation is 5°, but you must make sure you note whether it is East or West Deviation. As the Compass number is the highest, it must be West (error West, Compass best).

C	103°	
D	5°	West
M	098°	
V	2°	East
T	100°	

On a Compass bearing of 103° C you have a Deviation of 5°W to apply. The Variation of 2°E helps you to determine your True bearing of 100°T or vice-versa if going from True to Compass. The Compass Adjuster determines the corrections for Deviation at 10° intervals from 000 to 360° on the compass, and he or she then records this information on the vessel's Deviation card.

<u>Variation</u>: In most parts of the world there is Variation. Variation changes with position, e.g. in the eastern Mediterranean Sea, Variation is minimal, but in the central North Atlantic, Variation can be much more. Moreover, some places will have a westerly Variation and some an easterly Variation.

In addition to the changes in Variation due to position, the Variation amount also changes over time (in the same position/area). This occurs because the position of the Magnetic North Pole slowly moves in a small circle. The movement of the Magnetic North Pole is known as Secular Variation or Secular Change and is indicated in the compass rose.

The Secular Change is indicated by the figure in brackets, next to the current Variation on the compass rose on your chart. For example: on Chart AUS 252 it states:

8°20′E 2009 (1′W)

This means that in 2009 the Variation was 8°20′E. Every year it moves 1′ West. From 2009 until 2013 is four years, so if you are using this chart in 2013 you would apply 4′West to 8°20′ (one minute for each year).

Therefore, you have 8°20′E and now you have to apply 4′W, which means you will have 8° 16′ E. See the diagram below:

If we apply 4′ West, then you can see that moving in a westerly direction 8 °20′ East becomes less (e.g. subtract the total yearly change).

If the Secular change was East, you can see that 8 °20′ East would become more (e.g. add on the yearly increase).

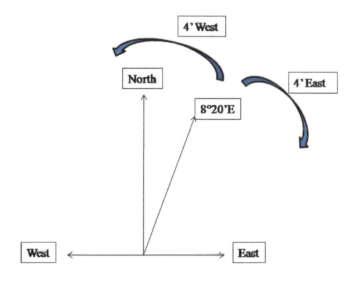

The degrees of Variation are more important than the minutes, it would be difficult to alter course by 20′!

In this example applying a Variation of 8° East is all you need to do.

Electronics
All your different electronic systems should run on their own individual circuits, so if one develops a fault you do not lose them all.

GPS - Errors
GPS contains errors and therefore your position should always be checked via other methods. *(See 'Position fixing' later on in this section.)*

Errors that occur within the GPS unit:
- Systematic: Some errors are caused by the changing satellite geometry. This is called Dilution of Precision (DOP). For a three-dimensional fix, you need four satellites. Ideally, one of the satellites should be directly overhead, with the other three separated by 120 degrees of azimuth. An arrangement other than this ideal situation will cause DOP inaccuracy. A good value of HDOP (Horizontal DOP) is between two and four, values in excess of this size are of poor accuracy - you can check the values on the GPS.

- Environmental errors: Moisture and salt in the air, poor weather conditions or lightning.
- Ionospheric delay: Signals from satellites bend on entering the ionosphere (this is also known as refraction) and their speed varies. (The ionosphere is the outer region of the Earth's atmosphere.)
- Multipath error: A satellite signal may be reflected off the water, or off metal objects on board your vessel. This may cause the GPS receiver antenna to receive the signal by two or more paths.
- Receiver errors: Mismatch of satellite signals.
- **Selective Availability**: SA is the military's ability to scramble the GPS readings. At the time of writing, the USA is not scrambling the signal (the SA was turned off in 2000). DGPS (Differential GPS) was developed to reduce SA.

Common errors in using the GPS:
- Offset: The main position fixing error occurs when using the GPS in combination with older charts. The correct offset from the chart needs to be applied to the GPS reading *(see 'Chart Errors' earlier in this section for full details).*
- Ensure your GPS settings match the spheroid of your chart. The GPS is usually operated on a spheroid called World Geodetic Spheroid 84 (WGS84). In the past, charts have been based on various spheroids, e.g., Australian Geodetic Datum 1966 (AGD66). You must check your chart to find out whether it is based on WGS84 or AGD66 (for example) and set your GPS accordingly.
- Magnetic or True: You can select Magnetic or True settings for bearings and courses. Ensure you have selected your preferred setting before completing these calculations. *(See 'True to Compass or Compass to True' under Charts, earlier in this section.)*
- Measurements: Are you reading statute miles or nautical miles for distance? Check your unit is set to nautical miles.
- Measurements: Are you reading knots for speed? Ensure your GPS is set correctly.
- Measurements: To reduce errors, check your GPS is set to degrees, minutes and decimals of a minute instead of seconds - to match your charts.
- Location: Follow the manufacturer's instructions when mounting your GPS. Obstructions can affect the signal and the GPS unit can affect the ship's compass.
- Input Errors: Double check the co-ordinates that have been inputted by you into the GPS. Ask someone else to read and check the numbers too.

GPS - Tracking Function
This function provides a track that, providing you have safely entered a harbour or port, you can simply follow the track back out and know that you are in safe water. This is a great advantage if you find yourself on a lee shore in the middle of the night.

Hand-Bearing Compass
This piece of equipment is invaluable when in a busy waterway.

You can take bearings of other vessels (relative to you) and jot them down. A few minutes later you do the same and compare with the first bearing. This will show you whether you are on a converging course. Remember, if the distance is diminishing between you and the target and the bearing is steady (or near to steady) you are both heading for the same bit of water. *(See 'Collision' earlier on in this section.)*

IALA International Association Of Lighthouse Authorities
The IALA is primarily known for its buoyage systems that are used in the pilotage of vessels at sea.

Regions: Two regions exist around the world. IALA region A and IALA region B. Region B covers the whole of the Americas, Japan, South Korea and the Philippines, while the rest of the world belongs to region A.

IALA buoyage system A: When entering a port or going upstream, green buoys (cones) will be on your starboard side, red buoys (cans) will be on your port side; when leaving port or heading downstream, the green will be on your port and the red on your starboard.

IALA buoyage system B: This is completely opposite to A. So if you are in a country that uses the B system, when entering port or going upstream, red will be on starboard and green on port.

Port & Starboard

Short story Port is so named as it is the side of the vessel that was alongside the wharf. Starboard comes from steerboard. Vessels were steered with a board on the 'steerboard' side (steered from the right), to protect the steer board they docked port side, hence port and starboard.

Latitude & Longitude
Writing latitude and longitude correctly is very important. The next person on watch must be able to read and understand what you have written on the chart and in the log book. Latitude should always be written first.

E.g.   00° 36' 12" S
                 080° 25' 42" W

Written above is: degrees (°), minutes (') and seconds ("). There are sixty minutes in a degree and sixty seconds in a minute. You can instantly spot an error if the minutes (') or seconds (") are sixty or higher. The highest number of minutes that can be used is fifty-nine. (001° = sixty minutes, therefore 000° 61' is written incorrectly and should be written as (and is the same as) 001° 01'.

Seconds can be written as decimals of a minute. This makes it possible (and easier) to use a calculator. For example, the above latitude and longitude would be written:
                 00° 36.2' S
                 080° 25.7' W

0.1 of a minute is 6 seconds, therefore:
12 seconds is 0.2 of a minute and 42 seconds is 0.7 of a minute.

To convert:
        To convert seconds to decimal divide the seconds by 60.
        To convert decimal to seconds multiply decimal by 60.

        0.1 of a minute x 60 = 6 seconds.
        Therefore 0.1 of a minute is 6 seconds.

To calculate the Lat./Long. examples above:

        12 seconds to decimal of a minute: 12 / 60 = 0.2
        42 seconds to decimal of a minute: 42 / 60 = 0.7

Our charts are in degrees, minutes and decimals of a minute and our GPS is set the same. To reduce errors, set your GPS to match your charts. *(See 'GPS Errors' earlier in this section.)*

(See Measurements & Conversions section for more calculations and all the decimals of an hour.)

Navigation Hints
Never rely on one source for determining your position *(see GPS Errors earlier in this section).*

Always study the charts for your journey with great care before departing. Check your position regularly. *(See 'Bearing fix' above and 'Position fixing' further on in this section.)* Double check the waypoints before and after inputting them into the GPS.

Never pass a significant landmark without checking it on your chart. Having lots of electronic navigation equipment is not an excuse for lack of knowledge or lazy navigation.

Square or rectangular shaped pencils are better for navigation, as they don't roll away.

The navigation got a whole lot easier in Canada. Narrow waterways left no doubt of direction, however the Lift Lock (or boat lift) gave a new meaning to our altitude on the GPS.

The Peterborough Lift Lock is a boat lift located on the Trent Canal in the city of Peterborough, Ontario, Canada.

Navigation Lights
You can tell which way a vessel is heading by their navigation lights. If you see both green and red lights of another vessel, it is heading towards you. Of course, the red light is their port light and green their starboard light, but ships can have many different lights. Their navigation lights can become lost within other lights i.e. cabin lights or deck lights.
Keep a book on board of the complete International Collision Regulations so you can identify their light signals, such as:

- 'Not Under Command' (two all round red lights, one above the other - vertically).
- 'Restricted In Ability to Manoeuvre' (three all round lights, red, white, red, one above the other - vertically).

The priority of the 'give way vessel' and the 'stand on vessel' changes for different vessels and different circumstances. You need to know the rules and how to react before a close quarters situation develops.

When coastal cruising, be aware that ship lights between you and the coast can be lost within the shore lights. Maintain extra vigilance, particularly in harbours.

Large ships can take a long time to stop and/or alter course. Their momentum carries them a long way.

Collision Regulations: Do you know what these signals mean?

They tell you what the boat is doing and which side is safe to pass.

What are the night-time lights for this vessel?

Answer: This vessel is Restricted in Ability to Manoeuvre (RAM) as it is dredging. It is safe to pass on the side of the two diamonds.

The black ball, black diamond, black ball in a vertical line tell us that the vessel is RAM.
The two black balls on one side tell us NOT to pass this side, this is where the area of danger exists.
The two black diamonds tell us that this is the side we must pass, i.e. it is the safe side to pass.

At night-time, or in restricted visibility, the RAM signal is a vertical line of lights: red-white-red.
The side to pass (black diamonds during the day) will be two vertical green lights.
The side of danger (not to pass), indicated by two black balls during the day, will be red vertical lights at night (or in restricted visibility).

Sunset To Sunrise: We've known some cruisers to turn their navigation lights off at night to conserve power, and some do not turn them on at all. I think this is a very bad idea and breaks all the rules of good seamanship. Fit LEDs. Aside from an emergency, if you do not have enough power to run lights then you should not be out there at night. The oceans may seem large, but on most trips we have had to change course for other vessels. What if they can't see you? If you've fallen asleep? If another boat is 'running blind' also?. . . Is it worth it? Invest in LED lights, particularly for the masthead lights.

Parallel Indexing

'Parallel Indexing' or 'Blind Pilotage' involves navigating along a pre-planned track in waters where standard methods of navigating are impractical because the waters are so confined, or where co-ordinates are offset as per the chart title information *(see 'Chart errors' earlier in this section)*. Usual methods of navigation, e.g. transferring radar ranges to the chart and transferring visual bearings to the chart, are impractical because it is not quick enough.

Parallel Indexing is where you use your radar's VRM (Variable Range Marker) and an offset bearing line. (Some modern radars have an electronic indexing line that can be utilised anywhere on the display.) It is a line drawn or displayed that is parallel to your heading line.

First a note on radar operation: The radar display can be set up to show North-Up, Ship's Head-Up (which is usually abbreviated to Heads-Up) or Course-Up picture. Some people prefer a North-Up presentation because the display is orientated to look the same as the chart, and the display is stabilised so only the heading marker moves and you do not lose the picture when altering course.

Others prefer to maintain Ship's Head-Up (usually preferred on open waters), because the view outside the window is the same as the radar; however, care needs to be taken. This is an unstabilised display and when you alter course, the heading marker remains upward while the whole picture rotates in the opposite direction by the amount of course altered. During course alteration the whole radar picture rotates, making the radar difficult to read until the vessel settles on its new heading. Course-Up stabilised and North-Up stabilised works well, as yawing is eliminated.

How to do Parallel Indexing: You place a line at a chosen clearance range from the centre (your boat), parallel to your heading line and on the side where the obstruction/headland exists (using an offset EBL (electronic bearing line) or a PI (Parallel Index) line if your radar provides one). Use the VRM (variable range marker) to set the EBL/PI line at the appropriate distance and make sure you do not breach that line. (See diagram below.)

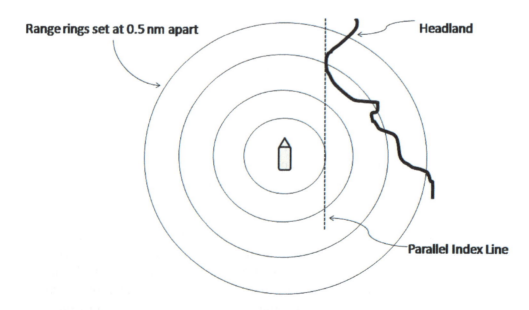

The vessel is in the centre of the range rings, the Parallel Index line is set at 0.5 nm away from the vessel.

Providing you keep the Index line on the headland, you will maintain the most direct course, staying the set distance (in this case 0.5 nm) from the headland.

If set correctly, this will keep you in safe water, away from navigation hazards. Your radar instruction book may not provide instructions specifically for Parallel Indexing. Ours doesn't, we simply use the bearing line (EBL) set as an offset bearing line, as our parallel line.

Patience

Sailing and patience go hand in hand. If being patient is not your forte, it soon will be after time spent cruising. Waiting to cross a bar, waiting for daylight, waiting for the right moment to take your dinghy ashore through waves . . . not having patience can be lethal. A wrong tide could pitchpole the boat or flip a dinghy. Making an unknown entrance into port at night could easily be a disaster. If it means you have to wait another ten hours for a safe entrance at dawn, well, you just have to wait.

Let time train you to keep calm and patient. Experiences will come to you; you will not need to go looking for them.

Short story Thirty miserly minutes too late: We arrived at Bahia de Caráquez, Ecuador at 6a.m. The 'waiting room' co-ordinates were spot on (this was an anchor spot outside the main channel where we had to wait for a pilot). On VHF we called 'Puerto Amistad, this is the sailing vessel Pyewacket II'. The radio stayed as silent as the calm sea; at 7a.m. it crackled into life, but by then we had missed the necessary high tide by an impossibly tiny 30 minutes. The entrance into Bahia de Caráquez was through an unmarked channel, uncomfortably close to the shoreline and shallow in places. It was cheap insurance, at US$30, to hire a pilot. Anchoring in the exposed 'waiting room' was our only option. For twenty-three hours we impatiently waited for high tide and daylight to synchronise. With visions of upping anchor during the night while riding the building swells, we tried to sleep in the afternoon. The 2,800 nautical miles from Acapulco (via a brief stop at Isle de Cocos) had taken its toll. Dirty-steel coloured water beneath persistent squalls and looming breasts of black clouds streaked with lightning had been our consistent company for too long! But even though we were close to the end of the trip, we <u>had</u> to be patient.

Ports

Prior to entering a new port, you must carry out as much research as possible. As well as books and manuals, if there is local knowledge available, seek it out. If the port is nearby to your present location and the opportunity arises to visit that port via land, grab this opportunity to view the entrance. It will provide you with some very useful information.

If you arrive at a new port at night, stand-off and wait for dawn before entering (unless it is a major port that you know well, it is well marked, charted accurately and your charts are up to date). A few hours of boredom is worth the wait. Bar entrances can be particularly lethal.

Water through hatches that are inadvertently left open when crossing a bar is to be expected. However, this picture was taken on the southern side of Cuba, after sailing in wind over tide. We experienced so much water over the deck; the dogged front hatch let water in, right on top of our bed! I am unhappily cleaning the bedding and mattress with fresh water.

Position Fixing

Fixing your position can be done several ways besides using your GPS. Batteries can fail and GPSs can break and have errors *(see GPS errors earlier in this section)*. Have some handy position fixing tricks up your sleeve.

To take a fix, <u>always</u> note the time the fix was taken. This is imperative for DR (Deduced Reckoning - read on for full information). It is fun to experiment with different ways to check your position, especially when coastal cruising. *(See 'Bearings' earlier in this section for another way to check your position.)*

Position: double the angle off the bow

This calculation takes advantage of the properties of an isosceles triangle. An isosceles triangle has two sides of equal length and consequently, it has two internal angles that are also equal. This rule is used when the second bearing between the bow of your boat and the target is double the angle of the first bearing.

<u>How to perform 'double the angle off the bow' on board</u>: See Figure 1(below) for a complete depiction of what double the angle off the bow refers to. Your first angle off the bow needs to be between 020° to 045° (less that 020° can reduce accuracy). So how do you measure this?

FIGURE 1 – DOUBLE THE ANGLE OFF THE BOW

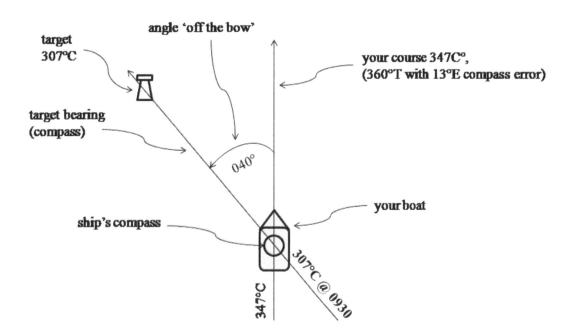

In this example the angle off the bow is a red bearing, i.e. Red 040° (Red-because it is on our port side). This is determined by reading your compass course (347°C), then reading the target's compass bearing (307°C). The difference between the two is the target's angle 'off the bow', i.e. 347°C - 307°C = Red 040°

Step by step: how to calculate distance off, using double the angle off the bow method:
1. Take note of the compass course you are steering. In our example, the course steered is 347°C (see Figure 2).
2. With your hand-bearing compass, or by sighting over your ship's compass, take a compass bearing of the chosen target (a lighthouse makes a good target).
3. Record this bearing, your log reading and the time. For example, Course = 347°C, bearing to Target (e.g. Nobby's Head Lighthouse) = 307°C, Time = 0930hrs, Log reading = 0.
4. The difference between course steered and the target's bearing is the target's angle off the bow. Study Figures 1 and 2.
   While steering a steady course of 347°C an identifiable land target (Nobby's Head Lighthouse) was sighted bearing 307°C.
   Angle off the bow = 347°C - 307°C = 040°
   As the target is on our port side, we can call this angle RED 040°. *(See bearings in this section for a full explanation of Red and Green Bearings and Relative Bearings.)*
5. If our first angle off the bow = RED 040°, then doubling this angle will give us RED 080°.
6. The compass reading required for the second bearing line to the target will equal the course steered minus the double the angle off the bow.
   See Figure 2.
   347°C - 080° = 267°C
7. As you are proceeding along the chosen course (347°C), keep an eye on the target's bearing. When the same target (Nobby's Head Lighthouse) bears 267°C, note down (again) the time and distance run (from the log).
   See Figure 2.
   Course steered = 347°C, target bearing = 267°C, distance run = 5nm, time of second bearing = 1030hrs.

8. The number of sea miles covered (assuming no current or leeway) equals the distance the vessel is from the target. So you can say, 'At 1030hrs we are 5nm from Nobby's Head Lighthouse, which is on a bearing line of 267°C.'

FIGURE 2 - DOUBLE THE ANGLE OFF THE BOW

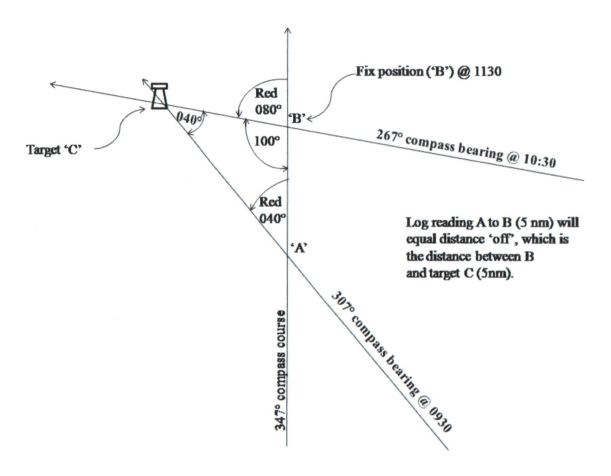

When you get the chance, have a go; it's actually quite simple and straightforward.

Another useful method is to guess 045° off the bow using your arm. Swing your arm from pointing at the bow to pointing abeam of your boat. Half of this swing (090°/2) is 45°. When the target is 045° off the bow, note the time and log reading, double the angle off the bow will be 090° or abeam.

When target is abeam, note the time and log reading. As before, the distance run will equal your distance off the target.

This method is easier, but it is not predictive, i.e. you may have to avoid a danger that is lying off a headland. By using an initial angle off the bow less than 045° (e.g. 030°), you can predict your clearance off the headline on arrival. By using 045° as your initial angle, by the time 090° (abeam) comes up, you could be in the danger zone!

Remember: to be able to plot the fixed position on a chart, convert all bearings to TRUE. We have used a total Compass error for the above example of 13°E. So we have to add 13°E to all the Compass bearings to obtain the True bearing for the chart work.

The Isosceles Triangle - how does it help us?
Refer to Figure 2. A straight line (our course) = 180°. We cut that line with the double angle of 080°, therefore 180° - 080° = 100° remaining.

This 100° forms the angle at the top of our isosceles triangle.

All triangles have three internal corner angles. The value of all three angles added together always equals 180°.

In our example, we have 100°+ 40° = 140°. We know triangles have a total of 180° internally, therefore the remaining angle must = 40°. There it is: our isosceles triangle!

We have a base line of a triangle, A to C and the two remaining sides (A to B and B to C) are equal in length because we have an isosceles triangle with two equal internal angles.

If we know the length of one side (our course covered, A to B) from our log reading, we then know the length of the side B to C.

A to B = 5 nautical miles, therefore B to C = 5 nautical miles.

We are 5 nautical miles from the target at 1030hrs.

Position - DR
In navigation, Ded Reckoning (DR) is the process of calculating your position by using a previously determined fix. You advance your first fix based upon known or estimated speeds over elapsed time and course. You must maintain the same speed, time and course for the duration (note length of time) or calculate an average. Of course, set and drift (effects of current) need to be accounted for at times to provide an Estimated Position (read on for more information on Estimated Positions).

To rely on a DR position, you must ensure your first fix is correct. As the new calculation is based on this position, if it is wrong the errors will accumulate. For example, you have obtained a good fix and for an hour you have been sailing at 5 knots. During this time, you have travelled five miles through the water. If your course has been the same, simply extend your course line and mark off five miles (measure miles off the latitude scale nearest to your location). This is assuming no set and drift.

The following example is a vessel travelling at 6 knots for one and a half hours *(see Speed, Distance, Time formula later in this section for more complex calculations)*.

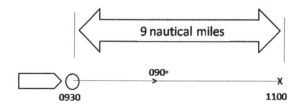

Course 090°, speed 6 knots.

After 1.5 hours distance = 9 nautical miles

The circle is the convention for a position fix by ranges and/or bearings. The cross is the convention for a DR position fix.

In one hour at 6 knots you would travel six miles, in another half an hour you would travel another three miles, therefore over an hour and a half you would have travelled a total of nine nautical miles. (The DR position is marked with an X and the time noted.)Remember, this example does not allow for set and drift. Estimated Position (EP) is DR with estimated set and drift applied.

Position - Estimated Position (EP)
Plot your DR position on your chart. From your DR position, lay off the estimated set and drift of the current.

For example, if the current is running to the north at 2 knots and you have worked your DR course over one and a half hours, then plot the EP from your DR position. This will be 2 (knots of current) x 1.5 (hrs), giving you a distance of three miles. Therefore, from your DR position, draw a line heading north (direction of current) and the distance of three nautical miles will be your EP. See diagram below.

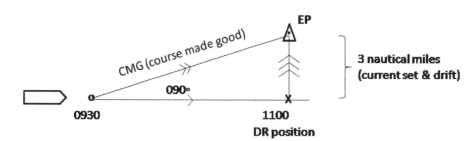

Northerly current is 2 knots, therefore over 1.5 hours the distance = 3 nautical miles.

Plot this on your chart to obtain your EP (Estimated Position). Note: the standard convention for EP is a triangle.

The line from your 0930 position to your EP position is your Course Made Good (CMG), you actually did this course.

(See 'Set and drift' later in this section.)

Position - Running Fix

A running fix is a fix using two bearings and it doesn't matter how far the course line is from the bearing object, therefore it is used when you have no means of measuring the range.

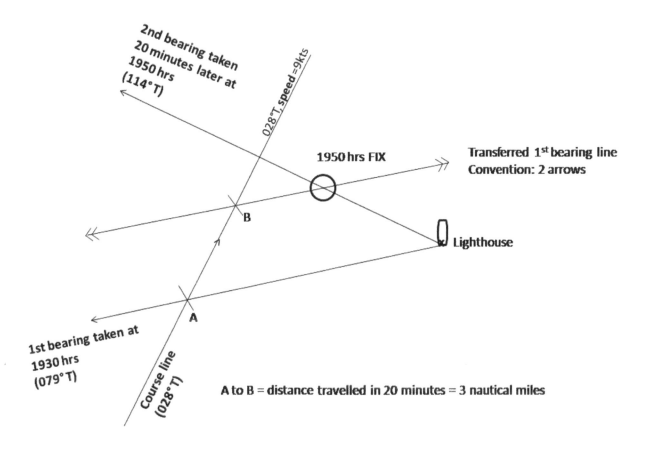

Step by step: how to plot your position using the running fix method:

1. Plot your course line. Label this line with your course and speed, in this example, 028°T at 9 knots. This is plotted in the area you are in and the direction you are going. At the moment you do not know where, exactly, you are - so this line indicates direction and speed only, NOT position.

2. Take the first bearing of a known charted landmark (079°T), lay this bearing off on your chart (ensure it is TRUE) and note the time (1930hrs) on your chart. You are on this bearing line somewhere at 1930hrs. This must cross your course line. (Some people prefer to lay off the first bearing line on the chart to start, so they ensure the course line crosses this bearing line. It does not matter where your course line is, providing it is in the right direction and crosses the first bearing line.)

3. For a period of time you continue on the same course (028°T).

4. Take a second bearing from the same landmark (now at 114° T in our example), note the time (1950hrs) and lay off on your chart (TRUE), this also crosses your course line.

5. From your first bearing line, along your course line (A), mark the distance travelled in the time period between bearings (A to B). The time period in this example is twenty minutes (convert to decimal = 0.33hr) speed is 9kts and distance 3nm. (9nm x 0.33 = 3nm).

6. On your chart, transfer the first bearing line (079°) to the distance covered in twenty minutes (B). Draw this line parallel (use your parallel rule) to your first bearing. This line is marked with double arrows at each end to denote its meaning (transferred bearing line).

7. The point where the transferred first bearing line intersects the **second bearing line** is your FIX.

8. The accuracy of the running fix depends on the accuracy of the estimate of the vessel's movement between A and B. (The movement made good between the two observed bearings or position lines.)

9. Your fix places you approximately four nautical miles off the lighthouse bearing 114°T.

Position: Correct Chart Work & Symbols

On the chart, use the following symbols so everyone understands the workings.

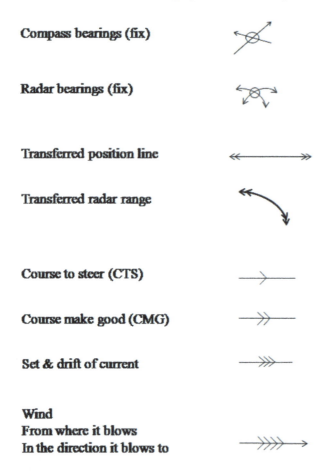

Compass bearings (fix)

Radar bearings (fix)

Transferred position line

Transferred radar range

Course to steer (CTS)

Course make good (CMG)

Set & drift of current

Wind
From where it blows
In the direction it blows to

Protractors &Parallel Rulers

We recommend using a Chart Protractor (e.g. Bi-Rola) as opposed to (or in addition to) parallel rules. You can place this protractor (like a big ruler) anywhere on the chart and rotate the protractor to line up to your grid lines. You can then read off the bearing that the ruler is lying on.

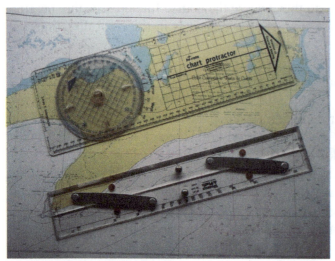

The top ruler is the Chart Protractor. Parallel rules are a good tool, but when 'walking' them across a chart it is easy to slip and slide, especially on a moving boat.

Position - Radar

Radar *ranges* are an accurate way to plot your position. However, radar *bearings* are not as accurate due to the movement of yawing and the horizontal beam width of the radar *(see 'Bearings' earlier on in this section).*

To fix your position from radar ranges, find two or three suitable landmarks and use your radar to establish the distance to/from these landmarks. Plot these ranges on your chart to obtain a fix. For example, if headland A is three nautical miles away and headline B is two nautical miles away, draw an arc using your pencil compass, set at three nautical miles from headland A, and two nautical miles from headland B. Where they intersect is your position. Three ranges are better than two as they reveal any errors that may occur; e.g. if lines are not all crossing on one spot.

Radar Reflector

Timber and plastic boats are poor radar reflectors and will not give a strong echo on screen. The beam goes straight through these materials. A simple radar reflector fixes the problem, and these can be homemade. Fix aluminium plates together at angles that would reflect a beam. Eight corner reflectors are placed back-to-back in an octahedron shape, this creates a corner reflector that will reflect radar waves coming from any direction. It is best to hang this type of reflector in the 'rain catcher' position, for better reflection. A reflector is a piece of equipment that I would not leave port without. When we've called up large ships from our fibreglass boat, to check that they have seen us, it's very reassuring to hear that they had spotted us on radar long before they saw us visually.

A quick fix would be aluminium drink cans crushed and hauled up in a net. Like all equipment on board, a radar reflector is an additional aid to navigation, not something you can rely on entirely.

Reciprocal Bearings

If you have reciprocal dyslexia, an easy way to calculate the reciprocal bearing is to plus or minus 200, then adjust by twenty accordingly. For example, for the reciprocal of 050°, add 200° = 250°, then just minus 20° = 230°.

Reefs

If you have to pick your way through reefs (even with waypoints to follow), if possible, do so with the sun up high and behind you. Position someone up high on the bow or up ratlines fitted to your mast shrouds to look out.

Wearing polarised sunglasses can be very helpful when locating reefs.

Rounding Capes

Most capes will have stronger winds than usual. The wind picks up speed around a sheer face, and this is known as an acceleration zone. Even in light winds, reef sails before these known zones, especially if you notice white water at the cape.

Safe Water (Navigation)

At all times know where your safe water is (i.e. good depth, no obstructions), for emergency collision avoidance or giving room to the stand on vessel. This is very important in busy waterways.

Set & Drift

Current will push you in a certain direction (called 'set') and over a period of time, the current will move you a distance (called 'drift'). To counteract set and drift, you need to know the speed and direction of the current. (You could do this by taking a good fix position and comparing that position to your DR position. The difference between your good fix and DR position will be the set and drift).

Finding the Course to Steer (CTS) allowing for a known current:
- The diagram below shows the vessel at A.
- From A the vessel wishes to get to point B.
- A to C shows the set and drift quantities of the current in one hour.
- A to B is the course to make good (CMG), (you actually travel along the line AB).
- A to D is the speed made good.
- C to D is the speed of the vessel through the water.

Constructing the triangle from Current and Wind to determine Course to Steer (CTS), allowing for known current and leeway.

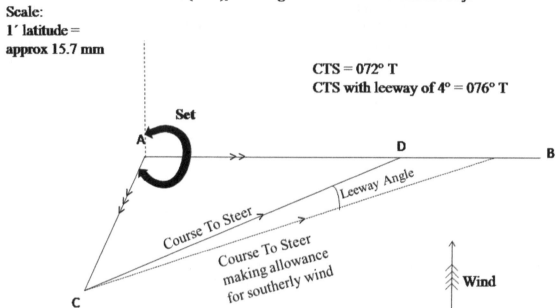

Scale:
1′ latitude = approx 15.7 mm

CTS = 072° T
CTS with leeway of 4° = 076° T

Due to the current, even though you are doing 6 knots through the water you are only doing 4.5 knots over the ground.

The current is effectively slowing you down by 1.5 knots.

From A, the vessel wants to make good a course of 090° TRUE, in order to reach point B.
The known current is set at 190°T at 2.2 knots. The vessel's speed is 6 knots.

Step by step: how to find the course to steer:
1. On your chart, lay off the course to make good, which is AB.
2. Draw a vector triangle over a one hour period. This will help you calculate how to steer your boat along the A to B line. To do this, plot one hour of current (the set and the drift) from A and label this as C.
3. From C as the starting point, lay off the distance the ship will travel through the water in one hour, (6nm measured off the latitude scale, 1′ = 1nm). The line should start at C and end on the original AB line, mark this as D.
4. The direction CD is the True course to steer from A, in order to counteract the current.
5. The distance AD is the distance you will cover in one hour, that is the actual distance made good (DMG) in one hour, and is therefore your speed made good (SMG), i.e. you cover

6. 4.5nm in one hour, therefore 4.5 knots is your speed. (Your GPS would say 4.5 knots due to the actions of the current; this is the actual speed over ground you will achieve, even though you are doing 6 knots through the water.)
7. The distance AB (7.1nm) is divided by the speed made good AD (4.5 knots) to find the ETA.

Time = D/S
Time = 7.1/4.5 = 1.58 hours   0.58 x 60 = 35 minutes   = 1 hour 35 minutes

Therefore if the ETD (Estimated Time of Departure) = 11:00, then ETA = 12:35

Leeway
We have so far calculated the current effects (above).

Understanding the effect the wind has on your vessel comes from experience. Different vessel structures have different windage effects. This is your vessel's leeway. *(See 'Leeway Angle' on the next page.)*

To counteract the leeway, in the above example the CTS (Course To Steer) is approximately 072°T. If your vessel is required to steer 072°T with a southerly wind that you expect to cause 4° leeway (determined through your experience on your vessel), then the vessel's track will be 076°T (072° + 4°). In other words, you have to steer this vessel 4° into the wind to make allowance for leeway that is caused.

When counteracting set and drift on your chart, always lay off the set of the known current first to determine the course to steer (CTS), and then apply leeway. As a matter of course, most helmsmen/women automatically steer to counteract these effects, if they can see their target. In the ocean, you have to calculate these compensations.

Doesn't all this make the GPS a wonderful invention? For those cruising under wind vanes or electronic steering, it is interesting to see and understand why your ship's compass reads different to your GPS.

Course To Steer
This is the True course to steer with allowance for set, drift and leeway. This CTS has been calculated on your chart in True. To steer by Compass you must convert the True course to Compass course. We do this by applying Variation and Deviation. *(See 'Compass' earlier in this section.)*

(CMG) Course Made Good (True)
This is the actual course over the ground between two observed positions. Or the course you wish to make good.

Distance & Speed
This is related to the vessel's movement through the water and is usually established from the ship's log.

(DMG) Distance Made Good
This is the measurement between two observed fixed positions, measured 'over the ground' not through the water. The effective distance you actually covered.

(SMG) Speed Made Good

This is related to the measurement between two positions, measured 'over the ground' not through the water, i.e. the effective speed obtained.

Set

This is the direction towards which a current and/or tidal stream flows.

Drift

This is the distance covered in a given time due to the movement of a current and/or tidal stream.

Rate Of Drift

This is the speed of the current and/or tidal stream, i.e. the distance, in nautical miles, the current covers in one hour.

Drift Angle

This is the angular difference between the track through the water and the track over the ground, caused by the current or tidal stream.

Leeway

This is the effect of the wind blowing the vessel to leeward. It depends on the wind's strength and direction, type of vessel and its draught. This is generally estimated from experience.

Leeway Angle

This is the angular difference between the ship's heading and the track through the water. Observe your wake compared to the fore and aft line of your vessel.

Position Line

This is a line on the chart on which the vessel lies or has lain. It may be straight for bearings or curved for ranges *(see Radar)*.

Sextant

We sometimes break up long sea journeys by taking star sights. It is good practice and very satisfying to find your position by the stars. It also provides the confidence to know you can get home if all else fails. Practice celestial navigation prior to your voyage and take all your books and equipment on board. A celestial computer is a great aid and speeds up the whole process, however they are prone to inherent failures of electronic equipment (usually a flat battery and loss of data).

Speed, Distance, Time Calculations

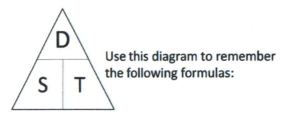

Use this diagram to remember the following formulas:

$$D = S \times T$$
$$S = D / T$$
$$T = D / S$$

D= Distance, S= Speed, T= Time.

Don't forget to convert the decimal figure into minutes. For example, to work out the time taken to travel 5 nautical miles at a speed of 10 knots using the formula above:

Time   =   D/S

Time   =   5 /10   =   0.5 of an hour

0.5 is half an hour, i.e. 30 minutes. You calculate this by:

0.5 (decimal of an hour) x 60 = 30 minutes

(For more information see 'Latitude and Longitude' earlier in this section.)

Speed

Boats have an optimum speed, which is their hull speed. The displacement speed is governed by waterline length.

To calculate the maximum displacement speed of your boat, a theoretical rule of thumb calculation is as follows:

<u>If the waterline length (WLL) is in metres</u>:
Maximum speed in knots = 2.43 x the square root of the waterline length (WLL) of the boat in metres.
e.g. for a WLL of 15 metres the maximum speed is 2.43 x $\sqrt{15}$

= 2.43 x 3.9 = 9.5 knots (maximum hull speed for WLL of 15 metres).

<u>If the waterline length (WLL) is in feet</u>:
Maximum speed in knots = 1.37 x the square root of the waterline length (WLL) of the boat in feet.

e.g. for a WLL of 49 feet the maximum speed is 1.37 x $\sqrt{49}$

= 1.37 x 7 = 9.6 knots (maximum hull speed for WLL of 49 feet).

This is an approximate guide, as the factor varies with different shaped hulls.

Speed vs. Wind

On board both our vessels we achieved the hull speed in 15 to 20 knots of wind. Wind speeds in excess of this are superfluous and just cause bigger seas and more discomfort. This is something we bear in mind when deciding on the day to depart.

Stronger winds apply pressure and stresses on your equipment and on you. Obviously we can't always pick our weather on long voyages, but this is worth considering for those first few days of a voyage.

Waypoints

We like using waypoints and a track on our charts to follow, this makes us more inclined to thoroughly study our proposed route on the chart before setting off. Take note of where danger lies and to which side of your intended route safety is found.

After studying your desired route on your chart, plot your course on the chart. Note and double check the waypoints and put them in your GPS. Always write the lat./long. on the chart with the bearing to/from the next waypoint. We both check the co-ordinates on both the chart and GPS, as errors can easily occur. Plotting regularly on a paper chart will clearly show any errors along the way.

Weather At Sea
Weatherfax is simple software that is easily downloaded from the Internet to enable you to receive synoptic charts and wind/wave charts over the SSB (HF) radio. *(See 'Weather' in the Voyage Preparation section.)*

Weatherfax resources: JVcomm32 is free to use for a trial period. Thereafter registration is required. http://www.jvcomm.de/index_e.html

Wind - Apparent & True
When your boat is moving, the wind indicator (or your wetted thumb) shows 'apparent' wind. This means that the direction and strength of the wind includes your movement, i.e. if you are going downwind, the wind feels less, but if you are going into the wind, it feels stronger. True wind is the actual force of the wind if you were stationary. Try to give your True wind when talking to other boats.

Resources: http://www.sailingcourse.com/keelboat/true_wind_calculator.htm

Wind vectors: See diagram below.

Step by step: how to calculate true wind:
1. Draw a line representing your True course and speed, for example: course 000° T, speed 5 knots. Choose a scale to use, say 5 centimetres for 5 knots (one cm per knot).

2. Place an arrow at the head of the line where your bow is pointing.

3. Draw the apparent wind speed and direction, i.e. where the wind is blowing to, with the head of the arrow pointing at the stern of your course and speed line. In our example, that is approximately 040° off the ship's bow at 10 knots, therefore the line would be ten centimetres long. (The drawing below is not to scale.)

4. The True wind is the resultant vector drawn from the tail of the apparent wind line to the head of your vessel's course and speed line.

5. Measure the True wind line using the scale you have been using for the rest of the vector (in this example, measure how many centimetres the True wind line is, that will be your True wind speed in knots).

6. Measure the angle of the True wind. You now have the True wind speed and direction.

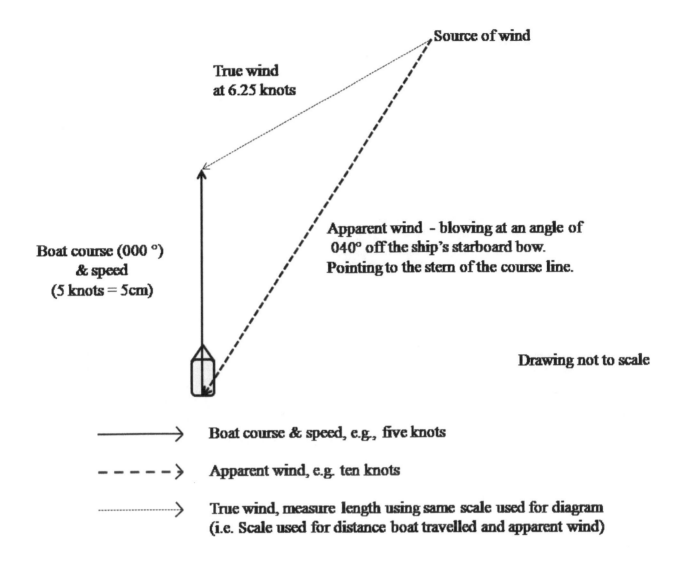

Source of wind

True wind
at 6.25 knots

Boat course (000 °)
& speed
(5 knots = 5cm)

Apparent wind - blowing at an angle of
040° off the ship's starboard bow.
Pointing to the stern of the course line.

Drawing not to scale

→ Boat course & speed, e.g., five knots

- - - → Apparent wind, e.g. ten knots

⋯⋯⋯→ True wind, measure length using same scale used for diagram
(i.e. Scale used for distance boat travelled and apparent wind)

Rules to follow

1. Speed is always drawn to the same scale for each line of the vector.

2. Direction is always drawn in the same type of bearing, e.g. True, Magnetic or Compass.

3. True is best, then you can calculate the True wind (direction the vessel is going to and direction the wind is coming from).

4. The head of the arrow must be placed at the head of the line, indicating direction.

5. Apparent wind blows to your stern (on your course and speed line).

6. True wind blows to your bow (on your course and speed arrow).

Mariah II running with the wind on her starboard quarter, with every scrap of sail up - perfect. This picture makes us teary with the great memories!

Additional Resources:
Boatsafe.com: www.boatsafe.com
NOAA (National Oceanic and Atmospheric Administration Downloads:
http://www.nauticalcharts.noaa.gov/mcd/Raster/download_agreement.htm
Cruising Guides: http://www.freecruisingguide.com/

Cruising Compendiums and other great info: http://www.svsoggypaws.com/index.htm
PC Chart Plotter and GPS Navigation software: http://www.sping.com/seaclear/
Free Marine Chart Planner: http://www.macupdate.com/app/mac/33427/polarview
Maximum Hull Speed Calculator: http://www.sailingusa.info/cal__hull_speed.htm

Navigation Worksheets: http://www.jsward.com/navigation/index.shtml

Calculate set and drift, DR, TVMDC, running fix, rhumb line, speed/distance/time:
http://marinersguide.com/software/

Chart Plotter and GPS Navigation Software: http://opencpn.org/ocpn/

Tide Program: http://www.wxtide32.com/

Find the correct local Variation from:
http://ngdc.noaa.gov/geomag/magfield.shtml
www.geomag.nrcan.gc.ca/apps/mdcal-eng.php
www.ritchienavigation.com/service/compensation.html

PERSONAL EQUIPMENT

Bikes/Bicycles

Finding space on board for bikes is not easy, but it's well worth the effort. Having bikes gives you the ability and opportunity to explore new destinations.

In San Diego while preparing Pyewacket for ocean voyages, we found the bikes a godsend.

Regularly spray your bikes with WD40, or any anti-corrosion spray. (Inox is really good.)

Stowing: If you do not have enough space to stow your bikes down below, stow them upside down on the outside of your cockpit's stanchions. Ours sat on their handlebars and seats, on the toe rail. Hold them in place using elastic with hooks on either end (bungee cord/Occy strap). Warning: take care using bungee cord, if the hook slips off while the elastic is tight, it will give you a nasty slap. *(See picture under 'Heating' in Health & Well-being section - look carefully you can see the wheels of our bikes!)*

Theft: New bikes can be a temptation to others. As well as having good locks, use old paint you have stowed away to make your new bikes look used. They won't attract so much attention and will be less tempting for sticky fingers.

Baskets: Do not solely rely on the basket bracket; they can easily get knocked off over the side. Use wire ties to hold it firmly in place.

A milk crate is a handy 'basket' atop of a standard bike rack. Simply use bungee cord to keep in place.

A canvas bag strapped onto your handle bars with a flat piece of wood in the bottom (to provide some stability) makes a makeshift basket too.

Folding bikes: Folding bikes are an option for space saving, but they are more expensive and harder to peddle on longer journeys as the wheels are that much smaller. Some people love them, some people hate them - if possible, try one before you buy one.

In our inflatable dinghy it is much easier to transport the bikes to/from shore than it was in our hard dinghy. However, we usually get some funny looks.

Camera

Invest in a good quality camera to capture your memories. We find the best options are cameras that are digital (ease of use), waterproof and drop proof (hoping not to test that part).

Our digital camera has two gasket sealed areas where water could penetrate if the seal is not perfect. We clean these areas and ensure they are closed properly before taking it into the water.

To improve the seal, wipe a very thin smear of Vaseline over the dry gasket or o-ring. This lubricates the seal and allows it to flow into the shape of the lid for enhanced water protection.

When shopping for spare parts, take a picture of the spare part/item you want to purchase. An idea of the size of the item is good to incorporate in the picture too.

Taking photos of all your equipment on board, including serial numbers, is an added benefit should you have to make an insurance claim (e.g. in case items are stolen or you suffer a lightning strike).

When leaving and arriving with other boats, co-ordinate your vessels for sailing shots. Good shots when underway are hard to achieve, but worth the effort.

Clothes

Don't throw away any unwanted clothes, cut them up and keep them for rags. Alternatively, if visiting poorer countries, they make great trading items and/or gifts.

Good times and great friends - celebrating Tahiti landfall, wearing our smart clothes in Suva Yacht Club!

Left to right: Spencer & Nana (SV Adverse Conditions), Noel & Jackie, Kian & Alim (SV My Chance), Elyse & Robert (SV Iron Mistress).

Socks and sleeves from tops make great 'gloves' for stowing wine bottles.

What clothes to take: We cover all bases: cool and light, through to snug and warm. You can experience four seasons in one day. Think about where you are cruising. If you are in the tropics, do not assume you will be warm all the time, and in any case your plans may well change. The trick is variety, comfort and not too much! Having good warm clothes is imperative for comfort on those night watches and to fend off hypothermia. *(See Health & Well-being section.)* In cold weather, we like lots of thin layers and cotton long johns. Protection from the sun is just as important as the cold.

Noel often wears long sleeved cotton shirts to protect his skin from the sun. I like t-shirts and shorts, but I have a supply of comfortable summer dresses and skirts. A range of sarongs is also imperative for my comfort. *(See the versatility of Sarongs in the Health & Well-being section or at www.1worldsarongs.com.)* On board in hot weather, a plain cotton dress or sarong is my preferred attire.

Recycling shops are a great way to stock up on sailing clothes.

One or two smart items of clothing are a must (don't forget shoes); you never know when you are going to receive that special invitation.

Have fun! We printed up Mariah II t-shirts for the 'team' traversing the Panama Canal.

Colin (Noel's brother), Jackie, Noel and Roy (Jackie's dad).

Short story Charity shops aren't just for clothes. In two different recycling shops in America, one on the east coast and one on the west coast, we found world atlas globes. On each boat we have sailed on we have had a globe and been surprised to find that we refer to it a lot. (Not for navigation, of course, but generally for geography, distances and scribing a proud line of our track travelled so far.)

It is hard to keep clothes on board stain free. For oil spots, I find that rubbing in a little washing up liquid or laundry powder right into the stain prior to washing can really help. *(See the Cleaning section.)*

If I am doing dirty work, e.g. in the engine room, I wear old jeans and shirts, gear that is stained and one step away from the rag bag (unless I managed to find a good set of overalls in a recycling shop).

Repairing clothes can be an inexpensive option, especially in third world countries.

Sea boots: We wore these just once on Mariah. We did not carry any on board Pyewacket. For colder climates, we would certainly invest in a good pair - be sure to try them on with thick socks before buying. If you have an open cockpit and are on watch, you are constantly exposed to the elements, so you will need good boots. It can rain constantly for days and soggy feet can be a bore.

Cultural respect: Ensure you wear appropriate clothes for the country you are in. In Oman, the showing of a woman's ankle can mean something quite provocative. Wearing appropriate clothing is particularly important when dealing with officials.

Short story Aside from cultural respect, wearing appropriate clothing can lead you to unexpected places. In Borneo, Noel and I were invited to a local wedding, indeed we were the honoured guests. We were simply invited in as we walked past. We noticed other cruisers walk past uninvited. Our arms and legs were covered, the other/uninvited cruisers wore the usual t-shirt and shorts. This clothing is tolerated, but not encouraged in some cultures. They missed out on a fabulous and unique experience due only to their attire, the wedding event was simply amazing.

Stowing clothes: Ensure they are not packed into cupboards too tightly; they will not be able to breathe and will end up with a musty smell. Good ventilation is important. Empty and clean your clothes cupboards at least twice a year, checking for any mould or mildew.

If you are lucky enough to have a wardrobe, ensure the clothes on hangers cannot swing when at sea, as it can cause chafing. Our wardrobe was packed full and the hangers couldn't move! Either pack your wardrobe out (toilet rolls, extra folded jumpers) or tie the hangers together to dampen the movement.

It is a good idea to have comfortable shoes for deck work. They can protect your feet and there are plenty of items to bash your delicate toes on, especially when 'finding your feet' on board. However, Noel and I only wear shoes if it is cold (then it is normally slippers in the cockpit, maybe trainers on deck). We prefer bare feet, but it has taken years of 'toe-bashing' to finally learn to miss all those hard objects!

Be cautious of flip-flops (thongs). They can easily catch on lines, equipment and in all sorts of unexpected places. Not recommended for on board.

Computer Equipment & Laptops
Most boats have at least one laptop on board, but the harsh elements mean this is not a good place for such delicate equipment. Have a purpose built bag for transport and protection. If you do not have a suitable case, wrap your laptop in a plastic bag, case, or a piece of canvas when not in use. Protecting it from the salt air will lengthen its life.

Laptop party in Aitutaki, Cook Islands.

It is usual for at least one laptop to be on board nowadays.

Spare parts: Carry spare keyboards and a spare mouse. When they stop working it is very frustrating and this will usually occur when you are far away from shops. There is a possibility that you can repair your keyboard if the keys stop working. I have tried this twice with only partial success, but others have had success:

- Before attempting to remove the keyboard, try vacuuming it to remove any stuck debris. Beware of sucking keys off though!

- If you want to try a home repair, first research 'how to remove your keyboard' using the Internet, as each model is slightly different. The trick is to place several layers of aluminium foil beneath the keyboard to improve 'contact'. Note: this will void any warranty you may have, so I would only try this as a last resort if the keyboard is not under warranty.

Charging: When my laptop battery is fully charged and plugged into the inverter, it uses far less power than when the laptop battery is low. If you are using the laptop at the same time as charging the laptop battery, you will drain your boat batteries quicker.

Software: You can purchase laptops that come installed with two different software operating systems. This is a good idea for receiving shareware; you have a better chance of running it on one of the two systems.

Securing your laptop: If using your laptop for electronic charts, you need a secure place for your equipment. On Mariah we installed a small pivoting, wall TV stand. We glued Velcro onto the stand and onto the bottom of the laptop (avoiding the parts on the bottom of the laptop that come apart, such as the battery). This worked in all weather for years. The stand was located down below decks (next to the chart table) and we could view it from the cockpit. When not in use, the stand pivoted against the side of the boat, out of the way.

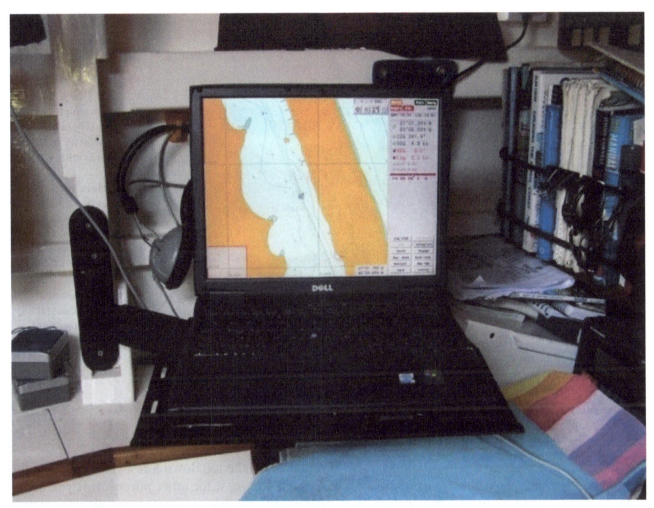

TV stand for our laptop on Mariah. The stand pivots out of the way when not in use.

On board Pyewacket we could have the laptop in the cockpit, as it is enclosed. We used non-slip material, which worked very well. We used electronic charts on the laptop for additional aid to navigating in and out of ports, but while out in the ocean we plotted our position on paper charts and the laptop was put away. (We followed our previously entered waypoints on our handheld Garmin GPS. This GPS was plugged into a 12 volt lead and used far less power than the large chart plotter.)

We have seen other vessels with a simple 'flap' type table, hinged to be flush with the hull or lay flat like a small table, with Velcro for the laptop. This works well if you can view the laptop from the cockpit, so you can use it for navigation.

Dive Equipment
We had a dive hookah on board Pyewacket, which has paid for itself many times over. Many friends have dive tanks that are easy to fill up in most destinations. However, there are times they can be difficult and expensive to refill. *(See 'Dive Hookah' in the Boat Equipment section.)*

Inevitably, at some point an item will be dropped over the side. If you are at anchor and you have the lungs to reach the bottom (check the depth sounder), then you are lucky. A good way to preserve breath is to have a line with a dive weight attached. Tie one end of the line to the boat, leaving enough length to reach the bottom. The diver holds the weight to help take them to the bottom without exerting too much energy, and once there (and hopefully retrieving the item) they can let go of the weight to float backup. The weight is then retrieved via the line.

Comfort and safety take priority in everything we do.

Here we have extended the tiller so I can see clearly while sitting on the edge of Mariah's cockpit, near good shade. (Intracoastal Waterways of America.)

Dry Bag
We have a large orange dry bag/sack, the type where you roll the top down a few times and clip the two ends together. This doubles as our grab bag. In port, we use it for other purposes. If you are at an anchorage, which gives a particularly wet dinghy ride to shore, you can put all your items, clothes and camera etc, in the bag to keep everything dry.

Short story Our grab bag was put to use daily when Noel and Den (SV Frodo) were building us a new dinghy in a brothel; because we had no dinghy, I swam to shore each day to where they were working, carrying lunch in this bag. *(See article, 'A Tender Moment In a House of Ill Repute' in the Maintenance & Repairs section.)*

Milk Crates (Plastic)
Milk crates are very useful. You can lash them to the bike rack or in your dinghy to neatly store life jackets, pump, spare paddles, lights, whistle and all safety equipment. Affix a net over the top and turn the crate upside down in the dinghy, to avoid 'showing off' items that maybe of interest to other people.

Use the basket/crate in the sail locker to keep spare odds and ends together. When on the hard, keep all your 'current job' tools together in the crate.

Precious Memories
My 'personal equipment' includes previous memories, which grow with each unique and precious moment.

In the Galapagos Islands, physically playing with the seals is one of my greatest memories.

When times are tough on board, the extraordinary experiences make up for it.

Reusing & Recycling

When receiving deliveries, I keep the envelopes and packaging (except large cardboard boxes where cockroaches can lay eggs). At some point I will need packaging and this way I always have some spare. Thin cardboard can be made into birthday cards if you are a little creative.

If you don't like the ribbons that are sewn into the shoulders of clothing, snip them out and stow somewhere handy (with your sewing gear). They are useful for kids' craft projects, ribbons on a gift or keeping keys together (I use one to keep all my thumb drives together).

Useful Items

Velcro: Carry spare Velcro, it will be used somewhere on board.

Cable/wire ties: are not just for cables. During spring time in Australia, you will see many bicycle riders wearing helmets with long cable ties sticking up (yes, it does look funny). These are there to fend off Magpie birds that protect their young by attacking cyclists! I have used them on our pulpit handrail to keep the birds off. Birds are lovely, but they can poo elsewhere!

Face cloths: or small towels are located in every cabin on our boat. I use these to wipe down the galley with fresh water, if I have cleaned with saltwater whilst at sea. They are useful everywhere; for drips when opening port holes or for quickly wiping up a spill, and it saves using copious amounts of kitchen paper.

Stockings or tights: are good for filtering fuel. I have also used them to filter out egg shell when eggs have become crushed in a dinghy run. I used different tights/stockings for fuel and eggs! *(See 'Diesel fuel filling filter' in the Maintenance & Repairs section.)*

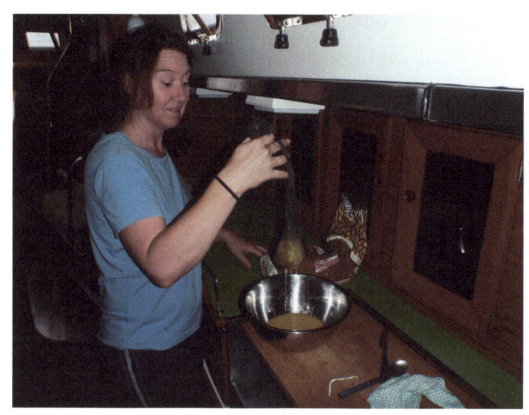

Jackie on board
Pyewacket,
saving eggs!

Short story In many third world countries you buy eggs loose and carry them in a plastic bag (if you are like me and always forget to take your empty egg carton when shopping). Inevitably, I break some of the eggs on the way home. The plastic bags were good quality and the egg didn't spill. When back on board I would tip the contents, shells and all, into a stocking and squeeze the egg through to make an omelette with no egg shell (the shell remained in the stocking). No waste! (Quite often I managed to tread on the bag of eggs in the dinghy, so simply picking out the egg shell was not an option!) So keep your egg cartons in your shopping bags.

Deep bowls: to eat from at sea; when the weather is rough they are easier to eat from than a plate. The food is contained and not so easily spilt when that big wave hits.

Knee pads: are a very important item on board - you will find yourself on your knees for extended periods of time. Maintenance and repairs are often low down.

Ziploc bags: are useful in the galley, but also for documents, thumb drives or your camera while riding in the dinghy.

They are also useful to collect parts and bits and pieces from equipment, e.g. screws, nuts, bolts etc. Keep these small items in Ziploc bags while you are working. Even in port, a boat with a large wake could pass by and suddenly all your little parts scatter! *(See the Galley section for more ideas.)*

Large plastic bowls are useful for catching up with laundry on shore.

Jackie in the Marquesas, having fun playing with water.

Handy Tools

A 'gopher' (pick up and reaching tool) is a very handy item to have on board. The 'hand' end squeezes together to pick up any item. This is perfect for reaching into those inaccessible places.

Bungee cord: Somewhere on board our boats we are always using bungee cord, with plastic hooks (known in Australia as Occy straps - which is short for Octopus straps). We use it to stow items securely, stop lines snatching and prevent halyards banging.

Dental floss: is not just for cleaning your teeth. You can use dental floss as sailing twine or whipping in an emergency. It can also be used as fishing line, for sewing, cutting fruit or hard-boiled eggs or even cake (wrap a length around your index finger on each hand), sliding under baked biscuits to lift them easily, securing mailed packages, quickie clothes line, stringing popcorn etc. *(See the Fun section.)*

If you use it on your teeth, stock up when you see it; it isn't available everywhere. Add some to your grab bag, for an emergency fishing line.

Trolley: to save your back.

Noel carrying our last supermarket shop before departing New Caledonia.

We carried a very heavy dive hookah on this trolley for two kilometres.

The trolley folds down for easy stowing.

Wet Weather Gear

Good quality wet weather gear is imperative if you want to avoid being miserable while sailing in rain. When buying new gear, buy one size too big and/or try it on with many layers of clothes. Most use will occur when it is cold as well as raining. You will want to be able to sail the boat and move around with the gear on. That won't be possible if it is too tight.

We like gear with Velcro around the ankles and wrists, it doesn't keep all the rain out, but certainly helps. Breathable gear is important too. Some brands have an inbuilt harness; these may not be tight enough, especially if you have purchased a larger jacket to be able to wear all your clothes beneath it. We prefer separate harnesses that incorporate a life jacket.

You can buy different coloured gear and we always wonder why they sell blue and white. The idea is to be seen: go for red, orange or fluoro green/yellow with reflectors sewn in. Aside from heavy duty wet weather gear, we have lighter jackets for short showers in warm weather. Once in port, wash the used gear in fresh water and dry it properly prior to stowing.

PETS ON BOARD

Here are some general Pet Considerations from various animal lovers. Continue reading for great advice from cruisers who lived on board with their pets while circumnavigating.

There is no way of knowing how a pet is going adapt to living on board a boat. Cats generally dislike water, but adapt to life afloat. Dogs are an entirely different prospect. We have seen dogs that love life on board and dogs that detest it. A trial period on a boating holiday would be a good start.

Questions To Consider:

- What happens if your pet becomes seasick?

- Is your dog a strong swimmer? At the very least you should take your dog to a lake or beach to see if it enjoys being near water, as well as to ascertain how much it likes swimming and how good at swimming it is.

- How will your pet get back on board?

- Are you taking your pet on board for you, as you cannot bear to leave it? In reality, would your pet be happier on land?

- Does your pet like living on the boat, or is it causing distress?

- Are you prepared to miss visiting certain countries that disallow pets?

- Are you going to be able to deal with animal poo if you are seasick?

Short story Noel's brother, Colin, has a campervan and enjoys travelling to various places in Australia. For companionship he got himself a lovely little dog and they enjoyed each other's company very much. One day when packing up, the dog disappeared and when Colin found him, he displayed an obvious reluctance when it came to getting in the van. Clearly, the dog did not like travelling and like anyone with a heart, Colin realised that it was unfair to the little fella to make him go. He luckily found a nice family to leave his pet with.

Dog Overboard

When the boat is moving, you may want to keep them down below. If the weather is bad you might confine your pet to the well of the cockpit, or have them stay below. Dogs should have a life jacket and lifeline and be attached like everyone else on board. Have a sturdy harness that your pet wears whenever you are on the move.

Develop a plan for your pet going overboard and create a platform that they can climb onto. Arrange a platform or boarding ladder, or any other way of boarding if you are ashore and your pet is on board and falls overboard. *(See SV Solmates' tips further on for some great ideas.)*

A new pet?

Neighbouring Tahiti is the island of Moorea. Here the stingrays are extremely friendly!

Getting Ashore

Getting a larger dog into the dinghy may not be that easy, so you may need an additional platform. If you have steep companionway steps, use a plank (which could be used from boat to dinghy too).

Other considerations:

- Sharp claws

- Carpeting prevents paws from slipping (buy a handheld vacuum for cleaning up hair)

- Vaccinations, certifications

- Play - old ropes with good knots

- Doggy bath - same as humans' shower, saltwater (deck wash pump, rinse with fresh)

Heat

Animals suffer from heat stroke too. Look for symptoms: panting, brick red mucous membranes, anxiety and agitation. Weakness and collapse follows quickly.

Identification

Ensure you have a significant picture (as well as paperwork) of you and your pet in a recognisable location (i.e. in front of a shop with your home town's name on the outside). This will help any problems if your paperwork is not straight or someone else makes a claim on your animal. A picture with you and your pet on the boat is a good idea too.

Procedures

Check procedures for each country and port you are entering. Some countries will not allow you to enter with pets on board. Check that you can take your pet into the marina at which you had planned to stop.

Potty Training
Buy a cat litter tray that is large enough for a dog. *(More ideas below from SV Solmates.)*

Thanks to Roy and Chris on board Solmates who circumnavigated with their dogs, for the following tips:

Comfort: The boat should have enough room for play and exercise. Think catamaran. Our decks became race tracks and the dogs were ever so happy. Boats with low bulwarks should have some type of netting, especially for boats that heel

Heeling can drive dogs crazy - actually, they just hunker down and don't exercise and don't poo or pee, which can lead to other problems. Catamarans are best for dogs. Even in our previous 70ft cutter/ketch the heeling made life troublesome for our dogs. (Our dogs have always been in the 40-80lb category.) Smaller breeds may have fewer problems.

Potty training: Very, very important. Designate an area which is good in all weather. Catamaran trampolines are the best and if the netting is too open and the dog's feet go through, identify a small area and place a small closed net on top, tied down with string, bungee cords, or plastic ties. Then the dog feels safe. Waves will usually clean everything away. On our monohull, we had a fenced-in stern and used artificial turf (about 2ft x 2ft) for 'duties'. This could be washed easily in seawater.

Safety: We lost one dog to drowning at the dock/marina while we were away for two hours, because there was no boarding ladder for the dog. Now this is our biggest concern, more than just about anything else. Catamarans or monohulls with scoops can use a swim ladder, angled at forty-five degrees (I prop a small inflatable fender between the swim ladder and scoop to create a forty-five degree angle) and put plastic mesh across areas so the dog's claws have something on which to grab. Without stern access, perhaps if the dinghy is left in water, a floating ladder arrangement could be made. You need various trials and efforts. Most important: constantly train your dog to USE your set up whenever at anchor, which also implies your dog can swim or at least be trained for this survival skill.

Lightning: Lightning is bad for dogs; they freak out. Put your dog in the head/bathroom with a comfortable towel from their kennel during storms. We cannot stress this enough.

Food: Dog food was generally available everywhere in the world, plus they can survive on cooked rice, veggies, meat scraps and multivitamins for weeks. The South Pacific was most difficult. French Polynesia was very expensive and we could only buy food in small sizes, like 10lbs, so we did stock up, otherwise it was never a problem.

Vets: Veterinarians are usually available everywhere. They will often house the dogs for very reasonable rates, allowing owners to go travelling for a week or so.

Identification: Dog tags are very important. Have the name of your boat, your dog's name and your email address on the tag on the collar. Also have your dog micro-chipped or tattooed. Owners should parade their dog via the dinghy all the time, letting other boats associate the dog with the owner and owner's boat. Many times Heather escaped and was saved by a town local or other cruiser simply because they made the association.

Photos: Have several photos of your dog. In Sydney, Heather escaped and we posted her picture all over town. After a few days, a Park Ranger found her in a park in Cammeray, not far from our boat. She was fixated on the cockatiels (those pretty, white, noisy, nasty birds that poop from the spreaders). He had seen her posted picture, which may have helped. We had the same problem in Thailand. Either her picture or the reward offered brought out the honesty in the local fishing community and she was returned within four days, well fed.

Bring an appropriately sized airplane-approved kennel. We use ours for their daily nest, but should an emergency arise and your dog needs to be transported by car or plane, the transport will be facilitated.

The lovely Chris, Roy, Heather and Stormy on their catamaran Solmates.

Medical kit: Same as for humans, plus anxiety pills (we sleep with Lorazapam and give the dogs half if they are to fly somewhere or are looking traumatized by lightning, fireworks, etc). It lasts six hours. Use antibiotics if their skin becomes infected (rare, but it happens). A 'Victorian Collar' or shield around their neck will keep your dog from scratching and gnawing annoying insect bites that get infected.

Monthly heartworm pills are mandatory. Similarly, monthly anti-flea pills are effective. Keep all shots current, especially rabies. Keep all the paperwork in a designated folder and keep it orderly, as this impresses the vet/animal control personnel when they visit your boat.

Water: Always rinse dogs well after a swim or a day on the beach. Even if you don't do this living on land, in the seawater there are many more irritants and a rinse is very important. Always, always, always have a bowl of drinking water available. The dogs know when they need it.

Security: Some cultures do not like dogs whatsoever - they are considered unclean. This can save the boat from being boarded by pirates, immigration, thieves, etc. Dogs that bark are great; ours usually greeted folks with wagging tails. A single dog hair can worry some religions to distraction. We have stories!

Paws Aboard is a provider of safe and fun supplies for active dog owners and their pets. They strive to deliver excellent quality products that focus on an active lifestyle on land, in water or on the go. Products are always inspired by their own dogs. Paws Aboard: www.pawsaboard.com

CATS
Thanks to Cindy and Faith on board Carmen Miranda who circumnavigated with their cat, Toulouse, for the following tips:

Requirements: We found that no matter what we had heard about a country's requirements when it came to arriving with a pet, it was always somehow different when we arrived. This meant we just needed to be ready for anything. We had heard that pets in Malta were a no-no, so we didn't even think about going there.

Food: Cat food is available just about everywhere. He really liked it when flying fish arrived on their own.

We stuck Velcro pieces on his food and water bowls and fixed them in place where he ate. This stopped them from flying around the cabin in bad weather.

Potty training: Our guy didn't care what was in his litter box, as long as it was clean. When the kitty litter that we started with was gone, we went to pebbles (washed in a net bag hung overboard). This worked fine until the bag got a hole and we lost all the pebbles; finally we stayed with torn strips of newspaper, which is available everywhere, usually for free.

His litter box had a plywood A-frame over it to make sure all stayed put in there. The whole assembly fitted under the companionway ladder.

The lovely Cindy and handsome Toulouse on board SV Carmen Miranda (picture by kind permission from Ann J Meyer).

Seasickness: When we first started travelling, the cat got seasick right about when I did. Soon he wasn't getting sick at all and I still was when the conditions got sloppy.

Safety: It's important for the cat to be below when the conditions get rough. Toulouse always went below on his own and into the safe spot we had made for him between a duffel bag and the bulkhead.

If a pet gets washed overboard, I don't think you'd be able to see him, much less get back to him.

Travelling and routine: I learned so much being with the cat 24/7 on the boat. I had raised him from when he fit in my hand, but on the boat I observed that he had very strict routines every day, like a little old man. He didn't mind all the travelling, but he didn't like change. He was always miffed when we upped anchor and went onward. Once underway, he was happy again.

A lot about travelling with Toulouse was easy for us because he was such an easy going guy. He happily rode in a car; he always asked to ride on my motorcycle (I always said no). He walked on a leash, and when we went to the vets he would sit next to me on the bench in the office to wait our turn. He purred while the vet cleaned his teeth. He was not afraid of anything.

Medical: Surprisingly in our country (US) if you bring a dog in, you need proof of rabies shot etc, but there are no such requirements for cats - of course that could change.

Short story The Last Word on Pets: Noel and I did not have any pets on board, but had a wonderful experience with a mangy dog! In the Marquesas (Daniel's Bay) we were setting off on a trek with several other cruisers. There was one house on the island and a dog that roamed. This dog was not silly, he took one look at the rabble that had to find their way by following cairns for several hours and took pity on us. He led the way and ensured we all kept together - there and back. Good dog!

Walking in Daniel's Bay with our guide.

THEFT & PIRACY

Keep temptation at bay: There are many things on board that would be very attractive to a would-be thief. Most boats have sophisticated gadgets and personal items. Even the boat itself could be the target. Keep a thief's temptation to a minimum and keep valuable items stowed below, not on display.

Secure dinghy: Always lift your dinghy on board or up the side of the hull at night and/or lock the dinghy to your boat. We know cruisers who have had their dinghy stolen while they were on board, even during the day!

Lock your outboard to your dinghy. Take the kill switch with you when leaving the dinghy, so it cannot be started.

Short story Regarding the kill switches, cruisers left their dinghy and outboard on a beach and paid local kids to keep an eye on it (we all did this in Cape Verdes). These particular kids started the engine and left it running. Without raw water to cool the engine, it suffered some severe damage. Take the kill switch; if it can't be started it can't be damaged that way or be driven off.

Boat security: Close windows that are over equipment or personal items, where a thief could stick his/her hand in and snatch a small item away. In remote places you may have to do this when on board. The Caribbean was one of our worst experiences regarding potential thieves and borders. *(See three short stories at the end of this section.)*

Keep your boat entry keys to things like cockpits and hatches separate from your boat's engine keys. (This is a debatable subject: in safer areas (which are the majority) you can leave all your keys together in the ignition, as there are usually other cruisers and honest people around). Some people like to leave their boat 'ready to start' in case their anchor drags while away - although, in that case, knowing if the seacock is on creates another huge debate and potential problem.

Ensure your cockpit lockers, hatches and other boat entry points have strong padlocks fitted, and use them. Make sure your life-raft is secure; it can be a valuable item to a thief and cause considerable problems and expense if you have to find a replacement.

Enable the companionway hatch to lock from the inside.

Some boats have a safe installed. Have an old/cheap watch or cheap jewellery that is easy to find and hide the good stuff well. Once they have something, they may stop searching.

In piracy areas, it may be prudent to turn your AIS transmitter off.

Short story While traversing the Gulf of Aden from Oman to Eritrea, we went in convoy with other cruisers, as we had heard reports of a Catamaran being attacked by pirates off the Yemen coast. Our route took us an equal distance from all land on either side. We did more miles this way, but were as far from any coastline as we could get. During our stay in Oman, groups were organised. In our group, there were nine boats. We had 900 miles to do together and agreed on 5 knots of speed. Being the smallest and slowest boat we were amazed to be leading the pack; we worked our spinnaker poles hard! If we wanted to speak to each other, we called on VHF channel 16, and simply said, 'fleet to channel number one, two or three.' These were pre-agreed channels on the SSB (HF). We did this so the pirates could not scan and listen to our conversations on VHF. We also ran with deck lights only, not masthead lights at night. With 400 nautical miles to go, Noel and I peeled away from the group. We enjoyed being in convoy, but figured the faster we could get out of the area, the better. We all arrived safely and were glad that part of the trip was over. Our celebratory dinner was in fine company, but poor fare. All we wanted was a beer and a steak, but the menu was rice, fish and water! We had just spent nine days eating rice, fish and water.

Insurance: Check your insurance, you may not be covered where piracy is a risk. Educate yourself and all on board about areas with any kind of risk.

Our theory: If ever it should happen, let them take what they want. Our goal would be getting away alive with the boat intact. We had a second wallet that was easily found with a small amount of cash and an expired credit card. We hid the real thing well. Always lock hatches and ports when leaving the vessel; we leave our galley light on (LED) and sometimes the radio playing. Say 'hi' to your neighbours and discuss if they/you, will or will not be around.

Security on shore: Leave your best jewellery on board; don't wear it out. Same goes with appearance, dress moderately and in keeping with the area you are in. Be aware of your surroundings as you walk around, and make eye contact with anyone behaving oddly around you, it will put them off.

Short story In Peru, we were walking in a fairly busy street (more people than cars). I was walking slightly ahead of Noel. He spotted two guys that he had seen just moments before and they were watching him closely. He felt as if they were closing in on him, one in front and one behind. He made obvious eye contact, which, he felt deterred whatever their next course of action was – it didn't feel friendly!

Carry a photocopy of your passport when ashore and leave the original on board. Some cruisers like to carry pepper spray. Be aware of how you are carrying your bag. Backpacks can be sliced at the bottom, with all your gear falling out without you even knowing it - in suspect areas, wear your backpack on your front.

If carrying a shoulder bag, keep the bag under your arm and ensure it is closed properly. If the bag is mostly over your shoulder or on your back, the handles can be cut away and the bag taken without you even knowing about it (happened to a friend of mine).

Hire a taxi. Make use of the taxi driver or a local in the marina (employee) to accompany you in town.

Take only the amount of cash you need.

Short story Keep these issues in perspective. We have done over 70,000 nautical miles and visited over fifty countries. We've travelled the Red Sea, Indonesia and South America. We have had one pair of shoes stolen out of the dinghy in French Polynesia and been robbed once in France by kids, on a remote dock - we had left the boat unlocked!

Short story We have heard of two pirate attacks in areas we were cruising at the time. The first was near the Yemen Coast. The high speed vessel approached the cruiser firing rapid-fire weapons, and they shot through the rigging (which only just held). The pirates were next to the boat, shooting, before anyone on board could do a thing – weapons or no weapons, there was no chance to even grab them. A knife was held at the wife's throat while the guy was ordered to give up/find all their cash. Equipment, money and personal items were taken, but they came away with their lives and the boat (albeit with damaged rigging). Our view on weapons? Guns are a worry, who would win in a shootout at sea?

The second attack was in a crowded anchorage in St Lucia. A boat was boarded by two men, who beat up the husband and wife and stole what they could grab. It was late at night and the pirates were on board before the boat owners knew what was happening. Our view on this? They were extremely unlucky with this incident, we'd rather have open windows and not be a prisoner on our own boat/home - a risk we are prepared to take.

Having said that, in Dominica we heard a rattle on our stern late one night; Noel had a look, thinking it was the Aries wind vane. He found two guys on a large surfboard wearing balaclavas. In astonishment, Noel yelled out very loudly '**%%##$@ off, we are calling the police'. They decided to paddle off. It may have been different if they had gained access to our boat before we heard them.

Resources:
See Jimmy Cornell's Noonsite for up to date information on problem areas: www.noonsite.com

Other useful research sites are:
Lists of incidents involving yachts in the Caribbean:www.safetyandsecuritynet.com
Search Latitude 38 magazine for piracy information:
http://www.latitude38.com/lectronic/lectronicday.lasso?
This is a guide from International Sailing Federation of how to cross the Gulf of Aden with the lowest possible level of risk:
http://www.sailing.org/tools/documents/ISAFGuidelinesForPreventionOfPiracy-[8521].pdf
This is the Australian Government Department of Foreign Affairs website which, which carries information on security conditions in countries around the world: http://www.dfat.gov.au

VOYAGE PREPARATION
Includes: Living On Board, Administration, YOU, The Boat, At Sea

LIVING ON BOARD
When making the transition to boat life, live on board for a good few weeks prior to departure. Becoming familiar with the smaller area (and all the bruises) is much easier when safely in port.

Big Trip Preparation
Keep a notepad to hand and jot down items you need/want for the trip, during the weeks leading up to departure. In my notepad I use the front to list things we need to buy. In the back, I write the list of jobs and this ensures nothing is overlooked.

Cheap Living
Living on a boat is not as cheap as some people think, but with good decision making, hard work and a little bit of luck it can be far cheaper than living on the land. Boats require constant maintenance, repair and improvement; this means time and money. We find that one job a day is the minimum necessary to maintain our vessel to our liking.

If you are less 'handy' or need specialist repairs, you will obviously spend more money. So gain a good balance of broad skills before setting out and be willing to learn as you go.

If you neglect your boat it will lose resale value and more importantly, it will quickly become unseaworthy. Problems will snowball and eventually the boat will be uninhabitable and a danger.

Not all anchorages are free and not all ports have anchor sites available. At times you will have no choice but to use the facilities and pay entry fees, mooring and marina fees.

Environment Laws: MARPOL
International Convention for the Prevention of Pollution from Ships (MARPOL-Marine Pollution) is the main Convention covering the operational or accidental pollution of the marine environments.

The Convention includes regulations aimed at preventing and minimising pollution from ships - both accidental pollution and that from routine. This is regulated by the IMO (International Maritime Organisation), see:
http://www.imo.org/about/conventions/listofconventions/pages/international-convention-for-the-prevention-of-pollution-from-ships-(marpol).aspx

Keep your bilges clean: Not only can debris and oil foul your bilge pumps, but if you pump oil or fuel overboard you could very easily find yourself facing an enormous fine for the environmental damage.

Noise pollution: Be aware of the amount of noise you generate. It has an impact upon the environment and will also affect the enjoyment of others, as well as any disturbance it may cause to wildlife.

The effects of chemicals, gases and solid wastes: Be aware of the chemicals and wastes you throw out. It can cause harm to shoreline flora and fauna. In narrow waterways, always take care to protect the environment.

A large wash: The wash from the back of your boat can erode the shoreline, destroy nesting grounds and upset vegetation.

Keep your engine well maintained: it will be more environmentally friendly.

Boat exhaust emissions: can contain carbon monoxide, nitrogen oxide, hydrocarbons and other pollutants.

No plastics overboard anywhere in the world, ever.

Resources: www.boatus.com/foundation/

Environment - Rubbish (Garbage)

There are international rules and regulations on what you can throw overboard and at what distance from land. These rules changed in January 2013, for current regulations see:
www.amsa.gov.au/Marine_Environment_Protection/Protection_of_Pollution_from_Ships/Discharge_Standards.aspand
www.amsa.gov.au/Marine_Environment_Protection/Revision_of_Annexes_I_and_II_of_MARPOL/index.asp

The plastic rubbish we keep on board e.g. milk cartons, are washed in saltwater and cut up into small pieces before being thrown in the ship's bin. You must have clean garbage! This prevents smells developing and cutting up the packaging means it takes up far less space.

Equipment

These days most cruisers have at least one laptop on board. In addition, thumb drives, printer and a scanner have been very useful items on our trips. We've used thumb drives to share photos, the printer to print multiple forms required for checking in and the scanner to scan in completed forms to send on to officials prior to arrival.

Flags

Etiquette: As guests in another country, you should fly their flag higher than yours and technically it should be bigger. However, our courtesy flag was rarely larger than our Australian flag and there was never a problem. The yellow flag (Quarantine flag) should be beneath the host's flag. Some (few) countries are not bothered by flags, but most will be very offended if you do not hoist their flag. It is not worth upsetting officials.

We made a big deal about hauling our flags. Why not? It's another successful voyage to another country. The enormity of our achievement never diminished!

Sailing into New York on board Mariah!

<u>Homemade flags</u>: For international travel, make up your own flags from spare material you have collected. If the flag is complex, make up the fundamentals (i.e. main colours). This will be enough to satisfy officials when you arrive and if you hoist the flag high enough, the details won't be seen. You can purchase a proper flag when you arrive, which is usually cheap and easy. I enjoyed making our flags during the passage. On arrival into a new country, always fly your yellow Q flag for Quarantine (I am a clean vessel and request free pratique). If you do not want to make your own, list the countries you want to stop at and purchase the flags of your proposed destinations prior to leaving. It may work out cheaper if you do this in your home country.

<u>Preparation</u>: Purchase a good book, or print off a colour sample of the flags of the destinations you are visiting. Your flags become great mementoes.

Here, Jackie is making the flag for Costa Rica. We stopped at Isle de Cocos, in the Pacific, to do repairs. We only stopped for two days as the mooring cost US$85 a <u>day</u>!

Short story A cruising buddy told us that they heard (over the VHF radio) the Port Captain, in American Samoa, deny a freighter entry to Pago Pago Harbour, because they did not have an American Samoa courtesy flag on board!

Flags - International Signal Flags
Your book of International Collision Regulations should list all the flags and their meanings (some flags have more than one meaning). These are mainly a requirement for commercial vessels, but you should at least be able to recognise a few of the more common flags.

Some examples:

Flag	Colour	Meaning
Alpha	Red with white diagonal stripe (or rigid blue/white vertical)	Diver down, keep clear and pass slowly, with caution
Bravo	Red (swallow tail)	Danger, I am taking on, or unloading dangerous and flammable goods, keep clear
Oscar	Red and yellow diagonally divided	Man Overboard (MOB)
Quebec	Yellow	I am a clean vessel and request free pratique

From Boat To Land & From Land To Boat

Transforming your life from boat to land (and back the other way) is a huge transition. On both our boats and on each transition (land to boat and boat to land), it took us several months to fully adjust. Patience is the key with your partner and yourself. There are many decisions to be made; we learned to take our time and just let plans and ideas unfold in their own time. This was far less stressful than forcing our plans into fruition.

Short story I am quite good at stressing about what is going to happen ('when we arrive back in Australia the first time', 'when we cross this bar for the first time', etc). Noel maintains his cool and says two things that calm me down. 'It will be okay' and 'something will happen.' It is amazing how calming a relaxed outwards appearance and comforting (although simple) words can be.

Ask yourselves some pertinent questions, when moving from land to boat:

- Do we sell the house?

- If we did sell, would that add stress to the trip if we had a major problem (i.e. nowhere to 'run' to)?

- Would renting be too stressful if we are out of touch for some time?

- What does storage of our personal items cost?

- What about our mail?

- Will we want a home to return to?

How we did it: We decided to rent out our house (and were lucky to have good tenants). It felt more secure to have a backup plan/somewhere to go, if all else failed.

We didn't worry about paying for storage, as it was an additional expense we did not want. We agreed with our tenants that we could use the attic of the guesthouse for non-valuable items. Other items were stored with or given to friends and family. What was left, we sold. We knew we would be away for years, so apart from a few small valuables (more sentimental than monetary), we got rid of most items.

Short story During our fifteen years together, Noel and I have spent less than four years living on land (most of the 'land time' was spent teaching commercial maritime). We have not accumulated many valuable 'land' possessions. If we had to toss-up between paying storage and keeping stuff, I would get rid of the lot, or at least arrange an alternative. For example, some of our furniture was purchased specifically for the BBQ area. Our tenants agreed to purchase the furniture, with the proviso that we would buy it back when we returned to the house.

Seasickness

There are a plethora of remedies. During your shakedown cruise, see what works best for you. Different remedies such as ginger, tablets and wristbands work for different people. We take half a seasickness tablet prior to each voyage, as a full tablet makes us drowsy. If you dissolve a seasickness tablet under your tongue, your body will absorb it quicker.

Keeping hydrated: Keep your fluids up, it helps stave off seasickness. We both become thirsty and quickly dehydrate when sailing. The day before departure, ensure you are fully hydrated. We make sure our pee is a very light colour and we try to maintain this when sailing. We drink a lot of water. This really helps me avoid being green.

Keep busy: Eat plain food, change the sails, watch the horizon and keep warm. Fresh air and being part of what is happening on board is a real help. However, as there are just two of us on board, Noel and I have to be 'off-watch' and lie down at some point. If I am feeling sick, once in my bunk the seasickness does ease enough for me to sleep. However, being down below will usually make it worse unless you are lying down. Always let the other people on board know you are suffering. They can make allowances and maybe help.

Engine room problems are a prime source for creating seasickness, as is using the head. Peeing in a bucket outside is not a bad idea if you really suffer when going below. Dealing with the engine is just something you have to do - the best advice is to keep coming up for air!

What we like: We like Stugeron and take half a tablet a few hours before leaving, whatever the forecast. Nerves at the beginning of a voyage are a contributing factor to seasickness. *(For more (and important) information see 'First Aid & Medication' in the Voyage Preparation section.)*

We never drink alcohol the night before leaving, or during the voyage.

Scheduling

Throw any schedule out of the window. Sailing is not like getting on a train or bus or travelling by car. Mother Nature determines your landfall and duration at sea. If family or friends are flying in to meet you somewhere, add in plenty of contingency time. You may not make it. Severe weather might force you to turn around, or a system might fail and returning to the port you have just left is safer and easier than continuing to your planned destination.

Getting ready to depart a port always takes us far longer than we anticipate.

Time: Never let time pressure have an influence on offshore sailing. Deadlines can be deadly!

Give ample leeway when arriving to meet someone or returning them back to the airport. Weather or equipment failure may not allow you to reach your desired destination in time.

Short story Our first offshore trip attempt from Coffs Harbour (NSW Australia) to Fiji was aborted; we hit a storm and turned back. The sixty knot winds were ferocious, so running with the seas (with a storm drogue) was our chosen option. That compass heading took us back to Mooloolaba in Queensland, Australia. After two weeks at sea we were relieved to be in a safe harbour. When we contacted my parents, they admitted that they had been on the verge of flying to Fiji to meet us as a surprise. Thankfully they didn't, and we have all learned that our proposed destination is only a possibility until we are actually there.

Shakedown Cruise
Know your boat inside out before taking on a lengthy (offshore) voyage. This can take time. It took us two years of coastal cruising, working on shore and working on board, before we were ready. It took several more years before we got the best out of our boat.

Stowing
Storage location is dynamic for the first few months. How you stow depends on the size and shape of your boat. Use of different sized plastic crates/baskets, containers and hanging baskets makes life easier.

When stowing tinned food or anything low in the boat where only the tops can be seen, write what they are on the top in pen, it makes life so much easier. *(See 'Stowing Food' in the Galley section.)*

Don't forget to stow some good clothes for those special times.

Bora Bora (from left to right: Alim, Kian, Judy, Noel, Barry & Jackie).

If you have many leads/power cords, buy a bundle of old/odd socks (or use your old ones) to store individual leads in. It stops them becoming entangled if stored together.

Location: Stow the items you use more often in an accessible place. If you buy dried goods in bulk, like rice and lentils, at the very least halve the bags and re-stow. This ensures that if one bag splits or goes off, you have only lost part of your supplies.

When stowing, always be aware of the trim of the vessel (fore and aft line) and avoid stowing heavier items on one side, otherwise you may create a list. Stow heavy items low and ensure they are lashed or held down.

You may end up having to stow some tools in your wardrobe, as it is the most secure place. This could also help maintain a seaworthy vessel by keeping the boat balanced (trimmed correctly).

Preparation: Top up smaller containers in your galley before you leave so you don't have to ferret around when at sea.

Many people have a list of where everything is stowed so items can be found quickly. However, the list will soon be out of date! Even after six months on board our new boat, we were still shifting items.

Ensure stowed items are not hitting or rubbing (and therefore chafing) wiring or piping. Even at anchor, you should ensure everything you are not using is stowed correctly. A wind shift and a lee shore can happen in moments, so you must be prepared for a quick getaway.

Space bag vacuum-seal storage bag: Vacuum bags are a great way to store and stow sheets, blankets and bulky winter clothes. If you don't have a vacuum on board to suck out all the air, simply lay on the bags (on your front), then do them up while you have the bag squished beneath you. They are a great space saver.

Protection and safety: Have a good supply of bungee cord (elastic) to help keep items in place. Also towels, foam and rags can be stuffed into plate and cup cupboards for when your boat is really rolling.

Don't throw out old socks, put wine bottles or jars in them to protect the glass at sea.

Use flat coffee filters between your dishes to stop rattles.

For precious items, have some bubble wrap to hand. Alternatively, use a Ziploc bag. Put a straw into the top of an almost closed bag and inflate, then seal the bag to make an air cushion.

Containers: Source plastic containers that suit the shape and size of your cupboards. Use these for food: tins will rust, cardboard will get wet and glass is dangerous.

If you have large, deep or long cupboards, purchase square plastic baskets/containers. These make searching and retrieving far easier (they are good in a deep fridge or freezer too).

Fuel and water containers: For stowing water and fuel containers on deck, affix a plank of wood to the stanchions. It is much easier to tie jerry cans to this wood. We have used this set up with holes drilled in the timber plank for better lashing ability.

Stowing gifts - Poster Tubing: Poster tubes on board are useful. We have collected original and colourful posters and paintings as gifts in various places, and can store them easily in the tubing. Plastic pipe works just as well and helps prevent damage.

Terminology

While the key elements of the boat should be named appropriately, as long as everyone on board calls the same thing by the same name, it will work. Quite often I will say to Noel, 'Can you pull the thingy while I adjust the wotsit'. We've done so many miles, Noel always knows what I am referring to!

Visitors On Board

Before visitors arrive, give them as much information as possible about the boat and how you live. Here are some examples that might shock visitors:

- Doing the dishes in cold water.
- Lack of freezer or fridge (or both).
- Lack of washing machine on board.
- No continuous power.
- Simple entertainment.
- Not the most salubrious restaurants every night.
- Holding tanks and toilet training.
- Water rationing, no lengthy hot showers or leaving the tap running when cleaning teeth.
- Lack of closet space.
- Small beds.

Spending/budget: When we have visitors on board, our normal spending is exceeded. Usually, visitors are on holiday and may spend more freely. This is our life and we work very hard on board to maintain this lifestyle for as long as possible before returning to life on land.

We have met cruisers who charge a fee for visitors to come and stay on their boat, even for friends and family. If you are uncomfortable asking for money, then accept an offer from your visitors to pay for a shopping trip to the supermarket or a meal out.

Hot water: What might be normal to you can seem quite bizarre to others. On board Mariah we did not have hot water (unless boiling the kettle). My mum was horrified that I washed up in cold water.

Kids: If you have a minor visiting and they are not with one of their parents, they will need a letter of permission from their parents (even if they are travelling with another adult). My dad came to Ecuador with my nephew (my dad's grandson) and it was necessary to show customs that my nephew's mother had granted permission.

Luggage: Inform visitors that they should travel with soft bags, as a hard suitcase has no place on a boat.

Importing goods via friends and family: Ask visitors to bring anything you are craving (if it's possible to transport, always check with customs/immigration). We always ask mum and dad to bring Vegemite! They find that all the customs and immigration officials smile when they declare it (declaring Vegemite in most countries is unnecessary, but if you are unsure, stick with the safety of declaring).

Visitors can bring equipment too. Be sure to check import duty. We have heard of some cruisers asking their friends/family to bring spare parts/equipment. They take all the original packaging off the items so they are classed (and look) second-hand to avoid possible import duty.

My dad joined us on board Mariah from the Cayman Islands to Panama. Even though he had little cruising experience, dad was fabulous on board. Cups of tea were regular, he stood as many watches as us and took less seasick tablets than us in some boisterous conditions! What a joyous time.

Water
Water preservation at sea is important. Have a backup for problems, e.g. separate tanks in case of a leaking tank, tainted water or Watermaker breakdown, etc.

Never drink seawater.

Manual or pressurised: Mariah had a manual foot pump in the galley, but on board Pyewacket we had a 12 volt pressurised pump. As with everything, there is a trade off. We liked the pressure pumps and ease of Pyewacket's system, but manual pumps allowed us to control the flow easily and therefore manage water usage better.

If you have a pressurised system on board for water, ensure you have a manual pump backup. You need to be able to get to your drinking water if your pump fails.

Quantity and usage: Before our first voyage, we tested how long our full tanks lasted. This was incorporated into our lifestyle (saving water where possible), and eventually we did not need to monitor our water levels on a daily basis. At the end of every voyage we always had plenty of water leftover.

Take care to preserve your precious water on board. Hauling water is work, but can be in the most pleasant surrounds. Georgetown, Georgia, USA.

Showering: Having a saltwater shower with either your deck-wash pump or bucket isn't so bad. On a boat with smaller water tanks, we rinsed off the soap (or shampoo) using saltwater and used just one cup of fresh water to wash off the salt (we did this for many years and never once suffered with sores or feeling sticky). On Pyewacket, we had enormous water tanks and we'd generally lather up after a swim with a tiny bit of shampoo and rinse off with fresh.

If taking a saltwater shower, use cheap shampoo, as it lathers up better than soap. When in port, jump in and have a swim, get back on board, soap up, have a good wash and jump back in to rinse off. Climb out again and use a little fresh water to rinse off the salt. You will never have a more refreshing 'shower'!

If you have an on board shower, use a bucket or bowl to catch all the cold water that comes through the system before the hot. Use this to wash up in.

If you do not have a shower below decks, or you prefer to shower outside in the cockpit, buy a garden chemical spray container. Our five litre container held one good shower per person. We made up a mixture of one full kettle of boiled water and topped it up with cold. It is a very easy way to control the amount of water used.

For real economy and/or speed, purchase a spray bottle and fill with warm or cold water and use as a spritz! Dilute shampoo into a spray bottle for a quick and economical shower, simply rinse off after.

Buy a black bucket, fill it with saltwater (or fresh if you have plenty) and leave it in the sun. In the afternoon/evening, scoop out the water and have a lovely warm shower. You may be in summer most of the time (following the trades), however cool currents can mean it is too cold to swim (e.g. in the Galapagos Islands).

Catching water: Using canvas can be tricky as most rainstorms are accompanied by wind, which tends to upset your carefully positioned canvas rain catchers. Different ideas work on different boats. We have seen successful ideas incorporating the pilot house roof with gutters built in. Some cruisers claim to have success using the mainsail cover beneath their boom to catch water off the mainsail when underway. We have found that by keeping our deck clean and by having conveniently placed water filling caps (on deck) leading directly to our tanks we can fill our tanks. For Pyewacket we created a simple dam using a length of timber with self adhesive foam strip applied to the edge. A couple of dive weights hold the dam firmly against the deck and bulwark up turn. This was sufficient to divert water into the tank filling caps. It was marvellous to watch and hear that precious water filling our tanks. And it didn't matter how hard the wind blew.

Jerry cans: Additional jerry cans of water are important, as they are isolated from any contamination or leaks in your main tank. If you have to abandon ship, take your jerry cans with you and tie them to your life-raft. They can be almost full and still float on seawater. We carried out an experiment to see how full a plastic container could be before it sank - we were able to completely fill the container with fresh water and it still floated in seawater! Test it yourself, with your own jerry cans/containers. (Saltwater is denser than fresh water.)

Filling up: When filling up your water tanks, always let the hose run for a while prior to filling the tanks, this gets rid of the plastic taste from your hose.

Noel tops up our supply at Aitutaki in the Cook Islands.

Top up with fresh water at every opportunity.

Clean water: You can purchase proprietary water cleaning aids. However, we simply follow the basic rule: if the locals drink it, we do. We have never had a problem with contaminated water.

Buying water: If you are in a country where you cannot drink the water from the tap, you can still use this water for laundry, cleaning and showering. Save the water you buy for drinking and cooking.

Watermakers

Manual Watermaker: You can purchase a manual Watermaker for a few hundred dollars. It may seem expensive at the time, but if you are in that life-raft, thousands of miles from anywhere, it will suddenly seem very inexpensive. (In 2003 we purchased a manual Watermaker for US$600.)

Short story We met Bill in Puerto Rico. We were working, fixing up friends' apartments, and therefore tied up in the marina. Bill had written a book about spending 66 days in a life-raft after his boat was sunk by Pilot whales in the Pacific Ocean. We learned a lot from Bill, but one of the fundamental pieces of equipment he said he had on board that had saved his life, was a manual Watermaker. This alone, in his life-raft, saved his and his wife's life. We bought one shortly after. You can buy his great book '66 Days Adrift' and read more of Bill's adventures at: www.wbutler.com/

If you are lucky enough to have a Watermaker on board, still practice conserving your water and top up whenever possible. It may breakdown.

Weather

Remember that they are called weather 'forecasts' and they offer no guarantees. The weather usually determines when you move. It is imperative to understand marine forecasts and how to obtain forecasts for the area you are in. Weather can be a complex subject. It is beneficial to study as much weather forecasting theory as possible.

In the Pacific Ocean, hundreds of miles from land. We knew this front was coming for several days, thanks to Weatherfax.

Weatherfax

Become familiar with the Weatherfax process and schedule prior to departure. If you are in a marina, the signal may not work very well due to interference from masts and equipment.

To utilise Weatherfax all you need is a good SSB radio (HF), a laptop and an earphone connection from the radio to the laptop. Free software for downloading Weatherfax is available on the Internet. http://www.jvcomm.de/index_e.html

We usually received a wind/wave forecast for 24 and 48 hours, and synoptic charts (isobars and wind strength) for 24, 48 and 72 hours. The wind strength arrows can cover a large area though.

Receiving weather via Weatherfax:
- You must deduct 1.9 kHz off the listed frequencies.
- To receive a good Weatherfax is easy, but the atmospherics can cause disturbances. Ensure you have done everything you can to receive a good picture.
- Turn off EVERYTHING:
  - the fridge
  - wind generators
  - solar panels
  - inverters
  - electronic steering gear (get someone to hand steer for a while or use the wind vane)
  - all electrical devices
  - solar panels (install a switch that lets you manually turn them off)

Deciphering pictures: We like the synoptic charts as they show you why the wind is doing what it is doing, and it can show you an escape route. You can clearly see what is coming.
Download the worldwide frequency list from: http://www.nws.noaa.gov/om/marine/rfax.pdf.

Do not forget:
- Subtract 1.9kHz from the given frequency.
- Some of the listed times are not exact and can change.
- Faxes can come a few minutes earlier and often later than the scheduled times.

Short story We were rounding Cape Vincent at the bottom of Portugal and had several destination options, Madeira being the favourite. At midnight, we received a Weatherfax showing gale force winds and nine metre seas off Madeira. The best conditions were at Casablanca. So, Casablanca it was; we had a great, safe sail and visited a fascinating place that we had not planned to see. Weatherfax certainly saved us battling huge seas. This was an example of when we drew a sketch from our electronic charts (as a backup should our electrics/laptop fail). We did not plan to go to Casablanca and therefore did not have paper charts.

GRIBs (GRidded Information In Binary) via the Internet: We do not use GRIBs as we do not have Internet on board, however they are a good comparison/backup to Weatherfax. The difference is that to receive Weatherfax you need only an SSB (HF) long-range radio and laptop. To receive the GRIBs you will need an Internet connection. SailMail is often recommended to us as a way of accessing an Internet connection on board. www.sailmail.com.

At anchorages, we compared our Weatherfax information with other cruisers who had GRIBs for a good overall picture. The Weatherfax covers a large area, but shows the big picture. On GRIBs you can select more localised weather.

Resources:
Weatherfax: www.jvcomm.de/downloadpre.html (trial period)
Weatherfax frequencies (worldwide): www.nws.noaa.gov/om/marine/rfax.pdf
NOAA Marine Weather Services guide: www.nws.noaa.gov
National Hurricane Center: www.nhc.noaa.gov/index.shtml?epac
Joint Typhoon Warning Center: www.usno.navy.mil?JTWC
Storm pulse: www.stormpulse.com
HurricaneZone.net: www.hurricanezone.net
Weather Underground: www.wunderground.com
Australian Weather - BOM: http://www.bom.gov.au/
Extreme Weather (Global Tracks Software): www.extremewx.com
Mexican Meteorology Service: http://smn.cna.gob.mx/
Internet access to download weather via: www.sailmail.com

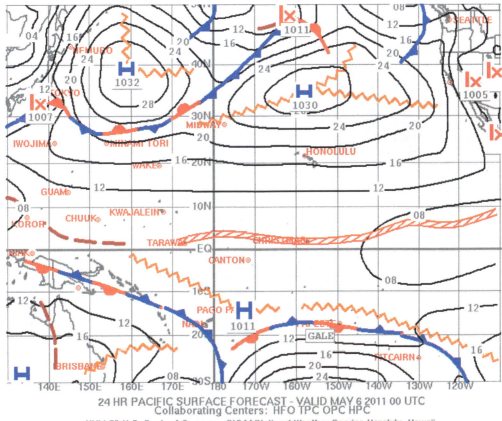

Courtesy of NOAA

This is a sample of a synoptic chart from NOAA (National Oceanic and Atmospheric Administration) in America. We received the black and white version.

You can see the Highs and the Lows either side of the equator. The thick striped line near the equator is the ITZC (Inter-tropical Zone of Convergence). There is a large cold front (blue), heading for Pago Pago (American Samoa). The sawtooth line is a high pressure ridge. The dashed red line on the bottom left over Australia is a trough. All of these systems would and could provide strong winds, squalls and would provide you with a fore-warning of unsettled weather.

ADMINISTRATION
Banking

Communication: Inform your bank and credit card company of your movements. If your credit or debit card is used in a new location, they may stop the transaction for fraud prevention if they do not know you are going there. If you have more than one debit or credit card, ensure you talk to each provider, prior to leaving.

Talk to your bank before you leave your country, explain your plans and discuss how they can best assist you while you travel. Request a personal contact during your travels. Our bank provided us with a personal contact who rapidly responded to all our queries/requests for assistance via email.

Withdrawing cash: If you cannot withdraw money via an Automatic Teller Machine or Cash Point in a foreign country, try over the counter; sometimes there can be a glitch with automated transactions.

Noel, banking in Cuba.

Bank charge saving: Check with your bank to see if they are affiliated with other banks in other countries. Using these affiliated counterparts can help avoid some withdrawal fees.

Security: When using Internet banking, always check for the 's' at the end of 'http' (https) in the address box; this means 'secure'. There should also be a picture of a lock somewhere in the address line; these two items show that you can use the website securely.

Fraud: Any irregular use on your accounts via Internet banking is fraud and unless the bank can prove negligence (i.e. you've not kept your passwords secure), you should be fully insured should fraudulent activity occur.

Budgeting & Money Matters In Preparation & When Underway

Using up foreign currency: When leaving a country, you inevitably have leftover coins in local currency. Count it up and spend it (I just love those penny candies/sweets/lollies!). Small shops (especially post offices) will be delighted to receive your change and you can avoid carrying piles of odd coins that are useless.

When leaving a country, we pay our marina or mooring buoy bill last. Most marinas are happy if we pay with all our remaining cash and make up the remainder with the credit card. This ensures we are not carrying lots of odd currency on board.

Emergencies: Keep a small reserve fund of American dollars (cash) on board for emergencies. American is the most internationally accepted currency.

Security: When out shopping, take care not to show your pocket or wallet full of notes. Hide the bulk of your money so that when you open your wallet to pay, you only show a few dollars. This works for bribes too and will hopefully help you avoid gaining attention from the wrong kind of people. *(See 'Bribes' further on in this section.)*

Budgeting: Being passionate about everything we do is important to us, including living on a budget. Finding an alternative that is cost effective is very gratifying. Sticking to a budget is not all about missing out; every dollar you save is one less you have to earn. It's not all about cutting back either; it's finding a better way to live.

Nana (SV Adverse Conditions) and Jackie having a great time at Aitutaki in the Cook Islands.

We joined the dancing troupe after their performance.

Good value entertainment.

Over time, you will be amazed at how resourceful you have become and realise that living on a budget is not repressive; it is actually a fun and exciting challenge. It improves your life and way of thinking. Do not cut corners for necessary equipment and supplies, just prioritise and think about what you actually need, not want.

Balance time, money and effort. Invest time in sourcing different prices and quotes for expensive items (sails for instance); but saving a twenty cent bus fare by walking five miles is a waste of time and effort.

It's easier than you think to make savings: learn to cut your own hair for example. *(See the 'Health & Well-being' section.)*

Short story I find having long hair is far easier to manage and it actually requires less maintenance. So why I cut my hair (and shaved the sides and back) in Tahiti baffles me; I was very hot at the time. To wear short hair I had to style it and ask someone else for a trim at the back. I will take a bit more time to contemplate the results of chopping my hair off next time!

With a glass of wine and good humour, I chopped off my locks while in Tahiti on Pyewacket!

More budgeting examples:
- Buy clothes, shoes, material and tools (if available) in recycling shops; many of these items can be new or nearly new, in great condition and incredibly cheap.

- Limit your dining out to only once a week when in port. *(See 'Eating Out' in the Galley section and the Kids On Board section for alternative evening entertainment.)*

- Buy your favourite wines less often, or accustom your palate to cheaper wine. It is amazing what you get used to.

Short story In the early days on Mariah we were on a strict budget, as were many of our cruising buddies. In the Mediterranean, you could purchase cask wine (by the litre) for 99 cents. We all purchased different wines and a fun time was had 'wine tasting'. The palatable wines were duly noted and bulk purchased.

Buying Equipment & Discounts
Always ask for a discount in a marine store; they are competitive and will more than likely accommodate you a little.

Good quality equipment can be 'cheaper' in the long run, so try to think long-term, especially for the pricier items.

Buying Equipment & Return Policy

When ordering equipment always check the return policy; that bargain you scored might end up much more expensive if you have to return the item.

The receipt may fade over time, so take a copy on A4 plain paper to avoid this happening. Staple your receipt in the manual, noting the time, date and place where the item was purchased. List the serial number of the item in the same place.

Checking In & Out Of Foreign Ports

<u>Paperwork</u>: Ensure you read and check <u>all</u> the official paperwork very carefully, especially dates. You can rarely go back and make changes if an error has occurred (and they do).

Understand what it is you have paid for and ask for receipts.

When meeting with officials, always carry spare photocopies of your documentation, e.g. passports, visas, boat papers, crew lists, etc, and extra copies of passport sized photos of everyone on board. At some port offices they will not photocopy your originals, but send you away from the official office until you have the required number of photocopies for them. *(See the full list of documentation required after the article 'Of Foreign Build, further on in this section.)*

<u>Flag etiquette</u>: When entering a new country always fly the 'Q' (Quarantine) flag, the flag of the country you are visiting and your flag ('your flag' is your boat's registered home port flag). These flags should be flown as you enter the territorial waters, but this is unrealistic (as territorial waters can extend several hundred miles from land) and we have never heard of anyone getting into trouble for not doing this. As you approach port (a few miles out) raise your flags then. Your host's flag should be larger and higher than your own, on your starboard spreader, above any other flag. The Q flag should be below your host's flag and taken down once you have cleared Quarantine. *(See 'Flags' in the Voyage Preparation section.)*

<u>Health and safety</u>: Research information on the health and safety standards of the country you are visiting and whether they apply to foreign vessels.

Every so often I would empty all the cupboards and clean them thoroughly. Entering a new country with strict rules gave me the motivation to present a spick and span boat.

Here, Jackie is clearing out a very deep cupboard behind the galley sink on Mariah.

Short story New Zealand previously had high safety standards that all vessels (including foreign) in their waters had to abide by, although this has since ceased. Some European countries have safety standards that will be enforced. Be sure to keep your research current and visit www.noonsite.com for pertinent information from other cruisers.

Requirements: Research the checking in requirements for the country you are visiting on the Internet and in your pilot books. If your pilot book is old, update it, as requirements can change. *(See article 'Of Foreign Build' below.)*

Be courteous: You are a visitor so be courteous, even if you do not share the same beliefs. Some (few) officials like to demonstrate their power. You really have to keep smiling and continue being polite. A soft drink and biscuits always helps (and are appreciated), if officials come on board.

Checking in can be in a boring office in a city, or a beautiful setting with colourful people.

Aitutaki in the Cook Islands, with the Quarantine and Customs officer.

Declare or beware: Where required declare items. Not only do you put yourself and your boat at risk of penalties if caught hiding something you should declare, but subsequent cruisers will be treated suspiciously and are not as welcome.

Short story Arriving at the Maldives was a dream come true. However, friends on an American registered vessel had their boat almost taken apart with a thorough search. All cupboards were emptied onto the floor, including all bathroom items! The unconfirmed story is that the Maldives has had so many American boats arriving with weapons and not declaring them, that they made a rule to search every American boat.

<u>Banned food</u>: Research each country's entry requirements as far as food is concerned. You may not be able to take in any fresh food.

Australia and New Zealand are particularly tough on what is and what is not allowed to be brought into the country. These rules are not just there to annoy you; they are protecting their environment and industries. Abide by the rules or expect fines or a difficult time. Usually if they can see you have followed their rules to the best of your ability and you have overlooked a banned food, they will bag it and take the food away to destroy it. Just don't hide anything.

If you don't want to follow their rules, don't go there!

Short story The first time we checked back into Australia prior to arrival, I diligently went through our galley and got rid of any disallowed foodstuffs. I missed one tiny packet of popcorn. The officials could see that I had followed their rules to the best of my ability and simply took and destroyed the item for me. 'Getting rid' of food can be achieved several ways: eat it, cook it (boil eggs for example), or throw it overboard (obeying MARPOL (marine pollution) rules). The second time we checked back into Australia, six years later, was far less worrisome and the rules had been relaxed somewhat. *(See the Voyage Preparation section for more information on MARPOL.)*

<u>Bribes</u>: Bribes are a part of life in some countries. If you know the checking in costs and have an idea of the amount of bribe that will be asked for (sometimes quite openly), carry enough money for only the checking in costs and a little extra for the bribe. Then it is easy to show the official that this is all the money you have with you and they will see that they are wasting their time asking for more.

Short story While in Bali, we learned through the cruising grapevine that a US$10 bribe was an acceptable amount in addition to the usual checking in costs. Noel kept the standard bribe amount in his shirt pocket and when US$20 was asked for, Noel took out the US$10 and said 'this is all we have'. Of course it was accepted.

Short story We had an interesting incident in Ecuador. It was necessary to obtain an 'official stamp' on our new (extended) visa, before we could be issued with a secondary essential document. This stamp could only be given in a town that was a nine hour bus trip away (one way). However, after some gently offered 'grease', the officials at a town one hour away were happy to do the deed. The cost (bribe) was almost insignificant compared with the bus ride and accommodation costs that we could have incurred. Our taxi driver figured out the acceptable amount and performed the transaction as a regular part of his hire services.

<u>Passports</u>: Most countries want you to have a passport with an expiration date at least six months after your anticipated departure date from the country you are visiting. Occasionally the required length of time prior to expiry is longer than six months, so do your research prior to arrival.

<u>Advance notice</u>: Some countries require advance notice of your arrival. Australia requires notice at least 96 hours prior to your arrival. There are serious consequences if you do not follow these rules. Despite the rumours, it is not complicated. When leaving your last port with your next destination being Australia, simply contact customs via email to inform them of your approximate ETA (yachtreport@customs.gov.au). Ensure you receive confirmation back saying that they have your details prior to your departure. Noonsite has all the information you need about checking in/arrival procedures. www.noonsite.com.

Short story Both times we have returned to Australia, we informed customs of our ETA from Noumea in New Caledonia, which is about one week's sail from Bundaberg in Australia. We gave them our ETA (explaining why it was approximate). They confirmed they had our details straight away. It was as simple as that.

Credit & Debit Cards
Not all cards are accepted everywhere. Ecuador has few places that will accept any credit card at all, but ATMs (Automatic Teller Machines) are prevalent, so obtaining cash is easy. Do not assume everywhere has the facility to withdraw money.

Short story On arrival at the Gambier Islands in the South Pacific Ocean, the post office had decided, just one week before our arrival, to cease offering international credit card transactions and exchange of foreign currency! We found one shop that would exchange American dollars and another that would accept credit cards. However, that shop was not well stocked and stipulated a large, minimum purchase. We had ample stores on board, which we supplemented with fresh bread and cheap chicken (by exchanging a few American dollars). We hardly spent a thing in six weeks because we couldn't. We still lived like kings and it was a relief to be in a place where we weren't able to spend up big on 'essentials'.

Currency
American dollars are accepted in most countries. (Keep an extra supply well hidden on board for emergencies.)

In some countries, especially South America, officials will not accept tatty US notes. Spend these in local shops and keep fresh, clean, crisp notes for officials.

Do not change too many dollars into local currency. You may not be able to change it back.

Short story In Eritrea, we withdrew too much local currency (Nakfa) from the bank. A few weeks later, that same bank would not change our surplus Nafka back to US dollars. We finally sought the black market, which actually gave us a better rate than the bank! During the exchange in the bank, I found it almost impossible not to giggle. Noel was wearing an old cruising hat, which was rather battered by this stage. To prevent it blowing off, he had cunningly attached luminous green and orange shoelaces to tie around his chin. Noel lives in this hat, inside and out, especially under flickering fluorescent tube lighting, such as in this bank. I couldn't help but grin when Noel was putting on his best 'meeting' voice with a 'suited' bank manager, while wearing what looked like a rag on his head!

Crew

We have heard both horror stories and wonderful stories about taking on crew. Our decision not to take crew on board was because Noel and I work very well together and we manage just fine.

Searching for crew
- Search for crew on the Internet and in magazines.
- Word of mouth is an excellent way to source crew.

What to ask/work out
- Get to know them a little and find out what makes them tick.
- Ensure you have an outline of what your intentions are and how things operate on board your vessel.
- They may want precise dates and destinations, but you can only provide these up to a point. Things can go wrong, delays occur. Not just bad weather, but parts breaking and having to wait for repairs/new parts where you didn't plan to. Most long-term cruisers have had to turn around and go back at some point.

Expectations
- What do you expect from your crew and what do they expect from you?
- Can they smoke?
- Will they stand watches?
- They will need to know where everything is, especially safety equipment and how to operate such equipment.
- What is expected of them during an emergency situation?
- Accommodation needs to be discussed and what is expected when you are in port.
- Will they be required to take on their share of cooking and washing up?

Pay

If you are taking on professional crew, of course you have to pay them and this is then classed as a commercial venture. If crew pay you for more than just their share of food, drinks and visas etc, it is a commercial undertaking and leads into insurance and liability implications. If you expect crew to contribute to boat expenses, that too will be considered a commercial venture.

However, if you want someone who has little or no experience (or sometimes lots, if you are lucky), then it can work several different ways.
- Food and board are offered in exchange for tasks on board.
- The crew pay a certain amount each day to cover food.
- Crew inevitably want something to do and feel part of the team, so asking them to be involved in different tasks in exchange for food may be the best option.

Gear
- What will be provided on board? Bedding? Life jacket? What will not?

Insurance/Medical
- Insurance is usually up to the individual.
- You must be made aware of any medical conditions/medications that your crew have and of course, the crew must be aware of any medical conditions you have.

Responsibility
- If you are taking anyone on passage, the captain of the boat is responsible for them in all ports. If crew get into trouble, the captain may have to pay for them to fly home.

Documentation
- Ensure everyone on board has the correct documentation, e.g. passports, visas.

Food
- What do they eat, more importantly what *don't* they eat?
- Eating ashore with paid crew, who pays?

Alcohol and drugs
- Rules and regulations on board.

Resources: Free Cruising Crewfinder: http://www.cruiser.co.za/crewfinder.asp

Documentation

Keep your original documentation and some money in your grab/ditch bag, when you are underway. If the worst happens, you will have some money and your passports for when you are rescued!

Purchase a boat stamp. Some countries think that you are not legitimate if you do not have a boat stamp and it can speed up the formalities. Design your own or purchase a 'do-it-yourself' stamp from a stationery store. The stamp should show your name, your boat's name, O.N. (official number) and contact information (an email address is fine).

Keep a copy of all your official paperwork on land (with family) too. An additional electronic copy is always handy; take a picture with a digital camera or scan them in and store on your laptop. (Keep a good stock of photocopies.)

Import Tax

When in foreign ports, before ordering new parts, carefully check the import tax requirements and costs.

Short story In Ecuador, we made the decision to purchase new sails. Researching the import duty we discovered that Ecuador could charge anywhere between 40% to 100% value of an item for import tax (depending on the type of item, it was impossible to find out which items carried which percentage). We sailed up to Panama to take delivery. At the time of writing, Panama charge about 4% import duty across the board.

Shipping: When shipping parts and equipment into foreign ports, ensure the package states 'Yacht In Transit', clearly near the boat name. A 'Yacht In Transit' package does not necessarily mean you will avoid import tax (as in Ecuador), but in most countries the tax will be less, or even totally avoided, as it is confirmation that you are just visiting.

Insurance

The variables of insurance are enormous and each individual's requirements are different. When considering whether to take up insurance, remember that most marinas and slipways will require evidence of insurance if you wish to make use of their facilities.

Check the details: When your insurance is in place, it is imperative that all documentation is read thoroughly; especially disclosure statements, what is not covered and what happens at renewal. Spend time reading any changes to your policy. Read the small print. If in any doubt about your insurance, contact the company for clarification and ensure this clarification is in writing.

Conditions: If you cruise in areas of unrest, special interest or cyclone/hurricane areas, your insurance company may require specific conditions to be met. One example is a requirement to be within certain latitudes during the hurricane/cyclone season.

Check geographic areas where your boat insurance company will and will not cover you. Quite often they have areas where you will not be covered.

Health insurance: is another personal decision. We met cruisers that did not have any cover at all and other cruisers who were horrified at that thought. It is a very personal decision based on your health, wealth and attitude. If you are from a country with healthcare, check the reciprocal agreements that may be in place for the countries you are visiting. Personally, we have our own 'personal health account', which means we can easily access funds for health issues.

Short story We have had some medical issues in other countries. Although they have never developed into serious concerns, there have been worrying problems. We sourced local medical help in places such as South America and Samoa and the medical facilities and professionalism of these Doctors was as good, and sometimes better than in the UK, Australia and North America! The cost was bewilderingly low.

Island Hopping On A Budget

Sailing to remote islands does not have to be expensive. Generally, the everyday groceries are more expensive, but with a bit of ingenuity you can figure out how to avoid, or at least minimise some of the cost. *(See 'Shopping/Victualling' in the Galley section.)*

Avoid visiting the touristy shops. Go where the locals shop and eat; you may have to change your diet slightly, but isn't travelling about new experiences?

You can stock up with items that will be more expensive on islands, prior to leaving a major port.

Short story Before leaving Panama to sail the islands in the Pacific Ocean, we purchased enough wine and beer, tinned and dried foods and bathroom supplies to see us across most of the ocean back to Australia. Having sailed these waters previously, we knew these items would be much more expensive on the islands. We also stocked up well with engine peripherals such as filters (fuel and oil), oil, diesel, sealing tape, etc. *(See 'Spare Parts' in the Maintenance & Repairs section.)* In the islands, locally grown fresh produce is the cheapest to purchase. Eight months later we returned to Australia with some small supplies of alcohol and even some original dried and tinned food. How much stowage space you have on board is an obvious factor. We were lucky enough to have cavernous cupboards that could store a year's supply of toilet rolls. Yes, you can buy these items everywhere, but we saved a small fortune having a good supply of these items, buying from where they were cheapest.

Noel transferring the goods from one of the many shopping expeditions in Panama.

International Dateline

The International Dateline is an imaginary line that separates two consecutive calendar days. It lies on the longitude line 180 degrees, apart from a few places where the line moves slightly off 180 degrees to accommodate certain countries. For example, the line diverts so that Kiribati is included in the eastern hemisphere.

To the west of the international dateline, the date is always one day ahead of the date to the east of the line. When crossing the date line, add a day going west, subtract a day going east. Samoa has recently (2011) voted to have the dateline shifted east, enabling them to join the economic weekdays of Australia and New Zealand and to watch the Sunday footy on Sunday! You can see how it is important to keep up to speed on these kind of changes.

If you are one side of the dateline and friends or family are flying over to meet you from the other side of the dateline, be aware that you could be talking about two different days!

Short story Noel's daughter Melanie came to visit us on our first trip to Tahiti. She gave us the date she would be arriving, but we did not realise that she was crossing the dateline, which put her arrival a day earlier. (The date she provided was the equivalent to the date in Australia, not where we were.) On sailing into Papeete (the day before her arrival – we thought), by luck we went into town to check our emails and saw that she would be at the airport in about one hour! We just made it by ten minutes, trying to look relaxed and organised!

Mail Management
We are lucky enough to have fantastic support from our families, including some who open and deal with our mail. (Thanks Mum xx.)

My mum handles all our mail. She periodically forwards it on to us if/when necessary. Most items we can handle over the Internet. If there is emergency mail while we are at sea, she understands our situation and can make contact on our behalf.

Mail forwarding traps: Forwarding mail to far flung destinations can be tricky. It can take twice as long to arrive as quoted and is often lost. I would only use this option in trustworthy locations and only if absolutely necessary; or you could find yourself stuck in port waiting for your mail.

Communication: Inform all your house administration contacts (insurance, banks, rates, council etc), of your situation. Ninety-nine per cent of them will correspond via email (if requested) and will not be perturbed if you do not respond straight away.

Don't forget to let the Electoral Commission know your new address for mail. You never know when an election will take place.

Short story Our mail in Australia was re-directed to my mum in the UK, which worked fantastically. However, I had forgotten to inform the Electoral Commission of our new address. An election took place and in Australia it is mandatory for every citizen to vote. We did not become aware of the fine until we returned (thinking for some reason they had our new address as we had notified everyone else, including the tax office). We wrote many letters and provided in-depth proof of our whereabouts, to prove we could not vote when the election was taking place. Fines and threats were mounting. They had to let us off in the end, as we proved we were on the remotest, inhabited island in the world at the time – Easter Island!

Mail forwarding companies: Having someone that you trust to open your mail is one less worry when underway. If you'd rather not ask friends or family, use a company that provides an address service. They receive your mail and forward it to an address supplied by you (e.g. marina or post office). Simply search the web for 'mail forwarding services' in your country. Here are some companies we have heard cruisers use:

America	Voyagers Mail Forwarding Service mailboat@vmfs.com, www.vmfs.com or Skypax www.skypax.com/
UK	My UK Mail contact@my-uk-mail.co.uk, www.my-uk-mail.co.uk
Australia	Pass The Post service@passthepost.com.au, www.passthepost.com.au/ or Campervan and Motorhome club, use this link to find several options of mail forwarding: www.cmca.net.au/pages/marketplace/marketplace/mail_forwarding.php

Making Money

Any self-employed person will tell you that this is hard work. Living on board makes it harder. But it is possible with dedication, motivation and lots of stamina.

Write: Put pen to paper, just look at the material you have. If you read a magazine you think you could contribute to, download (or request) their writer's guidelines. It is imperative to read and study suitable magazines. It is pointless sending a great piece of writing on a destination if the magazine does not publish destination articles. Talk to editors; ask them what they need. If you write an article, check and double check it and then check it again. Noel and I will edit all our articles carefully and still, sometimes, small errors sneak through. *(Let us know about any bloopers you spot in this book!)* Invest in a good camera. If you are writing sailing articles, you need high resolution pictures. Photographs are just as important as the text.

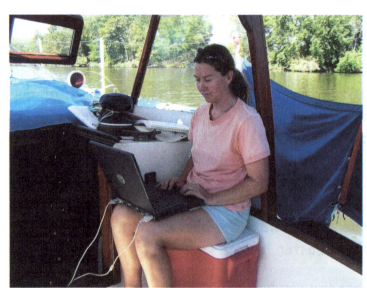

I took every opportunity to write about things I <u>wanted</u> to write about.

Here, we are traversing The Great Loop in America. There were lots of protected, flat waters . . . what an office!

You will need lots of patience as a writer. Magazines plan months in advance. For monthly publications for example, in October they may be putting January's magazine together. It can take many months to receive a response for just one article. Becoming a 'known and trusted' writer can take years, but once you are known it does become a little easier.

Perseverance is the key. If your writing is not quite up to scratch, keep practicing, it will get better. If magazines do not accept your stories, at the very least you will have a great diary of your travels to look back on. Articles can be rejected for many reasons, not just quality. Perhaps the editor has already accepted a piece on the same destination that you have submitted.

The pay is not that great. Bear in mind that many cruisers send in their stories, so there is a lot of competition. A unique event is a good start.

Make something: Decorative knots and paintings are something you can do on board. *(See 'Gifts' in the Fun section.)* Also:
  • Dying sarongs for sale.
  • Making kitchen oven gloves.
  • Making jewellery (e.g. beading).

Use your trade: What you did on land may be helpful to others on boats, e.g. carpentry, electrical work, computer repair, sewing (sail repair, canvas) and welding are just some very useful skills not everyone has and at some point will need. Cutting hair, nursing and bar tending are good skills that travel well too.

Photography: Market your pictures or artwork with http://www.imagekind.com. Take care with copyright (read their advice carefully).

Build your own online art gallery by sharing your photos with the world - then make money on your sales: www.instacanv.as

The Indian Ocean on Mariah. A photo does not have to be perfect.

I love the contrast in this picture of beauty and functionality; a good summary of cruising.

Marriage Certificate
Take a certified copy of your marriage certificate (or the original itself). In Tahiti, if there are just two of you on board, and the captain is from Europe and is married to the other crew member, no deposit is required (the normal deposit amount was the cost of airfares home for all on board).

Tax
Check for tax rebates in your home country. In Australia, we can claim a certain percentage of tax back on diesel used to run household items (heating and generating electricity), while living on board.

Time Zones: Greenwich Meantime (GMT), UTC (Universal Co-Ordinated Time) & Zulu
Have one clock on board that is always set to GMT time, preferably near the navigation station. Weatherfaxes and most radio Scheds will state their time as GMT/Zulu/UTC (which are all the same) to avoid confusion with time zones and daylight saving. *(See 'International Dateline' earlier in this section.)*

Short story On board at Easter Island we had three time zones: (1) Boat Time, (2) Actual Easter Island Time (mainland Chile time, which makes for a late sunrise at about 0830) and of course, (3) Zulu (GMT) to match up radio Scheds with other boats in other time zones. It was a little confusing, but had advantages. We could have several lunches in one day, and as early as 1100 it was 1700 in one of our time zones, i.e. sundowner time!

Visas
Different nationalities have different visa requirements. It depends on the reciprocal agreements in place (between your country and the country you are visiting).

Short story We met a cruiser that told us a story about requiring a visa for entering Australia. His colleague was arranging the visa, there was a miscommunication and the visa was not arranged properly. No one checked! On arrival into Australia, this gentleman was sent back to England. He was exasperated as he was 'integral to a meeting' occurring in Sydney. Be warned – the officials in any country do not give two hoots as to your importance in meetings! CHECK you have the right visa!

Short story On arrival into America, we had to wait on board for the officials to come to our boat to check us in. We were not allowed to step onshore. While waiting, we witnessed another foreign vessel arrive. After we were checked in, the officials went to the other visiting boat. The people on board did not have their visas and were ordered to leave immediately.

Short story Indonesia was our first foreign port and a CAIT (Cruising Application for Indonesian Territory) was required. We had completed the paperwork in Darwin (Australia) and had to wait for the visa. However, we were ready to leave and the weather was perfect. We arranged for the CAIT to be sent to our first port in Bali, estimated the date of arrival and left. Nine days later as we approached the anchorage in Benoa, a local came buzzing towards us in his leaky boat, waiving our CAIT above his sun kissed, skinny body. Our permit had arrived on that very same day. Resources: (http://www.sailindonesia.net/rally/rallypermit.php)

ARTICLE: in Cruising Helmsman magazine in 2007 (note the technology changes!).

Of Foreign Build
by Jackie Parry

What if I told you that two inch toy koalas, cans of coke and cigarettes assist a smooth entry into some countries. Well, the 'gifts' are by no means a prerequisite, but definitely an advantage.

Not quite checking in, but the collection of anchoring fees in the San Blas Islands is a very informal affair.

However the payments are collected, be courteous and follow their rules, you are a guest.

So you've bought the boat and spent months preparing. You've affixed every gadget financially viable, cajoled family into receiving your mail and even sold/rented/boarded up your home. You are ready to sail around the world. Have you thought about what other countries want, need and demand?

Rumour, hearsay and a little tittle-tattle has incongruently wormed itself into parts of our cruise around the planet. Boaties are a wonderful breed, always ready to lend a hand, a spare part or their wisdom, but sourcing hard facts is sometimes like a quick game of boat-to-boat Chinese Whispers.

There are many different ways to find out what the country you are visiting expects, in regard to Customs, Quarantine, Health, Port Police and Marine officials. But being prepared beforehand will save the stress of scampering into the bowels of cupboards and trying to complete required lists while po-faced, uniformed officials stare down their noses at you.

Diverse
Each country has different requirements, and the goal posts can even change at a different port within the same country. And don't always rely on the officials to explain everything. When we reached Tahiti and the grubby, bustling streets of Papeete, we wracked our soggy brains repeatedly, trying to avoid paying the 'deposit' of a return airfare to the country of our citizenship. The deposit is refunded when you leave but after opening a bank account (which costs), depositing the monies (which costs), retrieving the monies (which, funnily enough, costs), a few hundred dollars is quickly notched up. We did consider lying low and using the camouflage of the sixty-odd boats on anchor, but the thought of getting caught, fines and possible imprisonment put these daft ideas to rest. Strangely enough on a bus ride from the town with other cruisers, I found out that if the captain is European (and married to the crew, i.e. have marriage certificate) then you do not

have to pay the deposit. All of a sudden I am promoted to Captain and Noel is banned from the office (he may be remembered for his last, impatient visit); rubber stamp bang, shuffle shuffle - all done, not an extraneous fee in sight.

Jungle drums
Use your VHF and HF to gather facts en route from boats that have already checked in. Use them too, to pass on details after you have checked in. On arrival, some countries require you to stay on board until the officials visit you. That could be on anchor/mooring buoy or at the marina. Others require you to visit their offices and some (few) don't give a tinker's bell what you do. If you cannot contact anyone on shore from your boat and there are no other boats around to explain what to do (highly unlikely), wait on board for a few hours before venturing ashore. In this situation your first port of call is the Police or a government office. Be aware that some countries have designated ports for checking in. Australia is one, having the most stringent rules in all the thirty countries we visited.

Cool, calm and collected
Put on, and keep firmly attached, your patient head. It does not pay to lose your cool. On our arrival into Agadir in NW Africa, the officials eventually grace us with their presence and explain how they have left the rubber stamp and all the forms in their office; we will have to go with them. However, going with them means hiring a taxi. We pay for their errors. Noel gets a little hot under the collar, we are nearly asked to leave - into an oncoming storm!

Do it now
Okay, what can you organise now? A good start is to have a laptop and a printer, as someone will confound you by wanting something entirely new. Hand written lists are acceptable, in this case have plenty of carbon paper. My advice is to prepare as much as possible beforehand (see 'Essentials' list at the end of this article). You can type up the crew list, boat information, equipment list and desired ports list beforehand. Some countries will have forms to put this information onto, but some will want it printed/written out prettily and, often in multiples. A ship's rubber stamp makes it all look very official, even the most mundane crew list looks brilliant!

Visa requirements
Many of your visas will be processed when you arrive. However it is different for every nationality. It is YOUR nationality, not your boat's that has to fulfil the criteria. For an Australian boat (with Aussie Bloke and Pommie Sheila on board) we HAD to have a visa before entering US waters. There is no exception and foreign vessels WILL be turned away without a bona fide visa. Noel's visa lasts five years, mine for ten. It all depends on the country you are visiting and their reciprocal

agreement with your own country. Europeans and Americans can easily obtain a three-month electronic visa (extendable), over the Internet, to enter Australia. However, our Turkish and Thai friends had very real problems. For a six month stay they had to have chest x-rays by a selected Doctor who was on holiday for two months! For a three-month stay they completed forms, proved way beyond any doubt they were financially sound and of course, coughed up plenty of dough. But the three-month visa did not require a chest x-ray. Not every rule has logic.

Every country has Internet but out of the way places have tediously slow and expensive communication. You will have an idea which countries you intend to visit (this will, of course, change), but it does no harm to contact the places you think you might visit before you leave, to gain the information on checking in and visa requirements. Do it in the comfort of your home country - it gets difficult the further away you are. Officials will be only too glad to explain what is required, and prior knowledge of your arrival definitely earns you brownie points. Note that different rules apply if you arrive by boat rather than plane. Sometimes it is simpler to just turn up and sort the paperwork out on arrival (e.g. Panama).

Length of stay
Check regulations and your issued paperwork carefully, as length of stay can vary. Thailand, for instance, will charge thousands of dollars (rumoured to be 50% of your boat's worth) if you overstay your visa length (three months in year 2000).

Flying the flag
No matter what anyone else says or does, DO fly the yellow Q flag, the flag of the country you are visiting (higher and/or larger than your flag), and your boat's national flag. You can really offend some officials/countries if you fail to do this. A great job during a voyage is to make up the required flag.

Agents
Hiring an agent is stipulated in some countries. Normally the poorer the country the more likely an agent is required and the higher the costs (e.g. in Sri Lanka an agent was compulsory). We used an agent for the canal transit in Egypt as we had no choice. In countries where an agent is recommended, but not stipulated, we did all the paperwork ourselves. It may mean countless miles (comfy shoes a must), sore buttocks through waiting and much flicking through a language book, but it will save you a few bucks. And why are you there anyway? It's a great way to experience how the locals live and work.

Coping in the extreme
If you are quite attached to being alive and keeping hold of your possessions, a taxi in Colon, Panama, with a local driver is a prerequisite. It also helps greatly in checking in. For US$30 (2005) he will whisk you from one office to another, explain protocol and keep you safe - all this takes three long, hot days. Even with this knowledgeable assistance our stress levels still boarded the red. Fast food became a daily way to survive, grabbing a handy meal as we raced through our chores. The benefit of quick hits of energizing fodder helped us keep motivated and fuelled up. Building fat pockets, blocking veins and hideous levels of adrenaline that started to murder our heart cells were of no concern; just sorting through the quagmire of paperwork and staying safe became our priority. At least there is light at the end of the tunnel.

Clearing out
Clearing out is a similar procedure to checking in, but simplified. Take all the checking in papers you received with you, plus your normal folder of papers. You will find that sometimes your previous countries' clearance papers won't be asked for, but you never know when this will/will not happen. It not only depends on the country and port, but also on who is on duty - ALWAYS get your clearance papers. (Every country we visited issued clearance papers, except America).

Oh well, at least we had Panama's flag higher than ours!

Searching

We found that more American boats were searched than any other nationality. This is possibly because of the 'right to bear arms' in America. Do declare your weapons; some countries will do nothing, some will hold them until you leave. Not declaring weapons and then having them found has made US boats an easy target to strip search and although not done that often, they sure do go at it when they do. Right down to emptying tampon boxes all over the floor.(They don't clear up after!)

Costs

Charges vary for each country (and sometimes ports), from nothing to hundreds of dollars. Number of crew, tonnage, length and nationality will go in the mixing pot to bake up the costs. Also, cruising permits and an array of taxes can be added to the recipe. We estimate our checking-in costs for around the world, including cruising permits, but excluding visas, to be around US$2,500. The most expensive (excluding our return to Australia) being Sri Lanka (US$200) and least expensive France ($0).

The question of bribery

Rumours of alcoholic gifts in Sri Lanka aiding the expensive process of checking in were not quite right. Friends of ours slyly slid a small bottle of whisky to Customs while they were on board, we didn't. There was no monetary or friendly gain, except we had more booze left on board than our buddies! Bali officials openly ask for bribes, a $5 or $10 bill in a pocket with nothing else (on the man not the woman, if you have a choice), is a good idea. When asked for assistance in order to assist you(!), you can pull this out saying 'this is all I have', showing the empty pocket - it worked for us.

Country Etiquette

Observe etiquette. In Egypt the man checks in while the woman stays on board. (They did begrudgingly accept a woman, when there was no choice.) In countries where women are not so popular, keep quiet and keep your beliefs to yourself. When you do not receive a receipt for minor charges, it is best not to make a fuss. Yes, in some places it goes into the official's pocket. If you arrive after hours, pay the overtime fee, or stand off until the time is right. Remember men in uniform have power and can use it. Don't forget you are a guest.

Declare or Beware?

We declared all cigarettes and alcohol; we had nothing else to declare as we did not carry prescription drugs or weapons. Occasionally when the bowels of the bilge housed a few extra cartons of wine, we became a little absentminded. We were never fully searched; most countries are interested in boats housing refugees, not an extra bottle of grog.

Taking charge

Being polite and accommodating does not mean you allow officials to step all over you with their size nine boots and take advantage. In Cuba, it took four hours to check in, with sniffer dogs and men in large black boots from immigration, port, health and quarantine, all squished below like ugly sardines. Later, while safely tied alongside a wharf, we were approached by another official. He checked our papers and then demanded a gift for his Mother in Law's up and coming birthday! We politely but forcefully declined and watched him proceed along the wharf to the other boats.

You have to sort out the chaff and the blatant extortion. Practice, keeping your ear to the ground and common sense will get you through.

The best of the worst

Here we have highlighted the more colourful scenarios. Do not fear, most officials are polite, very welcoming and even, on occasions, approach with gifts. We were completely unprepared when we took off, but totally and successfully winged it.(See 'Short Story' following this article.) It worked for us, but with terrorism and pandemic viruses gathering momentum it pays to be prepared.

Mementoes

Your collection of paperwork will grow. Looking through the array of languages, coloured papers and types of questions when you return home, your smile will always broaden at your fond memories. My favourite is our certificate of clearance from the island of Niue (which is actually a country in its own right in the magnificent Pacific Ocean). I plan to have it framed, part of it reads:

Master or Commander of the yacht Mariah II burthen with 10.00 gross tonnage, navigated with 1 female, foreign built, bound for Tonga . . . .

Essentials

- *Q flag, courtesy flag, your boat's nationality flag.*
- *A full crew list: name; position (captain etc); occupation; DOB; place of birth, country; passport issue date, expiry date, number and where it was issued; male/female; address. If you take on additional crew, either update the list on a laptop or most places will accept a handwritten addition.*
- *Photocopies of passports (photo/details) - you cannot have enough of these.*
- *Passport photos, a dozen each, should be enough.*
- *Official country registration papers and many copies.*

- *Boat details listed: Name: registration: full description (colour, build, length, beam, draft etc).*
- *Official rubber stamp, with at least your names/boat name and registration number. In some countries it will be frowned upon if you do not have a stamp. (It transforms the plainest piece of paper into an official document.)*
- *Up to date passports with at least six months until it expires (with blank pages, some officials will not put their stamp on a page unless it is completely blank!).*
- *Check each country's requirements for the minimum time left on your passport before you can enter the country.*
- *Required visas.*
- *Stamp all your prepared paperwork with your boat stamp.*

Additional

- *Have plenty of copies of ALL papers. Not everyone will have a photocopier, or let you use it.*
- *Be prepared to write out which ports you intend to visit - in duplicate*
- *Be prepared to fill out duplicate forms, even though you have typed out the details.*
- *Create a list of all equipment on board. Radios, GPS, laptops etc, including make and model). We did not list our backup equipment - no one ever checked.*
- *Inoculations - this is debatable, most people have injections of some sort. For our circumnavigation we did not have any inoculations and were not asked for inoculation documents*. In South America on board Pyewacket we did have the yellow fever jab.*

(*We were actually asked for an inoculation document in Aitutaki (Cook Islands), we did not have one and our friends, who were checking in at the same time, simply gave us their documentation to show the official. This was done right in front of the official who just laughed and was just happy he was able to tick the box on the paperwork!)

Extra Tips

- *Language skills - just have a go, they'll love you for it (at the very least learn 'please' and 'thank you').*
- *Offer cool drinks (cola is a real hit in most countries).*
- *Requesting 'permission' to enter country and/or step ashore is always appreciated by officials (and is sometimes a requirement).*
- *Viewing a clean boat from the cockpit has helped avoid a search.*
- *Be courteous - let the sniffer dogs and the huge men in big black boots into your boat with a welcoming smile.*
- *Obey all the rules.*
- *Proof of ownership documentation may help.*
- *Dress smartly and be aware of cultural differences. In Oman if the locals can see a woman's ankles it means you are coming on to them!*
- *When officials search through personal papers, just bite your tongue.*
- *Small gifts from your country will always be received with a broad smile. Don't think of it as bribery, think of it as one nationality giving to another.*
- *Keep all your paperwork together in one watertight folder.*
- *Try to obtain local currency before entering (not always possible).*
- *Keep available your insurance papers.*

Visas (additional info)

- *Bank statements, proof of funds/property owned in home country - you may need these in some countries to prove you can fend for yourselves and have a reason to leave!*
- *Most visas are obtained when checking in. Don't wait until you arrive to find out! (There are different requirements for different nationalities.)*

Additional contacts:

www.noonsite.com for additional visa requirements and clearance procedures.
And check your country's government pages on destination trouble spots.

This article is all about bureaucracy, but dealing with the paperwork is a relatively small part of cruising. We were always so glad to make a successful landfall and catch up with our buddies, the tedium was soon forgotten.

On Board Paperwork
We have been asked for most of the following documentation at some point during our travels (not all at the same port). Ensure you check the requirements for the country you are visiting.

Imperative
- Visas
- Passports
- The ship's papers (original certificates)
- Crew lists - multiple copies at hand
- The original insurance certificate for the boat
- Passport photos for everyone on board
- Proof of ownership (of vessel)
- Vaccination certificates for all on board
- Pet inoculation details and certificates (check date requirements)
- Plus many photocopies of each item

You might also be asked for some of the following:
- Bank statements, proof of funds/property owned in home country (you may need these in some countries to prove you can fend for yourselves and have a reason to leave).
- List of medications on board. Anyone travelling with medications and/or syringes should carry a prescription. All medications should be kept in their labelled dispensing bottles or packages. If the medications are controlled or an injection type then it is also advisable to carry a doctor's letter authorising possession and use by the bearer.
- List of boat details, length, colour etc
- Ship's radio licence
- Certificate to operate the radio/VHF
- The skipper may need an International Certificate of Competence
- Fishing licence for the area you intend cruising
- Details of last haul out including details of type of antifoul paint used (keep receipts)
- Last termite inspection/treatment (keep receipts)
- List of previous ports visited and length of stay
- List of ports you intend to visit
- List of all equipment on board; radios, GPS, laptops etc, including make and model, (we did not list our backup equipment and this was not checked)
- Marriage Certificate
- Alcohol on board
- Weapons
- Engine details

Don't forget the courtesy and quarantine flag, and that an official looking boat stamp is a great help.

It is very important to remain polite and courteous.

YOU

Love the boat you have.

Mariah II was small and cosy.

The homely ambience we created reflected how much we loved her.

Food preparation

Prepare a good meal before setting off to sea, something easy to reheat like spaghetti bolognaise, not too spicy. Make up a large batch, as you may not feel like cooking for the first day or two.

If bad weather is forecast while you are underway, and you cannot make it to a nearby port safely, as part of your preparation (aside from reefing sails and battening down the hatches) prepare a meal and eat it if you can, as you may not have the chance for some time.

Overseas planning? Sometimes the unplanned events are best. This is one of our cherished memories: a simple walk on an empty beach with fantastic friends.

Palmerston Island (Pacific Ocean).

First Aid & Medication - Equipment & Knowledge
A standard kit is the minimum you should have available on board, but we suggest you should take more. Knowledge of how to use the gear is imperative. Completing a first aid course is just as important as a first aid kit.

How to build your own First Aid Kit:
First ask yourself some questions:
- How many of you will be on board?
- How long will you be self reliant?
- What medical help is available where you are cruising?
- What is the physical environment like where you are cruising? Is it hot or cold?
- Can you make-do jury rigging a splint or do you need the latest gear?
- Are there additional health problems to consider, like migraines or diabetes?
- What methods of communication do you have?
- Who on board has medical training or a first aid certificate?
- Is anyone on board allergic to anything, such as penicillin or aspirin?
- What information, such as first aid books, do you have on board? (A good medical handbook is imperative on board.)
- What age are the people on board? If you have kids with you, a liquid equivalent of medication maybe easier for them to take.

Short story Noel has been able to take aspirin all his life. In Ecuador, he developed an allergic reaction to aspirin and can now only take paracetamol (Panadol) for headaches/pains.

Basic medical kit supplies
- Bandages - assorted sizes
- Band-Aids/plasters - assorted sizes
- Butterfly bandages or strips
- Gauze pads - assorted sizes
- Eye pads (sterile) - assorted sizes
- Adhesive tape
- Splints
- Antibiotic cream
- Iodine
- Safety pins
- Scissors
- Thermometer
- Tweezers
- Cotton swabs
- Epsom salts
- Deep Heat rub
- Eyewash/bath
- Eye drops
- Cloves or oil of clove for toothache
- Insect repellent
- Hydrogen peroxide
- Sunscreen (this is kept in our general stores as we use it every day)
- Vicks decongestant
- Swimmer's ear drops

Medication
- Aspirin
- Paracetamol
- Decongestants
- Antihistamines
- Antacids
- Seasickness tablets - we find Stugeron the best (Stugeron is not available in the US).
- Antibiotics
- Allergic reaction drugs

For quantities and types of the above, ask yourself the questions listed and talk to your doctor.

Carry a bedpan. Injury or illness can prevent the important journey to the head.

Safety: As with all drugs, apply caution and seek professional medical help before taking any drug of any sort. In different countries, drugs can be purchased with higher individual doses and translating foreign instructions can increase the possibility of taking a high dose. (With all seasickness medication, we take half a tablet. A whole table makes us drowsy.)

Personal medication: Additional medications might include seasick tablets and personal medication. If you take medication regularly, prior to departure visit your doctor to stock up, and research where you can stock up again.

Legitimate narcotics: If you have medication that contains a narcotic, ensure you have a prescription from your Doctor to show legitimate use.

Vaccination: Check vaccine requirements for each country you are visiting.

Generic medications: Ask for the generic name of any medication you take. There are some places (like Ecuador) where you can buy prescription drugs over the counter.

Short story During our circumnavigation on Mariah, we did not have one vaccination, except the odd injection of coffee. Despite rumours, in all thirty different countries that we visited, not one had a 'required vaccination'. Our American friends still believe we should give our bodies over to medical science! On Pyewacket, we had a Yellow Fever injection (which lasts for ten years). Before we left to fly to America, we had a flu jab and Hepatitis A and Hepatitis B. Advice can be found on official web sites such as the World Health Organisation (WHO): www.who.int or from your own doctor.

Language
In most foreign lands, the locals speak reasonable English. However, the people in places tourists rarely visit speak less English. Learning 'please', 'thank you', 'hello', 'goodbye' and a few basics is important (and courteous). Not only is it fun to learn words in the local language, but it is also a sign of respect. Have a go, it's good to make a little bit of a fool of yourself and have a good laugh, the locals will love you for it and it may deepen the hospitality you receive!

Short story We often partake in an impromptu game of charades to try to communicate. In a Portuguese butchery, Noel did a great impersonation of a sheep (I think we bought goat though!) and in Thailand, Noel became an impromptu artist, drawing the different parts we needed. It brightens everyone's day to have the patience to make an effort to communicate well.

Safety

We have suffered no more than bruising on board by following these safety precautions:

- Always have one hand for you and one for the boat. When working aloft or underway, always keep one hand to hold you on.

- Concentrate on your current job, not what you are doing next or what is for dinner. Take your time and never rush; ultimately it will get the job done quicker and safer.

- Never pee over the side unless you are harnessed on. Lives can be lost this way. If you are new to sailing, don't sit on any gear, especially ropes, as these can move at incredible speeds.

- Be aware of the equipment around you, and where it moves to and what else it moves, for example the boom traveller and the boom itself. You can fix a scratch, knock or dent on the boat, but it is much harder to fix a broken or missing finger/hand or foot.

- Ensure all your safety equipment is checked and serviced regularly. Everyone on board should know the location of all safety equipment and how to operate it. It is pointless having great equipment if no one knows how to use it.

- Switch off all appliances when not in use. Ensure there is plenty of ventilation; carbon monoxide from solid fuel burners is a silent killer. *(See the 'Health & Well-being' section.)*

- Fit smoke and carbon monoxide detector alarms.

- Never stand in the bight of the line. This may sound obvious, but next time you have a boom preventer in use, or extra lines on your anchor chain (i.e. snubbers) and you are making adjustments, take note of where you and the crew are standing.

Short story We were about to gybe and I was adjusting the boom preventer line. A wave made us gybe too early and I was standing in the wrong place, suddenly I was pinned to the dodger. A turning block had failed and I was standing in the bight of the line without even knowing it. *(See article at the end of this section on our boom brake/preventer.)*

Safety Gear - What We Have On Board

You want to be as self sufficient as possible. That means all at once you are navigator, sailor, cook, cleaner, electrician, mechanic and so on; but maybe most importantly, safety officer.

Basic safety equipment:
- Life-raft
- Grab bag/ditch bag
- Jack lines, always clipped on
- Personal light and whistle on life jackets (our life jackets are our harnesses too)
- Flares
- EPIRB (registered, tested and current battery)
- Hand Watermaker
- First aid and medical kit
- Hand held GPS
- SSB Radio and VHF Radio (2)
- Access to weather (we use Weatherfax)

Keep the critical information about the boat next to the radio. Information such as the phonetic spelling of the boat's name, operation information and method for distress calling; even experienced crew might panic in a stressful situation and in an emergency it is imperative to relay this information properly.

Safety Thoughts

How you go about inspections in port is dependent on your level of knowledge. It is great to have expert surveyors to check all your gear thoroughly, but who can afford that regularly? Becoming an expert on every aspect of your boat is imperative. When at sea there is no help and no shops . . . just you, your tools and spare parts and if you're smart, maybe a detailed manual.

Resources:
Advanced First Aid Afloat by Peter F Eastman.
The Onboard Medical Handbook by Paul Gill. This book covers many scenarios that could occur at sea and provides information in layman's terms.

THE BOAT
Leaving The Boat
Whenever we leave the boat, we carry out the following:

Returning same day
- Double check gas is off at the bottle and the fresh water pump is off.
- Put anchor light on.
- Lock up.

Overnight/couple of days/weeks:
- All seacocks off.
- Full instructions placed on the boat for start up (i.e. location of engine seacock).
- Gas off at bottles.
- Anchor light left on.
- All electrical systems off (apart from solar panels, wind generators and engine start).
- Detailed instructions to neighbours at anchor, with location of key.
- Check bilge pump is working satisfactorily.

Protecting equipment in port:
When in port, we unplug and take down the radar screen from the cockpit and store it in a cupboard down below. Left on show in the cockpit, it would be very tempting for 'sticky fingers'. The exposed leads in the cockpit are covered with a canvas sock that is cinched at the top with Velcro.

Pre-Departure Checklist
Week leading up to departure:
- Fill fuel tanks and jerry cans (over time diesel will absorb water, so rotate diesel from jerry cans into main tank and then refill jerry cans with new diesel).
- Check gas supply and purchase more if required.
- Purchase distilled water for batteries.

Engine Inspection:
- Coolant
- Oil level
- Belts, tension/wear
- Fuel and oil filters
- Hydraulic oil
- Transmission fluid
- Impeller, hoses, hose clamps

Navigation:
- Monitor weather over the week before leaving.
- Obtain long-range weather forecasts, study weather systems.
- Monitor the barometer reading.
- Inform friends and family of your plans.
- Log on with Coast Guard/Marine Rescue, if service provided.
- Plot course on paper charts and enter waypoints into GPS, crew to double check numbers.
- Check charts thoroughly for navigation hazards, highlight.
- Check tide tables and discuss/set departure time.

Other:
- Clean hull, especially the prop, using dive hookah. This is a good time to check the boat thoroughly underwater.
- Check bilge pump and pump float (manual and automatic).
- Check all electronics are operating properly: steering, radar, GPS, plotter, depth sounder, radios etc.

Day before departure:
- Top up water tanks.
- Check all items on deck are lashed down properly.
- All items below decks stowed properly, doors and floor locked/clipped in place.
- Rig jack lines.
- Take grab bag out of cupboard and store on bunk (or wherever easily accessed in emergency).
- Remove storm sails from sail locker and place under table in saloon (or accessible place).
- Tie up lee cloths.
- Remove sail covers.
- Uncover steering gear and affix paddle to Aries.
- Prepare a meal for first night out.
- Test all running lights.

- Last garbage run.
- Final check on weather.
- Oven gimballed.
- Put out life jackets, foul gear and torches, for the ready.
- Check out with officials (Immigration, Customs, Health, Port Captain).
- Safety briefing with crew.
- Secure and lash dinghy on or below deck.

Shake, Rattle & Roll

No matter how well you have stowed your gear, there will be rattles, rolls, taps and clunks that need to be sorted out. These are very irritating for crew trying to sleep. The tiniest clunk, clunk, clunk, can drive a person a bit batty. It may take time to find everything, as the smallest movement can make a big sound. It is important to seek out the item and correct it. It may be a problem or may develop into a problem if left. A peaceful sleep is very important as far as safety and sanity is concerned.

Stability

Before heading off, think about your vessel's stability. Can water drain off the deck quickly? If you take on a huge wave, this will cause Free Surface Effect (FSE) and affect your vessel's stability. (Free Surface Effect is best understood by holding a tray full of water and trying to keep it horizontal. What happens when the water starts sloshing one way and another?) FSE by way of water on the deck also causes the centre of gravity of your vessel to rise. This negatively affects the stability. Ensure your scuppers and freeing ports are always clear.

Is your vessel trimmed properly? Ideally your boat should be slightly trimmed by the stern.

Strong Enough

This title could incorporate everything on the boat. But two pieces of important equipment come to mind that a lot of people neglect to consider.

Cleats: with backing plates: check them, the time to find out they are not strong enough is not in a storm!

Windlass: Your anchor rode or mooring lines should not be tied to your windlass. A windlass is not made for taking sustained, strong shock loads; use a snubber or devil's claw tied to your bollards or deck cleats. I know of one anchor winch coming clean off the deck on a brand new, very large boat. (The crew had used it for tying off a towing line.)

Short story Many times we have been invited over to other boats. As I have reached for the stanchions to haul myself up, I am told 'no, don't use that, it'll break'. Hopefully not referring to my weight! I realised that the stanchions had not been fixed to withstand a load! It makes me shudder to think about getting thrown against these in unkind weather at sea, to me they are a safety item, otherwise, why have them, just to trip you over?

Table

The space under the saloon table is sometimes ignored. Taking into account leg space, there is usually some spare space.

Hang a net to store soft items. We use this space for storm sails while at sea. In port they go back into the forward 'sail' locker. (We use bungee cord to secure the sails.)

Tanks, Fuel & Water
Baffles in the tank help with noise and stability. Free surface effect is an important issue on all vessels. *(See 'Stability' above.)*

You should have more than one water tank and be able to isolate one of the tanks. If one tank has a leak or becomes contaminated, you will still have good water in the other tank. Flexible water tanks must be lashed down properly; seatbelt strapping is best. Check regularly for chafing.

ARTICLE: Published in Cruising Helmsman in 2007.

Boom Boon From Generous Gent
by Jackie and Noel Parry

It had the potential to kill. The monster was sixteen foot long and solid. The aluminium boom swung at head height, an accidental gybe could be fatal. Although it's not always useful, I am quite attached to my head.

Necessity breeds invention and reluctantly we admit that one of our cleverest pieces of equipment on board was someone else's idea, gifted to us. It's not only the fact that this rudimentary concept saves lives and injuries, and assists us in being 'single-handed' when the other is asleep (read: avoids taking the risk of wrath in waking sleeping partner). The intriguing thing is that in a modern cruising world of escalating complexity, the clever part of this piece of equipment is not how it does what it does - but because it is fantastically simple. It is also cheap and anyone can rig it up in just a few minutes. Indeed, all you need is a boat, a long piece of rope and knowledge of a bowline knot. More remarkable is the nameless man that has helped prevent us becoming sacrificial skippers at the hand of a boom.

The liberator who freed us from the prospective murder weapon on board our boat, which is our home, resembled the epitome of 'Granddads'. Wisps of white stringy hair lifted by the soft breeze tickled his face. The spaghetti of lines that carved deep crevices along his unassuming face had become deeper by the sun's hand and a friendly, honest smile.

Moored alongside the quiet town called Laurieton on the east coast of Australia (in New South Wales), we were feeling pretty smug, after all we had survived another passage on the east coast of NSW (in our humble opinion this is one of the trickiest cruising grounds in the world). As the horizon quenched the shimmering sun with the onset of a calm evening, another sailing boat glided towards us. An ageing gent skippered this trim little vessel and with the minimum of fuss, stemmed the tide, came along side and tied up. We offered to take the lines, although he obviously was not in need of any assistance.

We then entered a period of only a few hours, which in the future we were to recall quite often and wonder why we had not taken record of the event as it was actually happening. We cannot remember the chap's name or the design of the vessel or even the vessel's name. However, the memory of his advice and modest appearance stays vivid. Our initial opinion was that he was someone that had just crossed the river and was heading into town. This thought persisted even while the slim glimmer of understanding was penetrating our even dimmer awareness. For the sake of this yarn, we shall call him Jim.

We instantly liked this humble human, who had no raging desire to give us an instant and vivid panorama of his entire life like so many people we meet. Jim presented Noel with his sextant and asked if he knew a way of repairing the cracked sextant arc. He said, 'It's a bit loose, I have had to sort of hold it all together while I take a sight with one hand, and adjusting the Vernier with the other.'

'Well', thought Noel, 'The old chap must be doing some practice sights standing on the beach. This shouldn't present too much of a drama, cracked or not, he can just turn around and read the street sign.' While Noel pretended to fiddle knowledgeably with the sextant Jim said, 'I find it a bit of a bother these days, my balance is getting a bit off, but the Fleming wind vane my wife insisted I fitted this time has at least left both my hands free, while I take the sun sights.'

'And just where were you taking sights then?' Noel enquired from beneath his creased forehead, whilst peering at the wobbly star reader. To our deepening perplexity, Jim explained that he had been on a course of around 260 degrees for the last two days. 'Eh?', we asked in unison (sometimes our conversation holds no bounds). 'Oh, I have just been out to Lord Howe for my annual jaunt,' said Jim.

We yakked for a while and we learned that Jim regularly takes off, solo, with his sextant. ('I can't stand all those buttons on the GPS'.) He sails for a few weeks to keep his hand in. This trip, he reckoned, his wife slept all the better back home in Pittwater, knowing he was sailing with his one concession, the wind vane. Jim, a quietly spoken man with no pretensions, except an enjoyment of sailing, went on to explain, 'I don't use a GPS; it robs me of a satisfaction of finding port with just the stars, sun, compass and log. I quite like all that.'

Noel and I had been having trouble harnessing our sixteen foot head-banging boom. Jim showed us his solution. A rope long enough to go right round the fore part of the boat onto the boom end, and back to a cleat in the cockpit. It all sounded too simple. Noel had been tossing up ideas involving jamming cleats, turning blocks, patented boom brakes and all sorts of paraphernalia. 'No, no, lad, just a rope will do, let's have a look.' And we all toddled off to Mariah and within two minutes Jim showed us how this preventer could run in front of our Samson post, around our timber cleats on either bow and run back to aft of the cockpit. 'You can re-tie it after each gybe to the end of the boom, or get all fancy with a snap shackle,' Jim added.
'Yeah, but don't I need turning blocks and another winch?' Noel asked, still stunned with the pure simplicity.
'No, no, lad, a boat's a simple thing, you'll get the hang of it.'

No longer do we fear our boom; the beast is harnessed and controlled with ease from the cockpit, especially on those darks nights when we are gibbering with terror on a windy night watch, running on the quarter. With the main run out all the way, we haul in the preventer and secure it on the windward quarter bit, then haul in the main sheet to make it all tight. This keeps the boom rigid and held down, maintaining a better mainsail shape, with no pumping of the sail. Backing the main is still to be avoided, but at least with an inadvertent gybe we stop the potential wrecking of gear, broken boom and gooseneck. And it has the added bonus of keeping our heads on our shoulders.

This set up also helps us in the gybing process. When the helm is eased over (slowly does it please), the preventer controls the speed of the gybe as we can ease it out with control whilst pulling on the main sheet. Before letting the main out beyond our reach we now connect the lee end of the rope onto the end of the boom (using our fancy snap shackles), and pull on the now windward end as we ease the mainsheet, then we pull on the preventer and make secure as before.

That revealing day, some eight years ago now, Jim went on to explain his desire to eat at the RSL (Returns Servicemen's League) and we did not have the wit or grace to ask him aboard. He quietly left the next morning. On night passages we ponder the chance meeting with this remarkable character from Pittwater, who calmly goes about doing what he likes best, sailing and navigating the seas. Over the years we have passed this neat idea onto several boats, helping them avoid injuries, breakages and stress. We have also raised our boom above head height, losing some of the enormous sail that we never raised in entirety. Now as we alter course two degrees as told by our GPS we often wonder if Jim ever repaired that cracked sextant.

This article is a reminder not to take short meetings for granted, they can be pots of gold.

AT SEA
Log Book
Filling out the ship's log book should be routine.

It is unnecessary to purchase expensive log books for your boat. Buy a hardcover blank book and draw in your own columns.

Our log book has a column for the:
- Date
- Time
- Position (latitude and longitude)
- Wind (strength and direction)
- Speed
- Course
- Barometer reading
- Bilge check
- Engine hours
- Comments (we include weather and sea conditions, sighting of other vessels, radio communications and miles to go)

Bilge: The bilge column is just a tick to show it is dry (or approximation of how much water is in there and why). This encourages us to check the bilge regularly and therefore find any problems in the early stages.

Engine information: In the back of our log book we kept a detailed account of all oil changes, filter changes and engine maintenance and repairs.

Referencing: Underline or highlight (with a highlighter pen), the destination and departure ports throughout the book to make referring back easier. Highlight fuel calculations, for quick reference.

Good seamanship: Complete an entry prior to handing over your watch. If the person taking over has not absorbed your verbal handover entirely, they can read the last log entry.

The ship's log book should contain the operation procedures, location of seacocks, weather, navigation plan, etc.

Backup: Log entries should be completed regularly, every few hours at least. This enables you to use up to date information, which is important if it becomes necessary to calculate DR (Deduced Reckoning). *(See the Navigation section.)*

Short story On the west coast of America near California, we had a short two night sail from one port to the next. I was up at about 2 a.m. for my watch. Noel did a complete verbal handover and I was so dopey I didn't take any of it in. When I get up, Noel always makes me a cup of tea and ensures I am okay to take over. The trouble is, I am not properly awake for at least another forty-five minutes. So, as usual, I just sat, sipped my tea and begrudgingly cast my eyes around the horizon. A short while later I saw the red and green lights of a rather large vessel heading straight for our starboard beam and two more not far behind the first. I dived below and scanned the charts to find where my 'safe water' was if necessary. The charts told me we were right in the middle of crossing a traffic separation zone (if crossing, always do so at ninety degrees to the traffic in the zone and give way). Panic over, the ships would go behind us. I learned my lesson and thereafter I paid a lot more attention when the handover was taking place!

Lookout
On grey days at sea, be extra vigilant on your watches/lookout. Grey coloured vessels can loom out of the foggy horizon and close quickly.

Moon
For the start of a lengthy voyage, we try to time our first few nights with a waxing three-quarter moon. This improves the night watches tremendously until you are fully in the swing of being at sea.

Ocean Miles & Passages
As with anything new, your confidence grows over time. Knowing you have a sound boat, systems, rigging, sails and an idea of what you are doing (because you have read lots and completed courses), certainly helps ease those fears.

The best thing for confidence is lots of sea miles. The sooner you leave, the sooner you will gain your confidence. Even after many years of sailing many miles and being around a vast array of boats, Noel and I always feel a little anxious before leaving on a voyage and settling into the travelling rhythm. This keeps us on our toes. We believe that ocean miles are easier than coastal miles; there are fewer things to hit!

Sea Berth & Lee Cloths
You may not always be able to comfortably use your cabin or bunk when on passage. Some sea-states can make the boat corkscrew or just move in a very bouncy or jarring manner. A good sea berth will be situated low down and in the middle of the vessel, although this isn't always possible. In severe weather, do not discount the floor - whatever it takes to get some rest.

We use extra cushions in really rough weather. Wedge into the bunk to help aid sleep. It is quite disconcerting to have your innards moving, while your outer body is held firm - that is rough sailing!

Lee cloths can be made tighter by adding ties to the ceiling from the centre of the top of the hem. This creates better stability for the person in the bunk on either tack.

Standing Watches
Schedules: Different schedules suit different people. We start with four hours on, four hours off. As we become accustomed to that, we extend the time to between five and six hours. This way we can both get a good sleep. Friends do three hours on/off. You have to find what works for everyone on board.

A rigid schedule on board, watch-keeping or otherwise, is impossible. Flexibility and adaptability from everyone is key.

When at sea, our routine settles in after three days; sleep requirements vary from one person to the other. Arrange a good routine/schedule that suits everyone on board. Everyone on board must feel they receive adequate and equal rest. Fatigue is a major contributing factor in accidents.

Having enough room to lie down in the cockpit is important for those short cat-naps (with alarm set) when on watch.

Keep busy: We plot our position every hour and complete the checklist.

Routine checks include:
- Sail trimming.
- All lines for chafing, wear.
- All rigging, loose, tight, any damage or wear occurring.
- Extra checks in the bilges, equipment.
- Items down below stowed, nothing loose.

Watch entertainment: Read with a small red light to maintain night vision.

Listen to the radio, but if you need to use headphones, just put one earplug in. Watch-keeping involves listening too. Your boat is a living thing and needs to be listened to.

Short story I like to keep busy on watch, otherwise the time drags and I become very drowsy. I do not worry about dozing if I really have to, as we use an oven alarm that is set to go off every eight minutes. I read a lot, using a red light to maintain night vision. I make bread (if the sea is calm enough), listen to music and sometimes do some simple exercises in the cockpit. I even make time for study and writing. Noel enjoys listening to audio books.

Obstacles: Keeping watch is not just about other boats; crab pots can be a real problem too. In some areas these are prevalent. They are a floating item (e.g. buoy or plastic bottle), attached to a line, with a crab pot on the bottom.

If we are in an area where there are many, we ensure our timing is right to help us. During the day we can weave our way through them (sometimes they can be in main channels, like in San Francisco!), and try our best to be in much deeper water for the night (too deep for the pots). You will need sharp eyes to spot some of them, as they are usually coloured 'sea' colour e.g. dark blue.

The thought of getting caught up at sea is terrifying. If you have ever swum around your boat at anchor when there is just a little swell you will understand how dangerous it would be, tens of tonnes of boat being thrown around near your head! If you have to get in the water, ensure you are tethered to your boat. A helmet (bike helmet?) is not a bad idea as an added precaution.

If in company, ask the other vessel to stand by you while you free your boat. Have dive equipment on board (e.g. dive hookah if you have a deep draft).

Night-time sailing: Sailing at night without a full moon can be very nice too, if the skies are clear and the stars light the water. This is the time to put out of your mind all those horror stories/possibilities others like to share, like thinking about the two miles of pure deep water below you and the possibility of shipping-containers lurking just under the surface!

Short story One night I was on watch and it was a very dark night. I had just completed a full 360 degree look around the horizon and sat back down (in the cockpit), to read a couple more pages. The horizon was clear of any boats, so I could relax for a while. Suddenly an enormous spotlight lit up the entire cockpit. I jumped up thinking I had missed a boat and that they were warning us. There was no sound or boat! I looked up and there was the most enormous meteor sailing through the sky, lighting us up. I have no idea how far away it was, but it appeared to be the size of a small car. It took some time for my heartbeat to return to normal.

Safety: If you are unsure of anything, always wake your partner or another crew member. If you are the one being woken, never have an angry word to say. When your crew catch a fish, gybe, reef etc, be prepared to be woken up to assist. Avoid becoming resentful at interrupted sleep, the crew may become too scared to wake you and a dangerous situation could develop.

There is nothing wrong with double checking, especially at night-time when you are tired. You are all in this together; help each other. It is too late to tell your mate 'I didn't want to wake you', when treading water!

Preparing for a voyage doesn't always mean thinking about oceans. Traversing the Great Loop in America created different preparation, such as focussing on depths, anchoring stipulations and more MARPOL regulations.
(http://www.greatloop.org/)

Short story With just two of us on board, Noel and I maintain that our lives are in each other's hands. We never grumble or complain if, when off-watch, we are woken several times by the other. When traversing a traffic separation scheme around the Straits of Bab el Mandeb in the Red Sea, we both stayed awake all night. The current was giving us a speed, over the ground, of over 9 knots. As a large ship overtook us we saw a light appear and both swore blind that the light was a smaller boat launched off the back of the ship, coming to rob us. As we moved further on and our eyes adjusted to the moonless night, we realised that the light we had seen was actually on top of a small reef that looked as though it was moving as the ship passed it! Fatigue can create weird imaginings, especially as we had just sailed the 'pirate' route between Yemen and Somalia.

Unexpected visitors on watch help pass the time. A beautiful Booby, near the Galapagos Islands.

CRUISING GUIDES & RESEARCH

Cruising Guides
A quick Internet search will tell you which guides you need. *(See end of the Navigation section for list of resources/guides and contacts.)* Search websites carefully, some guides are available for free online, for example Ecuador and Panama guides.

Pre-loved resources: At crossroad ports e.g. Panama, cruisers will be selling their used guides and charts for areas they have already tackled. Usually you can pick up fair priced second hand items.

Books: The Internet has opened up our world, but books are useful when at sea (pilot books) and when you're wandering around a town (tour guides).

Purchase a land guide too, this will help you better plan your time, especially for limited-stay visas.

Research
Research will be one of your primary jobs, whether you're a new cruiser, boat buyer or seasoned cruiser.

Chat to other cruisers, they usually have a wealth of information. Just one little tip can make your day easier and more fun. Do not assume new cruisers have nothing to offer, we've met many people who have just started out and have wonderful ideas to teach us. Keep in mind what your needs/wants are; it is your cruise.

Community sites on the web are very useful for subject discussions, for example:

Jimmy Cornell: www.noonsite.com

Yachting and Boating World: http://www.ybw.com/forums

Cruising and Sailing forums: http://www.cruisersforum.com/

Cruiser Log World Cruising: http://www.cruiserlog.com/

Or simply Google 'cruising forums' to find your favourites.

Research isn't just about which boat, where to anchor and what equipment you need. You should also research pertinent information about where you are heading, bearing in mind what you might need, for example specific medical items or clothing supplies.

Download or subscribe to local magazines for the areas you are visiting. For example, for Australia read Cruising Helmsman, for San Francisco and Mexico read Latitude 38 (a free magazine).

There are many great websites for cruisers. Try some of these:
http://www.cruisingquest.com
http://www.cruisingtips.net/

READING & RESOURCES

Books - Seamanship
Capt. Dick Gandy's Australian Boating Manual: http://www.australianboatingmanual.com
Chapman Piloting & Seamanship by Charles B. Husick (USA)
The Annapolis Book of Seamanship by John Rousmaniere (Illustrations by Mark Smith) (USA)

Books - Passage Planning
Cornell's Routes of the World by Jimmy Cornell
Ocean Cruising on a Budget by Anne Hammick
World Cruising Destinations: An Inspirational Guide to All Sailing Destinations by Jimmy Cornell
Nigel Calder's Cruising Handbook: A Compendium for Coastal and Offshore Sailors by Nigel Calder
The Voyager's Handbook: The Essential Guide to Blue Water Cruising by Beth A. Leonard

Books - True Survival Story
66 Days Adrift by William Butler: http://www.wbutler.com/

Books - Electrics
The 12 Volt Bible For Boats by Ed Sherman

Books - First Aid
Advanced First Aid Afloat by Peter F Eastman
The Onboard Medical Handbook by Paul Gill

Books - Kids
History Of The World by Susan Wise Bauer
Where's Wally? by Martin Handford
Swallows and Amazons series by Arthur Ransome
Tommy Tiller and His Dog Rudder by John Martin

Books - Galley
Sailing the Farm: A Survival Guide to Homesteading on the Ocean by Ken Neumeyer
Cruising Cuisine by Kay Pastorius
The Care and Feeding of Sailing Crew by Lin and Larry Pardey

Clean Seas
The MARPOL (Marine Pollution) Convention includes regulations aimed at preventing and minimizing pollution from ships - both accidental pollution and that from routine.

This is regulated by IMO (International Maritime Organisation), see http://www.imo.org/about/conventions/listofconventions/pages/international-convention-for-the-prevention-of-pollution-from-ships-(marpol).aspx

Clothing & Shoe Sizes
The following website has international size guides, converters, size charts and conversion tables; clothing sizes for women, men and children; charts for dress sizes, suit sizes and shoe sizes: www.sizeguide.net/

Community Web Sites (Useful for subject discussions)
Jimmy Cornell: www.noonsite.com
Yachting and Boating World: http://www.ybw.com/forums
Cruising and Sailing Forum: http://www.cruisersforum.com/
Cruiser Log World Cruising: http://www.cruiserlog.com/

Or simply Google 'cruising forums' to find your favourites.

Cruisers
Noel and Jackie Parry: www.jackieparry.com
Jimmy Cornell: www.noonsite.com
Lin and Larry Pardey: http://www.landlpardey.com/
Teresa Carey: http://sailingsimplicity.com/
A plethora of information: http://www.weliveonaboat.com/ and www.womenandcruising.com
For skippers and crew, plus their friends and family. Log your position, it's free and easy to use:
http://www.skipr.net/
Cruising Consultant: http://www.pamwall.com/

Cruising Guides
Cruising Guides: http://www.freecruisingguide.com/
Cruising Compendiums and other great info: http://www.svsoggypaws.com/index.htm (FREE guides - don't forget to buy them a beer when you meet them)
Visiting Indonesia: http://www.sailindonesia.net/rally/rallypermit.php
For Cruising Guides and lots more: http://yachtpals.com/cruising

Fashion Fun
1 WORLD SARONGS is the sarong source with sarongs of all types; plus sarong ties, sundresses, women's clothes, jewellery and gifts. www.1worldsarongs.com

Fun, Learning & Pleasure
Fun and Games - try your luck at: http://www.funny-games.biz/captain-chaos.html
Free Boat Clipart plus Ship Animations and Gifts: http://www.fg-a.com/stgifs7.htm
Decorative Knots are a nice idea, see: http://www.boondoggleman.com for gift ideas
Geocaching is fun for all ages: http://www.geocaching.com/
Learn a new language when travelling: http://www.linkwordlanguages.com/
For online learning, Animated Knots by Grog is brilliant for knot tying and lots of other useful information: http://www.animatedknots.com/indexboating.php
Radio: The BBC broadcasts worldwide: http://www.bbc.co.uk/worldservice/schedules/frequencies/
The Beachcombers' Alert! newsletter is published by Dr. Curtis Ebbesmeyer and distributed via subscription. Distributed four times a year, Beachcombers' Alert! features reports and articles concerning newly-discovered flotsam and other interesting beachcomber finds. http://beachcombersalert.blogspot.com.au/

Health
Travel health information - worldwide: www.nathnac.org/travel/index.htm
Centers for Disease control and prevention - travel information: http://wwwnc.cdc.gov/travel/
World Health Organisation - international travel and health: www.who.int/ith/en
The Travel Doctor: www.tmvc.com.au

Internet
The Wi-Fi free spot directory: http://www.wififreespot.com/
Internet: www.sailmail.com

Magazines
Latitude 38: http://www.latitude38.com/
Cruising World: http://www.cruisingworld.com/
Cruising Helmsman: http://www.mysailing.com.au/ link

Mail Handling Companies
America
Voyagers Mail Forwarding Service: http://www.vmfs.com
Skypax: http://www.skypax.com/

UK
My UK Mail: http://www.my-uk-mail.co.uk

Australia
Pass The Post: http://www.passthepost.com.au/
Campervan and Motorhome club, use this link to find several options of mail forwarding:
http://www.cmca.net.au/pages/marketplace/marketplace/mail_forwarding.php

Navigation
True and apparent wind calculator:
http://www.sailingcourse.com/keelboat/true_wind_calculator.htm
PC Chart Plotter and GPS Navigation software: http://www.sping.com/seaclear/
Free Marine Chart Planner: http://www.macupdate.com/app/mac/33427/polarview
Navigation Worksheets: http://www.jsward.com/navigation/index.shtml
Calculate set and drift, DR, TVMDC, running fix, rhumb line, speed/distance/time:
http://marinersguide.com/software/
Chart Plotter and GPS Navigation Software: http://opencpn.org/ocpn/
Tide Program: http://www.wxtide32.com/
Magnetic Declination Calculator: http://www.geomag.nrcan.gc.ca/apps/mdcal-eng.php
Compass Compensation: http://www.ritchienavigation.com/service/compensation.html
Find the correct local Variation from:
http://ngdc.noaa.gov/geomag/magfield.shtml, or,
www.geomag.nrcan.gc.ca/apps/mdcal-eng.php, or
www.ritchienavigation.com/service/compensation.html
Atlas of Pilot charts:
http://msi.nga.mil/NGAPortal/MSI.portal?_nfpb=true&_pageLabel=msi_portal_page_62&pubCode
=0003

Organisations/Information
Boat US: http://www.boatus.com/
UK Cruising Association: www.cruising.org.uk
Seven Seas Cruising Association: www.SSCA.org
Australian Hydrographic Service: http://www.hydro.gov.au/downloads/downloads.htm
Boatsafe.com www.boatsafe.com
Boating Safety and Clean Water: www.boatus.com/foundation/

Pets
Paws Aboard is a provider of safe and fun supplies for active dog owners and their pets.
www.pawsaboard.com

Photography & Artwork
Photography: market your pictures or art work with: http://www.imagekind.com
Build your own online art gallery by sharing your photos with the world - then make money on your sales: www.instacanv.as

Piracy
See Jimmy Cornell's Noonsite web page for up to date information on problem areas:
www.noonsite.com
Incidents involving yachts in the Caribbean: www.safetyandsecuritynet.com
The Australian Government Department of Foreign Affairs website which carries information on security conditions in countries around the world: http://www.dfat.gov.au

Products & Equipment
Safety Netting for Boats: http://www.ondecksports.com/Products/Sports-Netting
Weatherfax Software: http://www.jvcomm.de/index_e.html
For detailed winch information on anchor winches check out:
http://www.maxwellmarine.com/gen_which_winch.php
Anchor Buddy: http://www.anchorbuddy.co.nz
WD40 and its uses: http://www.wd40.com/files/pdf/wd-40_2042538679.pdf
Anchoring Techniques:
http://www.boattraining.com/waterways/issues/ww_00-spring/technique_anchor.html

Rallies
Latitude 38 Magazine (USA) organises the Puddle Jump Rally each year. This is a great way to make lots of new friends and experience French Polynesian culture to the full:
http://www.pacificpuddlejump.com/
Indonesia: http://www.sailindonesia.net/rally

Weather
NOAA (National Oceanic and Atmospheric Administration) Downloads:
http://www.nauticalcharts.noaa.gov/mcd/Raster/download_agreement.htm
NOAA Marine Weather Services Guide: www.nws.noaa.gov
National Hurricane Center: www.nhc.noaa.gov/index.shtml?epac
Joint Typhoon Warning Center: www.usno.navy.mil?JTWC
Storm Pulse: www.stormpulse.com/Pacific
HurricaneZone.net: www.hurricanezone.net
Weather Underground: www.wunderground.com
Australian Weather: BOM: http://www.bom.gov.au/
Extreme Weather: Global Tracks Software: www.extremewx.com
Mexican Meteorology Service: http://smn.cna.gob.mx/
Weatherfax: http://www.jvcomm.de/downloadpre.html
Worldwide Weatherfax frequencies: http://www.nws.noaa.gov/om/marine/rfax.pdf

Fair winds and calm seas in all you do.
Jackie and Noel

INDEX

9 780987 551504